"Only the dead have seen the end of war."
Plato

"If the dead can come back to this earth and flit unseen around those they loved, I shall always be near you; in the gladdest days and in the darkest nights... always, always, and if there be a soft breeze upon your cheek, it shall by my breath, as the cool air fans your throbbing temple, it shall by my spirit passing by. Sarah, do not mourn men dead. Think I am gone and wait for thee, for we shall meet again."
- From a letter to Sarah Ballou from her husband, Major Sullivan Ballou of the 2nd Rhode Island, in July 1861. He was killed just days later at the first battle of Bull Run.

"The dead were all around us; their eyeless skulls seemed to stare steadily at us... The trees swayed and sighed gently in the soft wind. As we sat smoking, an infantry soldier suddenly rolled a skull on the ground before us and said in a deep low voice: 'That is what you are all coming to, and some of you will start toward it tomorrow.'"
- A Union soldier recalling a night camped on the old Chancellorsville Battlefield

"War is at best barbarism... its glory is all moonshine. It is only those who have neither fired a shot, nor heard the shrieks and groans of the wounded who cry aloud for blood, more vengeance, more desolation. War is hell."
- General William T. Sherman

"It is well that war is so terrible, or we should grow too fond of it."
- General Robert E. Lee on the Union retreat from Fredericksburg in December 1862

"In the glades they meet skull after skull.
Where pine cones lay - the rusted gun, green shoes full of bones, the mouldering coat and cuddled-up skeleton; And scores of such.
Some start in dreams, and comrades lost bemoan."
- Herman Melville

SOLDIERS and the SUPERNATURAL

America's Haunted Forts, Prisons Battlefields & Military Ghosts

DAVID GOODWIN & TROY TAYLOR

© Copyright 2013 by David Goodwin and Troy Taylor
All Rights Reserved, including the right to copy or reproduce this book, or portions thereof, in any form, without express permission from the author and publisher

Original Cover Artwork Designed by
© Copyright 2013 by April Slaughter & Troy Taylor
Back Cover Author's Photo by Janet Morris

This Book is Published By:
Whitechapel Press
A Division of Apartment 42 Productions
Decatur, Illinois   1-888-GHOSTLY
Visit us on the internet at http: www.whitechapelpress.com

First Edition - September 2013
ISBN: 1-892523-87-6

Printed in the United States of America

SOLDIERS and the SUPERNATURAL

FOREWORD
By Roberta Simpson Brown

Ever since I saw my first ghost at age seven, I have been on a quest for answers to questions about life after death. I had feelings and experiences involving the paranormal, but I wanted to learn about scientific research methods used by experienced ghost hunters. I was lucky to meet two of the best and most trustworthy men in the business, Troy Taylor and David Goodwin. I have attended paranormal conferences with them, gone on ghost tours and paranormal investigations with them, and read their books with fascination and delight. I have always been impressed by their integrity in researching and writing about the paranormal. Both Troy and David have always had an interest in history and ghosts, and they bring a high level of professionalism and credibility to their writing. That is why I am so excited about their new book, *Soldiers & the Supernatural - America's Haunted Forts, Prisons, Battlefields & Military Ghosts.*

If you are wondering if this is just another book written about vague shadows on walls, footsteps on stairs, and moans in the night, the answer is no! This book does not rehash tales that have been told over and over. These stories tell of current happenings, and they cover haunted sites all over the United States and Canada.

The paranormal has become a very popular and profitable subject to write about, and there are hundreds of books to choose from. So how do we select the legitimately researched books over the ones that are not? I start by taking a look at the authors. Are they out for a quick buck, or are they sincerely interested in presenting well-researched, informative stories that not only entertain, but also give us compassionate insight into paranormal happenings in the past and present? I go for the latter, as I'm sure you do, too. David Goodwin and Troy Taylor have credentials as dedicated, ethical, well-informed ghost hunters that make them the ideal authors to tackle the subjects of haunted forts, camps and prisons, as well as haunted battlefields.

David Goodwin's book, *Ghosts of Jefferson Barracks*, began to take form when he was assigned to Jefferson Barracks in St. Louis, Missouri, in November 1998 as the Battalion Logistics Officer S4 for the 1138th Engineer Battalion. He was fascinated by the historical buildings and the stories the soldiers told him. After the publication of that book, he went on the serve two tours in Iraq as a distinguished military officer. Not only has David studied the history of the places he writes about, he also has had first-hand experience in combat.

Troy Taylor has written over 100 books on the paranormal, combining his knowledge of history and ghosts in a balanced, entertaining way. The popularity of his books speaks for itself. He is a compelling storyteller and a remarkable historian. Many of us who read his book, *Spirits of the Civil War*, were inspired to explore some of the locations he wrote about. He covers other accounts in *Haunting of America, Dead Men Do Tell Tales, And Hell Followed With It* and *A Pale Horse Was Death*.

Troy founded the American Ghost Society and the American Hauntings Tours. David is a long-time investigator for the American Ghost Society. Their co-authoring of this book of haunted forts, prisons, camps, and battlefields gives an accurate, unique perspective that will not be found in any other collection of stories.

In this book, we are transported through time to historical places to meet the dead who suffered and died, yet lingered on the sites where their lives ended. We learn that the ghosts likely had reasons for staying behind. Was the intensity of their experiences so strong that they did not realize they had died? Are they looking for peace? Do they need the help of us, the living? Even if the answers are not evident, these accounts give us cause to wonder and keep looking for an explanation.

The spectrum of paranormal happenings goes from pre-Civil War days up until the current time. The stories of haunted camps and prisons include some of the most haunted places in America, like Alcatraz, and Andersonville, the Civil War prisoner of war camp where an estimated 13,000 Union soldiers died of starvation and disease. My husband Lonnie and I visited one site they wrote about, the Alton Penitentiary in Illinois. It was easy to imagine going back in time and feeling the emotions of the prisoners who were incarcerated there. The haunted forts and battlefields draw large numbers of visitors, especially the Alamo and Gettysburg, which is believed to be one of the most haunted spots in the world.

With war and turmoil still a reality in today's world, people find themselves faced with the possibility of crossing over sooner than they had planned. They want to look through the veil to see what is waiting on the other side. They want the hope of eternal life. Though nobody has all the answers about ghosts, it is comforting to read a book by respected authors that supports the belief that there is life after death and that our lives have meaning by being a part of the great tapestry of history. We are all part of something bigger than ourselves.

When you look at this book, pick it up with the certainty that it was not thrown together for a quick profit. Buy it with the assurance that it has been carefully assembled to bring you a work that you will be proud to add to your collection. This is a must-read for anyone interested in our country's history and the subject of life beyond death.

Roberta Simpson Brown
Author of ten books, including *Spookiest Stories Ever: Four Seasons of Kentucky Ghosts* and *Kentucky Hauntings: Homespun Ghost Stories and Unexplained Mysteries,* published by University Press of Kentucky.

Soldiers and the Supernatural

INTRODUCTION
By Dave Goodwin

Baghdad, Iraq, Fall 2004.

I was asleep. There was nothing particularly special about my dreams, but I was content. I was finally getting some well-deserved rest. Shortly after 2:00 a.m., the first Katyusha rocket impacted nearby. In the dark recesses of my subconscious, the explosion's concussion was perceived as a loud clap of thunder. I barely stirred in my bunk, content to listen for the rain that for some reason I knew would never come. It was the mechanical whirring of the second rocket as it zipped along its unpredictable flight path that jolted me upright. Instinctively, I reached down and grabbed the body armor lying next to me, placed there specifically for situations just like this. Clutching the sweat-stained protective vest to my chest, I instinctively rolled over and threw myself to the floor. The second rocket's detonation was definitely closer than the first. I threw my armor over my torso hoping that if I were hit, the Kevlar vest and ceramic plates would at least protect my vital organs. Little comfort, I know.

As I laid there, prostrate and powerless to do anything, I broke out in a cold sweat. My heart beating wildly, I closed my eyes and braced myself for the inevitable carnage I felt sure was only moments away. Silently, I said my prayers while images of my wife and daughter and my friends played like a movie in my mind's eye.

At some time during this surreal chain of events, there was a third explosion, not as close as the first two, but close enough that the vibration from the blast could be felt through the floorboards of my hooch. The last rocket landed even farther away -- less reverberation, more relief. The silence that rushed in to replace the steel rain that preceded it was just about as disconcerting as the initial attack was. Emotionally spent, I thanked God for allowing me to live a little while longer, and after what seemed like an eternity, I slowly climbed back into my bed.

Lying there in total darkness, I was reminded of an old saying that dates back to the 1800s about "seeing the elephant." This uniquely American phase is typically associated with the overwhelming emotions that veterans feel during their first experience in combat. On this particularly memorable night, I may not have "seen the elephant," but I definitely heard the angry pachyderm stomp by my front door.

The thoughts, fears and physiological reactions I experienced that night in Iraq are extremely personal, and yet they are the same feelings that soldiers in combat or who are going into combat have felt since time immemorial. Whether they faced swords, arrows, minie balls, machine guns or improvised explosive devices IEDs , warriors through the ages have always wondered how they will react when the "elephant" glares at them for the first time or what will happen to them both physically and spiritually if the enemy sharpshooter finds his mark.

During this same deployment to Iraq, I had the opportunity to visit the now-infamous Abu Ghraib prison. Later, while writing an article about the ghosts of Abu Ghraib for my website and included as an epilogue to this book , I sat down and seriously pondered the link between soldiers whose lives are tragically cut short in combat and the ghostly impressions that are sometimes left behind.

Arguably, the best places to encounter the paranormal evidence that supports the intersection between the world we know and that of the phantom soldier are battlefields and historic military prisons.

Battlefields small and large dot our country from coast to coast. Some are mere roadside curiosities while others bewilder the visitor with their sheer expanse. Some battles were fought for freedom while others were open acts of aggression against an unsuspecting foe. Yet all were fought by brothers, sons, fathers, daughters and mothers and *all* bear the marks of the savage, unforgiving beast known as death.

At places like the Alamo, Shiloh, Antietam, Gettysburg and the Little Bighorn, scared soldiers stood shoulder-to-shoulder and leveled their rifles at the enemy, firing as fast as they could reload. Cannons belched and the ground shook. The air was filled with acrid smoke and the sickly sweet smell of atomized blood. The screams of men in the throes of death were drowned out by the spine-chilling shrieks of injured and dying horses. The pall of death covered the land as far as the eye could see. Blood was spilled, limbs were torn asunder and bloated, maggot-infested bodies rotted in the sun while the surgeon's bone saw played a grisly tune. It is here, on these solemn fields of honor, that the seemingly inconsequential lives of thousands of young men were snuffed out in the proverbial blink of an eye. Luckily for them if you could call it luck their deaths were usually quick. This was not the case for those unfortunates who were taken prisoner.

The men who died in military prisons wished above all else that they had perished in battle. In most cases, theirs was a slow, excruciating wasting away. It was the kind of downfall that rots away the sinew of the body and the singularity of a person's mind from the inside out. The soldiers who died at Andersonville, Alcatraz, Camp Chase and the Alton Penitentiary were not dispatched by bullets, bayonets or shells. Instead, their demise was due to incompetence, starvation, disease, and pestilence. They died a creeping, dismal, sometimes anonymous, death far from their homes and loved ones. For a soldier, there is no greater insult than to die in a God-forsaken "hellhole" and be forgotten.

It is probably for this reason that so many people who visit places like Gettysburg and Alcatraz today experience "intelligent" or "interactive" hauntings. This type of paranormal manifestation is what people typically think of when they think of ghosts. The "interactive" haunting is significant because as the name suggests, the spirit or residual personality of the deceased appears to interact in an intelligent manner with a living observer. This particular type of apparition is even more astounding when it haunts a location because it wants to be there.

Most religions expound that the soul or spiritual essence of the departed goes to heaven or some other metaphysical realm, but what if not all of the dead want to cross over to the other side? In instances of "intelligent" or "interactive" hauntings, the traumatic events associated with horrors of war and the essence of a life left unfulfilled appear to bind soldiers' spirits to the location where they died. Sadly, evidence suggests that there are rare instances when the spirit does not even know that he or she is no longer in the world of the living. If there is a hell, could it be worse than being trapped between two worlds for eternity?

Those are the reasons why battlefields and prisons are haunted, but why are ghosts and apparitions seen at forts and military posts? I offer the theory that these places are haunted for the same reasons that battlefields are.

During the Revolutionary War and the Civil War, many historic forts saw combat or sieges, explaining some of the paranormal activity observed there today, but for the rest of the outposts scattered across the countryside, their existence was more mundane. A soldier's life at one of these more humdrum military postings was fraught with both man-made and natural dangers. Summer days brought excessive heat and never-ending waves of mosquitoes and germ-carrying flies. With winter came numbing winds and freezing temperatures. Soldiers who were billeted in unhealthy quarters were always susceptible to a host of diseases such as cholera, yellow fever and smallpox. Garrison duty was dreary and monotonous. When not performing drill and ceremonies, soldiers found themselves assigned to guard mount and fatigue duty. Soldiers not on duty were left to their own devices. These often included fighting, drinking, fornicating, suicide, murder, desertion and any other form of debauchery a soldier could think of. The punishment meted out for these infractions varied from flogging to the firing squad. In many cases, there was little or no due process, which only served to exacerbate the injustice served upon the average soldier.

Today, soldiers do not have to face unhealthy living conditions unless they are deployed to Afghanistan or another distant local. The food served in the mess halls is plentiful and of very high quality. There has not been a cholera or yellow fever outbreak in the United States since the early 1900s. The last case of smallpox in the U.S. was in 1949. By the 1880s, flogging was officially abolished as a form of punishment and today the military justice process is comparable to its civilian counterpart. But for all the positive advancements that benefit the modern soldier, there are still some things that have not changed: Garrison duty is still dreary and monotonous and fighting, drinking, fornicating, suicide, murder and desertion are still prevalent in today's military.

Admittedly, the rollercoaster of emotions felt by soldiers assigned to bases then and now are not as volatile as those felt by soldiers in combat but they are no less intense. That said, there is no doubt that the psychic energy released as a result of these individuals' hardships and depravations is no less relevant to the hauntings they seem to spawn.

The most frequent type of ghost activity encountered at historic forts and modern military posts are residual hauntings. People who experience a residual haunting report hearing such things as mysterious knocking sounds, ghostly footsteps or muted voices and seeing doors open and close by themselves. Also generally associated with a residual haunting is the feeling of being watched, sudden, noticeable temperature fluctuations, strange odors and the feeling of "goose bumps" on the surface of one's skin. Some residual hauntings involve the appearance of apparitions, but in these instances they do not interact with the person who sees them.

For me, writing this book has been a catharsis. When I came home from my second deployment to Iraq in 2008, I was in a very dark place. My demons were intensely personal. Soldiers in my unit had died, and because of my position as chief planner, I felt responsible for their deaths. I did my best to hide my emotions from the people I loved or those I thought would never understand the conflict that was still raging inside me. I shied away from writing because I did not want my "ghosts" to interfere with the stories and history I have come to love over the years. I did not go to many ghost conferences, and when I did, I felt like a ghost myself. I was there, but I felt somehow transparent. Sometimes, I wondered if my emotional demons had doomed me to walk the same veiled realms that are discussed in the pages that follow.

I sought help and over time, I re-learned how to find solace in my writing. Thanks to the support of my good friend and co-author Troy Taylor, I started editing a lot of the ghost stories I had written over the years and even started writing new ones. It was not easy, but thanks to the support of my family and friends and my faith in God, I came to realize a fact of war that I had always known but never really embraced: No one, no matter how high their rank, can control the chaos of battle. It is up to the living to celebrate the heroic deeds of the departed.

Without a doubt, the valiant deeds of soldiers on the fields of battle create the hauntings we know today. History tells us the locations of troops, the number of dead and wounded, the quirks of generals and how one side maneuvered against the other, but if ghosts are born, they are born from humanity's most atrocious acts: war and mortal combat.

This book is not just a mere collection of folklore and spooky campfire stories. I don't think you'll find another book where you will imagine you hear the clash of battle so vividly that it stirs your soul as you will in the pages ahead that Troy and I have put together for you. You may want to prepare yourself.

You will be unnerved. You will be disturbed.

Between these pages, we have taken history and have interwoven it with the supernatural and the macabre in such a manner that I honestly believe you will feel the panic, horror and sadness of soldiers who have "seen the elephant" and then vanished forever through death's door.

Just keep the lights on when you reading this - that's what we did when we wrote it!

Dave Goodwin
Fall 2013

Soldiers and the Supernatural

HAUNTED FORTS & MILITARY POSTS

FORT MACKINAC
Mackinac Island, Michigan

When I look back at my childhood spent growing up in the wilds of Michigan's Upper Peninsula, my most vivid memories center around our family summer vacations.

Each summer, my father planned a vacation schedule that always included fun, fishing and visits to interesting places that were historic in nature. On one such memorable two-week excursion, when I was ten or twelve years old, my father loaded everyone into the car and took us to visit Fort Michilimackinac and Fort Mackinac pronounced Mack-in-naw . Both Fort Michilimackinac, located on the northern tip of the Lower Peninsula, near Mackinaw City, and Fort Mackinac, built on the high bluffs of Mackinaw Island, overlooking the emerald green waters of Lake Michigan, have guarded the Straits of Mackinac for over two hundred years. I fell in love with both of them on my first visit.

From the first time I stepped foot inside the windswept palisades of reconstructed Fort Michilimackinac, or when I walked under the 180-year-old limestone north sally port of Fort Mackinac, I remember feeling nothing but pure euphoria. For a kid, being surrounded by cannons manned by historically accurate reenactors and being able to chase your little brother around the walls of a real fort was heaven.

To my father's credit, he had one rule that was always strictly adhered to. Whenever we visited a historic location, my brother and I had to visit every display. My father believed that it was important for us to not only have fun, but also to learn about Michigan's history. In my later years, I grew to appreciate my father's wisdom, even though I did not understand it at the time.

Since my first trip to Fort Mackinac in the early 1970s, I have returned to the Straits of Mackinac on countless occasions. Each time, it never ceases to amaze me how I can still feel the thrill and wonderment of those two old forts, just as I did so many years ago. Now I am the one who insists that my kids not only have fun but that they also understand the importance of learning the history of the places we visit.

These days, when I visit a historic fort or battlefield and let me tell you, I have seen more than a few over the years , I am also there to learn about the ghosts that wander the dark recesses where few visitors dare to tread. For me, the Straits of Mackinac has never lost its allure and, like almost every other hallowed site I have discovered during my travels, the Straits -- and Fort Mackinac in particular - it has its own fascinating ghost stories to share.

Old Fort Mackinac

In the late 1600s, the French thrust themselves into the heart of the Northwest Territory in search of valuable natural resources, mainly animal furs. The European garment industry's demand for furs such as beaver, otter and muskrat had caused prices to skyrocket, and the fur trade in the New World was lucrative. The promise of fame and riches attracted many hearty French fur traders known as "voyageurs" to the Straits of Mackinac and the Canadian wilderness. The voyageurs' close association with the local Indian tribes, the primary suppliers of animal pelts and the main consumers of French wares, eventually led to the Indians becoming dependent on European trade goods. Over time, the Indians grew to rely on the blankets, guns, knives and alcohol that the French supplied. To get these items, the Indians worked feverishly to acquire the furs needed to ensure their survival. To maintain the status quo, the French, and later the British, established a series of forts in the region to protect their interests in the Northwest fur trade.

By the 1700s, French control of the Great Lakes region was being hotly contested by another great colonial power: England. Increasing political strife and saber rattling between two of the world's greatest sea-faring nations prompted France to build Fort Michilimackinac on the northern tip of modern-day Lower Michigan in 1715. For the next forty-eight years, this fort served as the epicenter for the French fur trade on the Great Lakes. In that time, the perpetual squabbling between France and Great Britain erupted into open hostilities. From 1754 to 1760, both countries fought the French and Indian War to determine who would lay claim to North America and its seemingly never-ending natural resources. In the end, the British were the victors, and the Union Jack was hoisted over Fort Michilimackinac in 1761. Despite its new ownership, the fort continued to thrive as a meeting place for Indians, traders and settlers. This prosperity lasted until the start of the American Revolution in 1775.

Even though the first battles of the Revolutionary War had no direct bearing on operations at Fort Michilimackinac, British commanders feared that the fort would not be able to repulse an American attack. In July 1763, during Pontiac's Uprising, Indians had overrun the fort and massacred its garrison of ninety-three soldiers. With this terrible embarrassment still fresh in his mind, Lt. Governor Patrick Sinclair, the British commander at Fort Michilimackinac, decided that the fort had to be moved to a more defendable location. Sinclair's search for a new home for Fort Michilimackinac lead him to Mackinac Island, three miles east of the Straits in Lake Huron. The island had a natural harbor and high bluffs, which Sinclair realized were untouchable from the water because a naval vessel's cannon could not be elevated enough to fire a round and have it impact on the heights.

After selecting Mackinac Island as the site for his new base of operations, Sinclair set in motion the logistical process required to move men and a considerable amount of equipment across the Straits. In the winter of 1779, a handful of British troops moved to the island and started laying the foundations of Fort Mackinac. The arrival of these few hardy men signaled the beginning of a military presence on the island that lasted for the next one hundred and fifteen years.

Within a relatively short period of time, the fort began to take shape. Land was grubbed and cleared of trees and in their place grew stone blockhouses. Each succeeding winter, more and more of Fort Michilimackinac was dismantled and laboriously pulled across the ice to Mackinac Island. By 1781, the last vestiges of the once-proud Fort Michilimackinac lay burned and abandoned along the shoreline of Lake Michigan.

For eight long years, the flames of rebellion consumed the American colonies, but with the signing of the Treaty of Paris in 1783, peace and stability returned to the Great Lakes. Technically, Mackinac Island now belonged to the fledgling United States, but it took another thirteen years before the transfer of power became official.

On September 1st 1796, U.S. Army Major Henry Burbeck took command of Fort Mackinac from his British counterpart. In the same year, the British, who were eager to maintain entrepreneurial interests in the region, established a new fort on St. Joseph Island.

The Stars and Stripes flew gallantly over Mackinac Island for the next sixteen years, but on the morning of July 17, 1812, the dreaded Union Jack returned with a vengeance. Under the cover of darkness, a British contingent under the command of Captain Charles Roberts landed on the backside of the island. Quietly, Roberts's assault force of regular soldiers, voyagers and more than two hundred Indians took up a position on the heights overlooking the fort. The lethality of this British army of occupation was increased with the addition of a cannon, which was hurriedly prepared for action.

When news of this military incursion reached Lieutenant Porter Hanks, the commander of Fort Mackinac, he was stunned. Even though a state of war had existed between Britain and the United States since June 12, 1812, news of the conflict had not yet reached the American garrison at the fort. Hanks and his fifty-six men did their best to prepare for the British attack, but the seriousness of the situation became clear when the English fired the first shot from their cannon. With the British in control of the high ground, Lt. Hanks knew his was a lost cause. Rather than face the possibility of needless bloodshed, Hanks surrendered the fort without firing a shot in return. By 11:30 a.m., the battle for control of Mackinac Island was over.

On August 4, 1814, the United States made a veiled attempt to reclaim the island. The disastrous incursion, under the joint command of Colonel Crogan, U.S. Army, and Captain Sinclair, U.S. Navy, was an abysmal failure. The casualties that were inflicted on the American forces were staggering for the time. With fifteen soldiers dead and fifty or more wounded, any hopes of an American victory were lost.

Fortunately, the second British occupation of Fort Mackinac was short-lived. The Treaty of Ghent, signed in February 1815, returned the island to the United States. Over the next several years, tensions continued to exist between Great Britain and the United States. The British, who again refused to abdicate their influence in the Straits, had built Fort Collyer a scant forty miles away on Drummond Island. Despite the relative proximity of these former adversaries, the clash of arms was never again heard on Mackinac Island.

For the next eighty years, the U.S. military maintained a nearly continuous presence at Fort Mackinac. During that time, troops from the fort were called to serve in the Indian Wars, the Mexican War and the War Between the States, but following the Civil War, Fort Mackinac's military significance began to wane.

In 1875, Mackinac Island was officially designated as a national park and the soldiers at Fort Mackinac had their rifles replaced with garden rakes. The U.S. Army, specifically the enlisted soldiers of Fort Mackinac, maintained the recreational facilities of the island for thousands of tourists until the fort was abandoned in 1895. Upon the military's withdrawal, the island fell under the auspices of the state of Michigan. In one anti-climactic flourish of a politician's pen, Mackinac Island had become the first state park in Michigan's history.

From Fort Mackinac's inception in 1779 until its eventual decline in 1875, it was constantly under construction or repair. While in operation, the top priority of the men stationed at Fort Mackinac was the protection and maintenance of the fort itself. As simple as this sounded, these rudimentary tasks were fraught with both mental and physical hardship. The various British, and later American, units that called the island home during that time period, provided a virtually limitless labor pool. When they were not building or maintaining the fort and grounds, soldiers spent countless hours conducting military maneuvers. This time was divided, not always equally, between firearms training, incessant inspections and fatigue duty. Military life on the frontier took up a good part of a soldier's day, and that was not always a bad thing because it left little time for the men to ponder the negative psychological impact of frontier life on the Great Lakes.

Soldiers assigned to Fort Mackinac were for all intents and purposes cut off from the world. The three miles of open water between the island and the mainland might as well have been a thousand. Men separated from their families, friends and previous lives found themselves longing to be anywhere but Fort Mackinac. During the winter months, when the island was encased in layers of thick ice and snow, the extreme isolation had a profound emotional effect on the fort's garrison.

To make matters worse, there were very few ways for the enlisted men and officers to cope with the tediousness of island life. The loneliness and inevitable depression caused by the absence of family and loved ones lead to a high rate of drunkenness and desertions. Military manuals of the day called for strict discipline to be enforced so as to ensure that army functioned effectively. To this end, quick and sometimes harsh punishments were meted out to soldiers who violated even the simplest rule. Punishments included, but were not limited to, time in the guardhouse, public flogging, court-martial, and reduction of rank with forfeiture of pay and privileges.

Errant soldiers who committed the crime of desertion faced the most severe repercussions. Author Keith R. Widder detailed one such incident in *Reveille Till Taps: Soldier Life at Fort Mackinac 1780-1895*.

In September 1860, Private William Henderson was found guilty of running away from the army, and his superiors dealt harshly with him. Henderson forfeited all pay due him and suffered severe bodily inflictions. In addition to receiving fifty lashes on his bare back, he had a one and one-half inch letter "D" indelibly marked under his left arm. Ten days later he had his head shaved and was drummed out of the army.

In some instances, nature exacted a worse toll on deserters than that inflicted by the officers of the courts-martial. One soldier who escaped the island during the dead of winter returned in disgrace with frozen feet. The frostbite was so severe that the post surgeon had to amputate both feet before infection set in.

If a soldier was lucky enough to avoid the disciplinarian's whip, he was not out of the woods yet. The hardship of a meager existence in the extreme winter climate of Mackinac Island was particularly unforgiving to those soldiers with weak constitutions. Not surprisingly, this created very unhealthy living conditions at the fort that were laced with periods of illness and injury.

For the most part, physicians at Fort Mackinac went to great lengths to keep all of the island's inhabitants healthy. The post's surgeon was constantly vigilant for a host of diseases. The most feared were cholera and typhoid. During the summer of 1832, the quick action of civilian and military medical personnel helped to avert a cholera epidemic that threatened to decimate all human life on the island. Later, in 1887, dysentery struck the civilians and soldiers living on Mackinac Island. It was the post surgeon, Dr. Charles Woodruff, who linked the dreaded outbreak to tainted drinking water. This could explain why the old fort hospital is still saturated with an "air of sickness" to this day.

Despite the best efforts of the post surgeon, the hand of death, whether summoned by lingering illness or by battle, sometimes reached out and claimed the lives of those who served at Fort Mackinac. The remains of one hundred and forty deceased soldiers and their family members were interred in the post's cemetery. Today, the tiny cemetery only yields the location of one hundred and seven of these graves. The final resting places of thirty-three unfortunates have been lost over the years. Sadly, only thirty-four of the marked graves have been identified. It is no wonder that the ghostly image of an unknown woman is frequently seen weeping over the graves of several children buried in the farthest corner of the cemetery

When not engaged in some official capacity, a soldier's free time was his own to do with as he pleased. Many men fished, engaged in sports, or availed themselves of the local farmers' daughters. Most importantly, a soldier's spare time was spent doing just about anything to ease the mind-numbing monotony of everyday life on Mackinac Island. One popular recreational activity was story telling, and ghost stories were always a favorite. One spectral tale that was whispered around the campfire centered on a ghost ship known as the *Griffon*.

In August 1679, Rene Robert de La Salle, launched the *Griffon*, the first large vessel known to have sailed on the Great Lakes. The sixty-foot wooden ship was a marvel in an age when simple canoes were the only means available to travel the emerald green waters of the lakes.

The *Griffon's* history was short and sordid. The "barque" was alleged to have been crewed by thirty-two men, described as both "saints and sinners alike," and captained by La Salle, who was by all accounts a tyrant. La Salle was a hard man to work for. He expected a lot from his men and did nothing to reward them for their loyalty. La Salle's overall poor management skills created a dismal command climate, prompting many of his men to seek employment elsewhere. To make matters worse, La Salle had a violent temper and demonstrated a complete disregard for the well-being of his men. These less-than-desirable leadership qualities wore upon the nerves of the men and resulted in a great deal of hatred and contempt for their captain. This bitterness, fueled by withheld wages, ran so deep amongst the crew of the *Griffon* that it was reported that there were several instances where La Salle's own men tried to poison him.

On September 18, 1679, the *Griffon* sailed from Green Bay with a five-man crew and was never seen again. The lakes were uncharted and most people believed that she had foundered in a storm far from shore or that local natives had seized the ship and crew. La Salle, on the other hand, had his own ideas about the disappearance of his ship. He speculated that his motley crew had stolen the valuable cargo of furs and trade goods stashed in the hold of the *Griffon* and had scuttled her to hide the evidence of their crime. Her "bones" have never been found.

But what became of La Salle? Like the *Griffon*, he too experienced an abrupt but not so mysterious end. Years after the *Griffon* was lost, La Salle was murdered, shot in the back of the head. Ironically, the man who fired the fatal shot was one of La Salle's resentful former employees. He murdered La Salle in the midst of a mutiny.

The lingering question of what actually caused the demise of the *Griffon* remains unanswered. What is known is that within a year of her launching, she was lost, presumably the first recorded victim to be swallowed by the Great Lakes. Perhaps this unresolved riddle is the reason that the ghost of the *Griffon*, forever manned by the spirits of her crew, has haunted the Great Lakes for hundreds of years. Sailors, both past and present, have reported seeing the phantom ship silently plying the undulating waves of Lake Michigan. But she is not alone. The *Griffon* shares her untimely fate with more than six thousand unlucky vessels that have also vanished under the waves of the Great Lakes over the years.

Another unearthly story told around hearths and campfires served as both entertainment and as a warning for those soldiers considering desertion. As previously discussed, following the War of 1812, the British constructed Fort Collyer, sometimes referred to as Fort Drummond, on Drummond Island. Lack of provisions, intolerable conditions and low morale all took a toll on this lost garrison, which had been all but forgotten by the British high command.

It is said that five British soldiers who were frustrated with their assignment to the isolated fort thought it best to voice their protest by deserting the army. The fort's commander was outraged by the men's despicable action and offered a $20 reward for the capture and return of each soldier - dead or alive.

The commander of Fort Collyer believed the men were going to try to make it to the United States, where they could book passage on a ship home, so he sent an Indian war party to capture them. John Bigsby, secretary of the British Boundary Commission, described the outcome in his book, *The Shoe and the Canoe*:

Five soldiers started early in the morning across the strait to the American main, and made by the Indian path for Michilimackinac. On arriving there they would be safe. The commandant sent half-a-dozen Indians after them, who in a couple of days returned with the men's heads in a bag. The Indians knew of a short cut and got ahead of their prey and lay in ambush behind a rock in the track. When the soldiers came within a few feet the Indians fired, and in the end killed every one of them.

In another version of the story, two Indian runners found the men sleeping along the beach somewhere on Manitoulin Island. In a frenzy, the Indian braves descended upon the luckless men. It was not until the bloody deed had been done that the Indians realized they needed to bring some tangible proof back to Fort Collyer to show the commandant that they had remedied his desertion problem. The conundrum was easily solved with a few hacks of a tomahawk. In quick order, the braves chopped off the soldiers' heads, leaving their torsos sitting around the campfire. According to Samuel F. Cook, author of *Drummond Island, the Story of the British Occupation 1815-1828*, the soldiers' headless bodies, "remained sitting on the log and warming themselves by the fire which made the night lurid with its glare. And ever since, unburied, they wander on those shores, seeking the heads which there they lost while sleeping." The authenticity of the story, whichever version you subscribe to, might have been questionable, but I am sure that the commander at Fort Mackinac did little to dissuade anyone from telling it.

Fort Mackinac itself has its own ghostly stories to share. On misty mornings, visitors and park staff sometimes encounter a phantom piper pacing back and forth along the wall of the fort's north sally port. The faint sound of his music, heard only at dawn, is the only evidence of his passing.

Several of those who have visited the post commander's quarters while touring the fort find that they are in the presence of something not of this world. Here, visitors sometimes encounter small shadows, said to be the spirits of one of fort's previous commandant's children.

Even the old reconstructed guardhouse, home for many derelicts and scofflaws in its day, is shrouded in a pall of unearthly energy. When the site was being excavated, it was rumored that the skeleton of a man was found in the deepest bowels of the guardhouse known as the "Black Hole." No one knows for sure who the man was or what crime he committed to warrant a punishment so hideous that it ended with his existence being erased from the world as he knew it. Today, tourists frequently comment on the unusual chills that run up and down their spines when they walk through the old jailhouse, unaware of the reason for such unnerving feelings.

Ghosts are reportedly just as prevalent outside the fort, as well. People who take leisurely strolls along the Rifle Range Trail sometimes find their peaceful commune with nature interrupted by volleys of rifle fire initiated over one hundred years ago.

And what about the reported sightings of Indian braves, running wild through the woods at the north end of the island at night? Many of the island's inhabitants believe they are the ghosts of seventy-five Indians who were said to have been butchered there by the English during the War of 1812. My research failed to prove or disprove that an incident of this type occurred anywhere on Mackinac Island.

Fort Mackinac is truly a gem in the crown of the Michigan State Park system. From its inception, it was a genuinely formidable bastion that symbolized both Empire and Commerce. Taken by force only once in its history, the small fort, consisting of a triad of nineteenth century blockhouses, reminds us that soldiers who once manned the post were expected to defend the frontier settlement to the last man. There were many who died here. Some who called the fort home deserted it in its time of need and paid the ultimate price for their cowardice. Others served faithfully, only to die when their constitutions failed under the considerable hardships of the region.

These men and women, be they sinners or saints, young or old, shared their fate with the island. It is their ghostly voices that call to me when I visit the Straits of Mackinac, and it is one of the reasons I come back time and time again.

FORT TICONDEROGA
Upstate New York - Near Burlington, Vermont

During the French and Indian War, which wreaked havoc on the American colonies in New England, Fort Ticonderoga was a key stronghold for British forces. Located at the strategic intersection of Lake Champlain and Lake George in upstate New York, the fort controlled the frequently used trade routes between the British-controlled Hudson River Valley and the French-controlled Saint Lawrence River Valley. The name "Ticonderoga" comes from an Iroquois word meaning "at the junction of two waterways." It's a name that would be well-known to the Native Americans of the region - but certainly not to the Scottish Highlanders in the 1750s. And yet, in one of the strangest ghostly tales of the French and Indian War, the name Ticonderoga is linked to a terrible premonition that involved Duncan Campbell, Lord of Inverawe and major of the

42nd Regiment of Foot, also known as the Royal Highlanders, or the Black Watch.

It's an eerie tale that still reverberates to this day.

Fort Ticonderoga

The construction of Fort Ticonderoga took place because of its strategic location. Lake Champlain, which forms part of the border between New York and Vermont, and the Hudson River, together formed an important travel route that was used by Indians before the arrival of European colonists. The route was relatively free of obstacles to navigation, with only a few portages. One strategically important place on the route lies at a narrows near the southern end of Lake Champlain, where Ticonderoga Creek, known in colonial times as the La Chute River, enters the lake, carrying water from Lake George.

Native Americans had occupied the region for centuries before French explorer Samuel de Champlain first arrived there in 1609. Champlain recounted that the Algonquin, with whom he was traveling, battled a group of Iroquois nearby. In 1642, French missionary Isaac Jogues was the first white man to traverse the portage at Ticonderoga while escaping a battle between the Iroquois and members of the Huron tribe. The French, who had colonized the Saint Lawrence River Valley to the north, and the English, who had taken over the Dutch settlements that became the Province of New York to the south, began contesting the area as early as 1691, when Pieter Schuyler built a small wooden fort at the Ticonderoga point on the western shore of the lake. The colonial conflicts eventually led to the French and Indian War.

In 1755, following the Battle of Lake George, the Marquis de Vaudreuil, the governor of the French Province of Canada, sent his cousin, Michel Chartier de Lotbinière, to design and construct a fortress at this militarily important site, which the French called Fort Carillon, named for a French trader. The work in 1755 consisted mostly of beginning construction on the main walls. The main bastions and a sawmill were added the next year. Work slowed in 1757, when many of the troops participated in the attack on Fort William Henry. The fort contained three barracks, which were completed in 1758, and four storehouses. One bastion held a bakery capable of producing sixty loaves of bread a day. A powder magazine was hacked out of the bedrock beneath one of the bastions. All the construction within the fort was of stone.

A wooden palisade protected an area outside the fort between the southern wall and the lakeshore. Since the French built the fort to prevent access to the lake by the British, it faced north. The wooden palisade on the lakeshore contained the main landing for the fort, additional storage facilities and other features necessary for maintenance of the fort.

By 1758, the fort was largely complete; the only ongoing work thereafter consisted of dressing the walls with stone. Still, French General Louis-Joseph de Montcalm and two of his military engineers surveyed the works in 1758 and found something to criticize in almost every aspect of the fort's construction. The buildings were too tall and thus easier for attackers' cannon fire to hit, the powder magazine leaked, the masonry was of poor quality and worst of all - which the critics did not seem to notice - several nearby hills loomed above the fort, offering a vantage point for an attacking army. It would also later turn out that the storage space inside the fort was severely limited. The barracks were also too small and the quality of the water in the cistern was poor.

In August 1757, the French captured Fort William Henry in an action that was launched from Fort Carillon. This, and a string of other French victories in 1757, prompted the British to organize a large-scale attack on the fort as part of a strategy against French Canada. In June 1758, British General James Abercromby began amassing a large force at Fort William Henry in preparation for the military campaign directed up the Champlain Valley. These forces landed on July 6 at the north end of Lake George, only four miles from the fort. General Montcalm, who had arrived at Carillon in late June, engaged his troops in a flurry of work to improve the fort's outer defenses. Over two days, they built entrenchments around a rise between the fort and Mount Hope, about three-quarters of a mile northwest of the fort, and then constructed an abatis felled trees with sharpened branches pointing out below these entrenchments.

Abercromby's failure to advance directly to the fort on July 7 made much of this defensive work possible. Abercromby's trusted second-in-command, Brigadier General George Howe, had been killed when his column encountered a French reconnaissance party a short time before. It was said that Abercromby "felt Howe's death most heavily" and did not act immediately. When he did finally launch his troops, he sent them on a full-scale front assault on the fort on July 8 - a disastrous attack that led to a British defeat, even though the attackers outnumbered the French defenders nearly four to one.

And it would be in this bloody attack that the eerie tale of the fort has its roots.

The story began in Scotland in 1755, several years before the battle at what would someday be called Fort Ticonderoga. In the Scottish Highlands was the ancient castle of Inverawe, which had been the dwelling place of the Campbell clan for generations. Lord Duncan Campbell, according to all who knew him, was a good, kind man, known for his integrity and loyalty. So when a man came to his door one night, in torn clothing and a blood-drenched kilt, out of breath and clearly in a state of panic, the laird ignored caution and allowed the man inside. When he asked the man what the trouble might be, the man said he was being chased and asked for shelter for the night.

"What have you done?" Campbell asked him.

The bedraggled stranger replied, "I have killed a man."

While most would, at this point, turn away a stranger under such circumstances, Campbell did not. He knew that many murders had been committed in the Highlands for good cause, and he believed the man deserved a fair shake. The stranger fervently told him that the murder had been justified and asked again for shelter.

"No man has ever claimed hospitality of me without receiving it," Campbell assured him, never suspecting that those words would haunt him for the rest of his life.

The stranger begged that no one be told of his presence. Campbell agreed, but the man was not satisfied. He urged him to swear on his dirk, or dagger, the ultimate test of Celtic honor. Campbell swore, and then led the fugitive to a secret room in the castle, where he was hidden away with food and drink.

Soon, there was another loud knocking on the door. This time, it was two armed men. One of them informed Campbell that his cousin, Donald, had been murdered. "We are looking for his killer," they said.

Campbell turned them away, forced by his oath to say that he had seen no one. He was deeply torn between his loyalty to his dead cousin and his sacred promise to the man who had murdered him. He laid down to rest that night but was later awakened by the ghost of his cousin, Donald Campbell. The apparition groaned at him, "Inverawe! Inverawe! Blood has been shed. Shield not the murderer!"

Campbell ran from his bedroom and went to the murderer's hiding place, telling him that he could no longer offer him sanctuary. But he had sworn on his dirk, the stranger reminded him, telling him, "Woe to him who breaks this oath!"

Campbell was torn. If he broke the oath, he would not only suffer great shame but possibly death at the hands of his betrayed guest. If he honored it, he risked the wrath of the ghost. Trying to strike a compromise, Campbell took the murderer to a nearby cave and left him there, promising to tell no one of his whereabouts.

But the following night, he was once again awakened by his cousin's angry spirit, who repeated the warning from the night before. Shaken, Campbell hurriedly dressed and ran to the cave, only to find it was empty. The stranger was gone. Campbell was relieved. No one could accuse him of shielding the murderer now. Hopefully, his cousin's spirit could now rest in peace - but that was not to be the case.

That night, the ghost returned once again, this time with a portentous - albeit cryptic - message. The ghost intoned, "Farewell, Inverawe! Farewell, till we meet once more at Ticonderoga!" Then the spirit turned away and vanished.

Ticonderoga? Where, or what, was Ticonderoga? Mystified, Campbell tried to figure out the strange warning, but eventually, he gave up. The strange-sounding word, though, never faded from his memory.

Three years later, in 1758, Duncan Campbell, now 55 and a major in the Black Watch, the regiment assigned to keep order in the turbulent Highlands, journeyed with his men to America to join the British force under General James Abercromby in the French and Indian War.

The regiment was ordered to take part in the planned attack against the French at Fort Carillon. At a village along the way, the 42nd Regiment stopped at a tavern. A young woman struck up a conversation with Major Campbell. As the men were about to leave, she asked him, "Will you be coming back this way? After you take Ticonderoga?"

Campbell stood frozen in shock. He stammered, "Ticonderoga? But they said we were to attack Fort Carillon."

The girl explained, "That's what the French call it, but the Indian name is Ticonderoga."

As soon as she spoke those words, Campbell knew that he was doomed. His fellow officers, all of whom had heard the tale of the major's ghostly visitor and his fateful promise, tried to calm him by dismissing it as a coincidence. When they reached their destination, they argued with him that since the military considered the place to be Fort Carillon, the name Ticonderoga should be ignored. The following morning, though, Campbell emerged from his tent, looked exhausted and resigned.

He told his friends, "I have seen him. He came to my tent last night. This is Ticonderoga, and I shall die today."

On the morning of July 8, 1758, General Abercromby staged the frontal assault on the walls of the fort. Attempting to move as quickly as possible, Abercromby decided to forego field cannons in favor of sheer manpower. But his sixteen thousand troops were no match for the mere four thousand French defenders, who soundly routed the attackers. Among the worst hit were the men of the 42nd Regiment, who suffered massive casualties. Among them was Major Duncan Campbell. His arm shattered by a bullet, Campbell was carried to Fort Edward, where his arm was amputated. He only lived a few days before dying on July 17, leaving a legendary mark on Fort Ticonderoga.

This battle did not mark the end of the fort's place in American history. It gave the fort a reputation for being impregnable, which had an impact on future military operations in the area, notably during the American Revolution. Following the French victory, Montcalm, anticipating further British attacks, ordered additional work on the defenses. However, the British did not attack again in 1758, so the French withdrew all but a small garrison of men for the winter in November.

The fort was captured the following year by the British under General Jeffrey Amherst in the 1759 Battle of Ticonderoga. In this confrontation, eleven thousand British troops, using emplaced artillery, drove off a token garrison of four hundred Frenchmen. They did so merely by occupying the high ground above the fort and threatening to unleash a bombardment down upon the fort. The French withdrew, but not before spiking a number of cannons left behind and using explosives to destroy portions of the structure. Although the British worked in 1759 and 1760 to repair and improve the fort, it saw no more significant action in the war. After the war, the British garrisoned it with a small number of troops and allowed it to fall into disrepair. Colonel Frederick Haldimand, in command of the fort in 1773, wrote that it was in "ruinous condition."

During the Revolutionary War, the fort again saw action in May 1775 when the Green Mountain Boys of Vermont and other state militia under the command of Ethan Allen and Benedict Arnold captured it in a surprise attack. Cannons that were captured were transported to Boston, where their deployment forced the British to abandon the city in March 1776. The Americans held it until June 1777, when British forces under General John Burgoyne again occupied high ground above the fort and threatened the Continental Army troops, leading them to withdraw from the fort and its surrounding defenses. The only direct attack on the fort took place in September 1777, when John Brown led five hundred Americans in an unsuccessful attempt to capture the fort from about one hundred British defenders.

The British abandoned the fort following the failure of the Saratoga campaign, and it ceased to be of military value after 1781. It fell into ruin, leading people from the surrounding area to strip it of some of its usable stone, metal, and woodwork. It became a popular stop for tourists in the nineteenth century, which led to its restoration by private owners in the early part of the twentieth century.

To this day, Fort Ticonderoga holds a fascinating place in the nation's military history - and in the history of the supernatural, as well. The ghostly tale of the Campbell clan has never completely faded away and remains today as an example of how the battlefield can serve as a borderline between life and death.

FORT ERIE
Ontario, Canada

Located on the Canadian side of the Niagara River, Fort Erie was the scene of several violent battles during the War of 1812. In fact, it achieved dubious distinction as the site of the bloodiest battle in Canadian history. Many American, British and Canadian lives were lost there. It's no wonder, then, that the old fort is reputed to be haunted by a number of ghosts, including a famous headless and handless pair - two soldiers who wander the grounds in search of something unknown, but obviously valuable enough to keep them hanging around two centuries after their deaths.

Fort Erie was the first fort to be constructed as part of a network of fortifications after the end of the Seven Years' War, as the French and Indian War was known in Canada. The war was concluded by the Treaty of Paris in 1763, at which time all of New France was ceded to Great Britain. The fort was constructed in 1764 on the edge of the Niagara River and got its first taste of action as a supply base for British troops, Loyalist rangers and Iroquois warriors during the American Revolution.

During the War of 1812, more men fought at Fort Erie than any other place in Canada, and it was the site of the only siege in the country. Part of the garrison of Fort Erie fought at the Battle of Frenchman's Creek against an American attack in November 1812. In 1813, Fort Erie was held for a period by U.S. forces and then abandoned on June 9, 1813. The fort had been partially dismantled by the small garrison of British troops and Canadian militia as they withdrew. British reoccupation followed the American withdrawal from the area later, continuing the back-and-forth exchange of the fort during the grim years of the war.

Most Americans know little about the War of 1812. The combatants in the war were the United States and Britain, and it included the latter's colonies of Upper Canada Ontario , Lower Canada Quebec , Nova Scotia, Newfoundland and Bermuda. Hostilities lasted from 1812 to early 1814, although the Treaty of Ghent ended the war in late 1814. The immediate cause of the war was trade tensions - Great Britain had been at war with France since 1793 and, in an attempt to impede neutral trade with France in response to the Continental blockade, imposed a series of trade restrictions that the United States declared were illegal under international law. Two other incendiary actions were the conscription of American sailors into the British Navy and British military support for the American Indians' defense of their lands against encroaching American settlers. With massacres on the frontier and American sailors being kidnapped on the high seas, the United States declared war on Britain in June 1812.

In the early days of the war, American leaders considered Canada such an easy conquest that President Thomas Jefferson breezily called it "merely a matter of marching." It seems, however, that they underestimated the region's complexity. Upper Canada proved to be a surprise. Many Loyalist Americans who had migrated to Upper Canada after the Revolutionary War unexpectedly ended up siding with the British during the War of 1812. In Lower Canada, Britain found staunch allies among the English elite, loyal subjects of the empire, and the French elite, who were counting on the British to protect them from the American evils of Protestant religion and republican democracy.

The main theater at the onset of the war was the West, principally the areas near the Niagara River between Lake Erie and Lake Ontario, and near the Saint Lawrence River and Lake Champlain. The United States began operations in the Western frontier because that was where the idea of war with the British got the most support from a populace angered that the British had threatened American settlers by selling arms and preaching violence to the Native Americans of the region.

During the early days of the war, in 1812 and 1813, inexperienced American commanders got an unwelcome dose of British military expertise. After American Brigadier General William Hull's embarrassing retreat from Canada on July 12, 1812, and the subsequent victory of British Major General Isaac Brock at Fort Detroit, Americans began to realize that taking Canada would not be an easy task. Brock went on to the eastern end of Lake Erie but was prevented from invading American territory by a temporary armistice. As soon as that armistice ended, however, the Americans crossed the Niagara River on October 13, 1812. The Americans were soundly defeated, but Major General Brock was killed, which was a great loss for the British.

In the months that followed, the war raged. On May 27, 1813, the Americans captured Fort George, on the northern end of the Niagara River. On September 10, 1813, the Americans, under the command of Captain Oliver Hazard Perry, gained control of Lake Erie during the Battle of Lake Erie. Soon after, they incurred the wrath of the British and Canadians by setting fire to the village of Newark present-day Niagara-on-the-Lake , leaving the surviving inhabitants without shelter, freezing to death in the bitter cold. The British retaliated by capturing Fort Niagara on December 18, 1813, and destroying Buffalo.

By the middle of 1814, their army considerably more disciplined and experienced, the Americans continued the fight. They captured Fort Erie and won the Battle of Chippewa. On July 25, the British laid siege to Fort Erie, forcing the Americans back across the Niagara River. In November, though, the Americans took back the fort and deliberately destroyed it, ending the exchanges.

After the war, the British continued to occupy the ruined fort until 1823. After that, it was abandoned, only to be occupied yet again four decades later. In 1866, a brigade of Fenians Irish Republicans used the ruins of the old fort as a base for their raid into Ontario. The Fenian Brotherhood - an American group that was founded to overthrow British rule in Ireland -- invaded Canada on June 1, 1866 with more than five hundred American Civil War veterans by crossing the Niagara River a little north of Fort Erie. Their first order of business was to occupy the town of Fort Erie and demand food and equipment from the local population. The invaders offered Fenian bonds as payment but were refused by the townsfolk.

The Fenians then marched north to try and capture the town of Chippewa at the Niagara River exit of the Welland Canal. Before reaching their goal, and discovering a British and Canadian force had reached the town before them, they turned to face a weak Canadian militia brigade that was approaching Fort Erie from the west, routing it at the Battle of Ridgeway. The Fenians returned to Fort Erie, where they defeated a second small force of local Canadian militia, including a naval detachment from Dunnville. Unable to get reinforcements across the river and concerned over the approach of a large number of Canadian militia and British regulars, the Fenians retreated from Fort Erie to Buffalo. This brought an end to Fort Erie's use as a military stronghold.

Throughout the latter years of the nineteenth century, the old fort was used as a park and picnic area by local families. It also attracted a number of famous visitors, including the Prince of Wales and author Mark Twain.

The reconstruction of the fort was started in 1937. The reconstruction was jointly sponsored by the provincial and federal governments and the Niagara Parks Commission. The fort was restored to its appearance during the 1812-1814 period and officially reopened on July 1, 1939.

During the restoration, a mass grave of one hundred and fifty British and three American soldiers was uncovered. A memorial at the entrance to the grounds marks their remains. At the other end of the property is an old Native American burial ground. These graves, and the fact that Fort Erie saw such bloody fighting during the war, may be the reason why it has become famous for its hauntings. In fact, there have been so many ghost sightings at the old fort that it has become a must-see spot for ghost enthusiasts. A seasonal tour at the fort brings people from all over the region. And there's nothing contrived about it. As fort manager Peter Martin once stated, "We have real ghosts."

One of the lingering spirits is a red-jacketed British soldier who walks the grounds and always seems to vanish just moments after he is spotted. Dennis McGibney, a maintenance worker at the fort, told about a former groundskeeper who saw the soldier, but as soon as he turned around, "he was gone." The worker never returned to that part of the fort alone.

There is also a mysterious man wearing what appears to be a top hat, who has been seen in the northeast bastion area. According to the visitors who have glimpsed this strange figure, he appears for a few seconds and then disappears. Jim Hill, superintendent of heritage for the Niagara Parks Commission, pointed out that the hat the man has reportedly been seen wearing was part of the British Marines' uniform from the War of 1812 period.

One of the most famous spirits at Fort Erie is thought to be the ghost of Captain Nicholas Kingsley, paymaster to the 8th Regiment of Foot. The captain died of a fever in September 1813, following a violent convulsion. His family later donated his deathbed to the museum at Fort Erie, where it is one of the oldest artifacts on display.

No one is allowed near the folding mahogany bed with brass hinges, not even the staff members whose job it is to keep the area clean. No one is allowed to touch it because it's so fragile that any pressure might cause it to collapse. And yet, the bedding is often found to be rumpled, and the captain's pillow has been discovered in all sorts of odd places, including on top of the bed's canopy.

The captain apparently is not fond of having his bed on public display. People taking tours of the fort have often reported that objects seem to have moved by themselves. One couple claimed that when they tried to stop the door to the room from opening, thinking that wind had caused it to swing open, they were met with a strong opposing force that seemed to come from nowhere. The only thing that staff members could think of was that Captain Kingsley wanted some privacy.

But by far the most famous ghosts of Fort Erie are the headless American officer and his companion with no hands. According to the legend, the two soldiers wander the banks of the Niagara River and the grounds near the old fort on a quest of some sort. No one knows what they are looking for. Local folklore states that the two men need one another because the headless figure can't see to help find whatever it is they are searching for, and if found, the man with no hands cannot pick it up.

There is one clue as to the possible identity of the two ghosts that was found in the autobiography of a fourteen-year-old drummer from the 11th U.S. Infantry during the War of 1812 named Jarvis Hanks. His memoirs, written sometime between 1831 and 1847, relate a gruesome incident that he witnessed at Fort Erie:

As there were no regular barbers attached to the army, the soldiers used to shave themselves, and each other. One morning several were shaving in succession, near a parapet. Sergeant Waits sat down facing the enemy, and Corporal Reed began to perform the operation of removing the beard from his face, when a cannon ball took the corporal's right hand, and the sergeant's head, throwing blood, brains, hair, fragments of flesh and bones, upon a tent near them, and upon the clothing of several spectators of the horrible scene. The razor also disappeared and no vestige of it was ever seen afterwards. The corporal went to the hospital and had his arm amputated, and a few men rolled up the sergeant's body in his blanket, carried it out and buried it. Probably less than twenty minutes transpired between the time he sat down to be shaved and the time he was reposing in the home of the soldier's grave.

Since few people had knowledge of Hanks' memoirs, this gave the stories of the pair of ghosts even more credibility. Nonetheless, there was no hard evidence of the story until one day in 1987, when workers at Fort Erie made a chilling discovery. In a section of the fort where the dead were buried - just beyond the site of the original field hospital - the remains of twenty-eight American soldiers were unearthed. One of them was believed to be Sergeant Waits. The body was fully clothed and while there were no way to be certain of his identity, his uniform had telltale epaulets. Unlike British sergeants, who wore chevrons or stripes, American sergeants wore epaulets. The epaulet had a different hook on it than the normal button that a soldier would have on his uniform. This evidence, coupled with the fact that the body had no head, was enough to convince the workers that Sergeant Waits had been found.

And what about Sergeant Reed? His body was never discovered. According to Jarvis Hanks, he lost only one arm, not both hands. Of course, he might have lost the other hand later in battle - becoming the other half of the ghostly duo that roams the old fort's grounds. Or perhaps Sergeant Waits' companion is not Reed at all, but another unfortunate war casualty whom he met along his journey in the afterlife.

Whoever they are, these apparitions from more than two centuries past remain behind at Fort Erie. Until they find what they are looking for, they seem doomed to wander the grounds of this historic and once blood-soaked place.

Fort Dearborn - site of future Chicago

FORT DEARBORN
Chicago, Illinois

It may not have been a cold morning in April 1803, when Captain John Whistler climbed a sand dune around which the sluggish Chicago River tried to reach Lake Michigan, but chances are it was. A chilling wind would have been a characteristic greeting from the landscape that Whistler had come to change. His orders had been to take six soldiers from the 1st U.S. Infantry, survey a road from Detroit to the mouth of the river, and draw up plans for a fort at this location. The British had also planned to build a fort at the entrance to the Chicago River but Whistler managed to beat them to the site. One has to wonder how the city might be different today if the British had managed to show up first.

After claiming the site, Captain Whistler returned to Detroit to get his garrison and his family. He was forty-five years old and neither his poor army pay nor the dangers of the frontier stopped him from living a full domestic life. Eventually, he fathered fifteen children.

Captain Whistler's family was spared the arduous trek over erratic Indian trails to the Chicago River. While the troops marched on foot, the captain and his brood boarded the U.S. schooner *Tracy*, which also carried artillery and camp equipment. It sailed to the mouth of the St. Joseph River, where it met the troops. The Whistler family took one of the *Tracy's* rowboats to the Chicago River, while the troops marched around the lake.

There were sixty-nine officers and men in the contingent that had the task of building Fort Dearborn, which was named in honor of Secretary of War Henry Dearborn, a man who would go on to be considered one of the most inept leaders in American history. During the War of 1812, Dearborn was placed in command of all the American troops between Lake Erie and the Atlantic. He tried to capture Montreal, but his troops were so disorganized that they never even made it across the Canadian border. Dearborn was finally relieved of his command by President James Madison in 1813, after he narrowly avoided being court-martialed. In spite of this, a number of Chicago parks and developments were named in his honor, leading author Norman Mark to refer to him as "an example of one of history's most successful failures."

The hill on which Fort Dearborn was built rose eight feet above the Chicago River. The water curved around it until, stopped from flowing into a lake by a sandbar, it ran south until it found an outlet. To this spot, the soldiers hauled the wood that had been cut along the north bank. The fort was a simple stockade built of logs, which were placed in the ground and then sharpened along the upper end to discourage attackers. The outer stockade was a solid wall with an entrance in the southern section blocked by heavy gates. An underground exit was located on the north side. As time went on, the soldiers built barracks, officers' quarters, a guardhouse and a small powder magazine made from brick. West of the fort, they constructed a two-story log building with split-oak siding to serve as an Indian agency. Between this structure and the fort they placed root cellars. South of the fort, the land was enclosed for a garden. Blockhouses were added at two corners of the fort and three pieces of light artillery were mounted at the walls. The fort offered substantial protection for the soldiers garrisoned there, but they would later learn that it was not enough.

When the War of 1812 unleashed the fury of the Native Americans on the western frontier, the city of Chicago almost ceased to exist before it got a chance to get started. On August 15, 1812, the garrison at Fort Dearborn evacuated its post and, with women in children in tow, attempted to march to safety. But it was overwhelmed and wiped out in a wave of bloodshed and fire after traveling less than a mile. The story of the massacre will be repeated for as long as Chicago continues to stand. It marks not only the deadliest event in the city's history of the city, but also created a ghost story that endures to this day.

At the start of the War of 1812, tensions in the wilderness began to rise. British troops came to the American frontier, spreading liquor and discontent among the Indian tribes, especially the Potawatomi, the Wyandot and the Winnebago, near Fort Dearborn. In April, an Indian raid occurred on the Lee farm, near the bend in the Chicago River where present-day Racine Avenue meets the river and two men were killed. After that, the fort became a refuge for many of the settlers and a growing cause of unrest for the local Indians. When war was declared that summer, and the British captured the American garrison at Mackinac, it was decided that Fort Dearborn could not be held and that it should be evacuated.

General William Hull, the American commander in the Northwest, issued orders to Captain Nathan Heald at Fort Dearborn through Indian agent officers. He was told that the fort was to be abandoned, arms and ammunition destroyed, and all goods were to be distributed to friendly Indians. Hull sent a message to Fort Wayne, which sent Captain William Wells and a contingent of allied Miami Indians toward Fort Dearborn to assist with the evacuation.

There is no dispute about whether or not General Hull gave the order, nor that Captain Heald received it, but some have wondered if perhaps Hull's instruction, or his handwriting, was not clear because Heald waited eight days before acting on it. During that time, Heald argued with his officers, with John Kinzie, a settlement trader who opposed the evacuation, and with local Indians, one of whom fired off a rifle in the commanding officer's quarters.

The delay managed to give the hostile Indians time to gather outside the fort. They assembled there in an almost siege-like state and Heald realized that he was going to have to bargain with them if the occupants of Fort Dearborn were going to safely reach Fort Wayne. On August 13, all of the blankets, trading items and calico cloth were given out and Heald held several councils with Indian leaders, which his junior officers refused to attend.

Eventually, an agreement was reached that had the Indians allowing safe conduct for the soldiers and settlers to Fort Wayne in Indiana. Part of the agreement was that Heald would leave the arms and ammunition in the fort for the Indians, but his officers disagreed. Alarmed, they questioned the wisdom of handing out guns and ammunition that could easily be turned against them.

Heald reluctantly went along with them and the extra weapons and ammunition were broken apart and dumped into an abandoned well. Only twenty-five rounds of ammunition were saved for each man. As an added bit of insurance, all of the liquor barrels were smashed and the contents were poured into the river during the night. Some would later claim that Heald's broken promise was what prompted the massacre that followed.

On August 14, Captain William Wells and his Miami allies arrived at the fort. Wells has largely been forgotten today, aside from a few Chicago landmarks and streets that bear his name, but at the time, he was a frontier legend among soldiers, Native Americans and settlers in the Northwest Territory. Born in 1770, he was living in Kentucky in 1784 when he was kidnapped by a raiding party of Miami Indians. Wells was adopted into the tribe, took a Miami name - Apekonit, or "Carrot Top" for his red hair - and earned a reputation as a fierce warrior. He married into the tribe and his wife, Wakapanke "Sweet Breeze" was the daughter of the great Miami leader, Little Turtle. The couple eventually had four children and remained together after Wells left the Miami and settled at Fort Wayne as the government's Indian agent.

When Wells received word from General Hull about the evacuation of Fort Dearborn, he went straight to Chicago. His niece, Rebekah, was married to the fort's commander, Captain Heald. But even the arrival of the frontiersman and his loyal Miami warriors would not save the lives of those trapped inside Fort Dearborn.

Throughout the night of August 14, wagons were loaded for travel and the reserve ammunition was distributed. Late in the evening, Captain Heald received a visitor, a Potawatomi named Mucktypoke "Black Partridge", who had long been an ally to the Americans. He knew that he could no longer hold back the anger of his fellow tribesmen and he sadly gave back to Heald the medal of friendship that had been given to him by the U.S. government. He explained, "I will not wear a token of peace while I am compelled to act as an enemy."

Heald had fair warning that the occupants of Fort Dearborn were in great danger.

Early the next day, a hot and sunny Saturday morning, the procession of soldiers, civilians, women, and children left the fort. Leading the way was William Wells, riding a thoroughbred horse. Wells, in honor of his Miami heritage, had painted his face black. He was now a warrior prepared for battle - and for death.

A group of fifteen Miami warriors trailed behind him, followed by the infantry soldiers, a caravan of wagons and mounted men. More of the Miami Indians guarded the rear of the column. The procession included fifty-five soldiers, twelve militiamen, nine women and eighteen children. Some of the women were on horseback and most of the children rode in two wagons. Two fife players and two drummers played a tune that history has since forgotten, perhaps marching music to inspire the exodus.

The column of soldiers and settlers was escorted by nearly five hundred Potawatomi and Winnebago Indians. In 1812, the main branch of the Chicago River did not follow a straight course into Lake Michigan. Instead, just east of the fort, it curved to the south, struggled around the sand dunes, and then emptied into the lake. The shoreline of the lake was then much closer to the present-day line of Michigan Avenue. The column from Fort Dearborn marched southward into a low range of sand hills near what is now Roosevelt Road that separated the beaches of Lake Michigan from the prairie. As they did so, the Potawatomi moved to the right, placing an elevation of sand between them and the column. They were now mostly hidden from view.

The procession traveled to an area where 16th Street and Indiana Avenue are now located. There was a sudden milling about of the scouts at the front of the line and suddenly a shout came back from Captain Wells that the Indians were attacking. Captain Heald ordered his troops to charge and the soldiers scurried up the dunes with bayonets fixed, breaking the Potawatomi line. The Indians fell back, allowed the soldiers in, and then enveloped them. Soldiers fell immediately and the line collapsed. Eventually, the remaining men retreated to the shoreline, making a defensive stand on a high piece of ground, but the Potawatomi overwhelmed them with sheer numbers.

The soldiers' charge led them away from the wagons, leaving only the twelve-man militia to defend the women and children. Desperate to protect the families, the men fired their rifles until they were out of ammunition and then swung them like clubs before they were all slain. What followed was butchery. A Potawatomi climbed into the wagon with the children and bludgeoned them to death with his tomahawk. The fort's surgeon was cut down by gunfire and then literally chopped into pieces. Rebekah Heald was wounded seven times but was spared when she was captured by a sympathetic Indian chief. The wife of one soldier fought so bravely and savagely that she was hacked into pieces before she fell.

Aware of the slaughter that was taking place at the wagons, William Wells rushed to the aid of the women and children. Overcome by the massive number of Potawatomi, he never made it. Wells was said to have fought more than one hundred Indians, single-handed and on horseback. He shot and hacked at them until his horse fell beneath him. Indians pounced on him and killed him in the sand. One Potawatomi took Wells' scalp, while another cut out his heart, divided it into small pieces and gave them to other warriors. Honoring the slain hero, and hoping to gain a small amount of his great courage, they ate the heart of William Wells.

Then a Potawatomi attacked Margaret Helm, the wife of the fort's lieutenant. As the two fought, a second Potawatomi joined the fight, seized Mrs. Helm, and dragged her into the lake, where he proceeded to drown her - or that was how it appeared. The second warrior was Black Partridge, a close friend of Lieutenant Helm. The false drowning was actually a ruse to save her life.

Although it must have seemed much longer, the battle was over in less than fifteen minutes. Captain Heald, who had been wounded twice in the fighting and would walk with a cane for the rest of his life, agreed to parlay with the Potawatomi chief, Black Bird. After receiving assurances that the survivors would be spared, Heald agreed to surrender. Sixty-seven people had lost their lives in the massacre: William Wells, twenty-five army regulars, all twelve militiamen, twelve children, two women and fifteen Potawatomi.

The surrender that was arranged by Captain Heald did not apply to the wounded and it is said that the Indians tortured them throughout the night and then left their bodies on the sand next to those who had already fallen.

Many of the other survivors suffered terribly. The Potawatomi divided up the prisoners and most were eventually ransomed and returned to their families. Others did not fare so well. One man was tomahawked when he could not keep pace with the rest of the group being marched away from the massacre site. A baby who cried too much during the march was tied to a tree and left to starve. Mrs. Isabella Cooper was scalped before being rescued by an Indian woman. She had a small bald spot on her head for the rest of her life. Another man froze to death that winter, while Mrs. John Simmons and her daughter were forced to run a gauntlet, which both survived. In fact, the girl turned out to be the last survivor of the massacre, dying in 1900.

Captain Heald, along with his wife, was also taken prisoner. He and Rebekah were taken to Fort Mackinac and were turned over to the British commander there. He sent them to Detroit, where they were exchanged with the American authorities.

After the carnage, the victorious Indians burned Fort Dearborn to the ground and the bodies of the massacre victims were left where they had fallen, allowed to decay on the sand dunes of Lake Michigan. When replacement troops arrived at the site a year later, they were greeted by not only the burned-out shell of the fort, but also by the grinning skeletons of their predecessors. In 1816, the bodies were finally given a proper burial, likely around present-day Prairie Avenue and 17th Street, and the fort was rebuilt. Twenty years later, it was finally abandoned when the city of Chicago was able to fend for itself.

The horrific Fort Dearborn Massacre is believed to have spawned its share of ghostly tales. The actual site of the massacre was quiet for many years, long after Chicago grew into a sizable city. However, construction in the early 1980s unearthed a number of human bones around 16th Street and Indiana Avenue. First thought to be victims of a cholera epidemic in the 1840s, the remains were later dated more closely to the early 1800s. Due to their location, they were believed to be the bones of the massacre victims.

The remains were reburied elsewhere but within a few weeks, people began to report seeing the semi-transparent figures of people wearing pioneer clothing and outdated military uniforms wandering around an empty lot just north of 16th Street. The apparitions reportedly ran about in terror, silently screaming. The most frequent witnesses to these nocturnal wanderings were bus drivers who returned their vehicles to a garage that was located nearby, prompting rumors to spread throughout the city.

In recent times, the area has been largely filled with new homes and condominiums and the once-empty lot where the remains were discovered is no longer vacant. But this does not seem to keep the victims of the massacre in their graves. Current reports from the immediate area tell of specters dressed in early eighteenth century clothing, suggesting that the unlucky settlers of early Chicago do not rest in peace.

PLATTSBURGH AIR FORCE BASE
Plattsburgh, New York

The Lake Champlain region plays host to a number of unexplainable paranormal anomalies. The nagging question of exactly how deep Lake Champlain really is and the fact that it is reputed to be the home of a aquatic monster called "Champ" seem to lend credibility to the belief that many areas in and around the lake have ghostly tales to tell. One such mysterious location is the former site of the Plattsburgh Air Force Base at Plattsburgh, New York.

Located on the western shore of Lake Champlain, this once-prominent Air Force base continues to be haunted by faint echoes from its past. The historical significance of the land the base was constructed on and its pivotal role in the military history of the United States is definitely reflected in the spectral energy that manifests in the oldest sections of the now-defunct complex.

For over one hundred and fifty years, several different countries have vied for control of Lake Champlain and the surrounding countryside. In 1609, Samuel de Champlain, famed French explorer and founder of Quebec, discovered the lake which was named in his honor. But even before the arrival of Champlain, the lake was a hotly contested piece of real estate.

For centuries, two great Indian nations claimed the lake in the name of their ancestors. The fierce Iroquois Indian Nation controlled the west bank of the lake and the Algonquin laid claim to the east bank. The rivalry and savagery inflicted on any member of a rival Indian nation caught on the wrong side of the lake at the wrong time was unparalleled. The only thing these two warring nations could agree on was the fact that they despised the early white settlers who ventured into the region in the early eighteenth century even more than they hated each other. Settlers were lucky to survive an Indian attack. Chilling first-person accounts describe the gruesome horrors the Indians perpetrated on groups of unsuspecting settlers who were caught off guard as they attempted to set up new lives at the lake's edge, but by the end of the eighteenth century, the balance of power along Lake Champlain no longer favored the Indian tribes.

During the French and Indian War, both the British and the French used the waters of Lake Champlain as a military highway to move men and other instruments of war. Britain, the eventual winner of the Seven Years' War, coveted Lake Champlain because it was crucial to commerce and travel through the backwoods and mountains of the region that would one day become New York state.

At the start of the American Revolution, the strategic importance of Lake Champlain and the surrounding countryside did not go unnoticed by military leaders on both sides of the conflict. As such, the entire region was rocked by one military engagement after the other.

The most significant military campaign of the war was the Battle of Lake Champlain, which took place near Valcour Island, only four miles from the location of Plattsburgh Air Force Base.

On October 11, 1776, Benedict Arnold, commanding a tiny fleet of fifteen boats manned by nearly "five hundred half-naked, unskilled sailors" went head to head against twenty-eight British gunboats near Valcour Island. Arnold was keenly aware that his situation was grave and that his bold plan had to succeed. While fighting in Canada, Arnold had learned of the British plans to cut the colonies in two using two massive armies positioned so as to strangle the American Army into surrendering. Arnold's assignment was to delay the Northern British Army, which consisted of six hundred and twenty-four vessels and nine thousand men, for as long as he could. The British gunboats that Arnold faced on the cold gray morning of October 11 were only the advance guard of the looming British armada. Standing on the deck of the *Congress*, Arnold personally commanded his beleaguered and outgunned fleet in the pitched naval battle that ensued. By nightfall, Arnold's fleet was obviously crippled but instead of taking the initiative to put an end to their grisly work, the British fleet disengaged for the night with intentions of returning in the morning to finish off Arnold. That night at a council of war, Arnold and his fellow commanders came up with a daring escape plan. The plan called for what little was left of the American fleet to row silently past the recuperating British fleet in the dead of night. When the British woke up the next morning, they were astonished to see that their enemy had vanished. Even though Arnold's victory at Valcour Island was more of a draw, it served to delay the English long enough for the Americans to prepare for the crucial battles that lay ahead.

Following the Revolutionary War, peace again returned to the Lake Champlain region and the land became ripe for settlement. Towns and villages began springing up all across the newly opened frontier of New York and Vermont. Attracted to this new land boom were families like that of Zepheniah Platt. Platt, along with several other families, moved into the area in 1784, and in 1785, Platt formally established the town of Plattsburgh. The town grew quickly and by 1810, its population numbered well over three thousand.

During the War of 1812, Plattsburgh again found itself caught up in the battles and bloodshed of the conflict. As in the recent War for Independence, Plattsburgh and the land bordering Lake Champlain was of strategic military importance. The U.S. Army needed a base from which to conduct raids into British-held Canada, so a small two-hundred-acre military facility was established on the outskirts of Plattsburgh. The military's presence was both a boon and a bane. Store owners and businessmen in Plattsburgh saw their coffers grow due to the money brought in by the presence of the military, but the close proximity of the soldiers also attracted unwanted attention from the British.

In 1813 and 1814, a series of small skirmishes and battles were fought in and around the city of Plattsburgh. By the end of 1813, British warships had cleared Lake Champlain of the few remaining American ships that dared to venture out into her waters. In September 1814, the most crucial battle of the war was fought at Plattsburgh.

A British force of fourteen thousand soldiers had invaded the region from Canada. This seemingly unstoppable force marched unopposed until they reached Plattsburgh. The Battle of Plattsburgh took place between September 6 and 11, 1814. For five days, a small American force totaling only 2,200 regular army soldiers and militia under the command of Brigadier General Macomb engaged the British just outside the city. The battle culminated in a decisive engagement at a bridge over the Saranac River on September 11. Here, the outnumbered Americas managed to burn the bridge, finally putting a halt to the British advance.

At the same time that the English were being soundly beaten on land, they were also being routed on Cumberland Bay. On September 11, 1814, a young Navy lieutenant named Thomas MacDonough led his rag-tag fleet of American ships to victory against an overwhelming British naval force, signaling an end to the Battle of Plattsburgh and an end of the British invasion plans for New York. As with Benedict Arnold's victory at Valcour Island, the Battle of Plattsburgh had given American forces the needed time to regroup.

When peace was again restored to the region following the War of 1812, the U.S. military continued to maintain the original military installation at Plattsburgh. Over time, additional land was purchased and in 1838, stone barracks were constructed at the site. For the most part, the army maintained only a part-time presence at the Plattsburgh Barracks from 1814 to 1861. With the close of the Civil War in 1865, the Army re-activated the barracks and continuously operated the post until it was turned over to the Navy in 1944 for use as an indoctrination school for officers. The barracks was renamed Camp MacDonough in honor of Lt. MacDonough and was in operation for one year before it was turned over to the Army Air Force in 1945.

In 1946, the U.S. military abandoned the aging Plattsburgh Barracks yet again. The site was acquired by the New York State Housing Commission and became the home of Champlain College. The college converted the various buildings on the base into classrooms and student housing but ceased operation in 1953 when the federal government commandeered the school and its grounds for use as a new Strategic Air Command base.

Once officially re-designated as Plattsburgh Air Force Base, an additional 3,600 acres of land was purchased to make room for the new facility. In 1955, work began on an extensive runway that was required to meet the needs of the aircraft of the 380th Bombardment Wing, which arrived in 1956. Between 1956 and 1995, the base housed no fewer than twelve Atlas ICBM missile sites and actively supported the 380th Bombardment Wing's new sophisticated B-52G Stratofortress bombers, and later the new FB-111A bomber.

On September 30, 1995, Plattsburgh Air Force Base was officially closed by the Base Realignment and Closure Commission, after forty-two years of service as one of the nation's foremost Strategic Air Command installations. Since that time, the base has been converted into a civilian airport and industrial complex. The airfield is now knows as Plattsburgh International Airport.

Ghosts from almost every significant time period in the base's history have been encountered at various locations in and around the facility at one point or another.

At the heart of the oldest section of the base is a small cemetery and adjoining crematorium that is reputed to be identified as Building 666. Many of America's finest soldiers have been laid to rest in this cemetery through the years and it is said that the spirits of these deceased patriots still roam the cemetery grounds. Security officers who have been assigned to patrol this area at night routinely reported ghostly encounters with the restless spirits of long-dead soldiers who were wearing all manner of military uniforms and accoutrements.

Another paranormal hot spot is the old Finance Building. At one point in the building's history, it was used as a surgical hospital. It is said that during this period, a fire broke out in one of the wings of the building, killing many of the bed-ridden patients who were unable to flee from the flames. People continue to report hearing the tortured, desperate screams of these trapped souls, crying out for release from a fire that was extinguished years ago.

The Finance Building was alleged to be so psychically active that many of the security force's guard dogs refused to go into the basement. What would scare the dogs so badly? Possibly it was the smell of blood emanating from the basement's walls, walls said to have been painted red to hide the bloodstains and spattered gore from the days when the building was used as a surgical hospital.

Even the front gate of the former Air Force base is said to be haunted. Sentries who used to man the gate reported seeing the spirit of a soldier dressed in what they described as full regalia from the Revolutionary War marching back and forth between two pillars. The uniforms of the American Revolutionary War and the War of 1812 were similar, so perhaps the ghostly soldier was one of those assigned to the fort during its infancy in the early 1800s. Apparently this apparition is either unwilling, or unable, to leave his assigned post, even after all these years.

In addition to the specter of the ghostly soldier seen at the entrance of the base, the transparent form of a woman dressed in white is said to haunt a nearby grove of trees. Stories tell that the woman was the victim of a botched robbery that resulted in her death. The old cemetery contains a mass grave where a number of unknown soldiers from the Battle of Plattsburgh were reburied, as well as victims of the 1918 influenza epidemic, some of them children. The cemetery is said to be haunted by yet another woman in white, eternally searching for her baby.

Without question, the Plattsburgh Air Force Base's proud lineage makes it an ideal candidate to be haunted. What lies in store for the base's new occupants? Only time will tell, but one thing is almost guaranteed: It won't take long for the ghosts to make their presence known.

Even in death, some souls cannot be silenced.

THE GHOST ON THE STAIRS
Fort Belle Fontaine
St. Louis, MO

In most of my writings, I try to point out the history of many of the haunted locations that I have researched. Some of those eerie beginnings are events that involved large numbers of people, while others center on one particular person, item, or place. When writing about St. Louis, all roads seem to lead to Fort Belle Fontaine.

Fort Bellefontaine

In delving into the haunted history of Jefferson Barracks and the St. Louis Arsenal, I found that their stories always started with Fort Belle Fontaine. This little fort's prominence as the first U.S. military fortification west of the Mississippi, and its overall role in the St. Louis region during a tumultuous time in the nation's history, was the key to the later establishment of Jefferson Barracks and the Arsenal. Oddly, it would not be until I was doing research into other military posts across the country that I would come across ghost stories attributed to Fort Belle Fontaine. The various paranormal events that have taken place at the fort over the years have raised many questions, but to find out the answers, you must first know the history of this fort.

After the signing of the Louisiana Purchase in 1804, the Mississippi Valley literally became the Gateway to the West. In 1805, the U.S. military established Fort Belle Fontaine at the mouth of Cold Water Creek, near the confluence of the Mississippi and Missouri Rivers, in an effort to protect the City of St. Louis and the thriving river trade along the Mississippi River. Located on the south, low-lying bank of the Missouri River, just four miles downstream from the

Spanish Fort Don Carlos, which had been abandoned in 1780, this remote military fort and its small garrison greeted the first pioneers and settlers heading west into the new frontier.

The original site of the first fort, known as Cantonment Belle Fontaine was selected by General James Wilkinson, the first governor of the Louisiana Territory. A short time after a location for the fort had been established, three companies of the First Infantry, under the command of Lieutenant Colonel Jacob Kingsbury, arrived and set about the construction of the fort.

From the start, Cantonment Belle Fontaine served as a trading post or "Indian Factory" for the local Indian tribes but by 1808, the "factory" was moved from the fort. Trade goods previously stored at the fort were transferred to Fort Osage at the far western edge of Missouri and to Fort Madison in Iowa.

Being the only established military presence in the new Louisiana Territory, Fort Belle Fontaine served as an instrumental starting and stopping point for several notable explorers and expeditions. The famous pioneering military officer Zebulon Pike, who discovered Pike's Peak, started two expeditions from Fort Belle Fontaine. In 1805, Pike launched his expedition of the upper Mississippi River from the fort and in 1806, Pike used the fort as a starting point for his probe into the Spanish-held lands of the Southwest. During both expeditions, Pike left his family behind at Fort Belle Fontaine.

By far, the most famous explorers to visit Fort Belle Fontaine were Meriwether Lewis and William Clark. Members of the famous Corps of Discovery camped at Fort Belle Fontaine prior to starting their historic expedition on May 14, 1804. The Corps of Discovery later returned to the fort at the conclusion of their journey and spent the night there on September 22, 1806. The following is an excerpt from the *Journals of Lewis and Clark* upon their arrival at Fort Belle Fontaine:

Monday 22nd of Septr. 1806

"This morning being very wet and the rain still continueing hard, and our party being all sheltered in house of those hospitable people, we did not think proper to proceed on until after the rain was over, and continued at the house of Mr. Proulz. I took this opportunity of writing to my friends in Kentucky & c. At 10 a.m. it seased raining and we collected our party and Set out and proceeded on down to the Contonemt, at Coldwater Creek about 3 miles up the Missouri on its Southern banks, at this place we found Colo. Hunt and a Lieut. Peters & one Company of Artillerists we were kindly received by the Gentlemen of this place... We were honored with a Salute of blank space in MS. and a harty welcome. At

this place there is a publick store kept in which I am informed the U.S. have 60000$ worth of Indian Goods."

In 1809, Lieutenant Colonel Daniel Bissell took command of Fort Belle Fontaine. Upon his arrival, he found the Cantonment to be in a terrible state of disrepair and the fort's garrison plagued with illness. The shifting Missouri River was threatening the fort, which was situated on a flood plain. In addition, Bissell concluded that the fort was in a strategically poor position, as it was overlooked by a high bluff. In 1810, Bissell ordered the fort moved to the top of the bluff. By 1811, work on the new fort, which consisted of thirty buildings, several blockhouses and a rectangle palisade, was completed.

During the War of 1812, several military operations against the British and Sauk-Fox Indians were conducted from Fort Belle Fontaine and in July 1815, soldiers from the fort provided security for the great Indian council at Portage Des Sioux. In attendance at the peace negotiations were representatives from eleven different Indian tribes. Governor William Clark and Auguste Chouteau were among the most notable U.S. representatives at this momentous event. In the years that followed, Fort Belle Fontaine was a prominent command and supply point for several new military posts that had been established farther to the west, and the fort served as a starting point for Colonel Henry Atkinson's Yellowstone Expedition in 1819.

By 1825, Fort Belle Fontaine and its small arsenal had fallen into a sorry state of disrepair. At the time, conditions at the fort were considered to be unhealthy due to the effects of frequent flooding. When not fighting Indians or keeping the peace, soldiers drank and fought with each other. On at least one occasion, the monotonous duty contributed to the death of at least one man when a fellow officer killed a lieutenant during a duel. In 1826, military commanders decided that a new military post and separate arsenal facility was needed.

On July 8, 1826, troops from Fort Belle Fontaine helped establish a new military base of operations south of St. Louis near the village of Carondelet. This new military post was named Jefferson Barracks in honor of President Thomas Jefferson, who had died a few days earlier, on July 4. A small contingent of troops remained at Fort Belle Fontaine to protect the arsenal until a new one could be built on a forty-acre tract of land located three miles south of St. Louis, near modern-day Second and Arsenal streets in South St. Louis.

In 1827, the first building on the new arsenal grounds was completed, but the small facility at Fort Belle Fontaine continued to provide munitions and military supplies for troops operating in the Louisiana Territory until June 1828. Over the next few years, Fort Belle Fontaine was abandoned and officially replaced by the new St. Louis Arsenal and Jefferson Barracks.

Between 1828 and 1904, Fort Belle Fontaine remained unoccupied, silently standing guard along the Missouri River, a scant fifteen miles north of St. Louis. In that time, most of the wooden buildings of the fort on the bluff had rotted away, leaving only their limestone foundations. In a photograph taken in 1909, a single log cabin, believed to be the remnants of a soldier's quarters, was the only evidence that a military post had existed on the site. The site of the first cantonment at the river's edge had all but been obliterated by the currents of the Missouri River. Little or no evidence of the first fort could be found along the shoreline of the river by this time.

On April 5, 1904, the remains of the thirty-three officers, soldiers and family members who had been buried at Fort Belle Fontaine between 1806 and 1826, were moved to the Jefferson Barracks National Cemetery in south St. Louis County. The dead, including the body of Zebulon Pike's two-year-old daughter, were reburied on a high bluff overlooking the Mississippi River in the Old Post Section 1 of the National Cemetery. The St. Louis Chapter of the Daughters of the American Revolution erected a large memorial at the site, consisting of a granite boulder and commemorative plaque.

In 1913, the City of St. Louis acquired the property where the second fort once stood. The city built a detention home and training school for boys on the site. Life at the Missouri Home for Boys was rigorous, consisting of academic instruction in the morning and farm labor for the remainder of the day. Black and white boys were housed separately. The farming operation was phased out in the 1950s. In 1986, the County of St. Louis assumed control of most of the property that made up the boys' home. Just two years later, in 1988, the City of St. Louis ended its affiliation with the home. Today, the Missouri Hills Home is a residence for both boys and girls and is managed by the Missouri Division of Youth Services.

The presence of the home on the bluff has been a mixed blessing for the preservation of the old fort site. When the city of St. Louis and later the state of Missouri acquired the land, it prevented the site from being carved up by land developers, but construction on the site doomed many of the historical treasures located just beneath the topsoil.

Another critical event in the fort's history occurred in the 1930s, when President Franklin D. Roosevelt established the Works Progress Administration WPA as a means to jump-start the labor market during the Great Depression. Members of the WPA worked at the Missouri Hills Home to enhance the property and in doing so, made the land along the Missouri River into a picturesque landscape that would attract visitors from miles around. In 1936, the crown jewel of the project, the "Grand Staircase" was completed. The top of the staircase is an observation terrace which commands an impressive view across the Missouri

River towards St. Charles County and Alton, Illinois. The twisting expanse of limestone stairs, set into approximately five tiers, is still intact and usable today. In addition to the staircase, the WPA also constructed rest rooms and picnic facilities along the riverbank below the bluff.

Fort Bellefontaine's "Haunted Stairs"

Over the years, many different visitors to the site have claimed to see, hear, and feel things that they could not explain. Oddly enough, the most eerie ghost stories center around the Grand Staircase. It is said that pictures taken of the first or second tier of the staircase reveal the presence of what appears to be dark red smoke on the stairs. It has been said that people have experimented by taking photographs of the stairs using different kinds of cameras and film and in each instance, the anomalous red light always appears.

I guess it is possible that the red mist is a naturally occurring event. I have visited the site several times with my family, though, and I have yet to find a natural source that could account for the anomalous photographs taken at the site. The light could actually be a supernatural manifestation from beyond the grave. Perhaps the spirit a young officer killed in a duel still walks the site searching for peace, or one of the previous "unknown" occupants of the old fort's cemetery decided that he or she did not want to be moved to the Jefferson Barracks National Cemetery. No matter what or who is responsible for these mysterious incidents, they still continue to this day.

Today, the St. Louis County Parks Department maintains a picturesque overlook with historical markers on the bluff where the second fort once stood.

In addition, visitors to the site are enthralled by the Grand Staircase, and they are encouraged to walk along the Missouri River to explore the various WPA construction projects that still exist today. Unfortunately, nothing remains of the old fort except for a small limestone building that is believed to have been built in later years from the limestone foundations of the fort. Thanks to the history here, a trip to Fort Belle Fontaine is an outing that you will definitely not forget.

Jefferson Barracks

JEFFERSON BARRACKS
St. Louis, Missouri

Historic Jefferson Barracks, located on the high bluffs along the west bank of the Mississippi River, south of St. Louis, has served as a silent sentinel at the Gateway to the West for over one hundred and seventy-five years. In that time, historical fact and legend have been woven into a colorful tapestry, which makes this picturesque military post a true national treasure.

With the signing of the Louisiana Purchase, the vast untamed Western frontier was opened for settlement. Jefferson Barracks, selected because of its strategic and geographical location, served as a way station for explorers, traders, and pioneers seeking to establish a new life along the Santa Fe Trail.

Besides providing protection from marauding bands of hostile Indians, this prominent military reservation, spanning over 1,700 acres, served as an Army Infantry School, an influential federal hospital facility, engineer depot, calvary training depot, and one of the military's largest induction and demobilization centers in the United States. Over time, Jefferson Barracks was viewed as such a valuable resource in the training of soldiers and officers, that the military academy at West Point was almost moved there.

Prior to the 1900s, Jefferson Barracks was a key stepping-off point for troops and supplies bound for distant conflicts, such as the Black Hawk Indian Wars, Mexican-American War, Civil War and the Spanish-American War. Soldiers fighting in World War I and World War II were also trained at and deployed from Jefferson Barracks.

Considered to be the first permanent military installation west of the Mississippi River, Jefferson Barracks was a prison to Chief Black Hawk and several of his sub chiefs. Many years later, during World War II, Jefferson Barracks would again become an internment camp for over four hundred German and Italian prisoners of war.

During its heyday, Jefferson Barracks played host to a number of great leaders who would later influence American History. Three of these men, Dwight D. Eisenhower, Zackery Taylor, and Ulysses S. Grant, rose through the military ranks and became future presidents of the United States. One young lieutenant, Jefferson Davis, went on to become the president of the Confederate States of America. Several other young lieutenants and captains assigned to the post, such as Robert E. Lee, William T. Sherman, James Longstreet, and Winfield S. Hancock, saw their military careers culminate in generalship during the Civil War.

Jefferson Barracks would see itself flicker and fade into the history books one last time shortly after World War II. On June 30, 1946, this icon to the American ideal of Manifest Destiny was deactivated and declared military surplus. One hundred and thirty-five acres of the main post was taken over by the Missouri Air National Guard and five hundred acres of the military reservation would be turned into an historic park by the St. Louis County Parks and Recreation Department.

The long history of this legendary post would provide a breeding ground for ghosts.

Dueling

Though not officially sanctioned by the U.S. Army, dueling was commonplace at Jefferson Barracks in the 1830s. On January 19th 1830, 2nd Lt. Charles O. May, a member of the 6th Infantry, lost his life in a duel with a fellow officer near the north gate. Also in that same year, Major Thomas Biddle, post paymaster, and Pettis Spencer, a congressional candidate, killed each other with pistols in a duel at the post.

These tests of honor frequently occurred on post, but they also took place on nearby Bloody Island. Aptly named, Bloody Island, located in the center of the Mississippi River opposite St. Louis, had been the site of many famous duels - all of which had dire consequences.

Time and time again, it became obvious that dueling was draining the officer corps at Jefferson Barracks of promising young leaders. This needless loss of life prompted military commanders to issue proclamations stating that the continued practice of dueling would bring harsh reprimands and punishment for all persons found to be involved.

Illness and Epidemics at Jefferson Barracks

During its history, three great cholera epidemics descended upon Jefferson Barracks and the surrounding Mississippi Valley. With each passing plague, the post was clouded in sadness and death. Hundreds of soldiers died as a result of these epidemics. During one epidemic, there were so many deaths that a "dead house" or morgue, was constructed at the northeastern corner of the present-day parade ground, to house the remains.

In 1834, twenty soldiers at Jefferson Barracks died of cholera. As a result of the outbreak, medical officers ordered the post and surrounding properties disinfected with chloride of lime.

In most cases, the cure the doctors provided to stave off the deadly disease was almost as bad as the illness itself. Soldiers experiencing a bout of cholera were given a chalky mercury compound called calomel and large doses of laudanum. As if these "wonder cures" were not dangerous enough, post surgeons also employed bloodletting, a common medical treatment of the time, to combat cholera and other frontier diseases.

With the dawn of the twentieth century, the Mississippi Valley would see the last major outbreak of smallpox but in the 1940s, the post experienced an almost epidemic attack of spinal meningitis. This ravaging disease would take a grim toll on trainees and inductees assigned to the overflowing post.

Discipline

The early Colonial Army was heavily influenced by many of the foreign officers that saw it through the Revolutionary War. With these British, French and Prussian officers came the misguided idea that discipline would be the foundation of the new military order in the United States. Harsh punishment would become the mainstay of garrison life at many military posts along the Western frontier.

Incidents of drunkenness and desertion were the most common offenses perpetrated by enlisted men at Jefferson Barracks. On average, fifty to sixty soldiers each year were court-martialed at the post for these kinds of violations. In most cases, soldiers who were found guilty were reduced in rank and required to pay a fine. Repeated violations would see them lose their whiskey ration for twenty to thirty days at a time.

By the late 1880s, extreme measures of discipline and outlandish levels of punishment for petty infractions were a fact of life for soldiers stationed at Jefferson Barracks. Soldiers were abused, cursed at, threatened, and bullied by strong-arm tactics that traumatized the common enlisted man.

Medical services provided on post were virtually nonexistent and in many instances, food and meat were put out on the mess tables the night before, making it virtually inedible the next day. This unpleasant aspect of camp life led to over three hundred desertions from Jefferson Barracks between July 1, 1888 and June 30, 1889. That amounted to about one disgruntled soldier deserting almost every day that fiscal year.

Men who could not adjust to military life at Jefferson Barracks deserted the army by several different means. Some hid on board trains that had stopped at the barracks' train depot, some escaped by swimming the Mississippi River, and some fled in boats. One particular soldier devised a foolproof plan to get out of the army. He dressed himself in civilian clothing and walked nonchalantly out the front gate. The army paid a bounty of $30 dollars for each deserter captured and returned to Jefferson Barracks.

It is said that one early oppressive commander at Jefferson Barracks had the ears cut off two soldiers who had deserted. For this inhuman act, the officer was later fined one month's pay, but in most cases, it was the soldier who suffered.

Deserters who were recaptured were thrown into the post stockade or military jail. Once in the stockade, soldiers experienced truly harsh and sadistic punishment. Prisoners in confinement were exposed to cramped, filthy living conditions that were infested with swarms of bedbugs. To add insult to injury, prisoners were also subjected to physical torture by being hanged by their thumbs and from being shackled in leg irons for little or no reason.

In June 1889, a man named Frank R. E. Woodward enlisted in the United States Army. Private Woodward was assigned to Jefferson Barracks, Company B, Calvary Depot, for training. Normally, a private enlisting in the military would not cause much of a fuss, but in this instance it created one of the most interesting episodes in the history of the post.

As it happened, Private Woodward was an undercover reporter for the *St. Louis Post-Dispatch*, who had enlisted to learn the reason why so many soldiers from Jefferson Barracks were deserting. Private Woodward experienced camp life firsthand. He found the soldiers' living quarters infested with bedbugs and learned that mess sergeants were stealing the soldiers' food and transporting it off post and selling it. Woodward determined that this criminal activity was causing frequent food shortages on post. In one report, Woodward told the story of an African American soldier who was beaten to death by a non-commissioned officer who found him sitting in an area that was considered off-limits to black soldiers. Woodward did not personally witness the assault, but he had witnessed recruits being beaten during training, so it was easy to understand why he would feel that a secondhand story of this nature had merit.

The *Post-Dispatch* printed Private Woodward's observations, and his graphic exposé became front-page news in St. Louis and across the nation. Readers were startled to learn that harsh punishments, unsanitary conditions and poor food were contributing to a desertion rate from the Army of about ten percent nationwide. These news articles would become an embarrassment to many high-ranking officers at Jefferson Barracks. Due largely to Private Woodward's investigative reporting and the subsequent public outcry, the Army launched an investigation into disciplinary practices and physical conditions at the post. The findings of the inquiry called for the physical reorganization of the place. Additionally, many of the officers involved were reassigned to other military installations, and several non-commissioned officers found themselves demoted.

It taught many people an important lesson: Never underestimate the power of a lowly private.

Jefferson Barracks National Cemetery

Soldiers who did not survive their stay at the Jefferson Barracks hospital were buried in the National Cemetery, which was established south of the post in 1863. The cemetery did not have an auspicious beginning. It was originally just as a small piece of land set aside for soldiers and their family members who died while stationed at Jefferson Barracks. The first person buried there was Elizabeth Ann Lash, the eighteen-month-old daughter of an officer. She was followed by other victims of disease, duels and violence on the frontier.

The small burial ground grew and a wooden fence was erected around it in an attempt to keep out wild animals. But time was not kind to the post cemetery, and thanks to the fact that most of the soldiers who buried friends or loved ones there were usually reassigned or moved on, there was no one to take care of the graves. Soon, the cemetery fell into a state of disrepair. As the cemetery expanded years later, the old grave markers were forgotten, and in many cases, the identities of those buried beneath them were lost. The remains of these poor souls were reinterred with only a number or the word "unknown" carved on their headstones.

By 1862, it was obvious that more space was going to be needed to bury the men killed during the Civil War. Major General Henry W. Halleck, commander of the Department of Missouri, a command echelon of the U.S. Army in the nineteenth century, recognized that the post cemetery could easily be expanded and would make an excellent choice for a national cemetery, as it was easily accessible from both land and riverboat. Based on his observations, President Abraham Lincoln expanded the "Old Post Cemetery" in 1863 and formally designated the burial ground as Jefferson Barracks National Cemetery.

The gravesites began to fill quickly as the remains of soldiers from both the North and the South began to arrive at the post for burial. In addition, men who died at the post hospitals were also buried in the cemetery. Before the war ended, more than 1,140 Confederate soldiers were buried at Jefferson Barracks and were joined by over twelve thousand men who fought for the Union.

In 1867, Sylvanus Beeman was appointed as the first superintendent of the cemetery with Martin Burke installed as his assistant the following year. Under their care, the cemetery was enlarged and improved and divided into sections for ease of identification. A short time later, other military cemeteries from the region began to turn over their dead to Jefferson Barracks.

In 1876, the first graves were moved. The remains of four hundred and seventy people were taken from a place called Arsenal Island and were reburied at Jefferson Barracks. The island, which was also known as Quarantine Island, was little more than a glorified sandbar that had been created by the currents of the Mississippi River. Located just north of Arsenal Street in St. Louis, it was only a half-mile wide and three-quarters of a mile long. Arsenal Island served the city for many years as a quarantine camp, where soldiers and civilian river passengers were taken when they were suspected of carrying some sort of contagious disease. During its years of operation, it saw cases of cholera, smallpox, yellow fever and more. Steamboats were often directed to the island if suspicious illnesses were on board and the passengers could be held in quarantine for weeks. Doctors on the island inspected the passengers before allowing them into St. Louis, and if they were found to be sick, forced them to stay on the island until they either recovered or died. Those who died were buried on the island's north end.

The bodies from the island graveyard were moved because of the threat to the island caused by the changing channels of the river. By 1880, surveyors discovered that the island had moved nearly one-half mile downstream from its position in 1862. Frequent spring flooding had already washed away many of the graves of the diseased and it was not uncommon to find human remains floating in the river. For that reason, the bodies were moved and their graves marked with tombstones bearing the word "unknown."

In April 1904, the remains of thirty-three officers, soldiers and civilians who had been buried at Fort Belle Fontaine were moved to the National Cemetery. These "unknown" burials, which included the two-year-old daughter of explorer Zebulon Pike, were buried on the same bluff, near the grave of eighteen-month-old Elizabeth Lash -- who may not rest in peace.

As with many graveyards, the Jefferson Barracks National Cemetery has its share of ghost stories. One of these involves a spectral child who has been seen on a bluff in the cemetery. As she has often been spotted near the grave of little Elizabeth Lash, legend holds that it is her ghost who walks here. Unfortunately, little is known about the Lash family or how the girl died. She was buried in the Old Post Cemetery on August 5, 1827 and it's likely that she passed away from one of the many diseases that were prevalent in the Mississippi Valley in those days. But what might make her ghost become restless?

That part of the story remains a mystery but what we do know is that employees of the cemetery and at least one soldier assigned to Jefferson Barracks have seen the ghost of a small girl walking between the marble tombstone near Elizabeth's grave. But is it really Elizabeth Lash?

I'm not sure. There may be another explanation for a toddler's spirit to be wandering the cemetery. In 1900, shortly after the death of Martin Burke, who was by then the superintendent of the graveyard, a new caretaker took his place named Edward Past. Not long after filling this position, he discovered the remains of several unidentified children in the Old Post section of the cemetery. Their graves had long been hidden beneath bushes and undergrowth. While their identities and the reasons for their deaths could not be discovered, it's likely that they were the victims of some epidemic. It's possible that one of these children may be the little ghost girl who roams the cemetery, perhaps in an attempt to somehow not be forgotten after all.

There is another legend that has long been told of this cemetery, involving two ghosts. One of them is a Federal "Buffalo Soldier" and the other is a Confederate soldier. It has been told that the graves of these two men are located close to one another and that at certain times the black man from the North and the white man from the South both appear near their grave sites to acknowledge one another.

It is said that this ghostly greeting occurs around sunset or occasionally in the morning, around dawn. The two shadowy forms rise from their graves and have been seen moving across the cemetery toward one another. When they meet, witnesses claims that they extend a hand to one another in friendship.

Some have surmised that they are doomed to continuously try and make peace with one another, not only for themselves but also for the fallen soldiers who are buried around them.

The Ghosts of Jefferson Barracks

One could reasonably argue that per square acre, Jefferson Barracks is the most haunted location in the St. Louis metropolitan area. The post is comprised of one hundred and thirty-five acres containing forty-one buildings of various shapes and sizes. Military and civilian employees occupy thirty-five of these. Most of the occupied historic buildings serve as administrative offices, classrooms and maintenance facilities for the various National Guard and reserve units stationed at the barracks, while some of the structures are used primarily for storage.

Of the thirty-five occupied buildings, thirteen or more have stories of paranormal activity associated with them that I am aware of. I am sure that if truth were told, there are more ghost stories out there that are waiting to be unearthed.

Over the years, soldiers and civilian staff have reported a wide array of ghostly phenomena. Even Private Woodward, the undercover reporter, reported that ghost stories seemed to abound at Jefferson Barracks. These brushes with the supernatural range from phantom footsteps to incidents involving interactive ghosts.

The stories you are about to read come from various locations inside the current military reservation. I think that you will find, as I did when compiling this information, that no one story or encounter you will read about in the following pages is really like the next. But each account has one thing in common in that it will leave you feeling unnerved.

I believe that a Lieutenant Colonel whom I knew from my time at Jefferson Barracks said it the best when he said, "If you have ever worked late in one of these old buildings, you would be convinced that ghosts exist."

Early Ghost Stories

Many of the ghost stories told at Jefferson Barracks have been a part of local lore for years. Some of them even date back as far as the Civil War. One such tale is that of the specter who has been reported on the grounds near the post headquarters.

During the Civil War, and for years after, soldiers guarded the train depot and the railroad tracks located along the Mississippi River. They also guarded the headquarters building on the bluff above the depot. One night during the Civil War, a sentry was walking his post near this building. As he rounded the corner, he reportedly observed a solitary figure walking up the grassy hill from the train yard. As the soldier stood watching, he realized that the man was not a living person, but what he described as a blurry "spook."

There is also a long-running legend about a ghost who haunts the post's old powder magazine. The massive limestone building was built in 1857 as a secure location to store rifles, cannons and gunpowder. In 1871, the Federal Arsenal in St. Louis was closed and its contents were moved to Jefferson Barracks. The powder magazine remained in constant use until the post closed in 1946. In more recent times, it has become a museum run by the St. Louis County Parks and Recreation Department.

The story of the ghost here has its beginnings around the start of World War II. In the dark days at the start of the war, sentries were posted all around the fort to protect it from possible sabotage. One of the most important guard positions was the powder magazine. Armed sentries were often seen patrolling around the building or walking across the top of the stone wall that surrounded the magazine.

Several of the soldiers who stood guard here reported seeing a ghostly sentry who would occasionally appear and challenge the guard who was standing at his post. The spirit was said to have a bullet hole in his head, running red with blood, and was said to be so frightening that several guards allegedly threw down their weapons and fled their posts after encountering him. One story had it that a certain soldier was so frightened by the specter that he not only left his post one night, he also left the Army. According to the story, the spectral sentry was a guard who had been killed years before, when a raiding party attempted to steal munitions from the powder magazine. He was believed to have confronted his living counterparts because he thought they were trespassers. Even after many years had passed, he was still on duty, even in death.

Another old story tells of a ghost who long haunted the grounds around the post's old north gate. It was believed to be the spirit of Second Lieutenant Thomas May, who was killed in a duel near the north gate in 1830. Legends also tell of a ghostly woman who has been spotted at the Laborer's House, which dates back to 1851. It was once used a residence by civilians who worked at the ordnance depot and today is a gift shop operated by the parks department.

First-hand encounters with the unknown still continue to take place on the post today. There are many haunted buildings here, where strange and unusual things have happened for years, but in these pages, we'll take a look at what might be consider the most haunted sites of Jefferson Barracks.

Building 1
Standing proudly at the eastern end of the parade field, high on a grassy hill overlooking the Mississippi River, is Building 1. Constructed in 1900, this three-

story brick building serves as the post's headquarters. The large room on the south end of the second floor was used as a ballroom. Many of the ornamental wood fixtures still remain there today. On the north wall of the old ballroom hangs a large, wooden, hand-painted map of Jefferson Barracks, which was made by an army private in 1938.

Jefferson Barracks' Post Headquarters

Recently refurbished to its former glory by the Missouri Air National Guard, Building 1 plays host to a multitude of ghostly encounters that have taken place both inside and outside. One entity frequently seen at Building 1 is that of an elderly Confederate Civil War general who has been observed in the post commander's office.

Sergeant William McWilliams, who was assigned to the Funeral Honors Program as a team leader, once had a hair-raising encounter with this ghost. When Sergeant McWilliams first started as an employee of the Funeral Honors Program in 1998, he was living in Building 78. One night, he was bored and decided to jog around the post to get some exercise. He stopped to catch his breath near where the display cannon from the Spanish battleship *Oquenda* is located behind Building 1. While recuperating from his physical exertion McWilliams observed what he believed to be candlelight coming from an office on the first floor, near the north end of the building. This piqued his curiosity, so he approached the building, hoping to determine its source.

What he found to be the source of the light was not what he expected in the least. As he got closer to the window from which the light dimly shone, McWilliams could see an older man, wearing what he believed to be a Confederate general's uniform and slouch hat, seated at a desk inside the post commander's office. The man appeared to be engaged in writing dispatches with a quill pen by the light of a single candle. Sergeant McWilliams watched the Civil War-era officer in awe for three or four minutes before the figure rose and walked toward the door of the office with his pen in one hand and the candle in the other. As the officer neared the doorway, he simply faded away into nothingness, right in front of Sergeant McWilliams' startled eyes. Needless to say, McWilliams did not stick around to see if the "general" reappeared.

Several employees working in Building 1 have observed a shadowy ghost of a man sitting at a desk near a window on the second floor of the building, writing by candlelight. It is possible that this is the ghost of the "old general," but we may never know. When the employees attempted to investigate, the ghost would be gone, leaving only the sound of footsteps walking away.

According to Sergeant McWilliams, restless spirits are also active in the basement of Building 1. When the Funeral Honors Program was first established, their office and training area were located there. As part of their training, soldiers were required to practice with a full-sized casket, which was stored in the basement. Sergeant McWilliams said that every morning, he would walk into the training area and find the casket lid open. It appeared that someone or something had rummaged through the training items kept inside.

Another person who had first-hand experience with the spirits inhabiting Building 1 was Security Officer Richard Dickson. While working for the Missouri Department of Public Safety, Officer Dickson was assigned to Jefferson Barracks for a number of years.

Dickson recounted an unusual experience he had in Building 1 one evening. On this particular night, he was working by himself and had gone to get a soda from the vending machine in the basement. After getting his soda, Officer Dickson started to walk back up the stairs to the first floor. When he reached the open landing, he could hear a typewriter busily clicking away from somewhere on the second floor.

This was a concern because as far as he knew, no one was supposed to be working in the building and all of the lights had been turned off when the last employees had gone home for the night. When Dickson started to walk up the landing towards the second floor to investigate the further, the typing abruptly stopped. Dickson thought this was unusual, but when he did not hear any further typing, he thought that maybe there was a natural explanation for the sound he had heard.

However, when he started to walk back down to the first floor, the typing sound started again. Dickson said this unexplained encounter with the unknown "freaked me out." He immediately left the building for the lighted safety of the guard shack.

Interestingly, even the large flagpole in front of Building 1 has a ghost associated with it. This grand flagpole with its ornamental cannon display, located just east of the parade field, was the focal point of many of the post's special events and activities. One night, an unnamed security officer was patrolling the grounds and conducting building checks. As the officer neared the east end of the parade field, he saw a person sitting near the flagpole. As the officer drove by in his security vehicle, he continued to observe the mysterious person and noted that as he got closer, the person seemed to disappear before his eyes. When the officer completed his rounds, he drove by the flagpole a second time, and observed the same mysterious stranger seated near the flagpole. This ghostly encounter allegedly scared the officer so much that he would not come out of the security shack for the rest of the evening.

The ghost at the flagpole could be related to another transparent figure that was observed on the grounds behind Building 1 by soldiers during the Civil War.

The late Tony Fusco, author of *A Pictorial History of Jefferson Barracks*, told me that during the Civil War and the wars that followed, soldiers guarded the train depot and the railroad tracks along the Mississippi River, below Building 1. Armed guards also patrolled the grounds around the building.

In this instance, a sentry was walking his post around Building 1. When he walked behind the building, he observed a lone figure walking up the grassy hill towards the building from the train yard. As the soldier stood watching, he realized that the person was not a living man at all; it was a transparent, wispy "spook."

Several Air National Guard employees working after hours in Building 1 have experienced some unusual paranormal events there as well. Employees reported hearing ghostly footsteps when no one else is in the building, the sounds of chairs and furniture moving around, and lights turning on and off by themselves. In one case, these noisy spirits caused such a racket, that the employee who heard it turned up the volume on his radio, just so he would not hear what was going on around him.

On one occasion in 1974, Master Sergeant Jerry Faust, training manager for the Missouri Air National Guard, had his own unsettling experience while working in the basement of Building 1. Faust said he will always remember this particular evening because it was the night that he heard heavy objects falling with a thud on the floor above. During normal business hours, this was a common occurrence because a friend working in the copier room above would jokingly drop boxes of paper of the floor and then Faust would respond in kind by pounding on the ceiling. On this particular night after hearing the noises, Faust went upstairs to see who was working in the copier room. When he dashed up the stairs to ascertain the source of the commotion, he found nobody in the room. Everything appeared to be in its place. This series of events occurred three more times, and each time when Faust went to investigate, he found the area above his office undisturbed. After the fourth time, he thought it best to continue his work at home.

Prior to this, Faust said he was never really bothered by the atmosphere of the building. Following his experience, he decided to keep the incident to himself. "People just don't talk about these things, they try to brush it off," he said. It was not until he was having a discussion with another officer who worked in the building, and the topic of hearing footsteps and other strange noises came up, that Faust would finally tell his strange tale.

Master Sergeant Judy Jarvis, an information manager for the Missouri Air National Guard, also encountered several unexplained situations in Building 1 after hours.

In the fall of 1992, Jarvis was working in her office on the first floor of the building, near the main foyer, when she started hearing what sounded like desks being moved around on the second floor.

The second floor of the building had tiles on the floor, which magnified the sound of the moving furniture. Jarvis remembered hearing other employees talk about planning to move the furniture around upstairs, and she concluded that they had finally gotten around to doing it. As the noises continued, she decided to call it a day.

After yelling "I'm leaving now!" several times up the stairs, Jarvis turned out all of the lights and locked the exterior doors of the building. When she got to the parking lot, she observed that there were no other cars there but hers. She decided to re-enter the building to see if anyone was in fact inside moving furniture. When she unlocked the door, she found the hallway light was on. This was one of the lights she was sure was turned off when she left the building minutes before. Jarvis said she checked the entire building, but there was no one else inside. She never found what was making the loud noises she heard earlier.

"I always have my doubts about the noises I hear because they can be explained as the normal noises of a shifting building," Jarvis said later. She said she had spent the night in Building 1 several times. Of those times, she said that she had to leave twice because of "an overwhelming need to get out of the building."

Another time, Jarvis was working in Building 1 in the early afternoon when she heard the distinctive sound of a can of soda dropping out of one of the vending machines in the basement. She went to the basement and checked to see if anyone was there. She found all the doors near the vending machines were locked. At the time, only two other people were working in the building, and Jarvis later learned that they had not purchased any soda that day.

Building 28

This former barracks was built in 1897 as a double barracks with a three-story tower in the center. It had been designed to hold up to four companies of cavalry soldiers and their non-commissioned officers.

Throughout the 1970s, people working inside the building reported hearing ghostly footsteps pacing the corridors. One night, a man was working on some training records for an upcoming inspection when he heard someone walking around on the second floor above his office. He didn't think that anyone else was in the building, but as it simply sounded like another soldier was working upstairs, he never bothered to check on it. Later, though, more footsteps joined the first set and the noise became very distracting as he tried to finish his reports. Finally, he tossed aside his papers and went upstairs to see what was going on, but when he got to the area where he believed the sounds had been coming from, he found nobody there. He looked around for a few moments and then decided to write the whole thing off to his imagination. However, as soon as he got back downstairs to his desk, the footsteps started again. This time, he decided to just wrap up his reports and go home.

One evening in the fall of 1980, Chief Master Sergeant Eugene Anacker and several other Air National Guard NCOs non-commissioned officers were working late in the building. When they were ready to leave for the night, they turned out the lights, locked the doors and walked out into the parking lot in front of the building, where they stood talking for a few minutes. As they started to leave, Anacker happened to look up and noticed that one of the lights on the third floor had been left on. He dispatched the lowest ranking of the group to go back inside and turn it off.

The young NCO unlocked the main doors, climbed the stairs to the third floor and turned the light off. A few moments later, he re-appeared downstairs and locked the door behind him as he left the building again. As the young man walked toward him, Chief Anacker looked up and noticed that the same light was on once again, even though they had just seen it turned off. Thinking that the wiring in the old building was going bad, he sent the same NCO back inside to turn it off.

When the NCO returned to the parking lot once more, Anacker was stunned to see that the same light was once again shining. Again, he sent the NCO back inside to turn the light off. This time, when the man came out, none of them looked to see if the light had turned itself back on. They simply got into their cars and went home.

Building 78

Erected in 1912, Building 78, also known as Atkinson Hall, served as the post's main dining facility. Atkinson Hall, with its distinctive whitewash exterior, replaced the post's old dining facility, Building 36, known as "Cockroach Bogey." There are conflicting reports of how many soldiers this building was capable of feeding. Published reports tell that it was capable of feeding four thousand soldiers at one time. A document written by a major who was assigned to Jefferson Barracks during the 1940s, though, indicates that the building could hold 1,600 soldiers at one sitting. Either way, the building was extremely busy and filled to capacity during chow time. Atkinson Hall served as a focal point for soldiers stationed at Jefferson Barracks until the post's closing in 1946.

Many years later, the Army Reserve and the National Guard renovated Building 78 for future occupation. During this restoration, a secret room was discovered on the third floor, near the main stairway. Inside, carpenters found military personnel files, books, and pictures from a bygone era. This mystery is compounded by the rumor that the contractor who built the building in 1912 committed suicide there years later.

Today, Building 78 is home to several units from the Missouri National Guard: Battery A, 128th Field Artillery, Detachment 1, 1137th Military Police, and the 1035th Maintenance Company. The building also seems to house its fair share of residual and interactive ghostly phenomena.

Several military and civilian employees on post have reported that the ghost of a World War I veteran frequently returns to Building 78 to check and make sure that everything is all right. But this is just the tip of the iceberg when it comes to Atkinson Hall.

Major William "Willie" Smith recounted a personal experience he had in Building 78 when he was the Battalion Logistics Officer assigned to the 1138th Engineer Battalion. Building 78 had been the previous home of the 1138th Engineer Battalion prior to the unit's move to Building 27 in the early 1990s.

Major Smith had been working in the basement of the building by himself after hours. While walking down the hallway, on his way to the restroom, Major Smith suddenly felt like some unseen person was watching him. The feeling quickly passed and Smith dismissed his apprehension, attributing it to the general "creepy atmosphere" of the building after hours. Continuing down the hallway towards the restroom, which was around a corner, Major Smith observed a "shadowy transparent form" cross the hallway in front of him.

"It was like catching a quick glimpse of something or someone moving in your peripheral vision," he reported. According to Smith, "The presence of this transparent shadow startled me because I was sure that I was the only person in the building at the time." But the Major's encounter was not over yet.

Continuing down the hallway towards the intersection where just moments before, he had observed a shadow flit across his field of view, Major Smith got the shock of his life.

Just as he was about to walk around the corner into the intersecting hallway, Smith observed a shadowy form peer around the corner at him. The transparent form lingered for a split second, seeming to watch Smith's approach and then fading into thin air. When the shadow "just disappeared," Smith said that he was justifiably scared. "I turned on all of the lights that I could find in an attempt to see if anyone else was in the basement. It was different, it was like someone was really there," he said.

Sergeant McWilliams, the same person who encountered the Confederate general at Building 1, also recounted an experience he had in Building 78. When McWilliams and another guardsman first started working with the Funeral Honors Program, they lived in Building 78 for a short period of time. McWilliams described several instances during the night and early morning, when he and his friend would feel "vibes," as if someone were in the building with them, watching them.

McWilliams described how he and his friend would wake up at night and hear an unknown, unseen person walking up and down the stairs. He also reported how he experienced "hot spots" in various parts of the building on evenings when the air conditioning was working normally. In one particular instance, McWilliams said that he woke up and the room in which he was sleeping was "icy cold, so cold you could see your breath." Moments later, the room was warm again. After these disturbing encounters, McWilliams sought out a place to live outside the post.

Building 27 &27A

Located almost exactly at the opposite west end of the post from Building 1 stands Building 27. Building 27 was built in 1896 as enlisted cavalry soldiers' quarters. This large, rectangular building, with a three-story center and two story wings jutting out to each side, could hold up to four companies of soldiers and NCOs. The original mess hall was located in the basement, but in the early 1940s, a smaller one-story building, Building 27A, was built directly behind Building 27 and was used as a mess hall. Today, Building 27 is the home of a joint reserve military intelligence program run by the Army National Guard's

35th Infantry Division, headquartered at Fort Levenworth, Kansas. Building 27A serves as an administrative area.

Both buildings play host to phantoms that are both residual and interactive in nature. One veteran battalion supply sergeant commented that he was always looking for a light switch to turn on when he was working in the building alone because he sometimes felt "apprehensive" or like "someone was watching" him. A battalion staff officer who frequently spent the night in Building 27 said that on at least one occasion, he thought he heard the sounds of "muffled footsteps" and doors opening and closing when no one else was present in the building.

Security Officer Richard Dickson, mentioned earlier, told me during my interview with him, that "everywhere you go on this post, you feel like someone is watching you." This was apparently the case one evening when Dickson was working the midnight shift. Dickson was sitting in the old guard shack next to Building 27, when he observed a six-foot-tall human form dart behind the building. As Dickson had just completed a check of the area and was sure that no one was working in the building at the time, he went to investigate the situation further. He exited the guard shack and proceeded to the other end of the building in an attempt to intersect with the path of the unknown figure. When Dickson got to the far end of the building, he waited - and then waited some more. He could hear someone or something walking through the dead leaves that had accumulated between the buildings, but no one ever passed him. After waiting for what seemed like an eternity, the intrepid security officer decided that he would check the doors in between the buildings and found each one secured. The phantom had vanished without a trace.

In September 2000, Specialist Nicole Howell, a personnel clerk for the 235th Engineer Company, was stunned when she observed the phantom of a cavalry scout in the main foyer of Building 27. Howell described the Civil War-era soldier as having shoulder-length brown hair and wearing striped uniform riding pants, with a sword worn at the side. When Howell first saw the figure, she could see only the boots and pants walking around the foyer. As the figure moved, she said it appeared to "phase" in and out. She first saw the boots and pants, and then she observed the soldier's upper torso and hair materialize right before her eyes

She later observed the same "scout" on the landing stairs leading to the second floor of the building, and a third time in the building's mailroom. Each time she described the phantom, she reiterated that the soldier appeared to be translucent and to appear and disappear in a pulses. According to Howell, she felt that the cavalry scout fancies himself a "ladies' man" and would only appear or make himself known when female soldiers were present in the building.

Howell also told me that she frequently felt like someone was watching her when there was no one else in the building. She stated that she had a really unusual experience in July 2000, as if seeing the transparent figure of a Civil War cavalry scout were not unusual enough!

She said that she became a little unnerved when her electric typewriter suddenly came to life as if it had a mind of its own and the carriage started to "return" by itself. As she watched in amazement, the typewriter continued to function by itself for several seconds.

But Specialist Howell was not the only member of the Howell family who experienced something supernatural in Building 27. Her husband, Sergeant Charles Howell, Administrative NCO for the 203rd Engineer Company, also had several "unnerving" encounters in both Building 27 and 27A. The strange events started to unfold in April 2000, when Sergeant Howell was working by himself in the building. During the early morning or early evening hours, he started to get the feeling that someone or something was watching him, and even in some cases, following him around the building.

According to his account, this unseen energy "made the hair on the back of my neck stand up" and he would get "weird vibes all afternoon, and just know something would happen." He explained, "You will be sitting there working, and all of a sudden you will get the creeps and think to yourself, what the hell was that?" Sergeant Howell estimated that a lot of strange things seemed to happen in the early morning hours or between 4:00 p.m. and 7:00 p.m. "You know that you are not alone, and yet you know you are the only one working in the building," he stated.

He suggested that the second floor command area, which included the office used by the battalion's commander, was the most unsettling part of the building. One time, Howell said he had work to do on the second floor, and he felt like he was "interrupting the ghosts or that they did not want me there." When this happened, he said he boldly stated out loud, "I have work to do, and I have every right to be up here working." In addition to the second floor of the building, Howell also indicated that he believed that the mailroom in Building 27 was extremely active with paranormal energy.

On a cold morning in April 2000, Sergeant Howell had another encounter with one of the spirits in Building 27. On this particular morning, Howell was working by himself in the unit's old supply closet, located in the basement of Building 27.

While he was busy counting equipment, he again felt that someone was watching him. He continued to count various items, and a short time later, he thought he saw a brown boot out of the corner of his eye. Thinking that someone was standing in the room watching him, he turned to see who it was, but immediately discovered that no one was there and that the boot was gone. Now, really feeling uneasy, Sergeant Howell decided that it was time to leave. When he turned off the lights inside the room and started to walk out the door into the hallway, the lights suddenly turned back on again. By this time, Howell was becoming frustrated. He used the time-honored military tactic of swearing when things get rough, demanding that the ghost, "Knock it the f---k off! I don't have time for your s---t!" Sergeant Howell never did tell me if he stuck around to see if the ghost replied.

Howell later reported other experiences with lights turning on and off by themselves. This time, he was in the Annex, Building 27A. He was going home for the evening and after turning off the light, had locked the heavy wooden door separating the Annex from the main building. As he turned the lock, he observed that the lights were turned back on. When Howell unlocked the door and looked at the light switch, he found that indeed, someone or something had turned the switch on.

On another occasion, Sergeant Howell was leaving after locking the Annex, and the lights mysteriously turned on by themselves again. When he unlocked the door, and turned the lights off, they turned back on while he was re-locking the door.

In March 2001, Sergeant Howell was again working late in Building 27A, going through administration files in the Orderly Room, located just inside the Annex. He again got the feeling that someone was watching him. When he looked up, he observed a man in the office leaning toward him. The visitor was husky in stature and was wearing a blue Spanish-American War uniform shirt, khaki pants, and a cowboy-style hat. Because of the way this ghostly visitor was dressed, Howell was struck by the thought that this soldier looked as if he could have been with Theodore Roosevelt and the Rough Riders during their famous charge up San Juan Hill. Sergeant Howell remarked that he thought that the soldier was probably an enlisted man because he did not see any officer rank or stripes on the soldier's shirt or collar.

Howell looked back down at his files, not really realizing the significance of the moment, and immediately, he did a double take and looked back at the soldier. Just as he looked up, he observed the phantom fade away. He said he knew that he had finally identified the building's prankster.

In April 2001, Sergeant Howell experienced another "creepy" encounter with this prankster when he was working late again in the Orderly Room. He had locked the hallway door and had turned off the hallway lights. He had left the door to the Orderly Room open and was working quietly, when all of a sudden, he heard the hallway door slam open. Then he heard heavy footsteps tromping down the hall towards his office.

Howell knew he had locked the hallway door and got up to see if anyone was there. While he was making his way toward the doorway, he heard the footsteps continue to approach his office. He waited to see if anyone walked by, but instead, the ghostly footsteps continued past his office and down to the end of the hall. Howell never saw who or what made the footsteps but he guessed that it was the ghostly soldier he had seen previously. After collecting his wits, he checked the heavy hallway door, and found it was locked. Realizing that he still had work to do, he closed his office door and turned up the volume on his radio so he would not hear any more noises in the hall.

Building 27 has two more ghost stories to tell.

The first tale comes from Corporal Melissa Squires, another soldier who worked in Building 27 for several years prior to being transferred to another unit. Almost from the time she started working in Building 27, Corporal Squires began to hear unexplained noises. When she would mention her observations to other employees working in the building, they told her that it was just her imagination.

In October 1999, Squires was working late by herself. As she continued to work into the night, she started to hear someone walking around on the second floor of the building in the squad bay right over her head. This occurred several times during the next couple of nights. Each time, she checked the building and the front parking lot. Each time, she found that no one else had come into the building after it was locked for the night.

In March 2000, Squires started to hear noises and banging sounds emanating from the basement below her work area. She described the noises as being similar to someone banging on the basement floor with a broom handle. Later, she started to hear unexplained thumps and bumps on the walls. Again, she mentioned the odd noises to her co-workers, and again she was told that she was imagining things.

Several months later, Squires got a scare she would never forget. She was working in Building 27 after hours, and again, she heard muffled footsteps on the second floor of the building. Summoning all of her courage, Squires went up to the second floor to see what was responsible for making these eerie noises. When she reached the hallway on the second floor, in front of the Battalion Commander's office, she suddenly was awash in intense heat.

She later recalled, "I started to get goose bumps and I immediately turned around and started to walk back down the steps." When she reached the main foyer, she collected her wits and returned to her office to do some more paperwork. A short time later, she heard the footsteps again, only this time, as she listened, she noticed that they were walking down the stairs to the main foyer.

She did not wait around to see who or what was walking down the steps. Instead, she immediately vacated the building at a high rate of speed, leaving her purse on her desk. "They told me that it was an old building, but I know footsteps when I hear them," she firmly stated.

Dave's Own Experiences in Building 27A

This chapter would not be complete if I didn't mention my own experience in Building 27A. I was working late one evening on some paperwork. The unit was preparing to go to annual training and a small contingent of soldiers from my unit were scheduled to leave early the next morning.

One soldier had come to the unit the day before because he lived quite a distance from the armory and did not want to make the long drive early in the morning. I knew the soldier might be staying in the building and was aware that he had spent the night there on many other occasions.

As the night wore on, I started to hear someone moving around on the second floor. I didn't really give it any thought because I assumed it was this same soldier getting ready to bed down for the evening. The rest of the night, I would periodically hear thumps and bumps as if someone were going about their business upstairs.

When I had finally concluded my business, I paged the soldier who I thought was staying in the building. I requested that he meet me in the front foyer so I could find out what doors needed to be locked for the night. I had just hung the phone up when I heard someone come running down the stairs from the second floor. I then heard the person come through the main foyer, enter the Annex, and come to a stop outside my office door.

I was packing my suitcase, and thinking that the person standing outside of my office was the soldier I had paged, I commented out loud that he did not have to wait outside while I finished packing. I asked the soldier to come into my office several times, and when no one came in, I started to get concerned. What made matters worse was the fact that I was sure that someone had to be in the hallway because I never heard anyone walk away. After waiting for a few more seconds, I looked out into the hall. No one was there.

I paged the soldier again and again requested that he meet me in the front lobby. Then I went to the lobby and waited for five minutes or more. No one ever arrived. I knew that someone was in the building, but I did not know where. First I checked the basement, thinking that the soldier could have gone there to pack some equipment for his trip. When I did not find him there, I searched the rest of the building, floor by floor. Needless to say, I was the only person in the building.

By now, I was getting a little spooked. I had been doing research on Jefferson Barracks' ghosts for some time and I was aware of the stories about ghosts in the building. Taking this into account, I did not want to blow the situation out of proportion.

The next morning, I met with the soldier who I thought was in the building the night before. He told me that as soon as he had been dismissed for the day, he changed his clothes and had gone to his sister-in-law's house. He said that at no time had he returned to the building the previous night. At the time I heard someone run down the stairs and stop outside my office he was eating dinner at a local restaurant.

I have been investigating haunted houses for many years and because I have a law enforcement background, I am more than a bit skeptical about things. On this particular night, though, I know for a fact that someone was moving around the building and that someone or something responded to my page. For me, my experience in Building 27A proved without a shadow of a doubt that there had to be some truth to the ghost stories I had collected from the civilians and soldiers working at Jefferson Barracks.

St. Louis Arsenal

THE LEGEND OF THE "BLUE MAN"
St. Louis Arsenal
St. Louis, Missouri

Fort Belle Fontaine, established in 1805 at the mouth of Cold Water Creek, near the confluence of the Mississippi and Missouri Rivers, provided crucial military protection for St. Louis after the signing of the Louisiana Purchase in 1804. This remote military fort and its small garrison greeted the first pioneers and settlers heading west into the new frontier and served as a way station for members of the Lewis and Clark Expedition prior to and following its historic "Voyage of Discovery" to the Pacific Ocean.

By 1825, Fort Belle Fontaine and its small arsenal had fallen into a sorry state of disrepair. Military commanders at the time considered the fort to be unhealthy due to the effects of frequent flooding, and it was decided that a new military post and separate arsenal facility was needed.

On July 8, 1826, troops from Fort Belle Fontaine helped establish a new military base of operations south of St. Louis near the village of Carondelet. This new military post was named Jefferson Barracks in honor of President Thomas Jefferson. A small contingent of troops remained at Fort Belle Fontaine to protect the arsenal until the new one could be built on a forty-acre tract of land located three miles south of St. Louis, near modern day Second and Arsenal streets in South St. Louis.

In 1827, the first building on the new arsenal grounds was completed but the small facility at Fort Belle Fontaine continued to provide munitions and military supplies for troops operating in the Louisiana Territory until June 1828. Over the next few years, Fort Belle Fontaine was abandoned and the new St. Louis Arsenal grew to house a large three-story brick building, completed in 1828, along with an armory, an ammunition plant, and several wagon repair shops.

In the years that followed, the St. Louis Arsenal would directly impact the St. Louis region, both militarily and economically. At the start of the Mexican War in 1846, it was estimated that the nearly five hundred civilians were employed at the facility. During the years leading up to the Civil War, the St. Louis Arsenal continued to supply arms and ammunition to settlers and soldiers alike.

By early 1861, the dark tide of the pending war between the North and South settled upon Missouri and the Mississippi Valley. At the time, Missouri was considered to be a pro-slavery state, and its very future was threatened to be torn asunder by secessionist sympathizers, abolitionist factions and those who favored the preservation of the Union. The St. Louis Arsenal would play a pivotal role in determining what faction would control Missouri during the Civil War.

It was estimated that prior to the start of the war, the St. Louis Arsenal contained an estimated sixty thousand muskets, over 1.5 million rounds of ammunition, ninety thousand pounds of gunpowder and several cannons. As the battle lines started to be drawn, it was clear to the leadership of the Union Army that the arsenal would become a prime target of attack by pro-Southern secessionist militia units in the event war broke out between the states. To prevent such an attack, a military unit headed by Union Captain Nathaniel Lyon, a feisty military officer with strong anti-slavery beliefs, was assigned to St. Louis in early 1861 in an attempt to bolster the small garrison protecting the arsenal.

On April 12, 1861, the city of St. Louis and the surrounding region felt the resulting impact of the first shots of the Civil War when Confederate forces bombarded Fort Sumter. As a result of open hostilities between the North and South, Captain Lyon secretly transported twenty thousand muskets and one hundred thousand rounds of ammunition by steamship from the St. Louis Arsenal to Alton, Illinois.

On May 9, 1861, Captain Lyon learned that Missouri militia troops sympathetic to the Southern cause, camped at Camp Jackson, intended to attack the St. Louis Arsenal in order to secure the arms and munitions stored there for the Confederacy. Captain Lyon confirmed this information by dressing up as a woman and reconnoitering Camp Jackson in an open carriage.

On the morning of May 10, 1861, Federal troops, including units from Jefferson Barracks, the St. Louis Arsenal, and the St. Louis Home Guard, under the command of Captain Lyon, marched out of the St. Louis Arsenal and proceeded towards Camp Jackson.

Prior to leaving the protection of the arsenal that fateful morning, Captain Lyon had received a tersely worded dispatch from D.M. Frost, the garrison commander of Camp Jackson.

Sir; I am constantly in receipt of information that you contemplate an attack upon my camp; whilst I understand you are impressed with the idea that an attack upon the arsenal and United States troops is intended on the part of the Militia of Missouri, I am greatly at a loss to know what could justify you in attacking citizens of the United States, who are in lawful performance of duties devolving upon them under the Constitution.

Frost's letter did little to dissuade Captain Lyon from taking action against the Missouri militia members at Camp Jackson. Lyon and his troops encircled the pro-Southern militia camp, which was located near the modern-day site of Frost Campus on the grounds St. Louis University. This show of Federal force convinced D.M. Frost to surrender Camp Jackson without a fight.

The quick thinking of Captain Lyon would earn him great favor from his military superiors and keep Missouri in the Union but the day would not end without the blood of innocent St. Louisans being spilled on the streets of the city.

While en route back to the St. Louis Arsenal, the Federal troops escorting the pro-Southern prisoners were encircled by an angry crowd as they marched along Olive Street. The cramped and overcrowded street served only to magnify the already volatile situation. Eventually, shots rang out, but who fired the first shots remains a mystery. One report claimed that a drunken civilian in the crowd fired a revolver at soldiers in the passing military column. What is well documented by the newspapers of the time is that after the first sporadic shots were fired, nervous Federal troops began firing into the assembled mob. When the smoke cleared, three dozen dead civilians lay scattered amongst the scores of wounded who lay moaning in the street.

Due to the continued civil unrest and riots in St. Louis, General John C. Fremont, Commanding General of the Department of the West, declared martial law in the city on August 8, 1861. A short time later, the munitions and arms stored at the St. Louis Arsenal were moved by horse and wagon to the above-ground ordnance room and powder magazine at Jefferson Barracks.

While that may have been the most dramatic moment in the arsenal's history, its story continues today. The St. Louis Arsenal still serves the nation as an active military reservation. It is maintained by the U.S. Air Force and the Department of Defense Mapping Agency Aerospace Center.

And its long history has left behind at least one resident ghost.

In the spring of 2002, there was considerable commotion regarding an apparition that had been spotted by several different employees at the arsenal on at least two different occasions. During one of these encounters, the specter, dubbed the "Blue Man" due to his bluish complexion, was observed by two people at the same time. Further investigation by an employee at the facility revealed that workers at the arsenal have reported encounters with the Blue Man for over thirty years.

Accounts of each encounter vary, but for the most part, the Blue Man has been described as being a white-haired, stoop-shouldered elderly man, wearing a long, dark blue nineteenth-century military-style jacket with tails. One employee who reported seeing the Blue Man while working in Building 36 on the evening shift, stated that the elderly spirit appeared to be transparent. To the man's amazement, the wispy figure disappeared into the shadows right before his eyes. In another instance, an employee reported seeing the Blue Man in solid form. The employee later reported that from a distance, the ghostly visitor appeared to be a real person, but upon closer inspection, the old man seemed to simply fade away into the night.

The identity of the Blue Man remains a mystery, although his connection with the world of the living appears to be somehow linked to the older circa 1918 sections of Building 36. Since the founding of the arsenal in 1827, many older buildings have previously occupied the same location as that of Building 36.

During World Wars I and II, Building 36 was used by the Medical Supply Depot as a quartermaster warehouse and morgue. But even the grim presence of the morgue does not explain the existence of the ghost of a blue-skinned elderly man wearing a nineteenth-century military jacket.

The employees who have witnessed the Blue Man first-hand are understandably reserved about talking about their encounters with him. I have been assured by one of these anonymous sources, that in each instance where the Blue Man has been observed at the arsenal, the employees who reported the encounter were sincere about their brush with the elderly, bluish ghost.

We are likely to never know for sure who this mysterious figure might be, but accounts of his strange appearance at the arsenal are likely to continue for many years.

FORT BENNING
Columbus, Georgia

A curse, several mysterious deaths and rumors of a buried treasure. These are the basic ingredients of any really good ghost story. But what if a particularly malicious apparition -- and the riches it protects -- are still hidden in the center of one of the Army's most prestigious military posts? This would make for one hell of a paranormal mystery and a real page-turner for any horror reader. But what if I told you the story was true? And it's one that has lurked at the U.S. Army Infantry School at Fort Benning, Georgia for decades?

Fort Benning came into existence because of the need for better training for American soldiers. Intermittent states of open hostility in America's early history, such as the War or 1812, the Mexican War, the Civil War and the Spanish-American War, were grim reminders of the poor quality of training the everyday infantryman in the field received after being inducted into the Army. As a result, soldiers were disorganized and generally undisciplined. This critical gap in the overall readiness of the U.S. Army plagued military commanders well into the early twentieth century.

Between 1778 and 1918, the army struggled to establish a formal infantry school to adequately train its ground forces. In 1826, the Infantry School of Practice was established at Jefferson Barracks, Missouri, but the school was closed after only being in operation for two years. In 1881, the School of Application for the Infantry and Cavalry was created at Fort Leavenworth, Kansas, but like its predecessor, the school for the infantry ceased to exist after 1892.

At the insistence of Lieutenant General Arthur MacArthur, the U.S. Army School of Musketry was established in 1907 to improve the overall marksmanship skills of soldiers, but even this stopgap measure proved to be too little, too late. With the outbreak of World War I, it was clear that a school expressly geared to teach infantry skills and tactics was needed.

On October 6, 1918, the Army purchased a sprawling, 182,000-acre working plantation called Riverside from Arthur Bussey, a Columbus, Georgia, businessman. Located south of Columbus, the former plantation became the official home of the U.S. Army Infantry School. The post was named Fort Benning in honor of Henry Lewis Benning, a native of Georgia and an accomplished soldier and statesman. Benning had been a Confederate general during the Civil War and later went on to become the youngest man to serve as an associate justice on the Georgia Supreme Court.

Fort Benning is considered to be the "Home of the Infantry" and has, over the last seventy-five years, produced some of the finest combat infantrymen the world has ever seen. Soldiers trained at Fort Benning have proudly fought and died in every U.S-involved military action since World War I. In addition, several prominent military leaders such as Omar Bradley, Dwight Eisenhower, George Patton and Colin Powell either received their initial infantry officer training or some form of secondary training at Fort Benning.

The fort's proud heritage is preserved at the National Infantry Museum, located in the Old Hospital Complex, which was built in 1923. The museum is just one of several buildings comprising a section of the Main Post that has been nominated for placement on the National Register of Historic Places. The National Infantry Museum is the only place where you can see General Patton's former headquarters.

It is imperative that we further discuss the history of the area that comprises Fort Benning's historic Main Post because it is here that the mystery of the hidden treasure -- and the killer ghost who protects it -- begins to unfold.

About twelve thousand years ago, the labyrinth of bluffs south of the Upatoi Creek, near modern-day Columbus, Georgia, was home to nomadic prehistoric hunters known as Paleo-Indians. Later, between 900 and 1540, the sandhills and forests along the Chattahoochee River were inhabited by an advanced Native American culture known as the Mississippians. The Mississippians were ceremonial mound builders whose complex agricultural-based society reached its height when Europeans were caught in the morass of the Middle Ages. Unfortunately, the Mississippian people would see their vast empire crumble with the arrival of Spanish explorers in 1539. The unquenchable Spanish thirst for gold and conquest virtually wiped the Mississippian, Aztec and Incan cultures from the face of the Earth.

In the early 1800s, early settlers began slowly infiltrating into the Fort Benning area. At the start of the Civil War, Georgia was a prosperous agricultural state but by the end of the war, the region was experiencing an economic depression. This was the sad state of affairs in 1916 when Arthur Bussey's plantation occupied the land where the oldest sections of Fort Benning can be found today.

Riverside was a little city in and unto itself. In addition to the luxurious home of Bussey and the home of Bucky Manford, the manager of the plantation, the settlement included a dairy, a general store and lodging for the other workers who were required to keep the plantation running.

One of the workers in the farm's dairy was a young Maryland man named Karl Dayhoof. On a cold, wet night in early November 1916, Karl was roused from a deep sleep by his boss, Bucky Manford.

There was no reason why Bucky would wake him up in the middle of the night, but even more puzzling was Bucky's question to him: "Are you afraid to go outside with me?"

"I don't suppose so," Karl half-heartedly replied.

Bucky then asked a question that puzzled the young man even more, "Do you think some people are good enough so that their mere presence protects others from evil spirits?"

Karl was at a loss for words but responded with a verse he had memorized from the Bible: "The effectual fervent prayer of a righteous man availeth much."

Seemingly satisfied with Karl's response, Bucky told him to quickly get dressed and follow him outside. Out in the darkness, Bucky ordered Karl not to say anything or make any sound, no matter what he heard or saw. Once Karl agreed, the pair walked off into the night. Karl really did not have to be told to be quiet because his head was still reeling from the strange course of events the evening had taken. What was his boss up to?

Silently, Karl and Bucky made their way through the settlement and into the woods west of Riverside, guided only by a shaft of light from Bucky's flashlight. It was well past midnight when Bucky finally stopped and turned off the flashlight. By that time, Bucky had lead Karl to the deepest, darkest part of the forest, to a gloomy place that could give a person the shivers even in the daylight. Bucky turned to Karl and again whispered his previous warning, "Whatever you see or hear, don't make a sound."

As the pair sat in silence, shrouded in almost total darkness, Karl's mistrust of Bucky mounted. The minutes slowly crawled by. It was during this darkest hour that Karl started to wonder if the stresses of running the plantation had caused Bucky to go insane. Before Karl could devise an appropriate exit strategy, something caught his attention in the distance, just beyond the bend of a nearby ravine. Focusing on the spot, Karl saw a blue light moving slowly through the bushes and vines towards the spot where he and Bucky were waiting.

As the glow continued its approach, it was heralded literally by the sounds of hell. The sound of clanking chains and inhuman shrieks and groans suddenly assaulted Karl's ears. The noise was so violent that the very ground beneath his feet seemed to shudder in response to the inhuman clamor. Just when Karl thought his eardrums could take no more of the pounding, the light rounded the bend. As Karl watched the light's advance with mounting trepidation, he was stunned to see that the epicenter of the deafening roar and the radiant blue glow was not coming from some monstrous demon, but from a little old man.

Glowing with a vividness as bright as lightning, the scowling old man stopped about ten feet in front of Karl and Bucky and glowered at them. From this distance, Karl could now see the apparition clearly. Dressed in a white shirt and string tie reminiscent of clothing worn in the 1800s, the elderly specter's appearance was anything but pleasing, due to the fact that there was a prominent mark in the center of the man's forehead that resembled a gunshot would.

After scrutinizing the duo for several minutes, the old man suddenly turned and walked silently back down into the ravine with Bucky and Karl in tow. Deliberately, the old man made his way through the brambles and thickets, stopping periodically to get his bearings and re-orient himself to his surroundings. Before long, the trio had reached a skeletal tree located high along the bank of the gulch. The old man found his bearings yet one more time and began to pace down the hill, appearing to be silently counting each step before eventually stopping at twenty. The ghost looked over his shoulder, and when he was sure that Karl and Bucky were watching what he was doing, he pointed down with a bony finger at the ground.

In the next instant, the old man was on the move again, peering over his shoulder at the old tree. He lined himself up with a large knot on the tree's trunk and proceeded to silently count out forty-five more paces. Again, the ghost stopped and pointed to the ground. Sensing the spirit's urgency, Karl committed to memory the exact locations where the old man had been standing each time he motioned to the ground. Suddenly, the light disappeared and the night came rushing back in. Unlike his laborious arrival, the spirit vanished in an instant this time, without the noise and fanfare of his initial appearance.

When Karl and Bucky's eyes had readjusted to the darkness, they found themselves alone in one of the most deserted sections of the plantation. Without a word spoken between them, the pair retraced their steps and returned home at 3:00 a.m.

For the next week, neither man spoke of their trip into the woods that frightful November night. Finally, out of the blue, Bucky cornered Karl in the dairy one day and hesitantly brought up the subject of their midnight rendezvous with the ghostly old man. Bucky admitted that his wife had been pressuring him to make more money. He wracked his brains but could think of no way he could get more cash. At his wits' end, he had resorted to visiting a fortune-teller in nearby Columbus in hopes that she would know how he could make his wife's dream a reality. Bucky said that it was the fortune-teller who told him that there was a treasure buried on the grounds of the Riverside plantation. Karl was now hopelessly enthralled by Bucky's tale.

Bucky recounted how, in 1861, the property where Riverside was located belonged to the Whitley family. The Whitleys were successful horse-breeders and trainers who operated their own profitable racetrack right there on the plantation. Bucky went on to tell how, just one week before the start of the Civil War, Old Man Whitley and his four nephews hosted the largest horse race in the state at their racetrack. To prevent any of the bettors from using counterfeit money, Whitley stipulated that all bets be placed using gold or silver coins. When race day finally came to a close, the Whitleys were the big winners. The old man walked away with $150,000 and between them, his nephews won the same amount. Following the race, the Whitleys threw a week-long celebration. It must have been quite a party, because when the week was over, the four nephews had mindlessly squandered their winnings. Old Man Whitley was now the sole holder of a small fortune.

The very next day, the first shots of the Civil War rang out at Fort Sumter. In a patriotic fervor, the nephews ran off to fight for the Southern cause. Only one of the four boys was ever heard from again. About a year later, the last surviving nephew returned to the plantation while on military leave. The night before he was to return to active duty, he demanded that his uncle loan him some money. When he refused, an argument ensued and the old man was never seen alive again.

Several days after the nephew had rejoined his military unit, slaves found the uncle's body in a field on the outskirts of the plantation. The old man had been shot once in the forehead, presumably by his infuriated nephew.

Following Whitley's funeral, rumors started to spread that he had divided his fortune in half and buried each half in a pair of wooden chests somewhere on the plantation. Several attempts were made to locate the missing treasure but it was never found.

Bucky was nearing the end of his story. He went on to describe how the fortune-teller had told him that if he waited at a particular place at a certain time, he would be shown exactly where the treasure could be found. Bucky admitted that he had made one attempt to find Whitley's money by himself but he got scared and ran away before he ever saw anything. To Karl's surprise, Bucky told him that on a return trip to the fortune-teller, she had said that it would be all right if Karl accompanied him the next time he went out searching for the money, but that there was one stipulation: Karl had to remain a passive observer.

Karl was visibly excited at the prospect of finding the buried cache of money. The old man's ghost had all but dug up the treasure for them. All that was left now was for him and Bucky to return to the woods and dig up their prize. Bucky saw Karl's optimism building and he quickly blurted out that he didn't want any part of the money. Surprised, Karl asked him why not. Wasn't it the whole point of visiting the fortune-teller in the first place to find out how he could lay his hands on some money? Bucky reluctantly mentioned that the treasure was cursed and that anyone who tried to recover it would die.

Karl thought about the buried $150,000 for a long time, but his thoughts always drifted back to his terrifying encounter with the ghost of old man. He knew without a doubt that Whitley's ghost was real and that there was no way he was going to tempt fate by exploring the possibility that Whitley's curse could exist, as well. Two years later, most of the plantation, with the exception of the main house, was bulldozed by the U.S. Army and Fort Benning was built in its place.

In the early 1920s, Karl, who still lived in the area, innocently told a major stationed at Fort Benning about his encounter with the ghost of old Mr. Whitely. Based on Karl's detailed account of what happened that harrowing evening, the officer raced back to post, obsessed with the idea that a hoard of gold and silver coins could be buried virtually beneath his feet. Knowing that he couldn't pull off this endeavor by himself, the major enlisted the aid of two non-commissioned officers from the Fort Benning baseball team to help him.

Armed with a metal detector that only one of the sergeants knew how to operate, the three would-be treasure hunters started out on their quest. Using Karl's explicit instructions, the men prowled around the old ravine until the sergeant holding the metal detector heard the unmistakable "click-click" in his earpiece indicating that something metal was hidden beneath his feet.

At this point, the story takes another unlikely turn.

At the start of the hunt, the major had promised the two sergeants that they would each receive one-third of the treasure, but unbeknownst to the brash officer, the two NCOs had decided to deal him out of the picture altogether. Instead of digging at the spot where the metal detector had indicated that something was buried, the sergeant stepped aside and directed the others to dig in another place. Finding nothing there, they returned to their residences that evening empty-handed.

The next day, the two sergeants returned to the site, knowing that the major was on duty and would essentially be out of their hair long enough for them to claim the treasure for themselves. Again, with the help of the metal detector, they quickly located the true location of the money, just yards from the hole they had dug the day before. Within a short period of time, the sergeants had literally struck it rich. All they had left to do was lug the heavy wooden chest that held the coins to the house of the conspirator who lived the closest to the scene of the crime.

When the major got off duty, he returned to the dig site and was aghast at what he found. He saw the second hole, saw the imprint of a chest in the freshly dug earth, and immediately knew he had been double-crossed. But what could he do? The entire operation was done clandestinely without the permission of his superiors so he could not go to anyone for help. The major knew that if he was to get any of the money for himself, he had to deal with the sergeants directly, but by the time he had come to this realization, it far too late to take any action.

The very next morning, Whitley's curse claimed its first victim. The sergeant who had been in possession of the chest unexpectedly collapsed in his home from complications due to a pneumonia-like virus. A short time later, the second soldier fell unconscious while in the middle of a baseball game after suffering from the same pneumonia-like symptoms. Both soldiers died later that same day at the post hospital.

When the major heard of the unfortunate demise of his fellow collaborators, he immediately dispatched several armed guards to the house of the first soldier who had fallen from the mystery illness. The men had strict orders to recover the chest and bring it to the major at his house. Within hours of receiving Whitley's money, the major was hospitalized after being stricken with pneumonia.

Before he died, the major confessed to his involvement in the unsanctioned treasure hunt that had claimed the lives of his two companions. Post doctors stated that whatever killed the men may have appeared to be pneumonia at the outset, but that it was far too virulent and fast-acting to have been pneumonia. The Army conducted a thorough investigation into the major's seemingly far-fetched story in an attempt to verify if it had any bearing on the series of strange deaths at the base. Fearing that the matter would be an embarrassment to the Army as a whole, the investigative panel's findings were never released to the public. Instead, the government confiscated the money and acted like the incident never happened.

As far-fetched as this story may seem, there are several key elements that have a basis in solid fact. First, the current site of the infantry school and the statue of the World War I Doughboy mark the approximate center of the Whitley family's racetrack. Second, in an article written by Eleanor Dayhoof titled "Ghost Still Guards Buried Treasure at Fort Benning," published in the April, 1967 issue of FATE magazine, Dayhoof suggested that the Whitely fortune may have in fact been buried in the vicinity of the Officers' Club, which is listed as point 7 along Fort Benning's Historic Trail. Last but not least, official military documents dating back to 1932, when the Officers' Club was built, indicate that the building cost $150,000 dollars to construct. The gold and silver coins in the chest that was dug up by the ill-fated soldiers would likely have been worth at least that amount. Coincidence? It makes you wonder, doesn't it?

Did old Mr. Whitley return from the grave to claim the lives of three soldiers who dared to disturb his treasure? No one knows for sure. One thing can really be inferred from this bizarre chain of events: If the legend is true, somewhere, hidden in the oldest section of Fort Benning rests a second chest that is filled to overflowing with a treasure that most people would give anything to get their hands on.

FORT CLINCH
Fernandina Beach, Florida

Fort Clinch is a major Civil War-era fortress located on Amelia Island, near modern-day Fernandina Beach, Florida. This tranquil historical location and adjoining park is surrounded by sprawling sand dunes and a scenic saltwater marsh. More than 167,000 travelers visit the fort annually and Fort Clinch's myriad of specters and spirits seem to reach out to all who enter its hollowed walls.

The Cumberland Sound and the land in and around the entrance of the St. Mary's River have played host to various military units as far back as 1736. In 1842, a generous section of land at the north end of Amelia Island was purchased for use as a military reservation. It would not be until 1847, around the time that the final bricks were being laid at Fort Pulaski, Georgia, that the actual construction of Fort Clinch would begin. Fort Clinch was built as part of the U.S. Army's Third American Building System, a series of key military fortifications built to protect the Eastern coastline from future enemy attack. Fort Clinch was built in the typical style of the day and was an impressive pentagonal fortress with brick inner and outer walls. In 1850, the fort was formally named Fort Clinch in honor of General Duncan Lamort Clinch, a renowned hero of the Second

Seminole War. Construction of Fort Clinch's defenses progressed at a snail's pace until the beginning of the Civil War.

In 1861, the more than six hundred Confederate soldiers began occupying Fort Clinch after militiamen under the direct command of the government of Florida took control of the fort. Southern control of the fort would be brief, however. In March 1862, Federal troops recaptured Fort Clinch, thereby giving the Union decisive control of the Georgia and Florida coastlines. Construction continued at Fort Clinch until the end of the Civil War, but by 1867, the fort was considered obsolete, due to the advent of new rifled cannons and improved gunpowder.

Fort Clinch saw duty during the Spanish American War in 1898, but at the close of hostilities with Spain, the fort was considered to be of no further military value and it was formally abandoned by the federal government. In 1926, the fort and grounds were put up for sale. A local businessman purchased the property but lost it during the Depression and the state of Florida purchased the land in 1935 for use as a public park. In 1938, the Fort Clinch State Park, one of Florida's oldest state parks, officially opened to the public. But in three years, Fort Clinch would again be pressed into military service as a key joint communications and surveillance command post during the Second World War. Following World War II, Fort Clinch again became a prominent part of the Florida state park system.

It was then that the ghost stories began.

Over time, visitors, boaters, and park staff have reported many strange occurrences at Fort Clinch. Boaters have told many stories and tales about ghostly lights that can be seen floating around the ruins of the fort after sundown.

One evening in late April or early May, three fishermen were returning to the boat docks at Fernandina after a night of offshore fishing. As the trio rounded the north end of Amelia Island and turned their boat toward shore, they observed what appeared to be a person carrying a lantern walking along the shoreline near the fort. As the fishermen continued to watch, they noticed that the light seemed to be getting closer to them. To the men's amazement, once they neared a point adjacent to the light's position, the lantern's flicker vanished and suddenly reappeared at the same spot where they had first observed it. It is said that the light is the ghost of a guard who is destined to search the shoreline for enemy ships, but this story is questionable. No self-respecting sentry, ghost or not, would search for enemy ships with a lantern at night.

It's possible that the ghostly sentry is not looking for ships at all, though. It is said that Union forces working on the fort during the Civil War were ambushed several times by Confederate troops. Several Union men reportedly died during these brief confrontations. During one such skirmish, a Union soldier was killed after he had written his wife a letter promising that he would not die until she saw her again. In 1996, a female volunteer working inside the old hospital at Fort Clinch reported seeing a ghostly figure carrying a lantern, but instead a lantern-toting soldier, the volunteer encountered the ghost of a woman, dressed all in white, like a nurse. The ghostly woman in white has been observed in the top floor of the storehouse at the fort, and in one instance, a volunteer even said that this mysterious visitor used the light from her lantern to help her find something in her handbag. The significance of the encounter did not register with the volunteer until she thanked another co-worker for helping her with the light. Needless to say, the volunteer was shocked when her friend told her that she was not even in the fort at the time. The origin of the ghost lights in and around Fort Clinch will probably remain a mystery forever, but the ghostly sentry and the woman in white are not the only spirits that are alleged to haunt this old military post.

One warm July night, two volunteers were sitting on the porch of one of the fort's interior buildings, which looked out over the parade ground at the heart of the old brick fortress. The volunteers watched in awe as the light from a full moon bathed the parade field in an eerie, luminescent glow. To the volunteers' amazement, the peaceful scene was shattered when they saw what appeared to be four Civil War soldiers run out from the northwest bastion tunnel and across the parade ground. In an instant, the figures dashed over the embankment, leaving the volunteers speechless. The next year, the same two volunteers made it a point to be at Fort Clinch on the night of the full moon in July. Just as before, the volunteers were amazed when the Civil War soldiers ran from the tunnel. But this time, something was different. There were only three soldiers where there had been four the previous year.

As the soldiers neared the embankment, one of the volunteers called out, "There were four of you last year. Where's the fourth man?"

To the utter bewilderment of the volunteers, one of the soldiers answered, "He's sick tonight. Couldn't come!"

There is one other notable supernatural entity that is known to intermittently manifest itself at Fort Clinch. It is the crying voice of a child that is sometimes heard echoing off the brick walls of the fort.

In the 1920s, a caravan of gypsies is said to have taken up residence at Fort Clinch. During the blistering summer of that year, the gypsies attempted to seek refuge from the heat in the dark, cool confines of the fort's southwestern bastion tunnel. That same summer, there was an outbreak of yellow fever, and several of the gypsies died as a result of the illness. Their bodies were hastily buried in unmarked graves near the fort. A small child was one of these unfortunate souls who never made it out of Fort Clinch alive that sweltering summer in 1920. It is believed that the woeful lamentations that are sometimes heard are the last desperate cries of a child delirious with fever. To this day, the cries of this phantom child can sometimes be heard in the unused southwestern bastion tunnel of the fort.

There is no doubt that the spirits that haunt Fort Clinch come from the many different time periods which make up the fort's history. It is quite possible that we will never know cause of the floating "spook lights" that have been observed by boaters and visitors to the fort over the years. One could surmise that the lights are in fact the ghost of a lonely soldier who is still looking for his lost love, or an ever-vigilant sentry who continues to walk his guard mount, on the lookout for a Confederate raid that will never come. More puzzling is the lady in white, whose origin remains a mystery that Fort Clinch is not ready to give up just yet.

Fort Fisher during the Civil War

FORT FISHER
Wilmington, North Carolina

At the start of the Civil War, the Confederate ground forces boldly took control of a peninsula south of Wilmington, between the mouth of the Cape Fear River and the Atlantic Ocean. Out-manned, and out-gunned by the industrial might of the Northern states, this thin sliver of land would become the lifeline of the Confederacy during its war of independence from Federal rule.

When the Civil War broke out, Federal military strategists knew that the South had very little industrial infrastructure to support its campaign. The

South's economy had always been based on the sale of cotton and tobacco. For the primarily agrarian South to fight a war, it had to import guns, gold and medicine from allies willing to do business with the fledging Southern government. With the start of hostilities in 1861, the Federal Navy blockaded all southern seaports in an attempt to stem the tide of manufactured goods and materials the South garnered through trade with England and Western Europe. It was believed by Northern tacticians that this stranglehold on the South's seaports would force the Confederacy to capitulate to the North's demands in no time at all.

Instead of capitulation, though, the South employed a new type of pirate to bring needed war supplies through the Federal blockade. These daring young seamen were called "blockade runners." This new type of buccaneer, using specially outfitted ships built for speed, hit the high seas and brazenly took on the might of the Federal Navy. They did all that they could to keep supporting the South through illegal goods, but many of the blockade runners went down under Union guns.

By 1864, the effects of the Federal blockade could be felt through the war-torn South. With all but one seaport closed, the Confederacy was dying. The one seaport that kept the South in the fight was located at Wilmington, North Carolina, twenty-eight miles inland from the Atlantic Ocean, along the Cape Fear River. At the mouth of the river was the one thing that kept the port at Wilmington out of the hands of the Federal Navy: Fort Fisher, known as the Gibraltar of the Confederacy.

Fort Fisher was without a doubt the most important earthwork fortifications in the South during the Civil War. Built on the southern end of Confederate Point, this huge L-shaped fortification was single- handedly responsible for the protection of Wilmington and its critical seaport. In July 1862, the new commander, Colonel William Lamb, discovered that the fort was little more than several batteries of cannon dug into sand earthworks. Under his direction, the paltry sand batteries became a true fortress.

Fort Fisher was not built in the same manner as many of the other brick and mortar coastal forts of the time. Instead, it was made mostly of earth and sand, which had been determined to be ideal for absorbing the damage of heavy explosive rounds. By early 1865, construction of Fort Fisher was completed. The fortress walls were twenty feet high and twenty-five feet thick at the base. The fort had a wooden palisade, protected by a shallow ditch and electrically controlled mines at the north end, and was made up of fifteen traverses built inside the walls to protect defenders from bombardment. Fort Fisher boasted an impressive complement of forty-eight long-range cannon capable of defending the fort from attack from sea or land. Any blockade runner who was able to reach the protection of Fort Fisher's guns, was safe from the Federal Navy, which lurked just outside the maximum effective range of the fort's biggest long-range cannon. From there, the blockade runners were guaranteed safe passage to Wilmington, where they would offload their precious supplies and war materials.

It was clear to Northern commanders that the guns of Fort Fisher had to be silenced once and for all. On December 24, 1864, a combined Union task force under the command of Admiral David D. Porter, attacked Fort Fisher for two days. This combined force of Navy ships and Federal infantry withdrew from the field after their commanders deemed that Fort Fisher's defenses, under the command of Confederate Major General William "Little Billy" Whiting, were too strong.

On January 13, 1865, the Union fleet returned with a vengeance. Admiral Porter again subjected the defenders of Fort Fisher to two days of merciless bombardment. Between the 13th and the 15th of January 1865, it was estimated that Union forces fired almost fifty thousand rounds at or into Fort Fisher. At the time of this attack, Whiting was meeting with General Braxton Bragg in Wilmington. The fort was defended by more than two thousand soldiers under the command of Colonel Lamb. During a lull in battle, General Whiting returned and announced that the fort would be sacrificed in an effort to stall Union forces long enough for Bragg and his army to evacuate from Wilmington. General Whiting, Colonel Lamb and his troops prepared to defend the fort to the last man. Their resolve was tested on January 15, 1865.

In the mid-afternoon of the 15th, eight thousand Federal infantry under the command of Major General Alfred Terry attacked Fort Fisher. The attack started when approximately two thousand sailors and marines attacked the northeast corner of the fort. Unbeknownst to the distracted Confederate defenders who were watching the Navy action to their front, four thousand Union infantrymen moved into position near the northwest corner of the fort. Just when it appeared to the Confederate soldiers manning the defense positions that the sailors and marines were falling back in disarray, a shout of alarm went up throughout the fort. The hapless Confederate defenders were stunned with horror as Federal troops stormed over the lightly defended northwestern corner of the fort.

General Whiting personally organized a Confederate counterattack in a vain attempt to push the Union soldiers out, but he was shot several times as he tried to wrestle a federal banner from its bearer. Minutes after the general was wounded, Colonel Lamb was also shot. The battle raged back and forth between the determined Union forces and the beleaguered Confederate defenders until late into the night.

At 10:00 p.m., Confederate Major James Reilly approached the Union line and surrendered. The battle of Fort Fisher was ended with more than two thousand men dead.

General Whiting was taken prisoner and transported to Fort Columbus, a Federal prison facility located on Governors Island in New York Harbor. On March 10, 1865, he succumbed to his wounds, despite the efforts of Union surgeons. "Little Billy's" body was later returned to North Carolina, the land that he loved. He was laid to rest in Wilmington's Oakdale Cemetery.

Fort Fisher had earned a reputation for bloodshed and death, which set the stage for the ghost stories that followed.

In the middle 1880s, the first ghost stories began to be circulated about Fort Fisher. A group of Confederate veterans visited the old fort for a day of revelry and reminiscing. As they settled down for the evening, one of the men looked toward the interior of the crumbling fort and saw an unbelievable sight. Standing near the third traverse was a figure wearing a Confederate general's uniform! As the veterans looked on in shock, the phantom continued to gaze out toward the sea. When the men had recovered their senses, they ran toward the figure calling out, "Billy! It's Little Billy, come back to join us!" As the veterans approached, the figure disappeared before their astonished eyes. Since then, the ghost of General Whiting has been seen at Fort Fisher by many people over the years. It is said that on certain evenings, the old general can still be seen looking out towards the sea from the fort's parapets and from other former fighting positions.

A couple of days after Hurricane Fran struck the Eastern Seaboard in September 1996, a man visited the park to see what effect the storm had had on Fort Fisher. The man walked a short distance along the beach, surveying the damage from the storm. Turning to head back towards the fort, he saw standing in front of him a man dressed in a Confederate general's uniform gazing intently out to sea. When the man opened his mouth to address the figure, it vanished into thin air.

Little Billy had been encountered once again.

In addition to housing the spirit of Little Billy, Fort Fisher also continues to attract the ghosts of the blockade runners it protected so many years ago. Many people claim that on foggy nights, if you stand along the inlet, you can hear the paddle wheels of invisible boats as they head upriver. If you listen hard enough, some say you can even hear the hushed conversations of the ships' ghostly crews.

Today, the huge dirt walls that once protected the fort from Union invaders still remain. However, weather, time and the unforgiving sea have taken their toll on this landmark of a bygone era. The once-impregnable traverses of the "Gibraltar of the South" are little more than dirt mounds these days and Fort Fisher lies in ruins - much like the dreams of the men who once defended the Confederacy.

FORT MCALLISTER
Richmond Hill, Georgia

By all outward appearances, Fort McAllister was anything but the crown jewel in the defensive ring that protected the prized harbor of the city of Savannah, Georgia, during the Civil War. Its sister fort, Fort Pulaski, was a modern technological wonder constructed using modern engineering techniques and elaborate brick masonry, while Fort McAllister was built using bricks made of sod and fill from the Ogeechee River bottom. As different as both of these Civil War forts are in appearance, they both have one thing in common: They both are still manned by long-dead defenders who still seem to cry out.

Construction of Fort McAllister's seven gun emplacements, almost completely protected by mounds of river mud and sod, was completed in 1861. The fort's massive earthen walls interconnected, creating a bomb-proof central spiral, which was used to safely house the post's hospital, powder magazines and barracks for the fort's two hundred and thirty defenders. In addition to the traversing weapons platforms, Fort McAllister housed an impressive ten-inch mortar battery that was constructed away from the main defenses because when fired, its blast tended to shake the fort's walls apart.

Compared to other Civil War fortifications that saw active service during the war, a soldier's life at Fort McAllister was considered relatively quiet and uneventful. Fort McAllister's defenders would hear the sound of battle seven times during the War Between the States. During those times of high drama, garrison life changed drastically when enemy cannon balls were directed at the fort's embankments and its defenders.

In 1862, Fort Pulaski fell to determined Union ground forces, supported by Union ironclads and other wooden support vessels. The loss of Fort Pulaski prompted Confederate commanders to place wooden pilings and other obstructions in the Ogeechee River within range of Fort McAllister's guns. This man-made obstacle course allowed only ships loyal to the Confederacy to navigate the river.

In July 1862, Fort McAllister's defenses would be tested for the first time. Union ships pursuing the side-wheeled Confederate blockade runner *Nashville* attacked the fort in an attempt to capture the ship. The *Nashville* had unsuccessfully attempted to run the Union fleet's blockade of Charleston harbor and now its captain looked to Fort McAllister's seven pieces of heavy artillery for protection from the Union steamers in hot pursuit. Union forces attacked Fort McAllister on four separate occasions during the final months of 1862 in an attempt to seize the fort and capture the *Nashville*. During each attack, the fort's earthen ramparts appeared to swallow up the enemy's cannon balls, thwarting the Union advance and protecting the *Nashville* lying at anchor nearby.

But the Union Navy refused to give up its attack on Fort McAllister. On January 27, 1863, the *U.S.S. Montauk*, a Federal ironclad vessel sporting eleven-inch and fifteen-inch smooth bore cannons in a huge revolving turret, attacked the fort, accompanied by several other wooden warships.

During the bombardment, the *Montauk* steamed within one hundred and fifty yards of the river pilings in front of Fort McAllister, its belching cannon plowing gaping holes in the fort's defenses. During the attack, Fort McAllister was reportedly struck by over four hundred and fifty cannon balls, each being absorbed by the fort's earth and sod embankments. Confederate gunners found their mark on the iron hull of the *Montauk* fifteen times during the battle, but the ship's armor deflected the rounds without significant damage or casualties. At the same time, the hardened defenders of Fort McAllister also reported no casualties or significant damage as a result of feverish Union shelling. At the end of the engagement, the *Montauk* and the remaining Federal fleet steamed away, vowing to return.

On February 1, 1863, the *Montauk* and several wooden support craft returned to Fort McAllister determined to win the day. During the first attack, both sides traded numerous volleys of cannon fire with nearly the same results as the previous attack the month before. It was reported that the *Montauk* was struck forty-eight times during this engagement, causing little more than slight dents and dings in the ship's armor.

During the second Union assault, the fort's commander, Major John B. Gallie, was killed by a fifteen-inch Union shell that ricocheted off one of Fort McAllister's cannons. Major Gallie was valiantly supervising one of the fort's eight-inch artillery positions when a Union shell fragment wounded him in the head. He fought on, despite the blood streaming down his face, until he was violently dispatched in front of the startled eyes of his comrades by a second Union shell. Some reports say the major was "scalped" by the round, while others say the blast "exposed his brains." Either way, the end result was the same.

Union forces, consisting of three ironclads, three mortar schooners and two wooden gunboats attacked Fort McAllister a third time on March 3, 1863. After seven hours of shelling, the fort experienced its second "unusual" casualty of the war.

Camp mascots were commonplace in both the Union and Confederate encampments during the Civil War. Soldiers on both sides of the conflict were known to adopt all kinds of animals to help relieve the monotonous rigors of camp life. Tom Cat, a coal-black cat, was Fort McAllister's cherished mascot. It was reported that Tom Cat would run back and forth along the fort's defenses during the maelstrom of combat. Each time, the defiant feline would wager one of his nine lives dodging the wall of lead cannon and musket balls that flew overhead.

On March 3, 1863, Tom Cat's luck finally ran out during a seven-hour battle, when a stray round killed the post's most cherished occupant. Tom Cat was the only casualty and his death was described in the official report of the battle. Tom Cat was buried with honors within the fort. He was later commemorated with a historical marker.

The death of Tom Cat would not signal the end for Fort McAllister. The fort and its defenders would fight on until December 13, 1864. On this date, Fort McAllister, the unmovable rock of the Confederacy, would find itself face to face with an unstoppable force: General William T. Sherman, a man intent on leaving his mark on history.

In fifteen minutes, four thousand Union infantry under the command of General Sherman, overpowered Fort McAllister's two hundred and thirty defenders, marking an end to the post's distinguished battle history. Sherman, observing nearby, called the battle "The handsomest thing I have seen in the war." The fall of Fort McAllister heralded the end of Sherman's famous March to the Sea.

But the tales of the storied fort were not quite over.

In the late 1930s, industrialist Henry Ford took an active interest in the historical preservation of Fort McAllister. Ford purchased the Civil War landmark and invested his own money in the extensive re-construction of the fort. Largely thanks to this, Fort McAllister is today regarded as the best-preserved Civil War-era earthen fortification in the South. Like many other historic sites from the war, this tranquil park has its share of ghostly occupants.

During the 1930s, workers who had been hired by Henry Ford refused to spend the night at Fort McAllister because it was reported that strange noises could be heard emanating from the grounds. It has been said that source of the eerie noises was never identified and that the same ghostly sounds are still reported today. In addition to the mysterious noises, Civil War reenactors, visitors and park staff have reported seeing the ghosts of the fort's two most famous casualties.

Scores of people have reported seeing a black cat nimbly running along the fort's earth ramparts or perched in the various "bomb-proof" rooms of the fort. Reenactors have recounted how they have seen the ghost of Tom Cat peering out towards the river, while others have said that they have felt the touch of an invisible cat rub along their legs. When questioned about the possibility of the existence of a flesh and blood cat at Fort McAllister, staff and park administrators adamantly deny that any cats live on the park grounds.

In addition to those who have reported a brush with Tom Cat over the years, many others have claimed encounters with the headless ghost of Major Gallie - a much more unnerving event. He has been seen many times on the park grounds at night, pacing near the ramparts where he lost his life in the defense of the fort.

On one February morning in the early 1960s, groundskeepers trimming the grass at Fort McAllister reported that their work was disrupted by an icy chill that seemed to engulf them, even though the sun was shining and there were no clouds in the sky. With their nerves jangling, they got a long look at the headless body of a man, wearing a Civil War-era officer's uniform standing in the same location where Major Gallie died that fateful day in 1863. They had no doubt that they were seeing the unlucky soldier's ghost.

FORT PULASKI
Savannah, Georgia

Savannah, Georgia, is the home of the Fort Pulaski National monument. Construction on this stately coastal fortification, built using more than twenty-five million "Savanna Gray" and "Rose Red" bricks, was completed in 1847. This valuable defensive position, which looks like a truncated hexagon, consisted of a moat, parade ground and two powder magazines and would play a critical role in the Civil War.

Early in the war, the Union Navy blockaded the Confederate coastline in an attempt to cut off all foreign trade and economic aid to the South. Fort Pulaski protected Savannah's prosperous seaport and the smugglers who dared to dodge Union ships to bring weapons, medicine and supplies to the beleaguered Southern Army.

In 1861, Confederate militia under the command of Colonel Charles H. Olmstead occupied Fort Pulaski, located on Cockspur Island. In the spring of 1862, Federal troops under the command of General David Hunter, landed on nearby Tybee Island, unopposed by the Confederates who watched from eight thousand yards away. Over the next two months, Union troops positioned thirty-six pieces of heavy artillery on Tybee Island.

Fort Pulaski

The resulting siege of Fort Pulaski would be the first real successful test of the Union Army's new rifled cannon and would lead to the eventual downfall of masonry fortifications in general. On April 10, 1862, General David Hunter began his bombardment of Fort Pulaski. The artillery barrage continued non-stop until the afternoon of April 11.

Even though there had been no Confederate casualties, Colonel Olmstead knew it would only be a matter of time before the Federal troops breached the walls of the fort. Seeing no other option, Colonel Olmstead surrendered Fort Pulaski to General Hunter later in the day.

In 1864, the former Confederate stronghold became a prison - for captured Confederates. Five hundred and fifty Confederate prisoners were held at Fort Pulaski. During their incarceration, the men endured starvation, scurvy, and crippling dysentery. Thirteen of the prisoners died and the rest were transferred to Fort Delaware one year later.

Could some of these doomed men be among the ghosts who haunt Fort Pulaski?

In the late 1980s, Savannah was again occupied by both Federal and Confederate troops. These Civil War soldiers were reenactors involved in the filming of the movie *Glory,* starring Morgan Freeman, Mathew Broderick and Denzel Washington. The film was shot at various locations around Savannah. One group of costumed reenactors took advantage of some of their free time and visited Fort Pulaski en route to the movie set. While these modern-day Civil War soldiers were exploring the fort, a young man wearing a Confederate lieutenant's uniform approached them. The officer reprimanded the reenactors for failing to salute him. To their surprise, the lieutenant then ordered them to fall into formation because a Yankee attack was imminent.

The reenactors decided to play along, believing that the young man was just trying to entertain the other visitors to the fort. The lieutenant sternly ordered the reenactors to face about turn away from him , which they did. This was the last time they would see the brash Confederate officer. According to the reenactors, the young man simply disappeared. They never saw him again.

FORT MONROE
Hampton, Virginia

During the War of 1812, the United States learned that it was ill prepared to defend its eastern coastline from the advancing British Army. In 1814, the necessity for adequate coastal defenses was exemplified when Washington, D.C., was captured and burned by the British. As a result of this embarrassing incident, a new coastal defense system was put in place. Fort Monroe would be the first of these new fortifications. With an armament of almost two hundred cannon, Fort Monroe controlled the channel into Hampton Roads and still serves as protection for Washington, D.C., today.

It is also regarded as one of America's most haunted forts, largely due to its connections to the Civil War.

The history of Fort Monroe stretched back centuries before the war. In 1609, the first English colonists built Fort Algernourne at the same location where Fort Monroe stands today. As early as 1608, Captain John Smith realized that military defenses were needed to defend the approaches to the colony at Jamestown. The same site, later named Old Point Comfort, was used as a defensive position throughout the Colonial period.

In 1819, Brigadier General Simon Bernard, a famous French military engineer, was assigned the arduous task of building a moated, heptagonal stone fortress that would rival any found in Europe at the time. When construction of Fort Monroe was completed in 1834, it was considered to be one of finest seacoast defensive positions of its day. Named in honor of James Monroe, the fifth president of the United States, Fort Monroe became the Army's new Artillery School of Practice.

Fort Monroe

At the start of the Civil War, Fort Monroe's armaments and defenses were quickly improved to protect it from possible Confederate attack. Considered the "Gibraltar of Chesapeake Bay," Fort Monroe served as the starting point of several land operations against the Confederate Army and was so impregnable that it was one of the few Southern forts not captured by the Confederacy during the war. For this reason, President Lincoln didn't hesitate to visit the fort in May 1862 to help plan the attack on Norfolk. In 1864, General Ulysses S. Grant stayed at Fort Monroe while he helped prepare the plans that brought about the end of the war.

During World War II, Fort Monroe bristled with an impressive complement of coastal artillery guns, long-range cannons and a series of rapid-fire weapons. Many of these advances in weapons technology were soon obsolete when the potential of the long-rang bomber and aircraft carrier was realized at the end of the war. Today, Fort Monroe serves as the headquarters for the U.S. Army Training and Doctrine Command.

In addition to still serving as a military post, it is also a very haunted place. There have been reports of military apparitions, the phantom clumping of boots, rustling of phantom skirts, the sound of disembodied laughter and the ghosts of several famous people, including General Grant, Chief Black Hawk and even Abraham Lincoln. The former president has been spotted many times in the plantation-style home called Old Quarters Number 1, clad in a dressing gown and standing deep in thought by the fireplace of the appropriately named Lincoln Room.

Another famous specter frequently observed in his former barracks, Building Number 5, is that of Edgar A. Perry, also known as Edgar Allan Poe. The author enlisted under a false name to avoid being arrested for unpaid gambling debts. Poe served four months at Fort Monroe before he sold his enlistment in 1829. During his stay at Building Number 5, Poe penned "The Cask of Amontillado," loosely based on a ghost story about a soldier who had been walled up alive inside the building.

On Matthew Lane, sometimes called "Ghost Alley," is the home of a spirit known as the "Woman in White." The "Woman" is alleged to be Camille Kirtz, a young woman married to a Civil War Army captain who was nearly twice her age. While he was away on assignment, Camille found solace in the arms of another man. Her husband came home early one night and caught them in bed together. The hot-headed captain drew his revolver and fired at his wife's lover - but hit Camille instead. Today, she haunts the house where she died and is also seen in a nearby grove of trees, where some say she tries to reunite with the spirit of her lover.

At another residence located along Matthew Lane, an angry unknown entity is said to haunt the home of an Army officer. This unseen presence apparently has a great disdain for roses. When past residents have left bouquets of roses anywhere in the home overnight, this malevolent energy scatters the petals all over the floor, where they are found the next morning.

The ghost of a toddler is said to haunt the basement of an enlisted soldier's home. Occupants of the residence have heard a child's phantom laughter in their basement and report that this mischievous spirit likes to hide their children's toys. The identity of the child ghost, and the cause of his or her death, has never been determined.

Numerous spirits lurk within the confines of Fort Monroe, but there is one well-known personality who is more closely connected to the fort than any other. His name was Jefferson Davis and he served as the president of the Confederate States of America.

Jefferson Davis was born in Kentucky in 1808. Ironically, he was raised just miles away from the birthplace of Abraham Lincoln. He graduated from West Point in 1828 and was sent to the infantry. He soon fell in love with Sarah Taylor, the daughter of his commander and future president, Zachary Taylor. He left the military in 1835 with a career that was only distinguished by several blow-ups with superior officers. Davis never believed that he had the temperament to be a common soldier. He was a man suited to command and in later years, would have preferred a military command to the presidency of the Confederacy.

Jefferson Davis

Upon leaving the Army, Davis moved to Mississippi, where he helped run the family plantations with his older brother, Joseph. The family had many slaves, but by the standards of those days, they treated their slaves quite well. Their food was never rationed, they were allowed to choose their own names and the slave quarters were superior to those found on most plantations of the time. However, they were still property and in Davis' eyes, rightfully his under the laws of the Constitution.

In 1835, Davis married Sarah Taylor without the blessing of her parents. Five weeks later, both of them fell ill from malaria and Sarah died at the age of twenty-one. Their marriage lasted only three months. Sarah's death became the first of many tragedies to come in Davis' life.

In 1845, Davis entered the political arena and was elected to Congress as a Democrat. That same year, he married Varina Howell, a beautiful young woman who was half his age. Davis served for one year in the House of Representatives before resigning to lead a group of Mississippi volunteers during the Mexican

War. As fate would have it, he found himself with a command under Zachary Taylor, who now greeted him warmly, their differences forgotten in their shared grief over Sarah's death. Davis was wounded at the Battle of Buena Vista and gained a reputation for bravery, which he used to his advantage during the next Senate election. He handily won the seat and remained in office until 1853, when he was named War Secretary by President Franklin Pierce.

In 1857, Davis reclaimed his Senate seat and became one of the most forceful advocates of Southern rights, regularly threatening secession if those rights were challenged. A few years later, Davis would test the waters for a run at the White House as a Democratic candidate in 1860. At the Baltimore nomination convention, his name was placed under consideration, but Davis never pressed the issue, knowing that he would never gain enough Northern support to win an election.

Later, when the Democratic vote was split between Stephen Douglas and John Breckinridge, they were defeated. Although cautious and still hoping to compromise, Davis pushed for Mississippi's secession. He made an emotional farewell speech to the Senate on January 21, 1861 and then withdrew from his seat with four other senators. He was soon named the commander of the militia in Mississippi and also a compromise candidate for the presidency of the six states that now made up the Confederacy. He was elected on February 9 and inaugurated nine days later in Montgomery. Despite his poor health, an ongoing illness related to the malaria he had contracted years before, he still would have preferred a military command.

The years that would follow Davis' election as the President of the Confederacy would be terrible ones and they weighed heavily on Davis, just as the concerns of the North brutally wore down Abraham Lincoln. And this would not be the only sadness and despair the two men would share during the war.

During the war, Davis lived in a house on Clay Street in Richmond, Virginia. There is every indication that the Davis family was happy living there, despite the pressures of the war and the long hours that Davis spent working. As time wore on, though, Davis' health declined to the point that friends and associates urged him to rest. It was said that his only respite from the long hours he spent working on behalf of the Confederacy was his family. He often said that they eased his mind for precious minutes every day, especially his children, whom he constantly indulged. Davis' special favorite was little Joe, who turned five in April 1864. He often remarked that Joe was the hope and greatest joy in his life. Unfortunately, like President Lincoln's favorite son, Willie, who died while Lincoln was in the White House, Davis' greatest joy was taken away too soon.

On April 30, 1864, Varina Davis left the children playing while she made lunch for her husband. A short time later, Joe, and his older brother, Jeff, wandered onto the balcony in back of the house. Apparently, Joe was climbing on the railing when he lost his balance and fell to the brick pavement below. The fall fractured his skull and he died a short time later.

Varina became hysterical and it was later recalled that passersby could hear her screaming inside the house throughout the afternoon and into the evening. President Davis was crushed. He sat beside his wife for more than three hours, turning away everyone who called, including a courier with an important message from General Lee. Then, he vanished into the upper floors of the house, where his footsteps could be heard, incessantly pacing back and forth.

Over the course of the next few days, condolence cards and letters flooded the Davis home, including a heartfelt message from Abraham Lincoln, who was returning a gesture extended to him by Davis when his own son had died. The funeral took place a short time later, and the Hollywood Cemetery in Richmond offered a free plot for the boy's burial. An immense crowd gathered at the cemetery on the day of the burial and it was reported that children from all over the city, many of them Joe's playmates, covered the grave with flowers and crosses. The children also collected $40 and bought a monument to place on the boy's burial site, which read "Erected by the little boys and girls of the southern capital."

The last year that Jefferson Davis spent in Richmond was one of extreme sadness and grief. The house had become a place haunted by the memories of Joe's brief life -- and his horrible death. Davis even had the balcony that the boy fell from removed and destroyed. The only moment of joy the Davises experienced in the house was the birth of Winnie Davis on June 27, 1864. She would be called the "Daughter of the Confederacy."

On Sunday, April 2, 1865, word reached Davis from General Lee that the army was evacuating the Petersburg and Richmond lines and soon the city would fall. As the Federal forces neared the city, Davis assembled his cabinet and staff and directed the removal of public archives, the treasury, and all records to Danville. Later that afternoon, Davis left the city on a special train.

The next twenty-four hours in Richmond were chaos as the residents struggled to flee the city as the Union Army moved in. Disorder increased with every hour as the streets filled with frightened people trying to make their way to the railroad depots. Two regiments of militia were supposed to be maintaining order, but the panic was beyond their control. Terror ruled the streets and left destruction in its wake. Plundering and looting was rampant; straggling soldiers seized and consumed massive amounts of liquor; windows were shattered and shops destroyed and four tobacco warehouses were set on fire. The flames from the blaze soon spread to nearby buildings, burning out of control through the night.

Richmond, the capital of the Confederacy, had fallen into Union hands.

But in all of the chaos, Davis and his family somehow escaped. After the fighting ended and after Lee had surrendered at Appomattox, Davis and Varina managed to avoid the soldiers who were looking for them and planned to start out for Texas. Out West, Davis would gather his still-loyal soldiers, then would establish a new capital of the Confederacy and continue the war. It was during this time of flight when Abraham Lincoln was assassinated. Patrols were stepped up and the gauntlet was tightened around Davis, for most believed that he had somehow been involved in Lincoln's death.

On May 10, 1865, a contingent of Federal cavalry surrounded a group of tents near the town of Irwinville, Georgia. It was there that Davis and his followers were hiding, and they were forced to come out. The Confederate president was quickly arrested. When the commanding officer informed him that he had been implicated in the Lincoln assassination, Davis immediately denied it. "I would rather have dealt with President Lincoln than Andrew Johnson," he is reported to have said.

Davis and Varina were taken into custody and transported by ship to the country's most escape-proof prison of the day: Fort Monroe.

President and Mrs. Davis arrived at the fort on May 19. Their ship docked at Engineer's Wharf and Davis was roughly taken ashore and hustled into a casemate cell, which was about one step above a dungeon. He was imprisoned there for the next several days, until sunset of May 23. On this evening, the door to his cell opened and Davis was greeted with the sight of Captain Jerome Titlow, followed by a blacksmith and his assistant. To the Confederate president's dismay, the assistant was carrying a set of leg irons and chains.

These men were followed by two privates from the Third Pennsylvania Heavy Artillery who entered the cell with fixed bayonets. Two more soldiers were stationed outside, while another pair guarded the casemate door. More sentries were positioned on the ramparts overlooking the area. Along with the armed guards on the other side of the moat, Davis had seventy captors in all. They were taking no chances that he might escape, either with, or without, assistance from still-loyal Confederate troops.

As Captain Titlow entered the room, he explained to Davis that he had been given orders to put him in leg irons. Almost apologetically, he insisted that he was just following orders. The instructions to place Davis in chains came from Edwin Stanton, Lincoln's Secretary of War. At that point, most still believed that Davis had been involved in Lincoln's assassination. Davis paced about the small cell and then nervously rested his left foot on a chair. Thinking that Davis was submitting to this indignity, Titlow instructed the blacksmith to go about his work.

The blacksmith knelt down to shackle the chains on the president's leg when suddenly Davis attacked the man holding the chains, sending him sprawling onto the floor of the cell. The blacksmith jumped to his feet and raised the hammer above his head to strike Davis, but Titlow pushed between them. It took four men to hold Davis down as the chains were shackled to his legs.

Captain Titlow was the last man to leave Davis' cell. As he walked out the door, he turned and looked back at the Confederate leader. He later recalled that Jefferson Davis was seated on the edge of his prison cot, his head in his hands and tears streaming down his face. Even though Captain Titlow held no sympathy for the Confederate cause, he said it was one of the saddest things he had ever seen.

The days that followed were filled with humiliation for Davis. The fort's chief medical officer, Lieutenant General John Craven, recommended that Davis' chains be removed. The Confederate president's health was fragile and being chained like an animal was simply cruel. Not surprisingly, his recommendation was ignored. Soon, however, word of the shackling leaked out and reached the newspapers. Public disapproval of the punishment, both in the South and the North, created such an uproar that the War Department finally ordered Davis to be unchained.

After more than four months in solitary confinement, Davis was moved to better quarters, although he remained a prisoner. Soon, the public would also begin to clamor for Davis' release. There was no proof that he had, in any way, been involved in the Lincoln assassination. Even men loutspoken opponents of slavery, like newspaper editor Horace Greeley and Senator Thaddeus Stevens got behind the effort and created a stir that was simply too big to ignore.

At last, on May 13, 1867, after two years of confinement, Jefferson Davis was released. He lived on for twenty-four years after the end of the Civil War, traveling extensively and writing about the "Lost Cause" and its consequences. When he died in 1889, he was buried in Metairie Cemetery in New Orleans, where he had been living.

A short time later, Varina Davis had her husband exhumed and moved to Beauvoir, their family home in Mississippi. This did not prove suitable either, because the estate was located on a narrow peninsula on the Gulf of Mexico. It was feared that flooding might someday destroy the site and Varina pondered what to do. Soon, a great number of Confederate veterans wrote to her and asked that she choose Richmond for her husband's final resting place. In the city's Hollywood Cemetery, he would rest among the honored dead of those who had fought and died for the South.

Varina agreed and moved Davis' body to Richmond, aboard a special train, in the spring of 1893. The trip took several days, stopping frequently in towns across the South so that people could pay their last respects to the Confederacy's first and only president. They arrived in Richmond on May 30 and the coffin was taken to the rotunda of the capitol building, where it lay in state for a day. On May 31, a black hearse, drawn by six white horses, conveyed the coffin to Hollywood Cemetery. It was followed by a band playing Dixie and a long procession that passed along streets draped in mourning for the late president.

But legends persist that Davis does not rest quietly in his grave.

Down through the years, numerous witnesses have reported sighting an apparition in and around the casemate at Fort Monroe where Jefferson Davis was confined. Most of the sightings have been of strange mists and a shadowy figure that most believe is that of Davis. Some believe that he is reliving the terrible ordeal that he suffered through at the end of the war.

Fort Concho

FORT CONCHO
San Angelo, Texas

Built in 1867, Fort Concho was constructed to protect settlers and the transportation routes between a chain of forts that stretched across the heartland of Texas. Situated at the junction of the North and Middle Concho Rivers, the site selected for the fort was strategic to the government's stabilization of the region because no less than five major trails passed nearby. Even though the fort was surrounded by miles of flat, treeless prairie, it was considered to be one of the most beautiful and best-ordered posts in Texas. But order was anything but the norm in the post's early beginnings.

Confusion over the exact location of the post and the construction materials to be used hampered the early stages of construction. The first site chosen for the fort was later rejected, but not before $28,000 had been spent to prepare the land for future construction. Once a site had been decided on, the next hurdle was what materials should be used in building the fort. Initially, the fort's buildings were to be constructed out of pecan wood, but it proved to be too hard. Adobe was then put to the test. Soldiers with little or no experience in the making of adobe saw their work go down the drain when their stockpile of adobe bricks was melted away by heavy rains.

Finally, it was decided that the fort would be constructed of sandstone from nearby quarries. As there were no competent stonemasons on hand, private contractors were called in from Fredericksburg to do the work. Even this was plan was not foolproof. Ongoing construction of the fort continued for the next twenty-two years as a never-ending comedy of errors plagued the post. Even when the fort was eventually abandoned it had still not been completely finished.

Construction problems aside, several successful campaigns against the Comanche were launched from Fort Concho. In addition, the post played a pivotal role in the suppression of illegal profiteering that was being conducted by Mexican and American traders known as "Comancheros."

One of Fort Concho's most illustrious commanders was Colonel Ranald Mackenzie. Mackenzie was such a prominent character at the fort that it is said that he still attempts exert his command influence there from beyond the grave.

In September 1872, Mackenzie and his troopers successfully attacked a large Comanche camp. The attack caught the Indians completely by surprise. When the firing stopped, twenty-three Indians were dead and another one hundred and twenty-seven women and children had been taken captive. The prisoners were marched back to Fort Concho, where they were imprisoned in a stone corral over the winter. The following spring, they were allowed to rejoin their families at the Indian reservation near Fort Sill, Oklahoma.

While attacks by Comanche and Kiowa Indians posed a threat to the soldiers stationed at the fort, disease was an even greater enemy. Bad water was to blame. When the North Concho River was low, it teemed with harmful microbes from putrefying animal matter, including buffalo carcasses. In October 1870 alone, the fort's surgeon reported thirty-five cases of typhoid fever, sixty-nine cases of acute diarrhea and dysentery and twenty-one cases of continuous fever of an unknown origin. Six soldiers died that month from typhoid.

On the morning of September 27, 1874, Mackenzie and his troops were again thrust into battle with the Comanche. As dawn was breaking, Mackenzie found himself looking down into Palo Duro Canyon. To his surprise, hundreds of Indian tepees dotted the valley before him. Mackenzie immediately ordered his troopers to attack. The Comanche would have again been caught by surprise if Mackenzie's soldiers had not been spotted by several Indians as they moved about the camp completing their early morning chores. Despite the early warning, the Comanche were routed and their village destroyed. In the fighting's wake, the carcasses of more than eleven hundred dead horses lay scattered across the valley floor. The soldiers knew that if they could destroy the Comanche way of life by slaughtering their horses to prevent them from being recaptured, they would whip them into submission.

By the middle 1880s, it had been decided that Fort Concho, along with Fort Richardson and Fort Clark, had helped to bring peace to the Texas plains. Since Comanche attacks no longer posed a threat, Fort Concho was no longer needed. On June 20, 1889, the post was abandoned.

In 1935, the city of San Angelo acquired the fort and began restoring it to its former glory. The city's plans for reconstruction of the site were so successful that in 1961, the fort was designated as a National Historic Landmark.

History remains here at Fort Concho - and so do the spirits of the past.

One of the most haunted locations at Fort Concho is the officers' quarters, also known as "Officers Row." Located across the parade ground from the enlisted barracks, this row of sturdy stone houses serves as the impetus for most if not all of the ghostly tales that are told about the fort.

Fort Concho's most distinguished commander, Colonel Ranald Mackenzie, is said to haunt his old residence at the center of Officers' Row. The ghost of Colonel Mackenzie has been seen by visitors and staff at the old house on more than one occasion. It is said that Mackenzie was fond of his house because its location allowed him to see almost everything that was going on in the fort at any given time. The house was also located in a position that gave him a full view of the old stone corral where the Indian captives were held over the winter of 1873.

While preparing for a event one December, a female staff member who was working in the Mackenzie house reported that she had heard the unmistakable sound of footsteps walking around the room behind her. Just as she turned to see who was there, she was knocked up against a wall by a blast of cold air. Frightened and disoriented, the women also noticed that the sound of knuckles cracking seemed to accompany the strange manifestation. Since Colonel Mackenzie was known for cracking his knuckles, there was no doubt in the woman's mind that she had come face to face with the spirit of the famous commander.

Another of the "Row's" many distinguished families was that of Colonel Benjamin Grierson, who commanded the Buffalo Soldiers of the 10th Cavalry.

Colonel Grierson's daughter, Edith, died in an upstairs bedroom of Officers' Quarters Number 1 on Sept. 9, 1878, shortly after her thirteenth birthday. Edith was a lively girl who enjoyed riding her pony and going to the dances in the mess hall. She lived at Fort Concho for three years, writing home frequently to friends and relatives back home in Illinois about regimental life on the frontier, until falling ill from typhoid fever. After thirteen agony-filled days, she succumbed to the illness.

Edith Grierson - Ghost of Fort Concho

Edith's body was buried with military honors in the fort's graveyard. In the 1930s, the graves were exhumed to make way for city expansion. Edith's body was reburied in San Angelo's Fairmount Cemetery, in the Samuel Smith family plot. Despite the location of her mortal remains, it is said that her spirit never left the house. Over the years, many people have encountered her. In most cases, she is seen quietly playing jacks. Those who have met this spectral girl say that the first thing they notice is that the room where she is playing is substantially cooler than any of the other rooms in the house. Edith is reported to acknowledge the presence of people when they enter the room by turning her head and smiling at them before she turns her attention back to her game of jacks, but she will rarely speak.

One day in the mid-1990s, B.D. Shaffer, a delivery driver who worked for local florist Tom Ridgway, dropped off some flowers to the former Grierson home for a reception that was going to be held there. He had been instructed to place two arrangements of flowers in the bedrooms at the top of the stairs, one to the right and one to the left. Reaching the top of the stairs, Shaffer turned and entered the first bedroom on the right. He felt something akin to static electricity that made the hair on his arms and the back of his head stand up. Something made him say "Excuse me," as he placed the flowers on a bedside table and left the room. From the corner of his eye, as he entered the opposite bedroom, he saw a young girl sitting on the floor of the room he had just left. She looked very real and solid, but as Shaffer turned towards her, she faded away.

The next day, Shaffer had to go to a house at Lake Nasworthy to pick up some artificial flower arrangements. The lady of the house and her husband had been responsible for the restoration of Officers Quarters Number 1 at Fort Concho, the house where Shaffer had his encounter with the ghost. When he told her about his experience in the upstairs bedroom, she said the girl he had seen was Edie Grierson, and she had died in that room.

The following December, Shaffer returned to Officers' Quarters Number 1 for a Christmas event. The docent, upon hearing about his encounter with the ghost of a little girl, took him into another room and showed him a photograph of Edith Grierson. It was the girl he had seen.

And it appears that Edith still occupies her old home. In June 2003, the new assistant city manager of San Angelo, Harold Dominguez, and his family were staying in the former Grierson home as they waited for their new house to become available. Harold's wife, Angela, came face to face with the ghost of Edith. She had been busy packing the family's things when she looked up and saw a young girl descending the staircase. The girl was wearing a long, peach-colored dress and had long brown hair that was pulled back from her face. They stared at each other for a moment and then the girl disappeared. Neither Andrea nor her husband knew anything about the supernatural history of the house before they took up residence there.

Convinced that the encounter with the girl had been some kind of optical illusion, Angela laughingly mentioned it to her husband, but Harold grew serious. He told her of other strange things that had occurred while they had been at the house, including a desk chair that inexplicably moved and the sound of a wailing voice that had been heard outside one of the windows at night.

After just four days at the former Grierson house, the Dominguez family decided that they would prefer to stay in a hotel until the work on their new house was completed.

Officers' Row is not the only location at Fort Concho where ghostly activity has been reported. The fort's headquarters building is also reputed to be a hotbed for paranormal encounters.

Once, during a historic Christmas tour at the fort, Conrad McClure, a staff member working in the headquarters building, saw a shadowy figure in a blue uniform brush past him while he was tending to the fireplace. Intrigued by his encounter with the unidentified ghost, McClure did a little detective work and learned that a Second Sergeant named James Cunningham was the only soldier to ever die in the building. Cunningham was a chronic alcoholic who was discharged from the army. He was hospitalized due to complications from liver disease. Knowing that he was going to die, the sergeant requested that he be moved back to the fort, so that he could spend his last days with his friends and fellow soldiers. The end for old Irishman finally came on a cold Christmas Day. After compiling all of this information, McClure was sure that the spirit he encountered in the headquarters building could be none other than that of Sergeant Cunningham.

Several of the other staff members believe that Sergeant Cunningham does not like females to be in the headquarters building, likely convinced they don't belong there. However, he does always watch protectively over the building and its occupants.

In addition to the ghosts of Colonel Mackenzie, Sergeant Cunningham, and Edith Grierson, several other lesser-known, but still-active spirits have taken up residence at Fort Concho. The disembodied voices of Chaplain George Ward Dunbar and that of a woman believed to be his wife, Addie, have been heard talking in the post's chapel. The bearded, bespectacled Dunbar lived at the fort with his wife and six children in the 1870s, when Colonel Grierson was post commander. One day, he was ordered to go to Fort Sill, which was being besieged. He had to leave his family behind, but he promised he would return to them. Some months later, his family learned that he had died. The grief-stricken family was allowed to stay on at the fort. It is believed that his ghost returned to comfort them and has never left.

Another unexplained phenomenon at the fort are phosphorescent lights, believed to be the ghosts of several drifters said to have been murdered in one of the officers' quarters in the 1890s, have been observed in what is now the museum's library.

To this day, Fort Concho continues to be a haunted location. The restless ghosts seem to be elements of the past that have simply never gone away.

FORT LEATON
Presidio, Texas

Fort Leaton, as it has become known, has a muddied and strange history. The fort, which was really a private enclave for the Leaton family, was built on the site of an abandoned Spanish mission in 1848. El Apostol Sabriago, the mission on the site, had been built in 1684. This adobe place of worship, later named El Fortin De San Jose in 1773, was abandoned in 1810. It became a private residence in 1848. Its owner, Ben Leaton, created a contentious history that was surrounded by bloodshed and violence - ending with rumors of spirits that still linger at the site.

Ruins of the old Leaton trading post

The land on which Fort Leaton rests was part of a La Junta district grant that was awarded to Lieutenant Colonel Ygnacio Ronquillo by the Mexican government in 1832. He was transferred to Baja California later that same year and he sold the grant to Hypolito Acosta, who in turn sold it to Juana Pedrasa in 1833. At some point between 1833 and 1840, Juana met Ben Leaton in Chihuahua, Mexico, and the two became lovers. Though they had three children together, they were never married.

Juana and Leaton moved to La Junta and enlarged their estate in 1848 by purchasing land from Juan Bustillos. Bustillos, however, had no title to the land, so Leaton paid off a government official to manufacture one. The fraud was soon found out, but the Mexican government could do nothing since the land in question was now part of the United States. Leaton expanded and fortified the adobe mission buildings into a square-shaped compound that he dubbed Fort Leaton. The forty-room fort was one of the largest adobe buildings in Texas and served as a home, a trading post along the Chihuahua Trail and a private fortification for the Leatons against Indian raids and attacks by bandits.

Ben Leaton's history at the fort was short-lived and troubled. He was accused by the Mexican government of encouraging Apache and Comanche raiding parties to attack Mexican settlements for livestock that were then traded to him for guns and ammunition. Leaton countercharged that his Mexican accusers had endangered the lives and safety of all the settlers along the border by putting a bounty of $250 on Apache scalps and hiring Anglo outlaws to carry out these killings. This practice was intended to reduce Indian raids into Mexico, but had the opposite effect. Those who participated in the scalpings were often indiscriminate and greedy, and the scalps that they presented for payment were frequently those of members of other Indian tribes or even of the Mexicans that the bounties were designed to protect. As a result, tribes that were once friendly became hostile, and Mexicans in the area became distrusting of the Anglo settlers. An investigation of the charges against Ben Leaton was ordered by Major General George M. Brooke, commander of the Eighth Department, U.S. Army, but it was cursory and inconclusive. Neither the charge against Leaton nor his counter-charge were ever substantiated.

Leaton died in 1851 of unknown causes some claimed yellow fever and following his death, Juana Pedrasa married a man named Edward Hall and continued to live in Fort Leaton and operate it as a trading post until the 1860s. The fort also served as the first seat of the unorganized Presidio County. Although Fort Leaton was not a military fort, it was the lone outpost of defense along a four hundred and fifty-mile stretch of the Rio Grande River, from Fort Duncan at Eagle Pass to Fort Quitman southeast of El Paso. Until the construction of Fort Davis in 1854, the U.S. Army made Fort Leaton its unofficial headquarters in the area.

In the 1850s, Secretary of War Jefferson Davis authorized the experimental use of camels as pack animals by the military in West Texas to determine if the animals could be used successfully for military purposes on the arid Western frontier. In 1860, Lieutenant William H. Echols was sent with thirty-one soldiers, twenty-four camels, and twenty-five pack mules to find an overland trail to San Carlos Crossing and survey it as a possible site for a fort. The caravan stopped along the way at Fort Leaton between July 17 and July 20. When Echols reached San Carlos Crossing, he did not find it suitable for building a fort and the Army continued to use Fort Leaton as an outpost for military patrols. During the Civil War, the fort was briefly occupied by Confederate troops.

After a series of financial setbacks, Edward Hall heavily mortgaged Fort Leaton. According to legend, he used a fake deed to the land, dating back to the phony title created by Ben Leaton. He obtained cash - some say to pay off gambling debts - from John D. Burgess in 1862 and then defaulted on the loan. Hall refused to relinquish the property, so Burgess sent a group of men to evict Hall and his family from the property. At some point during the encounter Edward Hall was shot and killed, reportedly while sitting at the dinner table. Burgess moved his own family into the fort afterwards, but in 1875, an angry William Leaton, the youngest son of Ben Leaton and Juana Pedrasa, shot and killed Burgess. Despite this untimely death, his family continued to operate the trading post at Fort Leaton until 1884. By that time, railroads had been constructed that linked San Antonio with the Gulf Coast, El Paso, and Mexico City, effectively closing the Chihuahua Trail. Trade died out in the area and business at Fort Leaton was greatly diminished. Furthermore, Indian raids had declined across West Texas by the middle 1870s and ceased altogether after 1880, ending the military's need to use Fort Leaton as an outpost.

After the Burgess family ceased to occupy Fort Leaton in 1884, the fort began to deteriorate. For the remainder of the nineteenth century and the first quarter of the twentieth century, Fort Leaton was occupied periodically by several tenant families. The Burgess family sold the property in 1925. Between 1927 and 1956 various rooms of the fort were used sporadically as living quarters or for storage.

The glory days of Fort Leaton seemed to be over for good.

In 1968, the Texas Parks and Wildlife Department acquired the property, but strange tales began to be told about the site in the decades just before their occupancy. In those years, treasure hunters scoured the ruins. One group had dug a large pit, looking for gold that Leaton allegedly buried in the fort before he died. Two park employees assigned to clean out the pit reportedly fled the fort in terror after they claimed that they felt something invisible trying to pull them into the hole.

Other park employees have reportedly observed the transparent figure of John Burgess in the room where he was shot to death. An elderly woman, possibly the ghost of Mrs. Burgess or Juana Pedrasa, has been observed several times by park employees in a rocking chair in the fort's kitchen.

Even today, it is rumored that during thunderstorms, a headless specter, a victim of a freak accident, rides around the fort's corral on a white horse. Apparently, this unfortunate cowboy was riding near Fort Leaton when he and his mount were caught in a sudden thunderstorm. It is said that the thunder and lightning spooked the horse, throwing the man out of the saddle. Instead of landing on the ground, the cowboy's boot became entangled in one of the stirrups, and he was dragged to his death behind his terrified horse. The day after the storm, several of the cowboy's friends from a nearby ranch went to look for him.

The cowboys were horrified when they found their friend's headless body wedged between a tree branch and a large boulder. His head was found several hundred feet away.

Whenever there is a thunderstorm near the fort, it has been said that a headless horseman has been seen riding around the grounds on a brilliant white horse - a chilling reminder of the danger that can be found on the West Texas plains.

FORT WASHITA
Durant, Oklahoma

In 1841, the U.S. Army, under the command of General Zachary Taylor, constructed Fort Washita north of modern-day Durant, Oklahoma. Considered isolated even by frontier standards, Fort Washita was constructed in order to establish law and order in the Southeastern territories and to protect the Choctaw and Chickasaw Indians from rival Indian tribes. The fort contained a large stable and corral to support the cavalry and dragoons who frequently patrolled the plains to protect Indians and settlers alike from the raiding Comanche.

At the start of the Civil War, in 1861, Federal troops abandoned Fort Washita. Confederate soldiers operating in the area later used the fort as a major supply depot and hospital facility. After the war ended, the fort was burned to the ground and abandoned. When the Department of the Interior assumed control of Fort Washita in 1870, it was considered obsolete.

Instead of reactivating the fort, the Department of the Interior deeded the property to a Chickasaw Indian named Charles Colbert and his family. Colbert rebuilt the barracks inside the compound for use as the family's home. A short time later, Colbert and his family, along with their thirty-two dogs, spent the night at their new home. When Colbert awoke the next morning, he found that all of the dogs had disappeared during the night. He spent the following day tracking down the animals and returning them to the fort. The next morning, he awoke again to find that all of the dogs had escaped. Colbert could not find any logical reason for the dogs' disappearance. He had no idea why they chose to flee the warm house for the cold darkness - or how they managed to slip out of a locked door. Unnerved, the Colberts moved out of the fort a short time later.

The next tenant of Fort Washita fared no better. A doctor named Steele and his sister moved into the renovated barracks that were formerly occupied by the Colberts. Dr. Steele's sister was responsible for taking care of the house, and it was not long before she was reporting strange, unexplainable experiences both inside the house and on the adjoining grounds. She began talking of ghosts - but was she really seeing them? Some claimed later that her ghostly encounters were the result of a troubled mind. Others claimed that spirits drove her mad. Eventually, she suffered a nervous breakdown. A short time later, the Steeles moved away. Since that time, no one else has ever dared to take up permanent residence on the property.

In 1962, the Oklahoma Historical Society purchased the buildings and grounds of Fort Washita. Weather and neglect had left their mark on the post over the years. At the time the fort was purchased by the Oklahoma Historical Society, many of the buildings had collapsed or were in drastic need of repair.

Restoration began, only to be met with a shocking surprise. As work was being done in 1965, one of the graves in the post cemetery was exhumed. To everyone's horror, the grave contained two bodies, one of them a recent burial. Someone had used the abandoned cemetery to hide a murder. Forensic evidence revealed that the original body found in the grave belonged to a sixteen-year-old boy who had died of meningitis. The more recent body was that of an unidentified Hispanic man who had died with a deep gash in his temple. His remains had been hidden in the grave many years after the original occupant had been interred there.

Could this murder victim be one of the many spirits believed to roam Fort Washita? There is no question that there seem to be ghosts here, many of their identities unknown.

But one spirit - the post's most famous - has been dubbed "Aunt Jane." It is unclear exactly who Aunt Jane was, or how she died. Over the years, several stories about her untimely demise have been handed down from generation to generation. Each time her story has been told, it is further embellished, making it extremely hard to validate. However, it is possible that she was killed at the fort some point between 1842 and 1861.

One story suggests that Aunt Jane was a free black woman who had come to Fort Washita during the Civil War to spy on its Confederate occupants. It is said that when the Confederates discovered what Aunt Jane was up to, she was summarily beheaded, and her body and head were buried in separate graves.

The second story is drastically different. In this version, Aunt Jane is a white woman and the wife of an officer stationed at the fort. Aunt Jane was rumored to have always carried $20 dollars in gold with her, no matter where she went. One day while returning from town, bandits who were after her gold accosted her. In the ensuing struggle, one of the bandits allegedly cut off Aunt Jane's head.

The third account of Aunt Jane's murder involves a love triangle. As in the second account, Aunt Jane was the wife of an officer stationed at Fort Washita. One night, her husband returned home from a patrol and found his beloved in bed with another soldier, who was also stationed at the fort. In a fit of rage, Aunt Jane's husband set upon the lovers and beheaded them both on the spot. Later, the outraged husband threw the heads of Aunt Jane and her lover in the Washita River.

Even though the possible causes of Aunt Jane's demise are open to debate, the nature and timing of her frequent appearances have been verified by a number of people. The ghost of Aunt Jane is said to search for her head - or her missing gold, depending on the story -- on the nights of the full moon in the months of March and October.

Today, visitors and historic reenactors have reported strange encounters with the ghosts of Fort Washita. During one of the many Civil War reenactments held at the fort, several visiting high school students were sitting outside on the second-floor deck of a recently reconstructed barracks. As the students looked across the courtyard toward the old stables, they saw what appeared to be a green apparition walk from the barracks to the stables.

In another instance, two female members of a living history group were staying in the Bonahan cabin, west of the fort. On their first night in the cabin, one of the women claimed that she was suddenly disturbed from her slumber by the sensation that she was being strangled. A few hours later, the second woman awoke and said that she could sense an invisible presence hovering over her. On the second night, a third woman joined the two reenactors. The next morning, each of the women reported that they had been plagued during the night by dreams involving suffocation.

What lurks at Fort Washita? No one can say for sure. There seem to be a number of spirits of the past that still linger at the site of the old fort. Stories of weird encounters have drawn ghost hunters from around the country to this mysterious site. Few of them go away disappointed.

FORT DEVENS
Ayer, Massachusetts

Located thirty-five miles west of Boston, Fort Devens holds a unique place in our strange history of supernatural forts. It is one of the few military posts where soldiers have reportedly encountered something that seemed so real, and so terrifying, that they actually engaged a supernatural entity with weapons fire.

Built as a temporary cantonment in 1917, Camp Devens, as it was then called, was the primary training site for soldiers from the New England area who were on their way overseas to fight in World War I. The post was comprised of over

9,280 acres and was located in Middlesex County, in the towns of Ayer and Shirley. Camp Devens was divided into three distinct parts: North Post, Main Post, and South Post.

In 1932, Camp Devens was officially renamed Fort Devens, and the post became the home of the Military Intelligence School for the United States Army. Soldiers who received their training at Fort Devens served in World War II, Korea, and Vietnam.

In July of 1991, Fort Devens, fell prey to the Defense Base Realignment and Closure Act BRAC . Under this federal cost-cutting mandate, the U.S. Army scheduled the closure of the North and Main Posts, while at the same time consolidating its military holdings on the South Post. As part of this initial series of closings, the Army Intelligence School was moved to Fort Huachuca, Arizona. In the end, the South Post faced the same set of circumstances as its predecessors, and on March 31, 1996, Fort Devens officially ceased to be a military installation. It still remains an active training site for Army Reserve and National Guard forces, as well as for regional law enforcement agencies.

While Fort Devens was still in operation, ghost stories were already circulating around the post. One haunted location was said to be Hale Hall, the post's military training center. Military Police MP officers were frequently summoned to Hale Hall to investigate unexplained noises and other strange goings-on. Officers reported that a ghostly presence, nicknamed "George," was known to slam doors and turn lights on and off on unsuspecting occupants.

In addition to George, it was rumored that the ghost of a World War II German prisoner of war haunted several of the buildings that comprised the old Intelligence School. The post housed a prisoner or war camp for captured German and Italian soldiers from 1944 to 1946. Like a scene taken directly from a B-rated horror movie, stories started to circulate about an MP who reportedly shot at the ghost of a German prisoner. Every time the tale was retold, several questions always seemed to go unanswered - like, did the shaken MP actually hit his target? And if he did, what happened to the ghost? Whatever the outcome, I am sure that someone had to go see the base psychologist before the case was officially closed.

When Fort Devens ceased to be a military post in 1996, the property was put up for sale. Much of the land is now used by private industry. Housing developments now exist where soldiers once trained, as well as hotels, restaurants and a golf course. No one knows what happened to George or the ghost of the German prisoner, now that their favorite haunts have been torn down, remodeled or abandoned.

In any case, I am sure that the ghosts of Fort Devens are glad that most of the new occupants do not carry guns.

Fort Leonard Wood postcard

THE RIOTOUS GHOSTS OF BLOODLAND
Fort Leonard Wood
Waynesville St. Robert, Missouri

In December 2002, I Dave was transferred from Jefferson Barracks to Fort Leonard Wood, located in Central Missouri. My reputation as ghost investigator and author preceded me to my new unit. Almost immediately after my arrival, I started hearing ghost stories about Fort Leonard Wood. One of the most humorous, yet interesting stories I heard is undeniably questionable at best - as you'll soon see. But I think that you will also agree that the second story about a haunted preschool has some rather chilling elements. I will let you decide whether the stories are evidence of a haunting or of a hoax.

The history of one of the nation's largest military reservations began with a modest groundbreaking ceremony in December 1940. Constructed as part of the Army's Expansion Program in 1940, the 71,000-acre fort was named in honor of Major General Leonard Wood. Major General Wood was a graduate of Harvard Medical School and later the commander of the Rough Riders during the Spanish-American War. Wood later served with distinction as the governor of Cuba and as the chief of staff of the U.S. Army from 1910 until 1914.

Between December 1940 and the spring of 1941, construction at the new fort continued at a hurried pace. Before long, enough buildings had been erected to house the new Engineer Replacement Training Center, but when the United States entered the Second World War on December 7, 1941, the post was thrust into the spotlight as a training center. Between 1941 and 1946, over three hundred thousand soldiers trained at Fort Leonard Wood. At its peak, the post housed over fifty thousand soldiers at one time. In addition to Fort Leonard Wood being a premiere basic training facility, it was also a prisoner of war camp for captured German and Italian soldiers.

In general, the conditions that captured Axis soldiers endured at Fort Leonard Wood were far better than the standard of living the soldiers faced in their own armies. Private Fritz Ensslin, a former member of Rommel's Afrika Corps who was incarcerated at Fort Leonard Wood, said that his barracks at the fort was comparable to a Hilton Hotel and that the food was of such high quality that a fine hotel could not have served better.

All Axis prisoners received a daily wage of ten cents, whether they worked or not. Prisoners could receive as much as eighty cents a day, or the equivalent of an American Army private's pay in 1941, if they volunteered for additional work. Axis officers were not expected to do manual labor. Instead, they were given a monthly stipend based on rank. Junior officers received $20 dollars a month while senior officers received as much as $40 dollars a month.

There were several Axis POW camps located in Missouri, in addition to the one at Fort Leonard Wood. In general, escape attempts were few and far between. It was the same across the nation. Of the 425,871 Axis prisoners incarcerated in the United States during the Second World War, only a little more than two thousand of them attempted to escape. All of them were quickly recaptured. The most notable escape from Fort Leonard Wood involved a man named Rudolf Krause. On September 10, 1945, a little more than four months after Germany's surrender, Krause escaped while on a trash detail. Three months later, the FBI captured him in Orlando, Florida. His plan was to sign on as a sailor on a neutral merchant ship and make his way home that way. Not one to bear a grudge, Krause returned to Fort Leonard Wood from his home in Germany for a POW reunion in 1993.

Much like Jefferson Barracks, Fort Leonard Wood was deactivated in 1946, after the end of the Second World War. A small contingent of civilians and Army officers remained on site to safeguard the post, but for the next four years, the post lay dormant, and over time, the buildings started to fall into a state of disrepair.

The military training demands brought about by the Korean conflict caused Fort Leonard Wood to spring back to life in August 1950. Once reactivated, the post became a replacement training center for the 6th Armored Division and in 1956, Fort Leonard Wood officially became the home of the United States Army Engineer Training Center.

Again, during the Vietnam War, Fort Leonard Wood became a hive of activity. Basic Trainees from around the country arrived at Fort Leonard Wood for Basic and One Station Unit Training OSUT prior to shipping out to Southeast Asia. This tradition of training the finest enlisted soldiers and officers in the U.S. Army continues at Fort Leonard Wood today as it serves as the headquarters for the Maneuver Support Center MANSCEN . Soldiers and officers from the Chemical, Engineer, Military Police, and Transportation Corps, are taught the combat skills needed to survive on the modern battlefield.

Fort Leonard Wood is also the home of one of the country's finest military museums. The John B. Mahaffey Museum Complex, formerly known as the U.S. Army Engineer Museum, features informative exhibits on the history of the fort, and detailed historical information about the Engineer, Chemical and Military Police Corps.

As part of its designation as a World War II Commemorative Community, a twenty-five-acre portion of the museum complex allows visitors a glimpse of life at Fort Leonard Wood during the Second World War. In 1981, twelve World War II buildings, including four barracks, two mess halls, three day rooms, two orderly rooms and a regimental commander's quarters were set aside as part of the fort's museum. The buildings have been completely restored and today they serve as the only interpretive World War II community in the army. In addition, several other buildings chronicle the life of Major General Wood and the prisoner of war camp that existed at the post between 1943 and 1946.

It should come as no surprise that with all of the soldiers over three million men and women who have passed through the gates of Fort Leonard Wood over the years, a few ghost stories have become attached to the place.

One of the most far-fetched ghost stories I have heard deals with spectral residents of the small town of Bloodland. It is a little-known, but established fact, that the U.S. government used the right of eminent domain to acquire much of the 71,000 acres where Fort Leonard Wood was built. The history of the post may have started with a celebratory groundbreaking event, but the fact remained that the residents of many small towns and villages were forced to move from their homes to make way for the new post.

Bloodland was a town of approximately one hundred residents. It was a very old settlement, a town of hard-working people, mainly of German decent.

On the night of October 31, 1940, the residents of Bloodland had gathered for an annual community celebration. It was at this holiday party that it was unceremoniously announced that the town, including all of the buildings and land, was being taken over by the U.S. government to make way for the future construction of a new fort. The citizens of Bloodland were outraged by this news. It was later reported in a local newspaper that their anger towards the government, spurred on by a day of drinking, resulted in a small riot breaking out. Later, it became apparent that the former citizens of Bloodland were destined to get the last laugh at the government's expense.

According to local newspaper stories, a soldier named James Klown was court-martialed and imprisoned for a year in 1942 after he was found intoxicated and unconscious while on guard duty. Klown had been assigned to patrol a part of Fort Leonard Wood where Bloodland once was. Klown stated that while he was on sentry duty, he heard strange noises near his post. He claimed that when he went to investigate the source of the eerie noises, he was taken captive by riotous ghosts who were speaking a language he did not understand, and that the band of ghosts forced him to drink hard cider through a straw until he passed out.

In 1943, the rowdy ghosts of Bloodland struck again. This time, a young soldier named Randall Ellsworth suffered the same fate as Klown. Rather than court-martialing Ellsworth, though, military commanders allegedly placed the part of Fort Leonard Wood where the haunted town of Bloodland was once located off-limits to all military personnel.

Thirty-one years later, in 1974, the ghosts of Bloodland struck for the last time. This time, as in the previous two incidents, the ghosts' victims were three soldiers from the post. Each soldier later claimed to have been taken hostage by a group of ghosts and forced to drink hard cider through a straw until they were so drunk they collapsed.

In an article printed in the *Gateway Guide* on October 30, 1975, an unidentified reporter recounted the experiences of Klown, Ellsworth and the three unfortunate soldiers. When author Joan Gilbert researched the story for her book *Missouri Ghosts*, she contacted the newspaper but found that whoever had written the article in 1975 was no longer on the staff. Gilbert also learned that no one at the paper remembered the article or the incidents that it portrayed. The only thing in the article that Gilbert could verify were the facts surrounding the demise of Bloodland at the hands of the U.S. government.

What became of Bloodland? The site of the former town became a small arms firing range. According to the unnamed author of the article on the *Gateway Guide*, all that remained of the little town in 1975 were the foundations of an old school and the boarded-up remains of the Methodist church. Today, two reminders that Bloodland ever existed can be seen along westbound Iowa Avenue, within just a few miles of the main post. The Bloodland Cemetery is located near Range 11. This tiny historical burial ground predates the creation of the fort and it is the only remaining physical evidence that the little town had once thrived nearby. The only other testament to the former presence of Bloodland is the fact that the fort's command and control building for the various ranges on post is called Bloodland Range Control in the town's honor.

In pondering the story about the riotous ghosts of Bloodland, there is no doubt in my mind that the citizens of the small town were outraged by the way the U.S. government treated them. It is quite possible that the anger of the townfolk could have spawned supernatural energy in the area. It's possible - but doubtful. More likely, I think this story actually shows how bits and pieces of information from a practical joke can be woven into the tapestry of folklore for generations to come. A prank carried out by some of the former residents of Bloodland on some unsuspecting sentries took on a life of its own and became a ghost story.

But, erring on the side of caution, I would advise against accepting a glass of hard cider if you happen to be wandering around Fort Leonard Wood at night.

The second ghost story associated with Fort Leonard Wood is definitely more traditional fare.

Located in the heart of the fort is the Partridge Preschool. Allegedly, a four-year-old girl was killed at the school. To this day, it is said the spirit of the little girl refuses to pass on. People have observed what is said to have been the child's favorite swing moving back and forth by itself on the playground. Each time this is observed, witnesses report that the air is deathly still and that none of the other swings are moving. Visitors to the school have reported that if you rattle a doorknob inside the building and sit back and wait, the ghost of the little girl will rattle the doorknob back, as if acknowledging your presence. Workers who have been in the building late at night have heard the sound of music emanating from the classroom closest to the "haunted" swing. Sometimes the music stops abruptly. Other times, it is played as loudly as possible, depending on the little girl's mood. Another one of the ghost child's pet peeves is the placement of her favorite playground toys. Observers have commented that she likes *her* toys to be put in *her* special spots and it is not uncommon to find them moved back to their original places once their backs are turned.

I was unable to find any concrete evidence that a child died at the preschool. While it is sad to think that a young life may have come to an end at the preschool, what I find more puzzling is the fact that if the spirit of a little girl is not causing the paranormal activity there, then who or what is?

KEESLER AIR FORCE BASE
Biloxi, Mississippi

Compared to many of the other military forts and posts we have visited thus far, Keesler Air Force Base is a relative newcomer to the military scene. Don't be fooled, though; its strategic importance and the number of ghostly legends that seem to circulate there put it in the same category as haunted fortifications that have stood for hundreds of years.

At the start of World War II, the United States Army Air Corps realized that it needed a state-of-the-art technical training base for airplane and engine mechanics. In 1941, the city of Biloxi, Mississippi, deeded over fifteen hundred acres of land to the Army Air Corps and a short time later, Keesler Air Force Base was established. The base was named in honor of Second Lt. Samuel Reeves Keesler, Jr., an aerial observer from Greenwood, Mississippi, who had died heroically in France after his plane was shot down while performing a reconnaissance mission during World War I.

During World War II, Keesler Air Force Base graduated a majority of the B-24 Liberator bomber mechanics who were ultimately responsible for keeping these mighty flying fortresses in operation throughout the duration of the war. In addition to the soldiers who graduated from the B-24 copilot and emergency rescue schools held primarily at Keesler, over 142,000 aviation mechanics and 336,000 new recruits were also trained there.

In 1943, women and foreign nationals from around the world began training at Keesler, making it America's premiere electronics and aviation training center. Following World War II, Keesler AFB continued to grow, unlike many other military posts at the time. Courses in helicopter mechanics, military police training, meteorology and even cooking were held at Keesler.

In 1947, the Air Force's radar school moved from Boca Raton, Florida, to Keesler. In 1949, two very important moves affected Keesler. First, the post lost its airplane and engine mechanics school when they were moved to Sheppard Air Force Base in Texas, but at the same time, the radio operations school moved from Scott Air Force Base in Illinois to Keesler, effectively making Keesler the "Electronics Center of the Air Force." During the 1950s, when the continuous threat of the Cold War loomed on the horizon, training facilities at Keesler continued to be upgraded and modernized. As a result, four new academic buildings and a hospital were built at this time

By 1958, even more communications and control courses at Scott were moved to Keesler. These courses over time evolved into specialized electronic operator and maintenance programs and air traffic control training programs. This highly technical training culminated when Keesler began hosting digital computer training courses specifically geared for the Semi-Automatic Ground Environmental Defense System.

Between January 1967 and May 1973, pilot training again returned to Keesler. During this time, many foreign nationals completed their undergraduate pilot training in T-28 and T-41 training aircraft. By 1968, Keesler had graduated its one-millionth student. This was no real surprise, since astronautics and space systems courses had been added to the continually growing curriculums that same year. Keesler continued to supply the nation with trained electronic technicians throughout the 1970s and 1980s.

Today, Keesler Air Force Base is the home of the 81st Training Wing and it is the primary location where all Department of Defense weather forecasters and observers receive their training. In addition to the countless electronics and meteorology courses held at Keesler each year, the base has hosted C-12 and C-21 pilot flight training since 1994.

And from there, the base's most famous ghost story has taken root.

In the Air Force, training schools or specialized units are broken down into squadrons. "Wings" are the buildings where a training squadron is housed or conducts its training. The 335th Training Squadron would be like any other at Keesler AFB except that, unlike the other training units on base, the 335th has a haunted wing associated with it. It is said that a young airman hanged himself in one of the squadron's wings while in training. Since the airman's untimely death, the wing where he committed suicide has been kept closed and locked, although new trainees continue to live in "bays" adjacent to it.

On one particular occasion, an airman who lived in a wing next to the one where the suicide occurred, began to experience something he could not explain. Over a period of three days, the airman got up each morning to find that someone had tied several knots in the laces at the toe of his boots. The airman thought that this was highly peculiar. After the third morning, the airman was truly frustrated by the mischievous nocturnal antics of his invisible antagonist.

That evening, the airman decided to lock his boots safely inside his wall locker. He thought that this was a foolproof plan, because he had the only key to the locker. Upon waking the next morning, the airman was befuddled to find that, despite his attempt at extra security, unseen ghostly hands had tied knots up and down the laces of his combat boots. The airman surmised that the ghost had added the extra knots to teach him a lesson because he had attempted to thwart the spirit by locking up his boots.

PARRIS ISLAND MARINE CORPS RECRUIT DEPOT
Beaufort, South Carolina

Without question, the Parris Island Marine Corps Recruit Depot near the coastal town of Beaufort, South Carolina, is a significant proving ground for young "leathernecks" who wish to enter the Marine Corps. But what people seldom realize and something the Marine Corps will never admit is that this world-renowned training site is also a hotbed for ghostly encounters and paranormal activity.

Parris Island is a four-mile-long, three-mile-wide island with a rich history that dates all the way back to 1525, when it was "discovered" by a Spaniard named Pedro de Quexos, who named the point of land jutting out from what is now Port Royal Sound "La Punta de Santa Elena." Charlesfort, the first fortification constructed on the island, was built by the French in 1562 as a refuge for Huguenots seeking to escape persecution from Catholics in their homeland. This growing French threat in the Carolina wilderness concerned the Spanish, who re-occupied Santa Elena in 1566. During later British colonization in the 1700s, Colonel Alexander Parris purchased the island, thereby becoming the island's longest-standing namesake.

During the Civil War, Parris Island, with its slave-maintained farms and plantations, was steeped in all the antebellum traditions of the time. Following the Union naval victory at the Battle of Port Royal on November 7, 1861, Parris Island officially fell under United States control. The North's domination of the island went unchallenged for the remainder of the war.

Between 1909 and the present, the military's presence on Parris Island ebbed and flowed with the significant world events of the time. At first, the Marine Corps presence on the island was quite small. In 1909, the Marine Corps established an officers' training school on the island, and two years later, in 1911, the U.S. Naval Disciplinary Barracks, Port Royal opened its doors at the station. On October 25, 1915, the Marine Corps officially took control of the naval station and support facilities at Port Royal. It was at this time that the station's name was changed to the Marine Barracks, Port Royal. Over the years, the official name of the station changed a number of times. In 1983, the station officially laid claim to the name it bears to this day: Marine Corps Recruit Training Depot, Eastern Recruiting Region, Parris Island.

During the First and Second World Wars, more than 286,000 Marine recruits were trained at Parris Island. By the close of WW II, the base's importance started to wane. This respite was short-lived, because the Korean conflict loomed on the horizon. Following the Korean War, many of the station's oldest buildings were demolished and replaced with unsightly brick barracks. Many of these barracks are still in use to this day.

Over the years, the Marine Corps Training Depot at Parris Island had many names and guises, but the station continues to be the Corps' premier recruit-training center. Every year, more than seventeen thousand men and women who join the Corps learn the meaning of what it is to be a Marine at Parris Island.

Many of them also leave with stories of ghosts and hauntings.

Of all the locations on post that could be haunted, the one that garnishes the most ghostly attention is the old barracks rifle range. At this site, stories abound about the ghosts of recruits who cracked under the rigors of training and either committed suicide or even worse - murder.

In addition to the old rifle range, many of the older barracks and buildings on base, most of which are on the National Register of Historic Places, have their own spectral stories to tell. It is in many of these dark historic recesses that ghostly apparitions are encountered by the unsuspecting, and it is here that unexplained moaning sounds can be heard late at night.

The female recruits at Parris Island shun one old barracks in particular. The building is one of several that make up the only female Marine recruit training battalion in the Corps. Day-to-day coexistence with ghosts is a fact of life for the trainees assigned to live in these barracks, which are known as "White Elephants." Here, a rather noisy spirit randomly slams bathroom stall doors. This same invisible culprit also stands accused of flushing toilets and turning water faucets on and off without warning. Two female recruits who lived in one of the barracks while in training later talked about their ghostly experiences. The first recruit said that she sensed that there was an "overly oppressive feeling" in her barracks while the second female recruit, who claimed to have some psychic aptitude, said that "there was something very bad" in the building where she lived.

One of the most interesting ghost stories told about Parris Island is directly related to the station's most tragic -- and most scandalous -- training accident. On the evening of April 8, 1956, six recruits from Platoon 71 drowned after their drill sergeant, Mathew McKeon, forced them to march into Ribbon Creek.

In 1956, Marine basic training was as rigorous as it is today, but with one notable exception: Drill sergeants in the 1950s were given a great deal of latitude when it came to methods of discipline and punishment. Physical abuse and mental torture were commonplace, but the one tried and true form of punishment that drill sergeants used to weed out the less-than-stellar soldiers from their beloved Corps was the dreaded "Marsh March." Night after night, drill sergeants led their training platoons, consisting of between seventy and eighty recruits, into the flooded gullies, ditches, swamps and marshes around Parris Island. It was intended to not only discipline the unit's sick, lame and lazy, but also to boost sagging morale, even though it really had the opposite effect.

Unfortunately, on the tragic evening of April 8, 1956, an outing for the recruits of Platoon 71 ended in disaster. According to official court documents from Sergeant McKeon's court-martial, which took place in July and August 1956, the trouble started when several of the recruits failed to follow McKeon's instructions. This breakdown in the chain of command effectively turned a training event into a recipe for disaster.

Further testimony heard in the court indicated that many of the men of Platoon 71 were "joking, kidding around and slapping each other with twigs." This horseplay continued until suddenly, the hike turned deadly. Before long, a series of cries for help from men floundering in the dark water of Ribbon Creek pierced the night. Almost immediately following the first signs of trouble, complete and utter pandemonium swept through the previously unaffected recruits. In the wake of the panic, six Marines drowned in the shallow, muddy waters of Ribbon Creek.

In addition to being accused of causing the deaths of six Marines in his charge, McKeon, a combat veteran of World War II and the Korean War, also faced accusations of being drunk on the night of the incident. However, the reviewing physician who testified at Sgt. McKeon's court-martial indicated that while the sergeant had consumed a few drinks the afternoon of the march, there was no evidence to support the allegation that he was intoxicated at midnight, when the incident occurred. Unfortunately, Sgt. McKeon's mistake in judgment was a political quagmire for the Marine Corps as a result of widespread public condemnation of the "brutality" of Marine Corps training. In the end, McKeon was acquitted of manslaughter and oppression of troops. He was convicted of negligent homicide and drinking on duty and was sentenced to nine months of hard labor later reduced to three months . In addition, his rank was reduced to private. McKeon never regained his former rank. He was given a medical discharge in 1959. Many people who have reviewed the Ribbon Creek incident over the years have come to the conclusion that McKeon was used as a scapegoat by both the commandant of the Corps and the commander of Parris Island.

As a result of the tragic event, the Marine Corps instituted many sweeping reforms in its basic training program. Today, drill sergeants are forbidden from physically abusing or hazing recruits, but they are still allowed to push them to their limits.

The dreaded "Marsh Marches" are all but forgotten today, but the six Marines who drowned in 1956 still make their presence known to the modern-day recruits at Parris Island. To this day, strange, ethereal orbs of light are said to be seen floating around the old rifle range, and in one place in particular, along a silent stretch of creek bed. Many believe that the mysterious balls of light are the disembodied spirits of the six Marines who met their deaths more than a half century ago along Ribbon Creek.

It is possible that these restless spirits wander the swamps and marshes around Parris Island because it is the only way that they can be remembered? The tragedy at Ribbon Creek, as far-reaching as its outcome was, is not even mentioned in the post's official history. Could this by why they stay behind? Or could their spirits be trapped there, lost in the psychic ether of the area as effectively as if they were trapped in quicksand - bogged down in the limbo between this world and the next?

CHERRY POINT MARINE CORPS AIR STATION
Morehead City, North Carolina

Late in the summer of 1941, the U.S. government purchased eight thousand acres of farmland at Cherry Point, North Carolina, for use as a Marine Corps Flight Training Center. Little did the government negotiators and architects know that within just a few months of closing on the sale of the land, America -- and specifically the men and women serving at Cherry Point -- would be called to war. As a testament to American ingenuity and patriotic fervor, the airfield and support facilities at Cherry Point were fully operational by May 1942, a scant five months after the surprise Japanese attack on Pearl Harbor.

Originally, the air station was named Cunningham Field in honor of Lt. Colonel Alfred Cunningham, the Marine Corps' first aviator. The station's name was later changed to Marine Corps Air Station Cherry Point due to the fact that there was an abundance of cherry trees growing in and around a nearby post office.

From its inception, Cherry Point played a critical role in the nation's defense, both at home and abroad. During World War II, Cherry Point was not only a basic training center for Marines destined to fight in the Pacific Theater, but it also served as a pivotal base for anti-submarine operations along the Atlantic coast.

When the North Korean People's Army launched a surprise attack on Seoul in the early morning hours of June 25, 1950, America and its military became entrenched in the conflict. During the course of this widely publicized "police action," Cherry Point dutifully provided initial training to the replacement aircrews and support personnel who were badly needed to fill critical vacancies that threatened to cripple many front-line combat units. This training continued to the end of formal hostilities in July 1953.

In May 1961, the U.S. military again answered the call when North Vietnamese Communist insurgents threatened to topple the unstable democracy of South Vietnam. Just as in World War II and the Korean War, Cherry Point provided a constant stream of trained replacements for aircrews and support personnel lost in the seemingly never-ending and increasingly unpopular conflict that enveloped the whole of Vietnam. In addition to filling the training needs of the United States Marine Corps, Cherry Point also for the first time deployed three A-6 Intruder Squadrons to the war-torn region.

This practice of sending both man and machines into combat was the main purpose of Cherry Point's recent wartime missions. AV-8B Harrier squadrons, A-6E Intruder squadrons, as well as EA-6B Prowler squadrons based at Cherry Point have served valiantly in Desert Storm, Operation Enduring Freedom and Operation Iraqi Freedom.

But the ghosts who linger at Cherry Point may date back to before the base ever existed.

Historical records indicate that prior to the establishment of an airfield at Cherry Point, there were several chicken farms located within the confines of the land designated as a military reservation in 1941. According to local legend, an elderly widow known only as "Miss Mary" owned one of these farms. It is said that when the U.S. government forced Miss Mary to move from the only home she had ever known, the emotional distress caused her death a short time later. Whether Miss Mary died of a broken heart or old age is up to debate, but some people believe that the old woman continues to make her presence known even to this day.

For several Marines stationed at Cherry Point over the years, there is no question that Miss Mary continues to haunt the ground where her home once stood. Today, that same parcel of land is a secure storage facility surround by a double-layered security fence located at the core of the air station.

The first recorded encounter with Miss Mary is said to have taken place in 1947, five years after the base was officially operational. During this and each subsequent encounter, Miss Mary is always described as being a kindly old woman who seems to be both curious and cordial. Appearing in vintage nineteenth-century clothing, Miss Mary never ceases to baffle and confound anyone she meets.

One such notable encounter took place on November 11, 1975. On this particular evening, Sgt. James Segura was on guard duty at the storage facility when an elderly woman wearing a long-sleeved calico dress approached him from behind some stacked oil drums. Segura was taken aback by the fact that the woman standing before him reminded him of his late grandmother. For all outward appearances, she looked harmless.

Before Segura could react or really comprehend who or what he was seeing, he and the old woman entered into an eerie dialogue. During the course of this once-in-a-lifetime exchange, the old woman asked Segura his name and introduced herself as "Mary." Without prompting, "Miss Mary" seemed eager to prattle on about how nice the weather had been and about her nearby chicken farm. She said she was upset because the government was going to force her to move. For Segura, time seemed to stand still, and with each passing second he could not help but notice the feeling of dread that slowly enveloped him. How could an old lady suddenly turn up in the middle of the night on a military base that was lit by floodlights and protected by a double set of chain-link fencing?

Somewhere around this point in the conversation, Segura's military training kicked in and he decided to report the intruder to the sergeant of the guard. After politely asking his elderly visitor to wait where she was, Segura quickly double-timed it to the nearest guard post and contacted his supervisor. When Segura and the sergeant returned a short time later, the old woman in the calico dress was nowhere to be found. The spirit of Miss Mary had lived up her reputation and had vanished into the cool November night, leaving no evidence of her presence.

Even though Sgt. Segura's supervisor was convinced that there was no reason to disbelieve the soldier's account of what happened that night, Segura sought extensive medical tests to prove that he was not hallucinating. Base medical personnel later commented that Segura appeared to have been "shaken" by the events of that evening, but he did not appear to have experienced a delusional episode, nor did it seem that he the victim of a hoax. Segura, who is no longer in the military, was so emotionally moved by his chance brush with Miss Mary that he told his story to Dr. Louis Nabb, a sociologist and paranormal researcher.

Over the last several decades, it is estimated that Miss Mary has made an appearance at Cherry Point at least once every six months. Undoubtedly, many of these encounters go unreported for obvious reasons. All totaled, nearly a half-dozen Marines have been brave enough to admit that they have met and conversed with the elderly apparition. All of them have managed to come through the experience unscathed.

I don't think the Marine Corps has a medal for anything like that, but you have to admit that it takes guts to spend time conversing with a ghost - and then tell someone about it.

SOLDIERS and the SUPERNATURAL

HAUNTED PRISONS & CAMPS

Its huge doors swung open and we were in the presence of... I do not know what to call them. It was evident they were human beings but hunger, sickness, exposure and dirt had so transformed them that they more resembled walking skeletons, painted black.
   Lucius Barber, Union sergeant, on the Confederate Prison at Andersonville

The supply of wood issued to the prisoners during the winter was not enough to keep the most modest fires for two hours out of every twenty-four, and the only way to avoid freezing, was by unremitting devotion to the blankets... For my part, I never saw any one get enough of anything to eat at Point Lookout, except the soup, and a teaspoonful of that was too much for ordinary digestion.
   Anthony Keiley, a Confederate officer and a prisoner of war at Point Lookout, Maryland, in 1864

Atrocity came in many forms during the Civil War, from the shedding of blood in battle to outright slaughter. In combat, the art of killing becomes part of the strategy of winning the battle, but other kinds of cruelty and killing took place during the war -- in both the North and the South.

When we ponder the prisons of the Civil War, images of horror from places like Andersonville immediately spring to mind. However, not all of the prison commanders were sadists who enjoyed torturing their prisoners. Most of these men were diligent and honorable soldiers who were doing the best they could with a bad situation.

Prior to 1861, there was simply no precedent for the care of prisoners of war. During the American Revolution and the War of 1812, prisoners of war were ransomed or exchanged as a matter of honor. In the days prior to the Civil War, the United States Army had less than sixteen thousand officers and men of all ranks, most of whom were serving on the Western frontier in scattered companies. One year later, after the surrender of the Confederate garrison at Fort Donelson, General Grant captured nearly that many men after one battle. It was the first large surrender of the war and at that point, how to house, feed and control such a massive number of prisoners was a complete mystery.

Possibly the best way to handle the situation with prisoners, it was thought, was to continue to exchange them. This was the practice in Europe at the time and how it had been handled in America's previous wars. Prisoners were exchanged on a regular basis through formal treaties and gentlemen's agreements between officers. But by 1862, President Lincoln refused to agree to a formal exchange treaty. To agree to a treaty with the Confederacy, he maintained, would mean that the United States was recognizing the Confederacy as a bonafide nation, rather than as an illegal collection of rebels.

Regardless, the Union and Confederate generals made their own informal exchanges beneath the flag of truce. By 1862, a formal agreement was made between the opposing armies that prisoners would be exchanged within 10 days of capture, but this didn't last. The system quickly broke down and prisons and prison camps on both sides began to fill with prisoners awaiting exchange. A new system would soon be needed to combat the terrible overcrowding in the camps.

As a result, a rather unusual plan was hatched. From the beginning of the war, civilians suspected of disloyalty or spying for the opposite side were not imprisoned, but were "paroled." The military decided to try this also, and some prisoners were returned to their own lines in exchange for a promise that they would not return to duty until they were "formally exchanged." This plan turned out to be a complete failure. After his victory at Vicksburg, General Ulysses S. Grant found himself burdened with more than 31,000 Rebel prisoners. Rather than try to feed and guard these men, he decided to parole them instead. Then, during the Chattanooga Campaign, Grant discovered that a great many of the Confederate prisoners who were captured were the same men that he had paroled at Vicksburg. After Grant was given command of all of the Union armies, he called a halt to all prisoner exchanges in April 1864.

Not only was Grant irritated by the Confederate violations of the parole system, he also knew that the Confederacy desperately needed its prisoners to be returned to the battlefield. They were already short on men and greatly outnumbered. By refusing to return their prisoners, the Union could hurt them even more. Grant was also aware of the tremendous cost involved in keeping the Federal prisoners in the Southern camps. This would put an additional burden on a government that was already having trouble feeding and clothing its own army.

Grant was forced to make a grim decision when he halted the prisoner exchanges -- and one that he would be harshly criticized for. He knew that the conditions in the Confederate prisons were unspeakably filthy and dangerous. The Federal prisoners were given only starvation rations and that disease was rampant. He also knew that by not allowing these men to be exchanged, many of them would likely die, but he felt that he had no choice. Grant believed that the needs of these men were overshadowed by the needs of the entire nation.

Conditions that were deplorable in the prison camps were about to become worse.

In the early days of the war, the prison camps on both sides were fairly civilized places. Both the Federal and the Confederate armies treated their prisoners well, as it was believed that they would be only short-term detainees and would soon be exchanged. Local ladies, out of a sense of Christian decency, often would visit the prisons and bring the inmates bundles of food as well as socks, blankets and other small comforts.

However, as the war continued, and as supplies grew shorter, bitterness against the other side grew, and the desire for revenge grew stronger. Soon, it didn't seem unreasonable to give the prisoners just a little less to eat, or a little less firewood to keep warm with. In some cases, downright cruelty became the order of the day.

The Confederate military had been the first to have to deal with large numbers of prisoners. Even before Grant's mass capture at Fort Donelson -- and even before the attack on Fort Sumter -- the Confederates had forced the surrender of United States Army regulars stationed in Texas, who were then imprisoned in temporary camps. Then, after the Confederate victory at Manassas, the South had to provide for over a thousand prisoners who were captured in the fighting. These men were sent back to Richmond by train.

The officer placed in charge of these new prisoners was Brigadier General John H. Winder, a West Point graduate who was a friend of Jefferson Davis. To house the prisoners from Manassas, and the increasing number that followed,

Winder used several warehouses. One of them became known as "Castle Thunder" and was mainly used for political prisoners and other Confederate criminals.

In 1862, Winder took over another warehouse, this one owned by a ship chandlery and grocery company called Libby & Son. The building was unfurnished, but it did have running water and primitive toilets. Libby Prison soon became the housing for Federal officers, and became known as one of the most notorious places in the South. The floor plan of the three-story building measured only 100 by 150 feet, but into it was jammed nearly twelve hundred men. In 1864, one hundred and nine men escaped from the prison through a makeshift tunnel.

In the fall of 1861, the Union named Colonel William H. Hoffman as the commissary general of prisoners. Hoffman was another West Point graduate, and while he was known for his economical regulating of the peacetime Army, he was now faced with the prospect of controlling thousands of Confederate prisoners. He was woefully unprepared for the task.

Hoffman's first assignment was to find a central prison where captured men could easily be taken and incarcerated until exchanged. One temporary location was the Old Capitol Prison in Washington, D.C., which was used primarily for political prisoners and other civilians. He also commandeered several Atlantic forts like McHenry in Baltimore, Delaware near Philadelphia, Lafayette and Columbus in New York and Warren in Boston. The Army in the West took over a former medical college in St. Louis, which became the Gratiot Street Prison, and later moved prisoners into the abandoned Illinois State Prison at Alton.

Hoffman continued his search for suitable locations, and after inspecting several islands on Lake Erie, decided upon Johnson's Island as the site for a new prison. The island was a small piece of land, near Sandusky, Ohio, which was not only free of inhabitants but which discouraged escape by virtue of its being being located far out into the icy waters of the lake.

In 1862, Hoffman realized that he was in over his head. With the fall of Fort Donelson, he suddenly had more prisoners that he knew what to do with. He then turned to camps that had once been used to train Federal volunteers and had these turned into prisons. Among them were Camp Butler near Springfield, Illinois, Camp Randall at Madison, Wisconsin, and Camp Douglas in Chicago, which was perhaps the worst of the temporary prisons. The site was marshy, disease-ridden and filthy and had no sanitation to speak of. Even though his staff explained that the site needed a sewer, Hoffman considered this an extravagance. It would not be until 1863, when the death rate at the camp reached ten percent per month, that Hoffman allowed the site to be drained.

The buildup of prisoners on both sides came to an end in July 1862, when an agreement was reached between the opposing armies to permit prisoner exchanges. Under the agreement, prisoners were exchanged within days of capture and accordingly, the prison populations began to dwindle. Soon, the South was mainly using Libby Prison and a few other buildings in Richmond to temporarily house its prisoners. In the North, Hoffman was able to place most of the captured men at Johnson's Island, Camp Chase and at Alton.

The exchange program was very uneven throughout its short lifespan, but it did keep the prisons fairly orderly and uncrowded. Even when the program changed into the parole system, it managed to keep the prisoners from becoming a drain on the budgets of the two armies. It would not be until Grant's order in 1864 to cease the paroles that life in the camps would become completely unbearable.

Federal and Confederate reactions to Grant's order differed greatly. In the North, Hoffman immediately re-opened a number of prisons that had been previously closed and even opened two new ones at Rock Island, Illinois, and at Point Lookout, Maryland. In the South, though, there was little reaction at all. It was almost as if the Confederates believed that the exchanges, or paroles, would start up again. There was no doubt about it, there were many more Confederate prisoners in the North than Union detainees in the South and these were men that the Southern Army desperately needed to continue the war. They had no wish to continue holding the Federal prisoners and frankly, could not afford it.

Soon, however, they realized that the paroles were not going to begin again, and they realized that measures had to be taken to provide for long-term incarceration. At the time, most of the prisoners were housed in Richmond. As this was also the center for supplying the Confederate Army, and had a large civilian population, a food shortage quickly developed. The Union authorities soon got word that Federal prisoners were starving in the South and Secretary of War Edwin Stanton issued an order for Northern prison rations to be cut to the same levels as those being given to Union men in Confederate camps. The secretary declared this to be only fair, but many saw it as simply revenge.

Despite the lack of food on both sides, whether accidental or deliberate, hunger was not the only thing responsible for the deaths of prisoners. Many of the men received only meat and bread, and they began to grow sick from the lack of fruit and vegetables. In the Northern prisons, Hoffman only permitted the prisoners to have vegetables after an outbreak of scurvy. The Confederates provided vegetables even less frequently. Soon, dysentery and diarrhea were killing more men than starvation, and were turning the survivors into living skeletons.

Meanwhile, the food shortage in Richmond grew worse, and officials proposed a plan to remove the bulk of the prisoners from the city. There was a growing fear of a revolt at Libby Prison -- a fear that convinced the Confederate Army to plant a gunpowder mine under the prison in early 1864. It was hoped that this would deter the inmates from causing too much trouble.

General Winder sent two men to search out a location for a new prison in Georgia. After a location was discovered, Camp Sumter was constructed by erecting a wooden stockade. It was designed to hold ten thousand men and enclosed an area of sixteen acres. In February 1864, even before the fence was completed, rail shipments of prisoners began arriving from Richmond. There was no shelter and the men were forced to improvise huts, tents and burrows that were impossible to keep clean. There was no medical care, little food and the only water came from Stockade Creek, which also served as the prison sewer. At the height of its operation, the prison saw the arrival of more than four hundred men each day. By August 1864, it was packed with more than thirty thousand prisoners, three times the capacity it was designed for.

The camp became known as "the hellhole of the South" and most will recognize it from the name of the town that was nearby: Andersonville.

But the South was not alone in its poor treatment of prisoners. At Elmira, New York, Colonel Hoffman had a large fence erected around a former camp for Union recruits and began moving prisoners into it. It quickly became known as the worst of the Federal prisons. Even the guards' barracks were badly constructed and flimsy. The prisoners, of course, had it much worse, and many of them quickly sickened and died from lack of warm clothing and fuel for fires. Like Camp Douglas, the Elmira prison also suffered from virtually no drainage of waste. A small pond within the confines of the camp provided drinking water and was also used as the prison toilet.

In addition to disease, the prison also suffered from poor management and bad medical care. Records say that about one-fourth of the twelve thousand prisoners incarcerated there are still buried on the property.

At other Union prisons, retaliation for suffering in the South caused conditions to become even worse. Hoffman ordered that all Confederate prisoners be treated in the same way that Federal prisoners were being treated, which resulted in fewer rations, malnutrition and scurvy. It was said that at several prisons, inmates were so desperate for meat of any kind that they organized rat hunts.

The Confederate camps in Georgia were the first to release their prisoners, but not initially to freedom. In the late summer of 1864, there was a growing concern about Sherman's invading army. It was thought that if Sherman freed the Union captives, then the South would have little chance of gaining the release of their own men in the North. Soon, the Rebels began to move their enlisted men from Andersonville and the officers from a camp in Macon, Georgia. After placing them first in Savannah, they were then moved to a stockade near Millen, Georgia. After the immediate danger of Sherman's March had passed, most of the inmates were returned to Andersonville.

Other prisoners had been moved to Charleston, where they were housed in an old hospital, which was in immediate range of the Union siege guns. The Federals, believing that the Confederates had purposely placed the men under fire, reciprocated by moving six hundred Southern officers from Fort Delaware and housed them in a stockade on Morris Island near Charleston. Here, the Confederate prisoners were also in danger of being killed in the bombardment.

By 1865, it was over. Grant, believing that the war was nearly won, ordered a general exchange of prisoners. At City Point, Virginia, and at Wilmington, North Carolina, thousands crossed the enemy lines while fighting continued nearby. After the collapse and surrender of the Confederacy, the remainder of the prisoners on both sides finally went home. By the war's end, more than 56,000 men had died in the horror of the camps.

After the war, United States authorities attempted to hold a number of camp commanders responsible for the deplorable conditions in the Southern prisons. Several of them were tried in court and one of them, the commander of Andersonville, actually went to the gallows. In the end, though, there was blame to be found on both sides. Why were such terrible conditions tolerated by the commanders and private citizens of the respective sides? Was it bitterness and revenge? Lack of food and a poor economy? Or simply the darker side of human nature? These questions will never be answered, and even though the war has been over for a century and a half, the devastating effects of the prison camps are still reverberating today - with ghosts and hauntings.

JOHNSON'S ISLAND
Near Sandusky, Ohio

In the frigid waters of Lake Erie lies a piece of land called Johnson's Island. It was here in 1861, that Colonel William Hoffman proposed the construction of a prison camp for captured Confederates. The site was located about three miles north of the city of Sandusky, Ohio, and was determined to be close enough to the shore to be easily supplied by boat, yet far enough that escape was nearly impossible. The island consisted of three hundred acres of land, half of which was timbered, so there would be plenty of wood for fuel. While it seemed the perfect place for an "escape-proof" camp, to the Southern soldiers, who had rarely seen snow or frigid weather, it was a forbidding place in the winter months.

Many of them would never leave it alive.

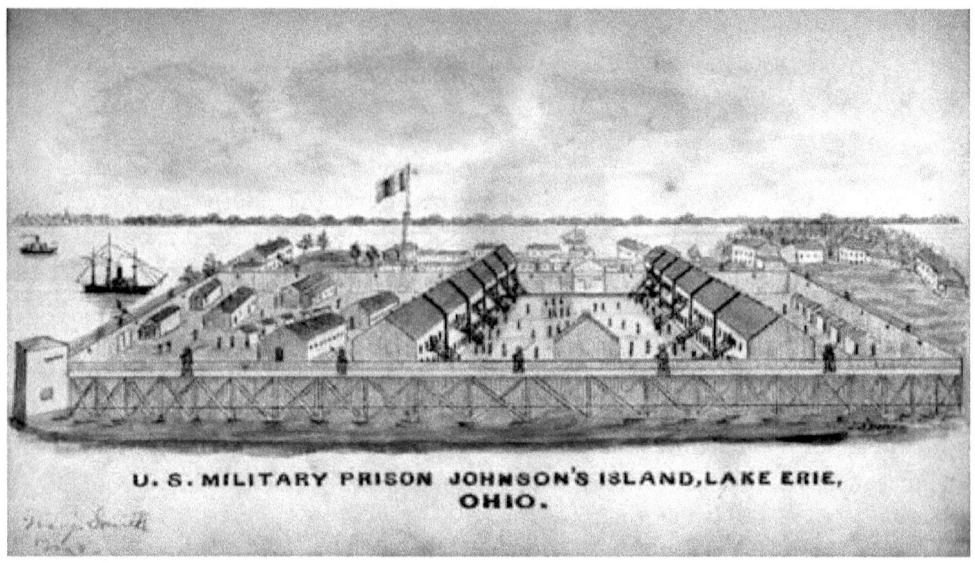

U. S. MILITARY PRISON JOHNSON'S ISLAND, LAKE ERIE, OHIO.

The land for the prison camp was cleared from fifteen acres of forest at the southeast corner of the island. The area was surrounded by a wooden stockade, and within the confines were built thirteen barracks to house the prisoners. The buildings were constructed of a single layer of knotty pine lumber, nailed to upright beams. No plastering was done and the cold and damp air soon caused the boards to warp and crack, creating wide gaps through which the wind howled. There was little protection from the cold, northern Ohio weather.

The first prisoners arrived at Johnson's Island in April 1862. They were a mixed bunch at first, comprised of officers, enlisted men and civilians, but by June, orders from the military commanders made Johnson's Island a prison for Confederate officers only. These men would grow to include as many as seven generals, and they constantly worked to keep up morale and order among the men. They managed to organize their own government, hold debates and even teach dancing, music and French.

There have been many estimates as to how many men the prison actually held, and while it had been built to contain one thousand men, even conservative estimates place the number of actual detainees at around twelve thousand. Somehow, shelter managed to be adequate, although food and clothing were in short supply. In the early days of the war, the men ate, if not well, at least regularly. It would not be until 1864 that the changes implemented throughout the Northern prison system managed to hit Johnson's Island. Rations were reduced sharply, care packages from home were stopped and even purchases made by the prisoners for food from outside sutlers were halted. This would continue for the remainder of the war.

The island prison was one-half mile from the nearest land. Confronted by this, only the most daring of prisoners ever tried to escape. In total, there were a reported twelve men who actually managed to vanish from the prison, which was a very small number compared to other Federal prisons.

The attempted escapes were more frequent during the winter months, when the ice was passable and the guards were less watchful while they tried to keep themselves warm. However, even a successful escape required scaling the fourteen-foot stockade wall and then crossing the open countryside in bitterly cold conditions. Several escapes were made when prisoners, dressed in stolen blue uniforms, casually strolled out of the gates with guard details that were leaving at the end of their watch. Their comrades would delay detection by answering roll call for the men who vanished.

But it was not the fear of individual escapes that bothered the Union commanders, but rather an organized revolt among the prisoners who vastly outnumbered the guards, or a raid against the island by Confederate sympathizers. This kept the Federal authorities in a constant state of worry, for false alarms and threats of attacks by Confederates in Canada were constantly reported.

After several rumored attacks, which never materialized, the threat from Canada came in September 1864. On September 19, a party of thirty paroled or escaped Confederates, armed with revolvers and knives, took passage on a steamer called the *Philo Parsons,* which traveled to Lake Erie islands. Near Kelley's Island, they seized the vessel and proceeded to sink another boat, the *Island Queen,* after letting off the passengers. That night, they cautiously approached the gunboat *Michigan,* which according to a pre-arranged signal, they were supposed to board and capture.

The signal would be a rocket, fired into the air by a Confederate spy named Charles Cole. For weeks, he had been living in Sandusky, posing as a banker, although he was actually a paroled officer from Nathan Bedford Forrest's cavalry. He had become friends with several officers on board the *Michigan* and arranged to have dinner on the ship that night. He and several compatriots were going to drug the ship's officers and seize the vessel.

Meanwhile, that same evening, a group of Southern sympathizers from Ohio were to arrive by train in Sandusky and seize the Federal arsenal there. They would arm themselves and the prisoners on the island, thus creating a three-pronged attack by land, by water and from within the prison itself.

Nothing could go wrong, they believed, and soon their Confederate force would be free to raid cities and ports on the Union's Great Lakes. Or, that was what supposed to have happened....

In reality, there was no dinner on board the *Michigan* and so, of course, no rocket. The authorities had been tipped off to the plan and Cole had been arrested that afternoon in his hotel room. Seeing no signal, the Confederates on the *Philo Parsons* lost their nerve and returned to Canada. The trains that arrived in Sandusky were thoroughly searched, although strangely, the armed Southern sympathizers were never discovered.

The misery and suffering caused at Johnson's Island was more the result of poor planning and short-sightedness than cruelty. The poor construction of the buildings, with single walls and no foundations, had been created for short-term residency, not for the twelve to sixteen months for which many of the men were incarcerated there. The buildings had not been made to withstand the cold winter temperatures and the gale force winds from the lake, nor had they been built to house the much greater than expected number of prisoners.

The camp was badly run and seldom were the facilities ever in complete working order. The supplies were constantly short, the food often rotten and the water pipes often frozen or broken. As mentioned previously, this bred disease and sickness among the men, leading to the deaths of scores of prisoners.

Today, Johnson's Island is a lonely place with little trace remaining from the time when it was a prison. The years and the elements have removed the remnants of the stockade and the prison buildings. There is nothing remaining of the Confederate soldiers who were held captive here, save for the cemetery, and if you believe the stories -- the ghosts.

The cemetery is a grassy spot, surrounded by an iron fence. Years ago, the graveyard was in a horrible state of decay. The area was overgrown and the wooden markers that had been used to locate the graves of the soldiers buried here were slowly rotting away. In 1889, a party of public officials from Georgia visited the site and, by private subscription, raised the money to mark the burial plots with marble stones. Each stone is carved with the name of the man buried beneath it, and his regiment, except for a few stones, which bear the word "unknown."

Over the years, the stories have persisted that not all of the men who died on Johnson's Island rest in peace. It is said that on certain nights, the spectral forms of Confederate soldiers still wander about the former grounds of the prison, and they have also been reported within the confines of the cemetery.

Their voices have been heard also. Many years ago, Italian workers at the stone quarry on the island began singing a song in English. This was unusual because many of them did not speak the language, yet the words were perfectly clear. When asked, they could not explain where they had heard the song, but to their American employers, it was eerily familiar.

The song the workers were singing? It was "Dixie."

CAMP CHASE
Columbus, Ohio

What could tether a melancholy ghost to a two-acre Confederate cemetery nestled in the capital of a decidedly Northern state? The answer would be two words: love and war. The legend of the "Lady in Gray" who is said to haunt the Camp Chase Confederate Cemetery, located in the sprawling city of Columbus, Ohio, is as much a story of steadfast love and the lengths that one woman was willing to go to see her soul mate one last time, as it is about the horrors of life in a Civil War prisoner of war camp. In this instance, a woman's fruitless search for a lost loved one, amongst the mortal remains of over two thousand Confederate soldiers, is a journey she is apparently willing to make over and over again, even in death.

With the opening shots of the Civil War in 1861, the relatively small city of Columbus suddenly came into its own. Heeding President Lincoln's call to arms for 75,000 volunteers to suppress the Southern rebellion, thousands of able-bodied Ohioans rushed to the state's capital for mobilization and initial military training.

The massive influx of men and war material necessitated the construction of an Army post in the vicinity of the city. A site on the western outskirts of Columbus, along National Road current-day Broad Street was selected. Work on the camp, which was named in honor of a well-known former Ohio governor, Secretary of the Treasury Salmon P. Chase, was completed in May 1861. Included in what was essentially a self-contained city was a small, 160-acre prisoner of war holding facility. The prison was completely enclosed by high walls and was of simple design. Divided into three sections labeled Prisons 1, 2 and 3, the complex was estimated to be able to hold between thirty-five hundred and four thousand detainees.

At first, only captured Confederate officers and political prisoners were incarcerated at Camp Chase. U.S. Army Captain Henry M. Lazelle of the 8th Infantry, himself a former prisoner of war, commented of the seven hundred initial detainees, "A large number of the prisoners, amounting to perhaps 200 confined here, whose cases I think are of unjust confinement...here are among the prisoners two idiots, two insane and several so maimed as to be utterly harmless in any community." By 1863, soldiers of all ranks were billeted in the prison following the early Union victories in Tennessee and Mississippi. In that time, the prison's inmate population peaked at between eight thousand and nine thousand prisoners of war.

As expected, the crushing tidal wave of new internees quickly overwhelmed the camp's limited resources. Buildings, already of questionable quality, which had been constructed on low muddy flats, became breeding grounds for disease. Open trench latrines, filled to overflowing with human excrement, contaminated the aboveground water cisterns. This served to exacerbate the already dismal situation.

Colonel W.P. Richardson of the 25th Ohio Volunteers documented the deplorable conditions at Camp Chase in an inspection report that he submitted to his superiors on April 14, 1864. In his report, Colonel Richardson listed just a few of his personal observations:

From this report and my own knowledge I have no doubt about the absolute necessity of the immediate removal of this prison. The entire eastern portion of the camp in warm weather is rendered almost uninhabitable by the stench from the ditch that carries off the filth of this prison. It runs the whole length of that part of the camp between the quarters of the officers and the men, and from the nature of the ground it cannot be changed to any other direction.

Men who were already weakened by malnourishment and subject to a fundamental lack of medical care were highly susceptible to a myriad of deadly illnesses, the most feared being smallpox. During the harsh winter months of 1863 and 1864, a particularly virulent smallpox epidemic swept through the prisoner population at Camp Chase. During this single outbreak, the dreaded disease claimed the lives of four hundred and ninety-nine men in the month of February alone. In all, at least 2,260 men died at Camp Chase while the prison was in operation. There may have been many more. Sadly, not all of these deaths were caused by illness.

Camp Chase was a place where carelessness and inattention to detail could get you killed. Initially, discipline at the camp was lax when compared to other Civil War prisons in operation at the time. Enlisted prisoners regularly received gifts from home, and purchased items from the sutler's store, while officers, provided they took an oath not to abscond, were allowed to leave the prison grounds during the day. Such leaves were granted on the honor system and were not uncommon at the time.

As more and more inmates arrived, conditions worsened, forcing the camp's administrators to revoke the prisoners' privileges to maintain order. Many of the various Northern regiments assigned to keep order at Camp Chase went to great extremes to see that no one stepped out of line. Prisoners were prohibited from gathering together in large groups. Failure to disperse or to follow simple instructions often resulted in the death of the offender.

One prisoner, J. Coleman Alderson of A Company, 36th Battalion, Virginia Cavalry, described what happened one night when a sentry thought a prisoner had not extinguished a light after being ordered to do so: "On one occasion the moon was shining through a back window in barracks No. 2, on the opposite side from the guard who called 'lights out,' and as the moon did not go out, he shot and killed two men sleeping together in their cold, narrow bunks."

When Camp Chase was constructed, there were no provisions made for an on-site burial ground. The first prisoners, ninety-nine in all, who succumbed to illness or who fell victim to the guards' legendary brutality, were interred in the Columbus City Cemetery on Livingston Avenue. In late 1863, a prison cemetery, surrounded by a low fence, was established at the south end of Camp Chase. The bodies of prisoners who had been previously buried in the city cemetery were exhumed and then reburied with the more recent dead at the new graveyard. Cheap, wooden markers were placed over each grave.

At the end of the Civil War in 1865, Camp Chase was closed and dismantled, leaving only the Confederate Cemetery behind. As the years passed, the cemetery, which never had been very popular with the anti-Southern citizens of Columbus, languished in obscurity. During this time, the wooden fence rotted away, and weeds and brush became intermingled with the remaining grave markers that had not already moldered away.

The deplorable condition of the Camp Chase cemetery captured the attention of a retired Union colonel named William H. Knauss. Much to the displeasure of the citizens of Columbus, Knauss worked tirelessly to improve the old cemetery. Under his tutelage, the grounds were cleared of debris and a permanent stone wall was erected around the entire burial ground. Much to his credit, Knauss doggedly reviewed loosely kept cemetery records and replaced the old wooden grave markers with new marble headstones. Later, in 1907, a memorial arch and a bronze statue of a Confederate soldier were added to the grounds.

Thanks to a renewed interest in the Civil War, the graveyard sees a large number of visitors every year. It is said the one of these visitors is not of this world.

No one really knows when the "Lady in Gray" first visited the cemetery. According to local legend, the mysterious woman arrived at the Camp Chase cemetery shortly after the end of the Civil War. Presumably, the young lady, who always wore gray when she visited the graveyard, was searching for the final resting place of a deceased Camp Chase prisoner who was rumored to be buried amongst the Confederate dead. Many believed the grieving woman was looking for some bit of evidence that would lead to the identification of her husband's grave, but she could just as easily have been looking for the remains of her father, brother, cousin or friend.

Camp Chase Cemetery

The unidentified woman came and went so frequently in her personal quest that over time, the townspeople simply stopped paying attention to her. She had literally become part of the cemetery itself, always walking the rows of headstones silently, periodically wiping away her tears with a handkerchief.

Days turned into weeks and weeks turned into months until eventually, the "Gray Lady" as she was now known, made one final visit. Broken-hearted, she never returned. After all those fruitless sojourns to the Confederate Cemetery, the Gray Lady never found the gravesite of her missing loved one. She never had a chance to bid her final farewell.

In time, the Gray Lady became a faded memory, but then strange things started to happen at the old Camp Chase Cemetery. Passersby who lingered in the cemetery on quiet evenings reported hearing the sound of distant weeping that seemed to emanate from somewhere within the heart of the hallowed place. Others later claimed that when they heard the faint lamentations and turned toward the direction of the mysterious sounds, they momentarily glimpsed a gray figure flit amongst the Confederate headstones and then vanish into the shadows.

Many people have encountered the Gray Lady over the years. She has been seen wearing either a gray traveling suit of the style that was typically worn by fashionable women in the mid-nineteenth century or a long gray dress and heavy veil that obscures her face from view. Even in death, the Gray Lady is so intent on finding the grave of her dearly departed, that she has been known to walk through trees and even through the iron gates of the cemetery itself. On more than one occasion, people who have seen the Gray Lady pass by have tried to catch up with her. In every instance, she has eluded her pursuers, leaving a few fluttering flower petals in her wake.

Oddly enough, flowers have become an important piece of this bizarre puzzle. It is believed that the Gray Lady is responsible for leaving flowers on the graves of Private Benjamin F. Allen, 50th Tennessee Infantry, Grave Marker 233 and on Grave 46, the only unknown soldier buried in the cemetery.

Before you scoff at the story of a ghostly lady who leaves botanic tokens on the graves of Confederate dead at the Camp Chase Cemetery, remember, truth is sometimes stranger than fiction.

There was, in fact, a real woman named Louisiana Ransburgh Briggs who was officially introduced as "The Veiled Lady of Camp Chase" at a gathering of Civil War veterans in Washington, D.C., in June 1917.

Louisiana Ransburgh, named after her mother's home state, was born on December 10, 1849 in New Madrid, Missouri. When Louisiana was fourteen, she moved to Columbus to live with relatives after the death of her mother. At the tender age of fifteen, she met and fell in love with a dashing young captain in the Ohio Militia named Joseph Briggs. The young couple were married in October 1867 and settled into the Briggs family estate, which was a stone's throw from the old Camp Chase Cemetery.

Like William Knauss, the man responsible for restoring the cemetery, Louisiana could not stand to see the scores of Confederate dead who were interred in the Camp Chase Cemetery forgotten.

Usually traveling at night, Louisiana Briggs visited the old cemetery and left flowers on the graves of the fallen "Sons of the South." Not wanting to raise the ire of her pro-Union neighbors, she often wore a thick veil to conceal her identity.

Louisiana faithfully performed this secret ritual year after year. It was not until the twenty-seventh annual reunion of the United Confederate Veterans in 1917, that a resolution was passed proclaiming her the "Confederate Angel of Camp Chase." Louisiana had finally been recognized for the selfless acts of kindness she had rendered the dead of Camp Chase over the years. Louisiana Briggs lived to be one hundred years old. In February 1950, the "Confederate Angel of Camp Chase" was called to join the men she fallen men that she had honored for so many years.

The similarities between the ghostly Gray Lady and Louisiana Briggs are irrefutable, but are the women one and the same person? It is quite possible that an unsuspecting visitor to the cemetery may have witnessed the gray-clad, veiled figure of what they believed was a supernatural entity when they had, in fact, observed the very much alive "Confederate Angle of Camp Chase" in action. This is a fine explanation, but how does it explain the distinct sounds of a woman weeping heard in the Camp Chase Cemetery during a Civil War reenactment in the summer of 1988, thirty-eight years after Louisiana's death?

The men who died at Camp Chase did not perish in battle; they died a slow, painful death in a disease-ridden prison far from home. To die and be forgotten is an even greater insult. Each of the men buried in the Camp Chase Cemetery left loved ones behind. If you were a mother, daughter or sweetheart of one of those men, what lengths would you go to be reunited with the one you had loved and lost?

The Gray Lady's continuing presence is proof that love and honor can in fact transcend the thin veil between this earthly realm and the great beyond.

FORT WARREN
George's Island, Massachusetts

Located in the middle reaches of Boston Harbor is George's Island. This twenty-eight-acre island, located approximately seven miles offshore from Boston proper, commands the city's outer harbor and historic main shipping channel. George's Island, first fortified by the French during the American Revolution, is the present site of Fort Warren, an impressive granite-walled fortress that is best known for its service as a prison for Confederate Soldiers during the Civil War. Today, this national historic landmark's most notorious restless spirit is known only as the "Lady in Black."

George's Island was created by ancient glacial activity. In the years prior to the early 1800s, the island was primarily used for farming and other mundane agricultural purposes.

The quiet serenity of this scenic island with its gravely beaches and tidal flats and pools was dramatically changed forever when the United States government purchased George's Island for coastal defense in 1825. During the next twenty years, the quiet island was transformed into one of the biggest and most impressive nineteenth-century classic walled fortifications that can still be found in America today.

Construction of Fort Warren began in 1834, and the bulk of the work on the two-story pentagon-shaped fortress was not completed until 1845. Dedicated in 1847 in honor of Joseph Warren, a hero of Bunker Hill, Fort Warren enclosed six acres on the upper end of the island. Almost all of the remaining vacant land on the island was used for other buildings or fortifications. The fort itself consisted of five bastioned pentagonal granite walls, generally thirty feet high, flanked by an earth-mounded cover face and a dry moat, which partially surrounded four sides of the fort. Progressive upgrades and the construction of the fort's interior quarters and gun emplacements continued until 1860.

Fort Warren

At the beginning of the Civil War, Fort Warren served as a training camp for several Massachusetts Army units, but soon it was being used as a military prison. Though Fort Warren was considered the "North's most tolerable prison," it was ill-suited for housing more than one hundred and seventy-five prisoners for any length of time. When the first steamer arrived at the harbor below Fort Warren, though, it was bearing over seven hundred and fifty-five men. This drastic overflow of prisoners of war, sixty of whom were suffering from typhoid fever, overtaxed the prison's meager resources.

The quarters occupied by the soldiers and prisoners were considered by some doctors and Army surgeons to be "too crowded for comfort" and "deficient both in neatness and order." Overcrowding was a major problem. It was not uncommon for one hundred and sixty men to be crammed into a room no bigger than seventeen by fifty feet. Prisoners who were housed in one of these notorious rooms, dubbed "Room Number Forty-Five" reported that "the atmosphere of number forty-five was almost unendurable."

Even though many of the fort's first prisoners missed several meals upon their arrival due to the overwhelming number of unexpected captives, the fort's meals became more routine and consistent as time wore on. Fort Warren was known for serving tea, coffee and bread with each meal. This was a luxury that was unheard-of at most, if not all, of the prisons maintained by the North or the South during the war.

Citizen aid from charitable local Bostonians was what really made Fort Warren the most tolerable military prison in the North. Local citizens donated large amounts of clothing, shoes and other necessities to the prisoners at the fort, thereby easing much of the pain and suffering experienced by the prisoners on a daily basis.

The commander of Fort Warren, Colonel Justin E. Dimick, a graduate of West Point, was known for his use of kindness to maintain discipline within the prison. Colonel Dimick brought this trait with him from his recent command at Fort Monroe. Colonel Dimick's "gentleman's attitude" and "Christian" bearing would earn him high praise from both prisoners and subordinates alike. Dimick was so well-liked by the prisoners that as a mark of appreciation for his humane treatment, several Confederate officers signed a letter that they gave to Dimick's son, Lieutenant Justin E. Dimick, Jr., requesting that he be well treated in the event he was captured. Sadly, Lieutenant Dimick was mortally wounded at Chancellorsville in May, 1863. Colonel Dimick was officially transferred from Fort Warren "for reasons of health" after he continued to protest the number of prisoners that were being moved to Fort Warren.

Massive overcrowding at Fort Warren caused many of the captives to experience severe bouts with many different types of illnesses. Remarkably, only twelve prisoners died at the prison. The camp's incredibly low mortality rate was attributed to the prison's physician, Dr. DeWitt C. Peters. Dr. Peters' efforts were bolstered by the citizens of Boston, whose donations provided Peters and his staff with a well-equipped medical facility. The twelve prisoners who died at Fort Warren were buried on nearby Deer Island, along with those prisoners who shared a similar fate at other prisons located at New York's Fort Lafayette and Governor's Island.

Between 1890 and 1945, Fort Warren was continuously upgraded and was an active military fortification until the end of World War II. In 1947, after over one hundred years of faithful military service, it was officially decommissioned. In 1958, George's Island and Fort Warren were purchased from the federal government by the Metropolitan District Commission for historic preservation and recreation.

Today, Fort Warren draws tens of thousands of visitors each year to its dark and musty casemates. There, inside the famous Corridor of Dungeons, local historians vividly entertain the onlookers gathered in the dimly lit hall with tales of the fort's grim history. Intermixed with this insightful lore, historians will faithfully recount the tragic tale of the "Lady in Black."

When the Civil War started, many young lovers were separated by the horrors of war. There are many documented incidents of young soldiers quickly arranging wartime marriages with their sweethearts before they marched off to battle. Such was the story of Andrew Lanier, a brash, young Southern soldier from Crawfordville, Georgia, and his lovely fiancé, Melanie. Andrew and Melanie had grown up together and had been childhood sweethearts. It seemed only natural that with the proclamation of war between the North and South, that they would consummate their relationship by getting married.

On June 28, 1861, Andrew and Melanie were married. The young lovers had only forty-eight hours to spend together. At the end of those two brief days, Andrew found himself marching off to war. Not knowing what his fate would be, Andrew's heart was heavy with loneliness. Several months later, Andrew was captured by Union soldiers during a battle. His loneliness and despair would only worsen when he learned what it was like to be a prisoner of war. Andrew and many of his compatriots who were captured at the same time, were transferred to the "Corridor of Dungeons" deep inside the bowels of Fort Warren. At the time, Fort Warren was considered by many to be a "Northern Bastille," from which there was no escape.

While it may have been difficult to escape from the dungeons of Fort Warren, Southern sympathizers working on George's Island and in Boston routinely smuggled contraband into the fort and likewise, smuggled out mail from the prisoners. Andrew, who had nothing but time on his hands, put pen to paper. He told Melanie about how he was taken prisoner, about his dismal life at Fort Warren, and about how he ached to be with her with every fiber in his body. Andrew's sad and moving letter found its way out of Fort Warren and was eventually received by Melanie in Georgia.

Melanie was by all accounts a headstrong young woman, possessing a steely resolve that was uncommon among ladies of her era. When she received Andrew's letter, she was horrified, and she decided that it was up to her to free her husband from the clutches of Fort Warren. Melanie traveled to Boston on a blockade runner and then made arrangements to stay with family friends who were loyal to the Southern cause.

In the following days and weeks, Melanie patiently reconnoitered Fort Warren with a telescope. She painstakingly noted the routines of the guards and the schedule of the boats that frequently docked at the harbor below the fort.

She made a particular study of the area of the fort where her husband was being confined.

Melanie decided that she would attempt to free Andrew under cover of darkness. In preparation, she cut her long hair short and dressed in a man's suit. On January 15, 1862, armed with only a pepperbox black powder pistol, Melanie rowed across the harbor to George's Island in the dead of night, during a frigid winter storm.

Melanie landed her small boat on George's Island and made her way up to the fort looming in the distance. On her way up the rocky embankment, she skillfully evaded several sentries standing guard and soon found herself hiding in a tangle of bushes outside of the granite casemate where Andrew was imprisoned. Melanie was a shrewd planner. She had passed a message to Andrew alerting him of her plans via Southern sympathizers who worked on the island. She had pre-arranged that she would signal Andrew by whistling a tune they used sing together when they were children. As sleet pelted down, Melanie began to whistle. A short time later, a makeshift rope was lowered from the wall and Melanie was pulled up into the darkness, where she entered the fort through a narrow slit in the granite wall.

Andrew and Melanie were finally reunited. They hugged and kissed and after they had wiped away their tears of happiness, Melanie revealed that she had smuggled in a pick and shovel, as well as the pepperbox pistol and ammunition. The Confederate officers gathered and decided how best to go about escaping. This was the chance they had waited for! It was decided that instead of simply tunneling under the wall and making good their escape, the prisoners would tunnel underneath the parade ground at the center of the fort. It was their hope to emerge inside the fort near the armory, break into the arsenal, seize the weapons stored there, and take over the fort in the name of the Confederate States of America. Confederate commanders dreamed of overpowering the small garrison of eighty or so Union soldiers and turning the two hundred and forty-eight cannons of Fort Warren on the unsuspecting city of Boston. Several of the high-ranking prisoners even believed this bold plan could change the course of the war in favor of the South.

Almost immediately, work was started on the tunnel. Weeks went by and the tunnel lengthened. The would-be Confederate engineers plotted and re-plotted the course of the tunnel as they neared the center of the courtyard. Each night, the prisoners worked. During the course of the excavation, piles of earth and rocks were moved to the "Corridor of Dungeons." Late in the evening, the prisoners quietly removed the evidence of their bold plan by throwing the dirt out of the narrow slits in the high walls of the fort. Finally, it was decided that the end of the tunnel was somewhere between the stone walls of the fort and the center of the parade ground.

The prisoners planned to remove the last bit of dirt from the tunnel early in the morning. They believed that they would be able to easily overpower their sleeping captors. Unfortunately, the Confederate engineers had miscalculated the length of the tunnel. When the final thrust was made against the top of the tunnel, the pick easily pierced the soft earth and smashed against a granite wall.

The prisoners were disheartened by the loud metal clang because it meant that they had missed their intended target -- the center of the courtyard -- and had tunneled underneath the most strongly fortified building inside the fortress. The loud sound of the pick striking stone also attracted the attention of an alert sentry nearby. The guard immediately reported his findings to his superiors, and the fort was placed on alert.

News of the suspicious activity was relayed to Colonel Dimick, who immediately ordered that the "Corridor of Dungeons" be searched. Union soldiers found the tunnel and the order was given to muster the prisoners in the courtyard. Once gathered, a head count was taken of the assembled Confederates, and it was found that eleven prisoners were absent from the ranks of their compatriots. Believing that the missing prisoners were hiding in the tunnel, Colonel Dimick yelled down into the tunnel, ordering them to show themselves. One by one, the missing prisoners exited the tunnel, their heads hung low with defeat. Andrew Lanier was the last man to leave the tunnel. The Union soldiers relaxed when another headcount was taken and all of the prisoners were finally accounted for. They didn't know that the prison contained one extra prisoner - Melanie was still hiding in the tunnel.

In a decisively bold move, she sprang out of the tunnel and pointed her pistol at Colonel Dimick, stating, "I have a pistol and I know how to use it." Colonel Dimick was known for thinking on his feet. He raised his hands in surrender and slowly approached the wild-eyed young woman while several of the other Union soldiers slowly formed a circle around the pair, weapons at the ready. When Colonel Dimick got close to Melanie, he quickly seized the imitative and attempted to knock the pistol out of her hands. As Dimick and Melanie wrestled for the gun, it went off. The pistol being old, rusty and not of the highest quality, exploded in Melanie's hands, sending a metal fragment into skull of her beloved husband. He died on his feet, instantly killed by the blast.

Andrew Lanier was buried in the fort's small cemetery two days later. A few days after that, Melanie went before a military court. She was found guilty of espionage and was sentenced to death by hanging. On the morning of February 2, 1862, Melanie's sentence was to be carried out. As was the custom of the time, she was granted one final request. Melanie told one of the guards that she was tired of wearing men's clothes. What she wanted, she said, was to die wearing a woman's gown. Soldiers searched the fort for a woman's dress, but none was found.

Instead, Melanie was allowed to wear a black robe that had been used in a play performed by the First Corps of Cadets the previous summer. Melanie was hanged wearing this rather bizarre costume. Later in the afternoon, her body was unceremoniously cut down and buried next to Andrew's fresh grave in the fort's cemetery.

One night, several weeks after Melanie's death, Private Richard Cassidy, one of the soldiers who had witnessed her execution, was diligently walking his assigned post. Suddenly, Private Cassidy felt a sharp pain around his neck. He looked down and to his complete horror, he saw that a pair of hands had slipped out of the darkness and were clutched around his throat. Cassidy twisted and turned in his attempt to break free. During the struggle, he turned around and found himself face to face with his attacker - a woman in black. He summoned his last ounce of strength and managed to struggle free of the spirit's icy clutches. Completely terrified, Private Cassidy ran back to the guardhouse yelling and screaming incoherently. When Cassidy had collected his wits, he told the story to the other guards who had assembled around him. Not surprisingly, the other soldiers refused to take him seriously and they laughed at his story. Cassidy's superiors also did not buy into the story that he was attacked by a ghost. As punishment for deserting his post, he was sentenced to thirty days of confinement in the Fort Warren stockade.

But Private Cassidy would not be the only soldier who would come face to face with the mysterious Lady in Black. In 1891, several years after the bodies of Andrew and Melanie were exhumed and reburied in Crawfordville, Georgia, four officers were walking through the fort's massive sally port after a recent snowfall. To the surprise of the officers, they observed what they believed to be footprints in the fresh snow that appeared to have been made by a woman's shoes. The tracks came from nowhere and seemed to go nowhere in particular. There were no women living at Fort Warren at the time and this strange occurrence was blamed on what would become known as the infamous Lady in Black.

In the following years, other soldiers stationed at Fort Warren had their own encounters with the Lady in Black. Some of them reported that the phantom had chased them from their post. In several instances, some of the soldiers even allegedly fired at the ghost, but in the end, those trigger-happy few always found themselves being reprimanded for accidentally discharging their weapons or for firing at shadows. During this time, soldiers stationed at the fort routinely played poker during the evenings in the old stone ordinance room. One night, around

10:00 p.m., the night's festivities were dampened when the card players and onlookers watched a small stone inexplicably roll by itself across the entire length of the storeroom floor. When the same thing happened during the next poker game, the ordnance room was deserted for a less haunted location. There was no explanation ever given for these strange occurrences so, of course, the Lady in Black was blamed for the trouble.

In 1931, a sergeant from Fort Banks visited Fort Warren. The sergeant's assignment required that he climb to the top of a ladder, which led to the dreaded "Corridor of Dungeons." As the sergeant neared the top of the ladder, he heard a voice say, "Don't come in here." The sergeant didn't need to hear anything else - he stayed out of the corridor.

During World War II, soldiers assigned to Fort Warren were allowed to bring their families to live with them on the island. During this tumultuous period in America's history, many Army wives living at Fort Warren reported seeing the Lady in Black. It was also during this same time that a sentry who was assigned to patrol in the general area where Melanie had been executed allegedly went stark raving mad before the end of his tour of duty. It was said that the soldier never recovered his sanity.

Official inquiry into the historical origins of the Lady in Black has indicated that the story is untrue. According to Civil War documents, a Confederate soldier named Samuel Lanier was imprisoned at Fort Warren. These same documents show that Lanier did, in fact, die on the island, but he reportedly died as a result of illness, not due to a wound received as a result of being shot in the head.

Moreover, there is no record of any woman being hanged at the fort, or anywhere else, during that time frame. The only woman to be hanged as a result of the Civil War was Mary Surratt, for her role in the conspiracy to assassinate President Lincoln. Surely, if Melanie had been put to death for attempting to free her husband and bring down the North, it would have made newspaper headlines.

Whether you believe that the Lady in Black is fact or fiction, there are still some aspects of the story that must be considered. Following the official deactivation of Fort Warren in 1946, reliable people have reported seeing the Lady in Black while visiting the fort. To this day, visitors and staff members alike continue to report strange encounters with a woman dressed from head to toe in a black gown and veil, but if she is not Melanie Lanier - a woman who apparently never existed - then who is this ghostly figure?

That part of the mystery remains unsolved.

FORT MIFFLIN
Philadelphia, Pennsylvania

Fort Mifflin, a small fortress on Mud Island in the middle of the Delaware River, played a key role in America's War of Independence. The six-week-long siege of Fort Mifflin in 1777, and its later use as a Union Civil War prison in 1863, make this historic location a haven for ghosts and would-be ghost hunters.

Fort Mifflin was the site of uncommon heroism during the Revolutionary War. Following the defeat of the Continental Army at the Battle of Brandywine, General George Washington desperately needed to regroup and rearm his ragtag troops. In contrast to General Washington's dilemma, the British Army fared far better in the way of troops and supplies. A British fleet of two hundred and fifty ships was poised to sail up the Delaware River in support of the British troops who were in pursuit of the fleeing Colonial Army, but first they had to get past Fort Mifflin. General Washington knew that he needed time to reorganize his forces, but he was keenly aware that if the British supply ships were allowed to sail up the Delaware River, the American fight for freedom would be a lost cause. General Washington, seeing no other alternative, turned to the small garrison at Fort Mifflin. He ordered the defenders to "hold to the last extremity" in hopes that they would be able to keep the British at bay long enough to buy his army the time it needed.

In the fall of 1777, the British surrounded Fort Mifflin with artillery batteries and began their bombardment of the little fort. During the darkest days of the American Revolution, the outnumbered and outgunned defenders of the fort were pitted against a far superior British adversary. The British rained over one thousand cannon balls each day upon the demoralized defenders of Fort Mifflin, but the ragged Americans withstood the punishment – and handed back their own.

Private Joseph Plumb Martin of the Continental Army wrote about his experiences during the siege, "I endured hardships sufficient to kill half a dozen horses. Our men were cut up like cornstalks." The ordeal lasted for six weeks. During that time, over four hundred of Fort Mifflin's brave garrison, an estimated seventy percent, died as a result of the British bombardment. When the fort's ammunition supply finally ran out, the fort fell into British hands.

The stalwart defense of Fort Mifflin by the American garrison was not in vain, however. The six weeks that the British spent trying to take the fort allowed the Continental Army to retreat to Valley Forge. The British, realizing that their supplies were running low, elected not to pursue General Washington, thus changing the course of the war in the America's favor. Washington later reported to the Continental Congress of the sacrifices made by the defenders of

Fort Mifflin during this crucial battle: "Fort Mifflin was evacuated, but only after a defense that does credit to American arms, and will ever reflect the highest honor upon the officers and men of the garrison."

In 1863, Fort Mifflin saw itself pressed into service once again. As the first battles of the Civil War were being fought at faraway places like Manassas Junction, Bull Run and Pea Ridge, the Union Army found itself inundated with Confederate prisoners of war. At the start of the war, both the Southern and Northern governments displayed befuddled indifference to the required planning and operation of prison facilities. Unfortunately, in most cases, it was the prisoners of war who suffered because of this gross incompetence.

As the war progressed, many Northern prison facilities became overcrowded and incapable of properly serving in the role for which they were established. This resulted in the creation of many "depot prisons." Fort Mifflin was just one of many small prisons that came into existence at this time.

Fort Mifflin, being constructed as a military defensive position, had no real accommodations for the housing of prisoners. The fort could comfortably hold only two hundred prisoners at any given time - and that was pushing the limit. The prisoners were broken down into three groups: Union soldiers being held on criminal charges, political prisoners, and Confederate prisoners of war. Each group was housed in one of the fort's three underground casemates. These structures were originally built to protect the fort's defenders from enemy artillery fire. They were poorly ventilated and were ill-suited for full-time habitation. At the height of the Civil War, Fort Mifflin housed two hundred and fifteen inmates. During that time, there were forty-two escapes and three deaths at the fort.

Today, historic Fort Mifflin sits in the shadow of the Philadelphia International Airport, but it does not appear that the sound of incoming and departing flights bothers the lingering spirits. The various phantoms observed at Fort Mifflin over the years seem to be directly linked to the roles the fort played in both the Revolutionary War and Civil War.

On many occasions, the image of a Continental soldier has been spotted by visitors and staff near the fort's artillery shed. Observers report that each time the young soldier, with flintlock musket in hand, has been seen, he appears dazed and confused. Perhaps this remnant of a bygone era took General George Washington's last order to defend the garrison a little too literally. He has simply never given up the fight.

The most famous ghost alleged to haunt Fort Mifflin is a spirit frequently referred to as the "Screaming Woman." This haunting seems to be centered around the fort's officers' quarters. Visitors unfortunate enough to cross paths with this particular unsettling specter report that ghost "screams out in terrible sadness." It is said that this tormented soul, who is observed wearing early nineteenth-century clothing, is the ghost of Elizabeth Pratt. Legend says that Elizabeth's daughter died at Fort Mifflin as a result of contracting dysentery. Pratt and her daughter were said to be at odds with each other and that the daughter died before the two could reconcile. Distraught by her daughter's death, the legend states that Elizabeth Pratt committed suicide. Now she is said to wander the vacant and deserted passages of Fort Mifflin, doomed to weep eternally because she will never have the opportunity to make amends with her estranged daughter.

The story has elements of truth, but much of it is clearly false. A woman named Elizabeth Pratt did, indeed, live at the fort. She was married to an Army Sergeant and had an infant son and a young daughter, both of whom died of illness, possibly yellow fever, in 1802. Pratt herself died the following year of an unspecified illness. She did not kill herself and there is no indication that she and her daughter quarreled.

Of course, she could still be the Screaming Woman. Losing two children within a year is enough to make anyone scream.

Several other ghosts, in addition to the Screaming Woman, have appeared to visitors and staff at various other locations within Fort Mifflin. Several people have reported seeing the ghost of a lamplighter lighting oil lamps in the barracks at the fort. A psychic allegedly identified the ghost as one Joseph Adkins, but his identiry has never been confirmed. On other occasions, the shadowy figure of a man is known to sit in a dark corner of one of the fort's casemates, quietly sewing. On more than one occasion, this ghost has been known to tip his crumpled hat to passersby, revealing that he has no face.

Today, Fort Mifflin, seven miles south of Philadelphia, is maintained as a historical park. It is a favorite destination for tourists and Civil War reenactors alike. But of course, the various ghosts who have been observed there over the years seem to feel right at home there as well. Obviously, Fort Mifflin is a landmark in American history where the dead do not rest easily.

POINT LOOKOUT
Scotland, Maryland

Located on a picturesque peninsula at the junction of the Potomac River and Chesapeake Bay, historic Point Lookout is arguably one of the most haunted locations in Maryland.

When visitors tour this popular recreation area today, it is hard to imagine that the ground they are walking on was the site of a notorious Federal prison facility, where more than four thousand Confederate prisoners of war lost their lives. Undoubtedly, the sheer number of tragic and needless deaths at one location is linked to a great many of the ghostly encounters that have been reported at Point Lookout over the years.

Point Lookout during the war

Originally explored by Captain John Smith in 1612, the area known as the "Point" has been a place of interest for many different people who had vastly differing opinions on how it should be used. In 1632, the Point was formally granted to George Calvert, Lord Baltimore, by King Charles I. Two years later, in 1634, the property was claimed by Calvert's younger son, Leonard, the first Colonial governor of Maryland.

During the Revolutionary War and the War of 1812, the Point was a hotly contested piece of real estate. Watchmen for the Colonial Army used the peninsula as a lookout point to keep tabs on British fleet movements on the lower bay. This crucial information was then relayed to American military commanders via a series of post riders. Because the Point was such an obvious observation post, it was frequently raided by the British in an effort to root out any American spies that might be hiding there.

In 1857, William Cost Johnson purchased much of the land that made up the Point. Johnson, a wealthy Maryland politician, had hatched a grandiose plan to turn the Point into a pleasure resort. Over time, a series of hotels, boarding houses and businesses dotted the landscape, but before Johnson could see his plan to fruition, the Civil War erupted, bringing with it all of the horrors of war to peaceful Point Lookout.

In 1862, Union General George McClellan made an unsuccessful attempt to capture the Confederate capital of Richmond, Virginia. The ever-increasing number of Federal sick and wounded from General McClellan's campaign, as well as others during the first years of the war, prompted the government to establish several hospital facilities throughout the region to treat its injured servicemen. The U.S. government leased most of Point Lookout and established Hammond Hospital at the north end of the present causeway. The 1,400-bed medical complex was made up of over twenty wooden buildings arranged in a circle that radiated outward like the spokes of a wheel. Doctors, surgeons and support staff required to run the hospital were housed in the existing hotels and cottages from when the Point had been a resort. Almost from the start, the hospital was busy. Wounded and sick soldiers from battlefields near and far began arriving for treatment.

The hospital is long gone now, replaced by a campground, but photographs remain that document the suffering of the soldiers who were patients there, many of whom fell victim to infected wounds, malaria, smallpox and typhoid fever. Old stories relate how desperate prisoners often tried to fake illnesses in order to be moved to the hospital, where they would try to escape. One of these unfortunate men may still be trying. Park ranger Don Hammett said that on several occasions, he saw what he described as "the form of a man running toward the woods, always at the same section of the road, at full speed, using long strides." It could be that this ghostly figure is the spirit of one of the men who died in the hospital, his last Earthly thought being of making a break for freedom.

It is said that for every soldier who died in battle during the Civil War, two died of disease. An 85-foot monument in the Confederate Cemetery marks the resting place of 3,384 soldiers who died at the Point.

Disaster offshore added to the wartime tragedy of Point Lookout. On November 11, 1862, a Union gunboat, the *USS Tulip*, en route from Point Lookout to Washington exploded, claiming fifty-seven lives. Eight mutilated, unidentified bodies washed ashore.

Even though the peninsula was located in close proximity to Virginia, Point Lookout was rather isolated and easily defended. This prompted Union General Henry W. Halleck to order Brigadier General Gilman Marston to construct a military prison just one-half mile away from Hammond Hospital.

In 1863, Point Lookout Military Prison, also known as Camp Hoffman, officially began receiving prisoners. The forty-acre prison camp was surrounded by a fifteen-foot-high wooden fence. The inner compound was divided into two sections, one area for officers and the other for enlisted prisoners. The prisoners were crowded into woefully inadequate, tattered canvas tents.

In July 1863, the POW camp housed 1,700 prisoners. By December of that same year, the prisoner population at Point Lookout had swelled to over nine thousand. At its peak, the camp held over twenty thousand prisoners at one time, making it the largest of the Union prison camps.

Union soldiers guarding the prisoners had orders to shoot any man who crossed an imaginary line inside the camp.

Without question, the camp was a hellhole, but overcrowding was just one of the prison's many devastating problems. Lice were everywhere, and during the winter, there was not enough wood or blankets to go around. One prisoner described the conditions that he saw when he arrived at the camp: "They were allowed only one blanket to several men...and their sufferings from the cold were intense." Anthony Keiley, a Confederate Officer imprisoned at Point Lookout in 1864, also recounted his experiences at the prison camp:

The supply of wood issued to the prisoners during the winter was not enough to keep the most modest fires for two hours out of every twenty-four, and the only way to avoid freezing, was by unremitting devotion to the blankets... for my part, I never saw anyone get enough of anything to eat at Point Lookout, except the soup, and a teaspoonful of that was too much for ordinary digestion.

Dr. Montrose A. Pallen, a physician who complained about the conditions on behalf of the prisoners, wrote: "Many of these men are without the necessary clothing even to hide their nakedness." Official military records indicate that more than five hundred and forty Confederate prisoners died due to exposure to the cold between November 1863 and February 1864.

One would think that sunshine would have offered the prisoners a brief respite from the bitter cold and dampness, but to add insult to injury, the camp was hellish even when the sun came out during the winter months. If and when the sun was able to cast its ambient light down upon the camp, it only added to the prisoners' misery. A combination of the sun's intensity and glare from the white tents and white beach sand wreaked havoc on the men's eyesight. Prisoners spending any amount of time outdoors without adequate protection for their eyes quickly developed a form of temporary blindness, which could last for days or weeks.

Even the very location of Camp Hoffman on the peninsula worked to the detriment of the prisoners. Since the camp sat on an area of low marshland, the site was prone to frequent flooding during the winter and spring months. Add to this the overall emaciated condition of the inmates and the camp's unsanitary conditions and you had a breeding ground for disease. During the time that the camp was in operation, smallpox, dysentery and scurvy took their toll on the prisoner population. One frightening statistic clearly demonstrates a prisoner's chance of survival at Point Lookout: Between 1863 and 1865 the camp housed over fifty thousand prisoners. Of those men, nearly four thousand died from sickness and disease.

Even though Camp Hoffman was considered to be isolated, it was the target of several unsuccessful Confederate attempts to free the prisoners. One daring plan called for Confederate General Bradley Tyler Johnson to free the prisoners and arm them so they could take part in an attack on Washington. News of Johnson's plan reached Union forces, prompting them to construct nearby Fort Lincoln in hopes that its presence would dissuade anyone from trying to free the prisoners at Camp Hoffman. It worked. Johnson never followed through with his plan when he learned that Union commanders had got wind of his intentions.

Following the Civil War, there was a move to turn Camp Hoffman into a home for veterans, but the federal government dismantled the camp and sold anything salvageable as scrap. Those buildings that were not torn down were later incorporated into a state park. Over time, the bodies of the Confederate soldiers who died at the prison were removed and placed in a federal cemetery just north of the park. Visitors to the site can still see the eroding open graves near the shore of the bay, even though the bodies of the dead were removed over a century ago. Most of the original prison site has been swallowed up by the bay itself.

But even though a large part of the prison is gone, the spirits of the past remain.

The ghostly encounters reported by visitors and staff at Point Lookout State Park are a testament to the fact that some of the spirits of the Civil War soldiers who were imprisoned there still linger today. Those tormented spirits are a reminder of the horrors of the past. Ghost stories not only seem to focus on the historical buildings at the site, they also seem to be directly linked to the very land where the prison once stood.

Staff members and visitors have seen and heard many strange things that they cannot explain in and around the park over the years. The sound of doors and windows slamming, phantom footsteps and even ghostly snoring has been reported in one of duplex buildings that was once used as a lighthouse.

In the 1970s, park manager Gerald Sword was sitting in his kitchen in the old lighthouse one evening when he had the eerie feeling that he was being watched. He turned to the window to see the shadowy face of a young man, wearing a floppy cap and a loose-fitting coat, peering in at him. Just then, a storm hit. When Sword opened the door to find out if the man needed help, the ghostly figure floated inside and disappeared before his startled eyes. Sword believed his visitor was a young crewman named Joseph Heaney, who died when the steamer *Express* broke up in a storm in 1878. Heaney's body washed up on shore and was buried near where it was found. A description of Heaney printed in a newspaper at the time matched the appearance of Sword's mysterious visitor. Other park employees have seen a ghostly woman at the top of the staircase in the manager's house.

Laura Berg experienced supernatural encounters during the time she lived in the lighthouse in the early 1980s, when she was Maryland's secretary of state. She and her husband sometimes heard footsteps outside their bedroom door at night. It sounded as if they were being made by a person wearing boots. They heard other odd sounds that they were unable to account for and smelled strange odors that came and went suddenly.

Paranormal investigators and psychics have repeatedly documented all manner of ghostly phenomena at the park. As if more evidence were needed that something strange is going on at Point Lookout, hundreds of ghostly encounters have been documented by everyday people who visit the site each year. Probably the most frightening experiences involve the phantom soldiers that are said to suddenly appear in front of vehicles traveling in the park and the ghostly voices of long-dead prisoners and guards that have been captured on audiotape.

Many historical locations tend to shy away from stories about hauntings because it is not the kind of reputation they want to be known for. Point Lookout is just the opposite. The park rangers keep track of each paranormal experience told to them and incorporate the information into a popular ghost tour they host each October.

The past is alive and well - so to speak - at Point Lookout.

THE GRATIOT STREET PRISON
St. Louis, Missouri

St. Louis was a city torn apart by the Civil War. Although St. Louis was largely pro-Union, it had to deal with the rest of Missouri, which was sympathetic to the Confederacy. Among those sympathizers was Missouri's governor, Claiborne Jackson, who came from a family of wealthy Kentucky slave owners. He grudgingly respected the state's decision in March 1861 to remain in the Union, but when war began a month later and President Lincoln called for four regiments of volunteers from Missouri, Governor Jackson called the request "illegal, unconstitutional and revolutionary." He refused to respond to the call for volunteers and four days later, Union leaders ordered Captain Nathaniel Lyon to muster four regiments into public service. Before nightfall, Lyon had his troops at the St. Louis Arsenal, supplied with both arms and ammunition.

The confusion continued for months. Secessionists met at the capital in Jefferson City so they could organize a state militia to defend against a Union invasion, while Union leaders met in St. Louis to discuss the defense of the city against the Confederates. In the end, battles were fought throughout the state, while St. Louis remained a Union stronghold, supply point and base of operations along the Mississippi River. Under the command of General Henry W. Halleck, St. Louis saw thousands of soldiers from both sides of the war swell its population to record numbers. The Federal men were there to train, convalesce or to protect the city, but the Confederate soldiers were not so lucky. Those men arrived as prisoners and were subjected to the conditions of one of the worst prison camps of the Civil War.

The Gratiot Street Prison was a crumbling stone structure that had been built in 1847. The imprisoned men starved, suffered, and sickened within its walls and most of those brought there as captives died before they could gain their freedom. Ironically, the horrific place did not start out as a place of imprisonment and suffering. It began, just over a decade before, as a medical college, organized by one of the most infamous, eccentric and possibly dangerous men in the city.

And when the prison closed, its ghosts were left behind.

The McDowell Medical College was founded in 1840 as the Medical Department of Kemper College. The medical school was headed by Dr. Joseph Nash McDowell, and it became the first to be successfully established west of the Mississippi. McDowell's school remained connected with Kemper College until 1847, when financial problems forced Kemper to drop the program. At that point, McDowell struck out on his own and constructed a building to house the school at Ninth and Gratiot streets.

It became one of the most prominent buildings in the city but its fame was often overshadowed by the eccentric reputation of the school's founder. Joseph McDowell was considered to be one of the finest doctors of his day. He was thought of as an excellent physician and a very capable surgeon in a city where medical standards were high. Many graduates of other medical schools in St. Louis would attend lectures at the McDowell's school as part of a graduate course. He came from a distinguished medical family as his uncle, Ephraim McDowell, was known as the first doctor to successfully perform an ovariotomy a surgical incision into an ovary .

In spite of this, it was McDowell's unusual personality traits that got him talked about in. He was described as having "an erratic temperament that approached insanity" and was horribly jealous of other doctors. He was also an ardent secessionist and believed strongly in the rights of the Southern states and in the institution of slavery. To make his volatile political positions quite clear, he often placed a loaded revolver on the table in front of him when discussing issues of slavery, states' rights or secession. While known for being generous in his treatment of the poor, he was also known for his hatred of immigrants, African Americans and Catholics. He would lecture on those subjects at street corners to anyone who would listen. After receiving numerous death threats, he made a breastplate of armor and wore it with his regular suit every day.

The McDowell Medical College in St. Louis went on to become the infamous Gratiot Street Prison during the Civil War.

The castle-like building on Gratiot Street was erected to McDowell's specifications. It was designed with two large wings and flowed outward from an octagonal tower. The tower had been fitted with an unusual deck around which six cannons had been placed to defend the school against possible attack. He also kept the school stocked with muskets that could be handed out to the students in case of emergency. During patriotic holidays, McDowell would pass out the rifles and march the students into the field along Seventh Street. After a short speech, he would give the command to fire off the guns and to set off the cannons in the direction of Mill Creek. The staff and students at the Christian Brothers College next door always made a hasty retreat when they saw the medical students assembling on the lawn.

The building had other unusual elements. The central column of the tower had niches that were intended to hold the remains of the McDowell family members after their deaths. The bodies were to be placed in alcohol-filled copper tubes. The building also included a dissecting room, a chemical room, a lecture hall, a laboratory and a dispensary where the poor were treated free of charge. There was also a rooftop observatory and offices for the doctors on staff. A massive anatomical amphitheater was fitted with six large windows so that dissections would be done in natural light. McDowell also opened a museum that contained more than three thousand specimens of birds and animals from North America. There were also minerals, fossils and antiquities, all of which could be viewed for a twenty-five-cent admission. Clergy and physicians were admitted for free.

McDowell was famous for his surgical skills and he emphasized anatomy in his classes. Students were required to take part in the dissection of human cadavers, a practice that would bring even more notoriety to the school. In those days, it was nearly impossible for medical colleges to get bodies for research because dissection was against the law. To obtain cadavers for study, McDowell and his students were forced to go on nighttime forays into the city's cemeteries. In this way, they introduced "body snatching" to St. Louis.

When rumors of grave robbing reached local residents, they were duly horrified. For the most part, the school began to be avoided as a cursed or haunted place, but occasionally, the more courageous citizens were stirred into action. On one occasion, the disappearance of a German immigrant woman started a riot at the McDowell College when rumors spread that she had been killed and her body dissected by medical students. Everyone knew that McDowell hated immigrants, so he was quickly regarded as a suspect. The woman was later found wandering the streets of Alton, Illinois, in a demented state.

It would be an incident involving one of McDowell's stolen corpses that would change his entire attitude about the possibility of ghosts and life after death. The incident so unsettled him that he turned away from his religious upbringing as a strict Calvinist and became an ardent Spiritualist. At one time, McDowell was an outspoken critic of anyone who believed in ghosts or other "such frauds without foundation," but that was before the spirit of his dead mother saved his life.

A German girl who lived in the neighborhood died of an unusual disease and McDowell and some of his students stole her body and hid it away in one of the laboratories. News spread of the theft and many of the local Germans became angry and vowed to break into the school and find the body.

McDowell received a letter that warned him that the locals planned to break into the school that night so he went to the college to hide the body. When he arrived, all was quiet and he went into the dissecting room with a light. He lifted the girl's corpse onto his shoulder, planning to carry it to the attic and conceal it in the rafters, or perhaps to hide it in a cedar chest that was out of sight in one of the closets.

"I had ascended one flight of stairs," he continued, "when out went my lamp. I laid down the corpse, and re-struck the light. I then picked up the body, when out went my light again. I felt for another match in my pocket, when I saw distinctly my dear, dead mother, standing a little distance off, beckoning to me."

McDowell said that he saw her rise up a little in front of a window and then vanish. Shaken, he nevertheless climbed the steps to the attic, where he hid the body. He came back downstairs in the darkness and when he reached the window, he saw two Germans talking. One of them had a shotgun and the other carried a revolver. The doctor eased down the staircase and when he got to the door of the dissecting room, he looked down the stairs into the hallway below. There he saw another five or six men, and one of them was lighting a lamp. "I hesitated a moment as to what I should do," wrote McDowell, "as I had left my pistols in the room where I took the body. I looked in the room, as it was my only chance to get away, when I saw my spirit mother standing near the table from which I had taken the corpse. I had no light, but the halo that surrounded my mother was sufficient to enable me to see the table quite plainly."

Suddenly, footsteps sounded on the staircase below and McDowell darted into the room. He lay down on the table where the girl's body had been and pulled a sheet up over himself. The men came into the room to look for the dead girl among the other bodies that had been placed there. Sheets were lifted from the faces of the corpses and when they passed the table where McDowell was hiding, one of them commented on the freshness of the corpse and that he had died with his boots on. However, they did not look under the sheet. McDowell was terrified that he would be discovered but claimed that he heard a soft voice in his ear, urging him to be still.

The Germans searched the building, but found neither the girl's body nor Dr. McDowell. When he finally heard them depart from the school, he breathed a sigh of relief. He had been saved and he gave the credit for his safety to the spirit of his mother.

At the beginning of the Civil War, McDowell's son, Drake, joined the Confederate Army under the command of General Meriwether Jeff Thompson.

He took two of the school's cannons with him. McDowell also went south to serve the Confederacy as medical director for the Trans-Mississippi Department.

In November 1861, General Henry W. Halleck took over as a commander of the Union Army's Department of the West, headquartered in St. Louis. Provost Marshall George E. Leighton seized the abandoned medical college and it was taken over by the Union military. The building was first used as a recruiting office for St. Louis and then it was converted into barracks for arriving soldiers. Finally, Confederate prisoners of war began being housed in the building to help relieve the overcrowding at a smaller, nearby prison, a hellish place known as Lynch's Slave Pen.

The job of converting the medical college to a prison was given to a Major Butterworth. In December 1861, fifty men, including fifteen former slaves, were put to work renovating the college and cleaning out what the medical students had left behind. The former slaves were given the distasteful task of removing the three wagon-loads of human bones and the assorted medical specimens that were found in the basement. Cooking stoves and sleeping bunks were constructed and McDowell's dissecting room was converted into a dining hall. General Halleck placed Colonel James M. Tuttle in charge of the prison's operations.

The first prisoners arrived on December 22. A large crowd of curious spectators gathered at the train depot to watch them come in but before the train arrived, the crowd became unruly and two regiments of soldiers from Iowa and Indiana had to be dispatched to the station to maintain order. As the train stopped, the Indiana regiment formed two lines from the cars to the prison. A military band, which had assembled at the scene, began to play "Yankee Doodle" as the men climbed from the train and "Hail Columbia" as they were forced to march off to the prison. The Confederates were in sorry shape when they arrived, having no uniforms and with whay little clothing they had being tattered and torn. Some had wrapped rags around their feet to take the place of missing shoes and their outerwear consisted of nothing more than blankets, quilts and buffalo robes.

The soldiers were taken to the Gratiot Street Prison and it was soon obvious that the prison had been poorly planned and prepared. The building's capacity was about one-third of the number that arrived on the first day. The holding areas were badly ventilated and unsuited for large numbers of people. The waste buckets that had been placed in the rooms were insufficient for the number of men who had to use them, as was the trench latrine in the yard area. In an effort to keep the prison as clean as possible, Colonel Tuttle issued an edict that would make the prisoners responsible for the cleanliness of their quarters. They were to sweep the rooms each morning and scrub them every two weeks.

Unfortunately, though, the overcrowded conditions made this impossible. When the scrubbing details were enforced, water sloshed around on the floor and seeped into the lower rooms, making the situation even worse.

Conditions here were chaotic because of the lack of organization of prisoners. Prisoners of all types could be housed in the same rooms. Held within the walls were not only Confederate prisoners of war, but suspected Southern sympathizers, bush whackers, spies, Union deserters and Union soldiers who had been arrested for criminal activity. The prison even held women accused of harboring fugitives or sympathizing with the South.

Discipline was harsh, especially in the beginning when St. Louis was still embroiled in the riots, murders and shootings that marked the early days of the war. Guards were ordered to shoot anyone who not only tried to escape, but even those who simply stuck their heads or other body parts out of a window. There were reports that some of the guards took potshots at prisoners just to practice their aim.

The prison was a filthy, horrifying place. The population soared and sanitary conditions and food rations further declined. The hospital was always filled, so the sick and dying were left lying on the floor. The dawn of each new day would reveal from one to four dead men stretched out on the cold stone. One prisoner wrote, "All through the night can be heard coughing, swearing, singing and praying, sometimes drowned out by almost unearthly noises, issuing from uproarious gangs, laughing, shouting, stamping and howling, making night hideous with their unnatural clang. It is surely a hell on earth."

The lack of space, poor food and lack of medical care plagued the prison. In March 1863, a smallpox epidemic raged through the close quarters and the polluted conditions in the lower rooms declined further. Lice and bed bugs invaded the prisoners, their clothing and everything else. Prisoners died at an alarming rate, largely thanks to new outbreaks of smallpox and typhoid.

In April 1863, the Western Sanitary Commission, a private agency that operated in the West during the war to help the army deal with sick and wounded soldiers, appointed two physicians to look into the situation at the prison. Among other things, they found that the bunks for the men were spaced so tightly together that a man could scarcely pass between them and that the prisoners' bedding had been reduced to scraps of blanket and pieces of carpet. The floors were so encrusted with filth that the stone had started to resembled dirt flooring. They concluded their report with, "It is difficult to conceive how human beings can continue to live in such an atmosphere."

A great many of them did not continue to live. Constant new inmates, many of whom were dead on arrival or died soon after, propelled the population at Gratiot Street to new highs in 1864. Horrified at the rate of death and illness within the prison walls, Union Surgeon General George Rex reported that despite the attention that has been called to the problem of overcrowding, the "evil still continues unabated." The prison remained open until the end of the war. By then, the conditions inside had collapsed beyond imagination.

In the summer of 1865, Dr. McDowell returned to St. Louis. He had survived the war and after traveling in Europe, came back to re-establish his medical school. He cleaned and renovated all of the rooms, except for one, which was left just as it had been when the prison was open. He called that room "Hell" and most likely, the description was a fitting one.

McDowell died in 1868 and the medical school was left vacant for years. In June 1878, the south wing was condemned as being unsafe and was demolished by order of the fire department. The octagonal tower and the north wing remained until 1882, when they were torn down. Nothing remains of the building today and it is merely a forgotten spot on the Ralston-Purina company's back lot.

But for years after the building closed down for good, it was anything but a forgotten place for the people who lived in the neighborhood around the old college. To them it was a haunted and forbidding place and not only because of the horrific experiments they believed had once been conducted by Dr. McDowell and his ghoulish students. The people in the area were convinced that the ghosts of men who died at the Gratiot Street Prison remained behind at the site.

According to the stories, cries and screams were often heard coming from the crumbling walls of the old prison. If anyone searched inside, they would find the place empty and abandoned. What could they have been hearing? Could it have been an eerie replay of the cacophony that was described by prisoners during the war? One of them wrote that on many nights, it was impossible to sleep because of the sounds that came from the lower levels of the prison. The natural sounds of incarcerated men were "sometimes drowned out by almost unearthly noises... laughing, shouting, stamping and howling, making night hideous with their unnatural clang."

Could these have been the sounds described by the terrified local residents as coming from an empty building that had once housed almost unimaginable horrors?

THE ALTON PENITENTIARY
Alton, Illinois

The Mississippi River town of Alton is a place steeped in history, legend and lore. Author Mark Twain called it a "dismal little river town." Today, it's considered one of the most haunted small towns in America. Perhaps one of the most horrific historical tales of Alton concerns the penitentiary that was constructed there in 1833 and used as prisoner of war camp during the Civil War. It was a place where tragedy, despair and disease became commonplace and where death came calling for hundreds of men. It is also a place where, even today, the dead do not rest in peace.

The old Alton Penitentiary foreground of photo was the state's first prison and went on to serve as a Confederate prison during the war.

Construction of what would be the first penitentiary in the state of Illinois was completed in Alton in 1833. There was no other building like it in the state and in fact, at that time there were few structures like it anywhere in the United States. While one of the first institutions brought to this country by the early settlers was the jail, a place where lawbreakers could be held while they awaited trial and subsequent punishment, penitentiaries as we know them today did not exist. It became an American invention that would have a profound effect on the rest of the country.

In the early 1800s, the Quakers in Pennsylvania began to search for a new method of incarceration for criminals in which "penitence" would become essential in the punishment of the lawbreaker. Around this same time, two prisons were built that would soon become models for the rest of the nation. Eastern Penitentiary was built in Philadelphia in 1829 to further the Quakers' idea of complete isolation as a form of punishment. Prisoners were confined alone in windowless rooms with running water and toilets. They would come into contact with no one during their entire sentence. This extreme isolation caused many of the prisoners to go insane and was fortunately not really feasible for most penitentiaries in the country.

Also in 1829, a rival system, which gained wider acceptance, was started with the building of a prison in Auburn, New York. Here, the prisoners worked all day at hard labor and then were isolated at night. The prisoners labored together but were forbidden to speak to one another in the early years of the institution. This system became more popular than the system devised at Eastern State because it was cheaper to operate and the buildings could house more prisoners.

The Alton Penitentiary was designed around 1830 and opened three years later as a loose interpretation of the Auburn system of prisons. The men incarcerated there were forced to work during the day, laboring mostly in the local quarries, and then were housed in their cells at night. Punishments for any sort of infraction could be brutal and mostly involved beatings and floggings. The prison had come into existence because the state legislature had amended the criminal code to favor confinement and hard labor, and to abolish the use of stocks and whippings as a punishment for crimes. Apparently, though, these punishments were allowed for those already in prison who broke the rules.

The first penitentiary building was completed in 1833 and held twenty-four cells. As more prisoners were incarcerated, additional cells and buildings were added to the prison, along with a warden's residence, which was located at the southwest corner of the site. In 1846, ninety-six new cells were added and more followed. By the time the prison closed down, there were two hundred and fifty-six cells with an average of two convicts in each.

The Alton Penitentiary was run under the lease system, which means that it was leased from the state by an individual who was then supposed to feed, house and guard the prisoners, also paying for their medical care. This person received about $5,000 from the state and took on the role of warden. He was then responsible for the conditions of the prison, as money allowed. Either the money provided was not enough to pay for the upkeep of the prison, or less-than-honest men were in charge but, whatever the case, conditions at the Alton Penitentiary deteriorated badly in a very short time. The prison became known as a grim and horrific place, plagued by rats, vermin and disease. There was always a lack of clean clothing, fresh water, edible food and medical care. Many of the men who served time there died within months of their release. Their health was so completely broken while incarcerated at the prison that they simply did not survive for long.

By the 1850s, conditions were so bad here that Dorothea Dix, a social reformer and leader in the movement to improve conditions for prisoners, the insane and the mentally ill, led a crusade to close the Alton prison. After visiting Alton, she was stunned by the conditions of the place. She wrote, "The penitentiary is badly situated too near the river, undrained and ungraded and generally, unsanitary. It is not fit for human habitation." This led to a heated controversy that eventually ended in a legislative investigation and the construction of a new prison near Joliet, Illinois.

In May 1859, the Alton Penitentiary was officially closed down. The prison in Joliet had been completed and the prisoners in Alton began to be transferred out in batches of forty and fifty men at a time. By June of the following year, the penitentiary was completely abandoned -- but it would not stay that way for long.

Early in the years of the Civil War, Alton became a military post, thanks to its location on the Missouri border and its access to the Mississippi River. The first garrison stationed here consisted of three or four companies of the 13th U.S. Regulars, under the command of General William T. Sherman. The local troops were commanded by Lieutenant Colonel Sydney Burbank.

It had become apparent by 1862 that the war was not going to come to a swift end, and more space was needed for the growing numbers of Confederate prisoners of war. In an effort to relieve the overcrowding at the Gratiot Street Prison in St. Louis, Major General Henry W. Halleck, commanding the Department of the Missouri, asked for permission to take over the abandoned Alton penitentiary, provided that he could get consent from Illinois governor Richard Yates. Governor Yates granted permission and at the end of January 1862, Halleck sent an agent to build fires in the penitentiary building to dry out the walls. By this time, the buildings had been empty for several years but they were perfect for what was needed. The site was an extensive one, bordering Fourth Street on the north, Williams Street on the east, Second Street on the south and Mill Street on the west. The "unsanitary" facility passed military inspection. A report by Augustus M. Clark, medical inspector of prisoners of war, contradicted the findings of Dorothea Dix and the Illinois legislative investigation by stating that the drainage for the prison was in "good order."

The prison had a main, three-story penitentiary building with two hundred and fifty-six cells and five long rooms, divided by partitions, which provided two enclosures each. There were also several stone buildings in the yard, which was surrounded by a high stone wall, and an old stable. Two buildings in the yard would be converted for confining Union troops who were under court-martial and civilian prisoners.

The first commander of the prison was also the commander of the Alton post, Lieutenant Colonel Sidney Burbank. He was an 1829 graduate of West Point and a veteran infantryman. The first prisoners arrived on February 9 by way of a river steamer. They were marched from the river landing to the prison and had to pass through a gauntlet of local residents, many of who shouted and spit on them. Not all of the prisoners were soldiers. They included spies, saboteurs, guerilla fighters and Southern sympathizers. Even a few women were incarcerated there and two of them died in Alton.

Within three days of the arrival of the first prisoners, the penitentiary was already overcrowded. The maximum capacity of the institution was estimated at eight hundred but throughout most of the war, it held between one thousand and fifteen hundred prisoners and often more.

Most of the prisoners remained in their cells or had limited access to the yard, where the drinking water and the latrines could be found. The prison had no water supply. A well was located on the grounds but soon after the prisoners of war were brought in, the water was found to be contaminated. The situation was remedied by hauling huge water kegs from the river, using a wagon drawn by six mules. The drinking water was stored in a trench that was located just a short distance away from a similar container that was used as the latrine. Jacob Teeple, a soldier from the Missouri Infantry who was among the first prisoners transferred to Alton, wrote, "Imagine, 1,200 men shut up in a prison with only Mississippi water direct from the river!"

There was little concern about these conditions by prison officials, for life was perhaps even more brutal here than in the days when it was a state penitentiary. While the prison was under the command of the U.S. Army, it was still managed by Samuel Buckmaster. He was a businessman who had leased the prison from the state from 1838 to 1860. He still held the lease when the military moved into it and the government paid Buckmaster a sum of $20,000 per year with which to maintain the prison and feed the prisoners. Any money left over was given to Buckmaster. As it had been when it was a state institution, the Alton penitentiary was in deplorable condition.

Augustus Clark, who had originally inspected the prison for the military, found nothing amiss when he returned for another visit. In fact, he wrote, "In this prison, more than any other, regard seems to be paid to the comfort of, as well as security of the prisoners. The military discipline maintained is not as strict as should be, yet every precaution seems to be taken to prevent escapes."

But Clark was as wrong about this as he was about the sanitary conditions of the prison. During the early morning hours of July 25, 1862, sentries along the back wall of the prison heard noises outside and at dawn, they discovered a hole in the ground about eighteen inches in diameter. Further investigation revealed that a tunnel exited the prison from an entrance in the washhouse, located in the prison yard. A roll call revealed that thirty-six prisoners were missing. The countryside was scoured but missing boats along the river suggested that the prisoners had escaped to Missouri. Only eight of them were ever recaptured and on August 9, General Halleck called for a court of inquiry into the matter. President Lincoln agreed that there seemed to be a problem in Alton and after the court obtained their sworn statements, Colonel Burbank and the 13th Regiment were transferred out.

The garrison was then taken over by the 77th Ohio Volunteer Regiment under the command of Colonel Jesse Hildebrand. After a disastrous rout of his men at Shiloh, Hildebrand had been transferred to Alton. He was ridiculed by his own men, by local townspeople, and even by the prisoners. He was not even settled into his new assignment before another escape occurred.

Heat was supplied to the prison by wood-burning stoves that had been set up in the corridors. In the yard buildings, stoves were located in the rooms, which used coal-oil lamps for light. The prison had also been equipped with "modern" gas lighting. The prisoners used this to their advantage on Sunday, November 16, when a fire broke out in a straw storage room north of the prison hospital. The Alton fire brigade was summoned and soon extinguished the blaze. Then, during the early morning hours of the next day, the same room suddenly burst into flames again. It was again put out but, as dawn broke in the sky, guards noticed a ladder that was propped up against the south wall of the prison yard. A braided bed sheet that was knotted at the top of the ladder dangled over the other side. A quick count revealed that four prisoners were missing.

The next day's *Alton Telegraph* reported in a scathing piece, "There are stationed here not less than 1,300 U.S. Troops as guards... there is gross negligence somewhere; for prisoners to have or get ladders and climb over prison walls within ten steps of a sentinel certainly argues a laxity of discipline which demands instant reform."

Officials in St. Louis sent off exasperated letters to Secretary of War Edwin Stanton. Colonel William Hoffman wrote, "I have urged for a more competent officer for the command than Colonel Hildebrand but have been told there is no one available... I therefore respectfully recommend that Captain H.W. Freedley, Third Infantry, be placed in command." In March 1863, Hildebrand was relieved of his command. He returned home to Ohio and died soon after.

Captain Freedley arrived in Alton on November 27. After only a cursory inspection of the prison, he was shocked and disgusted by what he saw. He reported, "There is inexcusable neglect here. So incomplete and incorrect were the rolls that at this time, there are names found on the rolls that are not found in the prison, as well as three persons found in the prison whose names were not on the rolls... Many of the prisoners are sadly destitute of clothing... I have found the guard duties were performed in a loose and careless manner, arising from a relaxation of discipline..."

As the war continued, new prisoners arrived in Alton on a regular basis. The facility usually contained many times the number of prisoners that it was designed for. In addition to constant health problems and continued overcrowding, the penitentiary continued to be plagued with dangerous situations arising from disorganization, mismanagement and inadequate security. Plots to escape were constantly hatched and while most failed, there was an escape attempt worth noting in July 1864. Forty-six prisoners working in a nearby stone quarry made a desperate effort against their guards. Acting at a given signal, the prisoners nearly overpowered the soldiers and seized a number of rifles before the guards could act. The weakened condition of the prisoners allowed the guards to quickly recover and they killed seven of the men and wounded five others. All but two of the Confederates were quickly recaptured.

Like this one, most of the escape attempts failed because of the poor health of the prisoners. Living conditions were sometimes unbearable and most of the men were badly clothed. Food was often withheld as a punishment or was not edible when it was available. Bathing facilities were not available and gnats and lice were common, as were rats and other vermin. The prevailing diseases at the Alton prison included malaria, pneumonia, dysentery, scurvy and anemia and they felled more men than gunshots ever could. Then, in 1863, several isolated cases of smallpox broke out among prisoners who had been transferred in from the Gratiot Street prison. The disease began to spread and quickly turned into an epidemic.

During the Civil War, of the more than six hundred thousand soldiers on both sides who died, two succumbed to disease for every one who died in battle. Dysentery i.e. chronic diarrhea was the biggest killer, followed by diphtheria, typhoid, measles, pneumonia and various infections. Smallpox was especially feared because it was spread by direct contact. The prisoners, at the time of the Alton outbreak, probably numbered almost two thousand in quarters that had been designed for less than half that number. They slept three to a bed, ate standing up and used a common latrine. Nothing was clean in the prison and the men were often unshaved and filthy. They could not bathe, their sleeping mattresses were never washed and the prison yard was filled with pools of stagnant water and urine.

The smallpox virus could live for hours on contaminated clothing and blankets and had an incubation period of two weeks. It was spread to others long before the carrier ever realized he was sick. There was little that could be done to treat the disease, other than to let it run its course. Those with smallpox would be completely dehydrated and as the sickness progressed, victims would develop oozing pustules on their legs, arms and faces. Survivors were often left badly scarred.

In 1863, men at the Alton prison began to get sick and soon, both prisoners and guards began to die. Before it was over, the disease spread into the city of Alton itself, killing many residents. In the early days, though, as the prison death toll first began to climb, Alton's mayor, Edward T. Drummond, refused to have any of the prisoners treated away from the prison. There were no hospitals in the city of Alton in those days. The patients were quartered in hallways, storage rooms and stables, as the prison hospital was woefully inadequate, having only five beds. Before the outbreak, there had been about a half-dozen deaths per week in the prison but soon, they were counting more than five each day. Once the disease started to spread, there was no way to stop it. The men were weakened by poor diet and filthy living conditions and were helpless against the ravages of the disease.

The sick and dying overflowed the converted sick rooms and no one knew what to do with the bodies of the dead. The prison "dead house" was simply a shed in the yard where bodies were kept until they could be buried. This soon became woefully inadequate, as did the former method of burial and disposal. Prior to the epidemic, the bodies of the men who died at the prison were floated by raft to the ferry landing upriver and then driven by wagon to an old goat pasture that had been converted to a cemetery north of Alton.

When news of the epidemic spread throughout the city, the residents of Alton quite naturally began to panic and they demanded the bodies be taken elsewhere, along with the men who had become fatally ill with the disease. The failing men, and those who succumbed to the illness, were taken to a small island located on the Mississippi called Sunflower Island. Located on one end of the island was a dilapidated summer cottage that was commandeered and turned into a hospital pest house - a ward to quarantine those with deadly diseases - and it too became quickly overcrowded. A number of healthy prisoners were ordered to act as hospital attendants and stretcher-bearers but the prisoners, along with the guards, feared going to the island, afraid they would never return. They also transported hundreds of bodies wrapped in sheets to Sunflower Island, placing them in hastily dug trenches.

An unknown number of men died and were buried in various locations during the epidemic. According to reports, the bodies were buried not only on the island, but on the prison grounds, as well. Jacob Teeple, who was incarcerated at Alton with his father and cousin, wrote, "Men died by the hundreds. My father died in Alton prison, and they would not let me see him buried, nor do I know whether he was buried or not."

The smallpox epidemic continued to rage throughout the winter and into the spring of 1864. Prison officials eventually gave up trying to keep an accurate account of the dead. Estimates made after the war ranged from one thousand to over five thousand deaths. Official numbers listed anywhere from thirteen hundred to fourteen hundred. Based on the abysmal conditions there, none of the numbers seem to be an exaggeration.

Throughout the epidemic, officials attempted to cope by using a number of makeshift accommodations to treat the disease, as they had no actual hospital facilities. In the summer of 1864, a group of St. Louis nuns from the Daughters of Charity arrived at the prison. They demanded better medical supplies, an actual hospital building and permission to conduct burial services for the men. A new hospital was authorized to be built on the grounds and construction was completed by that autumn. They also opened the first hospital in the city, a short distance away from the prison in a former boarding house. By the end of the summer, new cases of smallpox were no longer reported and the pest house on Sunflower Island was closed down.

Shortly after the war, the locations of the island graves were lost. An 1869 congressional report stated: "A number of Union soldiers and rebel prisoners of war, who died from smallpox, were buried on an island in the Mississippi River. The island has several times been overflowed since their burial, and all traces of the graves have been swept away."

The graves may have vanished, but the dead remained. In 1874, a wing dike built downstream on Ellis Island caused the shore of the Sunflower Island to erode, washing some of the bodies away. For years afterward, locals largely avoided the island and for this reason, failed to notice the continued erosion that took place, washing the island's rocks, stone and sand downstream. The waters also carried away the remains of many of the soldiers whose bodies had been left behind there. The island was shunned by the townspeople, some believed, because of the chance that traces of smallpox might linger here. Others believed that it was avoided for another reason altogether: because the ghosts of the men buried there in unmarked graves still roamed the island.

In 1935, a new locks and dam system was built on the river at Alton. Much of the island's sandy soil was used as fill around the southern leg of the dam and for a levee. Finally, in 1938, the locks and dam were completed, and as the water level behind the dam was raised, the remainder of the island was obliterated. Over the years, the site of the island has been lost, vanished beneath the waters of the Mississippi. All that remains of it is a sandy strip of land along the Missouri shoreline. There is no trace of what the island used to be but it is believed that many of the bodies that were buried there still rest beneath the water's surface.

But do they rest in peace? Many believe that they do not. Dating back to the late 1800s, Alton residents began avoiding the island because of the rumors of ghosts who wandered through the rocks and trees. Such stories are still told today. Many who walk along the shoreline claim that they have seen and heard the spectral occupants of Sunflower Island. Perhaps they are still searching for the spot where their bodies were once buried.

The penitentiary was closed down after the war and abandoned, despite a brief effort to once again have it used as a state facility. The walls around the prison yard were torn down between 1870 and 1875 and most of the stone was hauled off for use in other projects, including the Big Arch Railroad Bridge. A large number of stones from the walls were crushed and used to pave the streets of Crystal City, Missouri. The area where the prison yard was located was turned into a public park and playground called Uncle Remus Park, in honor of the fictional narrator of a collection of folktales created by post-Reconstruction Southern author Joel Chandler Harris.

During this time, though, the walls of the main prison building remained standing, and whenever Alton residents needed stone for any sort of minor construction, they would bring a wagon to the old prison and load up some of the already cut stones. By the 1940s, only scattered pieces of the prison buildings remained and the last section was finally moved in 1973 and rebuilt along nearby William Street as a monument to the past. The area where the prison once stood is now a public parking lot. Today, only a small portion of the wall still remains on the site of the penitentiary, where visitors can find historical information and displays about the prison and the Civil War.

As the years have passed, the old Alton Penitentiary has become the source of a number of ghostly legends around the area. The reason for this is simple: The events of the past are what create the hauntings of today. This is especially true when it comes to sites associated with death, brutality and tragedy. The Alton prison is a perfect example of all three. For years, the area where the prison once stood has been the scene of ghostly reports, both before the site was turned into a parking lot and after.

When the war ended, the prison building was returned to the state of Illinois but the city of Alton took charge of tearing down the other buildings on the site and removing them. The prison yard was turned into a public park in the 1870s and people from all over the city came there to listen to music, play games and to picnic - perhaps never even considering the dark history beneath their feet. In those days, the old prison building remained on the back of the lot, slowly crumbling into ruin. As one might imagine, the temptation of the spooky place proved too much for some visitors to resist, and many of them engaged in explorations of the now-empty corridors, abandoned cells and deserted staircases. However, these visitors were soon to learn that the old prison was not as "empty" as they first believed. Soon, tales began to be told about ghostly voices, strange sounds, screams and cries and eerie weeping and moaning that came from places where no living person could be found. On many occasions, curiosity-seekers told of looking through the prison in search of injured people or lost children, believing that the weird noises came from someone trapped inside. On every occasion, they found no one was there. The disturbing tales continued for decades, up until the time that the remainder of the prison was finally demolished.

In addition to the sounds, people also spoke of seeing the spectral images of former prisoners still wandering about on the property. These figures had the chilling habit of vanishing without a trace when approached or confronted. Even turning the old prison yard into a parking lot seemed to have had little effect on them. They have continued to be seen, even in recent years, when reports have emerged of men in ragged clothing seen stumbling across the empty lot.

The Alton Penitentiary is a disturbing example of how memories from the past continue to be experienced in the present. Death was a constant possibility for the men who were incarcerated at this place and history has chosen to remind us of this grim fact through the hauntings that continue to linger to this day.

ANDERSONVILLE
Sumter County, Georgia

The camp that would become the worst hellhole prison camp of the Confederacy had originally been intended merely to provide some relief for the city of Richmond. The city was already experiencing a food shortage in 1863 and after General Grant ended prisoner exchanges and paroles, the people of Richmond found themselves with many more Federal prisoners than they could possibly feed. No one could have predicted that it would become the Civil War's greatest example of man's inhumanity to man. Also known as Camp Sumter, the prison camp was so notorious for its brutal treatment of Union prisoners that to this day, the very mention of the name "Andersonville" can send shudders down the spine of any military history buff.

And so does the name of the camp's commander, Captain Henry Wirz, who was arrested after the war for "conspiring to impair the lives of Union prisoners of war." His two-month trial was a newspaper sensation and ended in his being sentenced to death. To the bitter end, Wirz protested his innocence, but to no avail. He was hanged on November 10, 1865, but as many have claimed, this was not the end of him.

Some say his ghost has never left the place of death and torture for which he took the blame.

In 1863, Confederate General John H. Winder sent his son, Captain W. Sidney Winder, to scout out a location for a new prison in Georgia. He discovered what he believed was the perfect site around November 24. The parcel of land was located deep in the heart of the Confederacy, and was far removed from attack. It was also a site where food would be abundant. Confederate officials planned a new prison on the property to be called Camp Sumter. It would contain a number of barracks, which were designed to hold between eight and ten thousand men.

The site Captain Winder chose was in southwestern Georgia, along Station Number 8 of the Georgia Southwestern Railroad. Because of this, it would be easily accessible by train. A local resident named Benjamin Dykes, who owned a sawmill and gristmill, offered a parcel of land for the prison which was extremely convenient for Dykes, since the Army would be forced to buy his wood and grain for the prison construction and for food for the prisoners . The piece of land was heavily wooded with pine and oak and the ground sloped down on both sides of a wide stream.

Orders were given from Richmond to start construction, but the local people were violently opposed to the prison being located so close to them, so much so that labor was impossible to find. Work was delayed for some time before finally, soldiers were forced to commandeer slaves from nearby farms.

Just as construction of the prison compound was getting started, conditions in the South made it impossible to build barracks for the prisoners. Rail lines and distribution centers were greatly stressed by the war, so out of desperation, the government ordered that a simple stockade be erected around the compound as quickly as possible. This work began in January. Trees were felled and then stood on end to form a large fence around the camp, enclosing an area of just over sixteen acres. Only two trees were left standing inside the compound itself.

On February 25, 1864, the first 600 prisoners arrived from Libby Prison in Richmond. One wall of the stockade was still not completed when they arrived. Confederate artillery pieces were trained on the opening until the wall was completed. Just shortly before the first prisoners' arrival, the camp's first commander, Colonel Alexander W. Persons, took over his duties. He continued to serve until June 17, when he was replaced by General Winder. In March, the camp's most infamous commandant, Captain Henry Wirz, arrived at Andersonville.

Heinrich Hartmann Wirz was born in Zurich, Switzerland, in 1822. He graduated from college in Zurich and then went on to medical school in Paris and at the University of Berlin, receiving two doctor of medicine degrees. In

1849, following the failed revolutions of 1848 in the German states, he emigrated to the United States and settled in Kentucky, where he married and established a medical practice.

When the Civil War began, Wirz enlisted as a private in the Louisiana Volunteers. At the Battle of Seven Pines, in May 1862, he was badly wounded and lost the use of his right arm. The Army found work for him, though, promoting him and placing him at prisons in Alabama and then in Richmond. Eventually, he was assigned to the staff of General Winder, the man in charge of Confederate prison camps, and ended up at the village of Andersonville in Sumter County, Georgia.

From the very first, there was no organized arrangement for the compound. The prisoners had simply been put in the stockade and then left to themselves. Many of the prisoners who were transferred from other camps were in horrible condition when they arrived, infested with disease and vermin, which quickly spread to the other men.

The first arrivals at the camp had built huts within the compound, using pieces of scrap lumber that had been left within the stockade. Later arrivals lived in tents or in holes they dug in the ground and covered over with blankets or scraps of cloth. In July 1864, the stockade was enlarged to accommodate more men, and within a week, the camp's population had risen to 29,000. Less than a month later, it would rise again to its highest point of more than 33,000. Bizarrely, Andersonville technically became the fifth largest "city" in the Confederacy.

As time progressed and the stockade became more crowded, food rations began to dwindle. The first staple to vanish was salt, followed by sweet potatoes, which had once been plentiful in the region. In time, the authorities reduced the amount of cornmeal handed out and later, meat was eliminated altogether. The rations continued to decrease and soon they were not even handed out every day. On one occasion, when the bread wagon entered the stockade to make a delivery, it was mobbed by the inmates and all of the bread was stolen. Captain Wirz responded by canceling all further rations for the day. According to some prisoners, the more sadistic guards usually those of the 55th Georgia would toss chunks of cornbread into the pen, just to watch the men scramble and fight over them.

Many of the prisoners began to devise ways to capture low-flying birds, which swarmed about the stockade in the evenings. The swallows that were snared were often eaten raw, such was the hunger of the starving men.

Security precautions at the prison camp became almost as legendary as the horrible conditions. The two regiments of Georgia and Alabama troops who guarded the camp were assisted by a battalion of cavalry and a large pack of savage bloodhounds. These dogs had been used before the war to track down runaway slaves and they now were being used to bring back any escaped Federal prisoners.

Conditions at Andersonville

Despite the ferocity of the bloodhounds, there were still three hundred and twenty-nine successful escapes from Andersonville during the fifteen months when the camp was in use. Most of them took place during work details, although the very first attempt occurred within a week of the camp's opening. A group of fifteen men managed to scale the east wall, using ropes made from woven pieces of cloth. All of them were recaptured, thanks to the dogs, but the attempt caused the establishment of the "deadline" within the stockade. This deadline was a boundary that was erected inside the stockade walls, made by placing a rail of pine logs about twenty-five feet inside and parallel to the walls. Guards sitting in "pigeon roosts" located every ninety feel along the wall were ordered to fire without warning if a prisoner crossed, or even touched, the line.

Soon, word got in the Northern press about the Andersonville deadline and it became infamous. The newspapers railed about the savagery of the Southern prisons and the barbaric design of the deadline. At war's end, it would even be publicly condemned by the Union government. The problem was that, despite all of the public posturing, the Federal condemnation of the deadline was sheer hypocrisy. All stockade-type prisons had some sort of deadline for security, including the Federal ones. This fact was hidden from the American public until after the war, when Confederate prisoners returned home. It is ironic that while the American press was fulminating against the deadline at Andersonville, Confederate prisoners were being shot for crossing the same sort of lines in places like Camp Hoffman, Rock Island, Camp Douglas, and other spots.

Once the deadline was established, tunneling became the preferred method of escape. With the digging came many problems. Every tunnel required a huge amount of secrecy and in a situation where thousands of men were packed into a stockade, privacy was hard to find and, as with most prisons, Andersonville had its share of informants.

In one well-known situation, in May 1864, the commandant entered the camp with a squad of guards, searching for escape tunnels. One prisoner, thinking that he might get special treatment for informing on his comrades, told the commander about a tunnel that was under construction. The Confederates punished the prisoners involved and forced them to fill in the escape route. That night, the informant was nearly beaten to death by other prisoners. He was pursued through the night and into the next morning and finally, he crossed over the deadline and called for protection from the guards. He was sure that he had earned it because of the assistance that he had given them. Instead, they shot him for crossing the deadline.

Soon, escapes grew more innovative. There were so many dead men being carried out of the camp that little attention was paid to them. When a prisoner died, he was placed in front of his tent and then carried away by a detail of other prisoners. Several quick-thinking men pretended to be dead and were carried outside the gate, then placed in a pile to await burial. As soon as darkness fell, they would escape. This plan was successful a number of times before Captain Wirz got wind of it and changed the burial policy. After that, all of the bodies were left inside the stockade until a surgeon could examine them.

There were certainly many opportunities for escape using this method, since death was no stranger to the camp. The main causes of death were scurvy, dysentery, typhoid, smallpox, gangrene and diarrhea but outright murder became commonplace as well. In fact, the murder of prisoners by guards, and even by other prisoners, became a daily occurrence.

Among the prisoners were groups of men referred to as "raiders." These groups ruled the stockade using fear and retaliation against any who opposed them. They preyed on the other inmates, taking food and belongings from them and even beating and killing anyone who crossed them. The largest and most vicious of the raider groups was led by William Collins of the 88th Pennsylvania Regiment. His men dominated not only the other prisoners, but the other raid as well, looting and murdering as they saw fit.

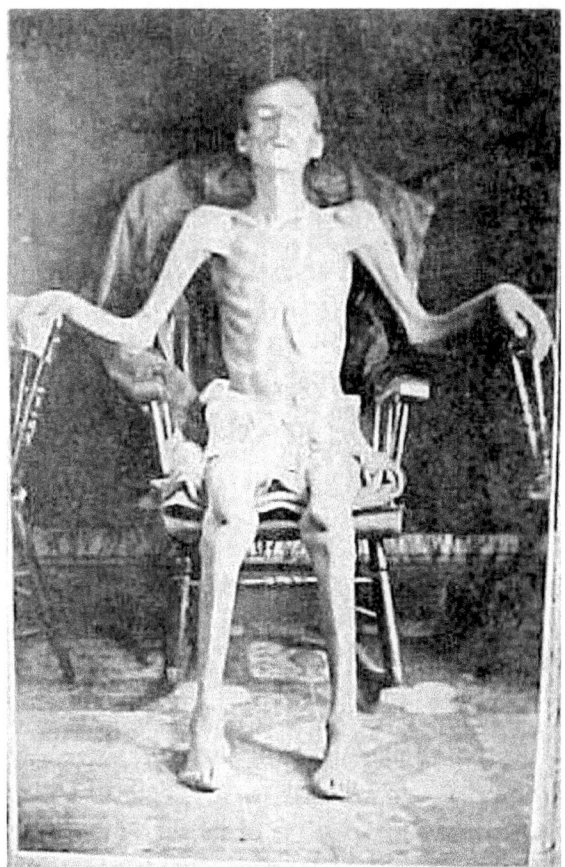

A survivor of the horrors of Andersonville

Finally, a group of prisoners banded together and they somehow obtained aid from the commandant. He allowed them to take matters into their own hands and they arrested the raiders. A military trial was held and twenty-four of the raiders were punished, with six of them hanged. Three of the other eighteen men later died from retaliatory beatings.

In the years that have passed since the closing of Andersonville, and the end of the war, the ghosts of the raiders have been blamed for most of the strange happenings in the area. This is perhaps merely legend, but many have claimed the raiders to be responsible for numerous weird events. The odd sights and sounds include apparitions of soldiers around the location of the former camp, the sounds of groans and echoing voices, and the sound of what seems to be a number of men tramping about the site of the former camp.

By September 1864, the majority of the prisoners had been transferred out of Andersonville due to Union activity in the area and because of the Northern occupation of Atlanta. In the weeks that followed, it was reported that as many as six thousand prisoners were sent to other camps. Those who were too weak or sick to travel remained behind, leaving just over eight thousand men in the camp. A huge number of those prisoners died in October, so by November just over thirteen hundred men were left.

In October, General Winder was transferred out and Colonel George C. Gibbs arrived to assume command of Andersonville. From that point, the camp took the role of a convalescent prison. As soon as the prisoners gained enough strength to travel, they were transferred to other facilities for a short time. The remaining Andersonville prisoners were paroled in May 1865.

This brought an end to the history of the Civil War's most notorious prison camp. Or did it?

To this day, the ghost of Henry Wirz is believed to haunt the site of Andersonville prison.

Legend has it that the ghost was also rumored to have haunted the Old Brick Capitol in Washington for a number of years but apparently, his spirit returned to the place of his greatest notoriety. Some believe that it may be Wirz's ghost that has been seen walking along the road near the site of the old camp. They believe that his spirit does not rest because of the terrible blot on his reputation that came about after the war. Captain Wirz always insisted that he was unjustly accused of crimes committed at Andersonville. He went to the gallows claiming his innocence. But was he?

Wirz was never a popular officer, even before his arrival at Andersonville. He was disliked by nearly everyone, including his subordinates and his own staff. He was especially hated and ridiculed by the prisoners for his heavy accent and overbearing personality.

In 1864, Wirz was sent to Andersonville as the commandant and continued in service there until after Lee's surrender. At that time, he turned over the camp to Union General J.H. Wilson and ended his career in the Confederate military. A short time later, he was placed under arrest by Captain Henry E. Noyes and charged with misconduct against Union prisoners at Andersonville. Wirz protested the arrest, stating that conditions at the prison had been beyond his control. He begged his captors to allow him to leave and take his family to

Europe. Instead, he was taken to Washington and officially charged with "impairing the health and destroying the lives of prisoners."

The arrest of Wirz was part of a much wider response to the American thirst for revenge against the Confederacy. It was believed that by arresting Wirz, the government might be able to placate the public. Whether Wirz was responsible for all of the horrors of the camp, though, was questionable. There was no question that terrible suffering took place at Andersonville and little doubt that Wirz was a harsh and possibly sadistic commander. However, Southern contemporary accounts insisted that he did the best job possible under extreme conditions. There was no question that Andersonville was the South's most impoverished and overcrowded prison. There are many today who believe that Wirz was nothing more than a scapegoat for the poor condition of the Confederate prisons and a victim of the post-war backlash against the South.

The trial of Henry Wirz began in August of 1865, ending a three-and-a-half month feeding frenzy by the press. While the former captain waited in jail, the Northern newspapers had already tried and convicted him many times over. He had been portrayed as a monster who maliciously sent scores of Union soldiers to their deaths.

Attorneys for the federal government began their case against Wirz, presenting evidence in the form of records, documents and testimony from former prisoners and from Union officers who had inspected the camp after its surrender. The witnesses were not always reliable, as several of them stated that they had seen Wirz "strike, kick and shoot prisoners" in August 1864, during a time when the commandant was absent from the camp on sick leave.

Of all the testimony, perhaps the most damaging came from a man named Felix de la Baume, who claimed to be a nephew of the Revolutionary War hero, General Lafayette. He spent several hours on the witness stand describing the defendant's cruel treatment of prisoners and his total disregard for the nightmarish conditions of the camp. Baume's testimony appeared in newspapers across the country and in the end, it sealed Wirz's fate. Baume was rewarded for his testimony with a position in the Interior Department. After the trial, it was learned that he had been a deserter from the Union Army and was not descended from General Lafayette.

On November 6, 1865, Wirz was condemned to death. Not long before his sentence was carried out, a secret emissary from the War Department offered him a reprieve in exchange for a statement that would convict Jefferson Davis of conspiracy to murder prisoners. Wirz refused.

Henry Wirz was hanged in the yard of the Old Brick Capitol on November 10, 1865. He was the only Confederate officer to be convicted and executed for war crimes. He maintained his innocence and was defiant until the very end.

As he said to the officer in charge of directing his hanging, "I know what orders are, Major. I am being hung for obeying them."

Was Captain Wirz ultimately responsible for the horrific conditions at Andersonville? Was he to blame for the deaths of thousands of Union soldiers? The question remains unanswered, but it seems that his spirit remains behind to try and restore his reputation. There is little doubt in the minds of witnesses that the apparition that they have seen pacing through the site of the former prison camp is that of the infamous prison commander. The officer in the neat gray uniform is, like Wirz, ruggedly handsome, with a short beard and the hat that the commander always wore. Often he wanders the grounds, restless and looking inconsolable, shaking his head or talking silently, yet wildly animated, to himself. On other occasions, he is seen standing in place, by the road or in the stockade area, a mute reminder of his possible innocence.

ALCATRAZ
San Francisco, California

"The Rock," the name given to Alcatraz Penitentiary, was the ultimate American prison. It was the end of the line for scores of the country's worst criminal offenders, bloodletters, badmen and escape artists but it began its history as a military prison. However, it gained its greatest infamy during the twenty-nine years that the damp, fog-enshrouded prison, located on a small island in San Francisco Bay, kept America's most notorious lawbreakers away from the rest of the world. The heavy mist, the cold wind, the freezing water and ominous foghorns made Alcatraz the loneliest of prisons. During its almost three decades as a federal prison, its steel doors clanged shut on more than a thousand convicts. It was a place of almost total punishment and minimum privilege. Those who survived Alcatraz often did so at the cost of their sanity -- and in some cases, their souls.

Alcatraz Island, located in the mist off the coast of San Francisco, received its name in 1775 when the Spanish explorers charted San Francisco Bay. They named the rocky piece of land La Isla de los Alcatraces, or the Island of Pelicans. The island was totally uninhabited, plagued by barren ground, scarce vegetation and surrounding water that churned with swift currents. In the late 1840s, the island was taken over by the U.S. military. It was a prime location for the establishment of a fort and a lighthouse was desperately needed there because of the many ships that were coming to San Francisco during the Gold Rush. Topographical engineers began conducting geological surveys and by 1853, work was started on a military fortress. One year later, a lighthouse was established the first on the Pacific Coast to guide ships through the Golden Gate.

Alcatraz as a military prison in its early days

A few years later, a military fort was erected on the island and in 1859, Alcatraz saw its first prisoners, a contingent of court-martialed, military convicts. Then in 1861, Alcatraz started to receive Confederate prisoners, thanks to its natural isolation created by the surrounding waters. Until the end of the Civil War, the prison population varied, consisting of soldiers, Confederate privateers and Southern sympathizers. They were confined in the dark basement of the guardhouse and conditions were grim. The men slept side by side, head to toe, lying on the stone floor of the basement. There was no running water, no heat and no latrines. Disease and infestations of lice spread quickly and not surprisingly, overcrowding was a serious problem. Prisoners were often bound by six-foot chains attached to heavy iron balls, fed bread and water and confined in sweatboxes as punishment.

After the war ended, the fort was deemed obsolete and was no longer needed. The prison continued to be used, though, and soon, more buildings and cell houses were added. In the 1870s and 1880s, Indian chiefs and tribal leaders who refused to give in to the white man were incarcerated on Alcatraz. They shared quarters with the worst of the military prisoners. The island became a shipping point for incorrigible deserters, thieves, rapists and repeated escapees.

In 1898, the Spanish-American War sent the prisoner population soaring from fewer than one hundred to over four hundred and fifty. The Rock became a holding pen for Spanish prisoners brought over from the Philippines. Around 1900, Alcatraz again became a disciplinary barracks for military prisoners. Ironically, it also served as a health resort for soldiers returning from the Philippines and Cuba with tropical diseases. The overcrowding caused by a combination of criminals and recovering soldiers resulted in pardons to reduce the number of men housed on the island.

By 1902, the Alcatraz prison population averaged around five hundred men per year, with many of the men serving sentences of two years or less. The wooden barracks on the island had fallen into a ramshackle state, thanks to the damp, salt air so in 1904, work was begun to modernize the facility. Prisoner work crews began extending the stockade wall and constructing a new mess hall, kitchen, shops, a library and a washhouse. Work continued on the prison for the next several years and even managed to survive the Great Earthquake of 1906. The disaster left San Francisco in shambles and a large fissure opened up on Alcatraz, but the buildings were untouched. Prisoners from the heavily damaged San Francisco jail were temporarily housed on the island until the city's jail could be rebuilt.

Construction of the new buildings was completed a few years later and, in 1911, the facility was officially named the "United States Disciplinary Barracks." In addition to Army prisoners, the Rock was also used to house seamen captured on German vessels during the First World War. Alcatraz was the Army's first long-term prison and it quickly gained a reputation for being a tough facility. There were strict rules and regulations with punishments ranging from loss of privileges to solitary confinement, restricted diet and hard labor. Especially violent or defiant prisoners were fitted with a twelve-pound ball and ankle chain.

Despite the stringent rules, Alcatraz was still mainly a minimum-security facility. Inmates were given various work assignments, depending on how trustworthy they were. Many of them worked as general servants, cooking and cleaning for families of soldiers housed on the island. In many cases, the prisoners were even entrusted to care for the children of officers. However, this lack of security led to a number of attempted escapes. Most of those who tried for freedom never made it to the mainland and were forced to turn back. Many others were never seen again. They had either reached the shore or had drowned in the cold waters of the bay.

During the 1920s, Alcatraz gradually fell into disuse. The lighthouse keeper, a few Army personnel and the most hardened of the military prisoners were the only ones who remained on the island. The mostly empty buildings slowly crumbled but this period would not last for long. A change was coming to Alcatraz that would make it the most formidable prison in American history and earn it the nickname of "America's Devil's Island."

The social upheaval that began during Prohibition and continued into the Great Depression brought new life to Alcatraz. President Roosevelt and the newly empowered FBI began a national "War on Crime" to deal with the gangsters, kidnappers and bandits that were terrorizing the country. Attorney

General Homer Cummings supported J. Edgar Hoover and the FBI in creating a new, escape-proof prison that would strike fear into the hearts of criminals. They decided that Alcatraz would be the perfect location for such a penitentiary. In 1933, the facility was officially turned over to the Federal Bureau of Prisons and the attorney general asked James A. Johnston of San Francisco to take over as warden of the new prison. He implemented a strict set and rules and regulations for the facility and selected the best available guards and officers from the federal penal system.

After being used as a military prison for many years, Alcatraz re-opened for the worst prisoners in the federal penitentiary system.

The Rock became largely Warden Johnston's creation. New construction was started on the project and practically the entire cellblock building was built atop the old Army fort. Part of the old Army prison was used but the iron bars were replaced by bars of hardened steel. Gun towers were erected at various points around the island and the cellblocks were equipped with catwalks, electric locks, metal detectors, a well-stocked arsenal, barbed and cyclone wire fencing and even tear gas containers that were fitted into the ceiling of the dining hall and elsewhere. Apartments for the guards and their families were built on the old parade grounds and the lighthouse keeper's mansion was taken over for the warden's residence. Alcatraz had been turned into an impregnable fortress.

Wardens from prisons all over the country were polled and were permitted to send their most incorrigible inmates to The Rock. These included convicts with behavioral problems, those with a history of escape attempts and even high-profile inmates who were receiving extra privileges because of their status or notoriety. Each train that came from the various prisons seemed to have a "celebrity" on board. Among the first groups were Al Capone, Doc Barker, George "Machine Gun" Kelly, Robert Stroud who would later become notorious as the Birdman of Alcatraz , Bonnie and Clyde's driver Floyd Hamilton and kidnapper Alvin Karpis. When each of these men arrived on Alcatraz, they ceased to exist as the colorful characters they once were and simply became numbers.

When Warden Johnston conceived of the idea behind Alcatraz prison, he did not even pay lip service to the principle of rehabilitation. This was a place of punishment, plain and simple, and nothing that these men had done or accomplished in the past mattered now. Inside, there would be no rewards for good behavior, it was simply expected and demanded. There were no perks for trustees, only punishment for breaking the rules. Johnston believed that a policy of maximum security, combined with few privileges and total isolation would serve as a deterrent to America's public enemies and those who emulated them. In the end, though, The Rock would be no more of a deterrent than the electric chair, the hangman or the gas chamber. In fact, despite the propaganda coming from the attorney general's office, comparatively few big-time gangsters were ever sent to Alcatraz. There were not enough of them who were captured alive to fill the cells. The felon that the FBI called a "notorious mail robber" was more likely to be a small-time loser who broke into some postal boxes. Unbelievably, some inmates were first-time offenders. If the new prison profited anyone, it was the wardens who were able to empty some of their overcrowded cells to populate Alcatraz. No court could sentence criminals to Alcatraz. Only those already serving terms could be transferred there, if the warden recommended it and the Bureau of Prisons approved.

Alcatraz was a brutal place of penitence, as the Quakers who had devised the American prison system intended all prisons to be. It was a place where the inmates had only five rights: food, clothing, a private cell, medical care and a shower once each week. Any, and all, of those rights could be taken away for even a minor infraction.

Each of the cells in Alcatraz measured four by eight feet and had a single fold-up bunk, toilet, desk, chair and a sink. A prisoner's day began at 6:30 a.m. with the clanging of a bell and the glare of bright electric lights. He had twenty minutes in which to dress and make his bed. If he wanted to shave, he had to shove a matchbox through the bars of his cell. A guard would place a razor blade in it and allow three minutes before returning to reclaim it. At 6:50 a.m. the bell sounded again and the floor guard took the morning count. A third bell would clang when all prisoners were accounted for. A fourth bell sounded when it was time for breakfast. The turnkeys, standing inside locked cages, pulled back a lever and all of the heavy steel cell door locks opened simultaneously. The prisoners then marched in a single-file line to the mess hall. The prisoners ate ten men to a table, with the black prisoners segregated. They all sat facing the same direction and all of them ate in silence. The first years of Alcatraz were known as the "silent years" and during this period, the rules stated that no prisoner was allowed to speak to another, sing, hum or whistle. Talking was forbidden in the cells, in the mess hall and even in the showers. The inmates were allowed to talk for three minutes during the morning and afternoon recreation yard periods and for two hours on weekends. This rule of silence was later relaxed.

The food was served cafeteria-style from a steam table. Bad food had caused more prison riots than anything else in history so Warden Johnston was determined to serve three palatable meals each day. Typical breakfast fare consisted of oatmeal with milk, fried bologna sausage, cottage fried potatoes, toast with margarine and coffee. Prisoners were required to clean their plates and if they did not, they received no food the following day. Johnston also issued three packs of cigarettes each week, and for heavy smokers, he installed tobacco and paper dispensers in each cell so that inmates could roll their own. However, he did not approve a commissary, as most prisons had, where the men could buy items like candy, chewing gum and soda pop with the few cents they earned each day in the prison workshops.

After breakfast, the prisoners were lined up again and marched back to their cells for another count. No prisoner was allowed to wear a watch. Bells told the time and they rang almost every half hour for one reason or another. After the next count, prisoners were lined up again according to their assigned workshop. Aside from breaks and lunch, the prisoners worked for most of the day, until 9:30 p.m. when the lights were turned out. The methodical routine never varied, except on Saturday and Sunday. On Sunday mornings, time was allowed for religious worship and on Saturday, the men were allowed their weekly shower. Both days offered two hours of free time for exercising in the yard or pursuing indoor hobbies.

In their cells, before lights out, prisoners could read books or magazines borrowed from the prison library, but to intensify their isolation, Johnston denied them newspapers and radios. Correspondence was also severely limited. A prisoner could write one letter a week to his family and receive no more than three. He could correspond with no one outside of his family except for his lawyer. Censors read all incoming and outgoing mail, deleted any part of it that did not confine itself to family affairs, and sent a typed copy of what remained. There were no set visiting days. Each monthly visit, limited to 45 minutes, had to be arranged through Johnston. A pass would be issued to the visitors and instructions given on where and when to board the boat to the island. A sheet of plate glass, which ran from floor to ceiling, separated the visitors from the inmates. At head level were two strips of steel, a few inches apart, which had small holes drilled into them. Visitors and prisoners could speak through these holes but they were designed to be so small that nothing could be passed through them. Guards were also present and could hear every word that was exchanged. They interrupted if forbidden topics were broached.

The guards at Alcatraz were almost as hardened as the prisoners themselves. There was one guard for every three inmates, which was stunning considering that most prisons assigned about one guard to every twelve inmates. Gun galleries had been placed at each end of the cellblocks and as many as twelve counts each day allowed the guards to keep very close tabs on the men on their watch. Because of the small number of inmates at Alcatraz, the guards generally knew each man by name. Although Warden Johnston forbid corporal punishment as a general rule, the guards did not hesitate, when met with any resistance, to knock a man senseless with water from a high pressure hose, break and arm or a leg with their clubs, or truss a prisoner up for days in a straitjacket. What was more usual, though, was solitary confinement in the punishment cells. While the cells in which the prisoners lived were barren at best, they must have seemed like luxury hotel rooms compared to the punishment cells. Here, the men were stripped of all but their basic right to food and even then, what they were served barely sustained the convict's life, let alone his health.

One place of punishment was the single strip cell, which was dubbed the "Oriental." This dark, steel-encased compartment had no toilet and no sink. There was only a hole in the floor that could be flushed from the outside. Inmates were placed in the Oriental with no clothing and were given little food. The cell had a standard set of bars, with an expanded opening to pass food through, but a solid steel door enclosed the prisoner in total darkness. Men were usually kept in this cell for one or two days. It was cold and completely bare, save for a straw-filled mattress that the guards removed each morning. This cell was used as punishment for the most severe violations and was feared by the prison population.

The "Hole" was a similar type of cell. There were several of them and they were all located on the bottom tier of cells and were considered to be a severe punishment by the inmates. Mattresses were again taken away and prisoners were given only bread and water, supplemented by a solid meal every third day. Steel doors also closed these cells off from the daylight, although a low-wattage bulb was suspended from the ceiling. Inmates could spend up to nineteen days there, completely silent and isolated from everyone. Time in the Hole usually meant psychological and sometimes even physical torture. Usually, convicts who were thrown into the Hole for anything other than a minor infraction were beaten by the guards. The screams from the men being beaten in one of the four Holes located on the bottom tier of D Block echoed throughout the block as though being amplified through a megaphone. Sometimes when men emerged from the darkness and isolation of the Hole, they would be totally disoriented and would end up in the prison's hospital ward, devoid of their sanity. Others came out with pneumonia and arthritis after spending days or weeks on the cold cement floor with no clothing.

And there were even worse places to be sent than the Hole. Located in front of unused A Block was a staircase that led down to a large steel door. Behind the door were catacomb-like corridors and stone archways that led to the sealed-off gun ports from the days when Alcatraz was a fort. Fireplaces located in several of the rooms were used to heat up cannonballs so that they would start fires after reaching their targets. Two of the other rooms located in this dank, underground area were dungeons. Prisoners who had the misfortune of being placed in the dungeons were not only locked in, but also chained to the walls. Their screams could not be heard in the main prison. Their only toilet was a bucket, which was emptied once each week. For food, they received two cups of water and one slice of bread each day. Every third day, they would receive a regular meal. The men were stripped of their clothing and their dignity as guards chained them to the wall in a standing position from morning until night, when they were given a blanket to sleep on. Thankfully, the dungeons were rarely used, but the dark cells of D Block, also known as the Hole, were regularly filled.

Alcatraz could test the limits of men's endurance, both physically and mentally. Over the years, a number of inmates attempted suicide, and a few succeeded. Those who failed always wound up in the Hole. A counterfeiter named John Standig tried to kill himself before he even got to Alcatraz by jumping from the train that was taking him there, but he survived. At the prison, he told a fellow inmate, "If you ever get out of here, tell them I wasn't trying to escape. I was trying to kill myself." He then began climbing one of the fences and was shot to death on the spot. An inmate named Jimmy Grove, a former soldier imprisoned after raping an officer's daughter, was saved by a blood transfusion after he cut the arteries in both of his arms. In April 1936, a prisoner named Joe Bowers was taken to the Hole after his broke his eyeglasses and tried to cut his throat with the glass. When he was released from solitary, he scaled the fence surrounding the work area, knowing that the guards would shoot him. They did, and his body fell seventy-five feet into the water of the bay below. Ed Wutke, a former merchant marine who was serving twenty-seven years for murder at sea, was found dead in his cell one day after severing his jugular vein with the blade from a pencil sharpener.

In 1937 alone, fourteen of the prisoners went insane and that does not include the men who slowly became "stir crazy" from the brutal conditions of the place. To Warden Johnston, mental illness was nothing more than an excuse to get out of work. If a man was capable of functioning physically, without disruption to the general population, his madness was ignored. If he was uncontrollable, he was confined to the hospital ward. A consulting psychiatrist visited the island at irregular intervals but offered little help to the inmates. One prisoner from Leavenworth screamed every time an airplane flew over the island. Another kept his head wrapped in towels to protect him from invisible assailants. Another one, nicknamed "Rabbit," was a docile prisoner until he scooped up every object in his third-tier cell, wrapped them in a bundle, and then hurled it over the railing when his cell door was opened. He was dragged clawing and howling to the medical ward and never returned to the cellblocks.

And then there was prisoner No. 284, Rube Persefal. A former gangster and bank robber, Persefal was assigned to work on the dock detail. One day, he picked up a hatchet, placed his left hand on a block of wood and while laughing maniacally, began hacking off the fingers on his hand. Then, he placed his right hand on the block and pleaded with a guard to chop off those fingers, as well. Persefal was placed in the hospital, but was never declared insane.

In 1941, inmate Henry Young went on trial for the murder of fellow prisoner Rufas McCain, his accomplice in a failed escape attempt. The two men, along with three other inmates - Doc Barker, William Martin and Dale Stamphill - had slipped out of the prison on the foggy night of January 13, 1939. An alarm sounded and the men were discovered on the beach trying to fabricate a crude raft. Two of the men started to flee and guards fired, killing Barker and wounding Stamphill. Young and McCain surrendered and were kept in solitary for almost a year. After they were returned to their cells in November 1940, the two argued on several occasions. McCain was assigned to the tailor shop and Young to the furniture shop, located directly downstairs. On December 3, Young waited until just after a prisoner count and then, when a guard's attention was diverted, he ran downstairs and stabbed McCain. The other man went into shock and he died five hours later. Young refused to say why he had done it.

Young's attorney was able to explain, however. During the trial that followed, his attorney claimed that, because of the terrible conditions at the prison, Young could not be held responsible for his actions. He stated that the guards frequently beat his client and that he had endured long periods of extreme isolation. This cruel and inhumane treatment had caused Young to become insane and his responses to hostile situations had become desperately violent. The attorney literally put Alcatraz itself on trial. He subpoenaed Warden Johnston to testify about the prison's conditions and policies and in addition, several inmates were also called to recount the state of their daily lives at Alcatraz. The prisoners told of being locked in the dungeons and of being beaten by the guards. They also testified to knowing several inmates who had gone insane because of such treatment. The jury ended up sympathizing with Young and he was convicted of a manslaughter charge that only added a few years onto his original sentence.

After the trial, Young was transferred to the Medical Center for Federal Prisoners in Springfield, Missouri. After serving his federal sentence, he was sent to the Washington State Penitentiary and was paroled in 1972. He had spent nearly forty years in prison. After his release, Young vanished into history and whatever became of him is unknown.

Al Capone arrived at the prison in August 1934. Upon his arrival, he quickly learned that while he may have been famous in the outside world, on Alcatraz, he was only a number. He made attempts to flaunt the power that he had enjoyed at the federal prison in Atlanta, where he was used to the special benefits that he was awarded by guards and wardens alike. He was arrogant and unlike most of the other prisoners, was not a veteran of the penal system. He had only spent a short time in prison and his stay had been much different than that of most other cons. Capone had possessed the ability to control his environment through wealth and power, but he was soon to learn that things were much different at Alcatraz.

It was deprivation of news from the outside world that led to Capone's first punishment. He spent a full nineteen days in the Hole for attempting to bribe a guard to bring him a newspaper. He also did two ten-day stretches for talking to other inmates when the rule of silence was in effect. Each time that Capone was sent to the Hole, he emerged a little the worse for wear. He was soon beaten down by the brutal prison system and was even forced to defend several attempts on his life. These attempts, the days of silence, trips to the Hole, grinding daily routine and likely what was, by now, an advanced case of syphilis began to take their toll on Capone. Eventually, he stopped going into the recreation yard, opting to practice his banjo instead. Once practice was over, he returned immediately to his cell, avoiding all of the inmates except for a few of his closest friends. Occasionally, guards reported that he would refuse to leave his cell to go to the mess hall and eat. They would often find him crouched down in the corner of his cell like an animal. On other occasions, he would mumble to himself or babble in baby talk or simply sit on his bed and strum little tunes on the banjo. Years later, another inmate recalled that Capone would sometimes stay in his cell and make his bunk over and over again.

Capone's mental health eventually fell apart and he spent his last days at Alcatraz in the hospital ward. His last day on Alcatraz was January 6, 1939. He was then transferred to the new federal prison at Terminal Island near Los Angeles. When he was paroled, he became a recluse at his Palm Island, Florida, estate and died in 1947.

During the twenty-nine years that Alcatraz was in operation, there were over fourteen escape attempts in which thirty-four men risked their lives to try and make it off The Rock. Almost all of the men were either killed or recaptured. Only one man was known to have made it ashore. John Paul Scott was recaptured when he was found shivering in the rocks near the Golden Gate Bridge. As for the men who vanished, it was believed that most of them succumbed to the cold water and the fast-moving currents that flowed past the island. Although no bodies were ever recovered, the authorities assumed that the escapees had drowned and marked the cases closed.

Of all of the escape attempts, two of them left a lasting mark on the history of the island. The most dramatic and violent took place in 1946 and was later dubbed the "Battle of Alcatraz." It began as an organized, carefully planned breakout from the "escape-proof" prison but it soon deteriorated into a bloody disaster about which one unknown prisoner left graffiti behind, etched into a steel bar, which simply read: "Hell broke loose - May 1946."

The accounts of what happened on Alcatraz in May 1946 vary in detail but May 2 marked the beginning of events that would lead to the deaths of two guards and three inmates. On that day, six inmates captured a gun cage, obtained prison keys and took over the D Block cell house in less than an hour. The breakout attempt might have succeeded if not for the fact that a guard named Bill Miller didn't return one of the keys to the gun cage as soon as he finished using it, as was required by prison regulations. This strange twist of fate completely disrupted the escape attempt. When the cons captured the gun cage, they found all of the keys except for the one that would let them out of the cell building. This was the key that Miller failed to return. The breakout was grounded before it even began.

But the prisoners, Bernard Coy, Joe Cretzer, and Marvin Hubbard, Sam Shockley, Miran Thompson, and Clarence Carnes, would not give up. Unable to get out of the cell house, they began trying to kill some of the tower guards and Coy succeeded in wounding one of the officers. As officers broke into the cell house, the inmates captured them and put them into two cells, 402 and 403 which were later changed to C-102 and C-104 . Half-crazed, Sam Shockley shouted,

"Kill all the sonsabitches! Kill the bastards! Kill them all! Don't leave any witnesses!"

Urged on by his fellow escapee, Joe Cretzer opened fire with one of the captured rifles, blasting wildly into the two cells. His shots critically wounded two officers, Miller and Corwin, wounded three other officers and left the others lying on the cold concrete floor, feigning death. They had no idea what the convicts would do next. Their inability to escape from the cell house had created a tense situation, leaving them trapped and desperate. They had no idea that, by this time, Miller had dropped the key that would let them out of the building into the toilet in cell 403.

Warden Johnston knew how serious the situation had become and he began organizing all of his back-up systems. Bureau of Prisons Director James V. Bennett received a teletype from Johnston that read:

Serious trouble. Convict has machine gun in cell house. Have issued riot call. Placed armed guards at strategic locations. Most of our officers are imprisoned in cell house. Cannot tell extent of injuries suffered by our officers or amount of damage done. Will give you more information later in the day when we get control.

J.A. Johnston, Warden

A radio message was sent to the Coast Guard and the San Francisco police, informing them of the trouble and asking that they swnd boats to form a perimeter around the island. All of the officers were called into duty and messages were sent to the press. As the story made headlines, thousands of spectators lined up to watch from the San Francisco waterfront as the police and Coast Guard boats began encircling the island. Dramatic headlines appeared in the newspapers and stories filled with rumors and exaggerations drew even bigger crowds on the mainland to watch events unfold on Alcatraz.

Other inmates in the facility were gathered and marched into the yard to be guarded, first, by Alcatraz guards, and then by U.S. Marines, who offered help by sending a detachment of men from a nearby base. Fear swelled on the island, not only among guards and officials, but also with the other inmates, who by their own choice did not want to be involved in what was going on. Once the alarms had sounded, everything began to happen very fast and the inmates knew there would be no careful selection of targets; all of them were in danger. Most of them had returned to their cells once the alarms had sounded, only to be marched into the yard a short time later. They were kept there all night before being taken into cellblock A. The inmates were cold, tired and hungry but most of all, they were scared. But they could not have been as terrified as the prisoners who had no part in the rebellion and yet were trapped inside the cell house with the six escapees. One inmate recalled, "They were more scared than anything else. They thought the whole place might go up in flames and smoke any minute. There was shrieking and cursing all night long."

The warden's main concern was to get to the guards who were being held hostage in cells 402 and 403. After that, he concentrated on isolating the armed prisoners. The guards, Marines and special personnel surrounded the building, keeping close aim on all of the doors and windows of the cellblock. Gas canisters were fired into the cells and rifle grenades were launched into D Block. One of them went off target, fell to the ground and started a grass fire. From San Francisco, it must have looked like Alcatraz was burning. The cellblock continued to be barraged with bullets, mortars and grenades. The helpless inmates inside the building took refuge behind water-soaked mattresses and tried to stay close to the floor and out of the path of the bullets that riddled the cells. But even after realizing that they could not get away, the six would-be escapees decided to fight it out.

The fighting lasted for two days. With no place to hide from the constant gunfire, Cretzer, Coy and Hubbard climbed into a utility corridor for safety. The other three men returned to their cells, hoping they would not be identified as participants in the attempt. They had no idea that one of the guards had scrawled their names on a cell wall.

In the bloody aftermath, Cretzer, Coy and Hubbard were killed in the corridor, their bodies riddled with bullets and shrapnel from explosives. Thompson and Shockley were later executed in the gas chamber at San Quentin and Carnes received a sentence of life, plus ninety-six years. His life was spared because he helped some of the wounded hostages. The cell building was heavily damaged and took months to repair.

The May 1946 riot may have been the most violent escape attempt from Alcatraz but it is, by all means, not the most famous. The classic "Escape from Alcatraz" occurred in 1962 and was carried out by three bank robbers who were serving long terms, Frank Morris and two brothers, Clarence and John Anglin. No one knows how long the trio planned their escape but it must have taken them several months to put it all together. Early that year, a fellow prisoner named Allen West helped the trio to devise a clever plan to construct a raft, inflatable life vests and human-like dummies that could be used to fool the guards during head counts. Over a period of several months, the men used everyday items and tools stolen from work sites to chip away at the ventilation shafts in their cells. They fabricated the life vests, the rafts and the dummies and they also created ingenious, duplicate grills that hid the cement that had been chipped away from around the vents. The quality of the human heads and faked grills was remarkable as they used only paint donated by prison artists and plaster created from soap, magazine pages and concrete powder to make them. They also collected hair from the barbershop, where Clarence Anglin worked as a barber, to make the dummies more lifelike.

These painstaking preparations paid off on the night of June 11, 1962. Immediately after the lights-out head count at 9:30 p.m. Morris and the Anglins scooted through the vents and scaled the utility shafts to the upper levels. Once they reached the roof, they climbed through a ventilator duct and made it to the edge of the building. After descending pipes along the cement wall, all three climbed over a fifteen-foot fence and made it to the island's shore, where they inflated the rafts and vests. They set out into the icy waters of the bay and were never seen again.

The escape was discovered the next morning when Morris failed to rise for the morning count. A guard jammed his club through the cell bars to wake him up and to his shock, a plaster head rolled off the bunk and landed on the floor. Alarms were sounded but by then, it was too late. The FBI pursued the case for a time but never found any active leads. Prison officials maintained that the trio drowned in the 34-degree water of the bay. A watertight bag was found floating in the bay four days later by a patrolling Army Corps of Engineers boat. The contents of the bag belonged to Clarence Anglin and mostly contained photos of a woman. A search was conducted for the three men's bodies but they were never found. More than forty years later, it is still unknown whether or not the trio made a successful escape.

After this last escape attempt, the prison's days were numbered. Ironically, the frigid waters around the island, which had long prevented escape, were believed to be the leading ruin of the prison. After the escape of Morris and the Anglins, the prison was examined and the structure was found to be deteriorating, mostly because of the corrosive effects of the salt water surrounding it. In addition, budget cuts had recently forced security measures at the prison to become more lax. On top of that, the exorbitant cost of running the place continued to increase and over $5 million was going to be needed for renovations. According to U.S. Attorney General Robert Kennedy, the prison was no longer necessary.

On March 23, 1963, Alcatraz closed its doors for good. After that, the island was essentially abandoned while various groups tried to decide what to do with it. Then, in 1969, a large group of American Indians landed on the island and declared that it was Native American property. They had great plans for the island, which included a school and a Native American cultural center. The

Indians soon had the attention of the media and the government and a number of meetings were held about the fate of Alcatraz.

The volume of visitors to the island soon became overwhelming. Somehow, during the talks, the island had become a haven for the homeless and the less fortunate. The Indians were soon faced with the problem of no natural resources and the fact that food and water had to be brought over from the mainland. The situation soon became so desperate that island's occupants were forced to take drastic measures to survive. In order to raise money for supplies, they began stripping copper wire and pipes from the island's buildings to sell as scrap metal. A tragedy occurred around this same time when Yvonne Oakes, daughter of one of the key Indian activists, fell to her death from a third-story window. The Oakes family left Alcatraz and never returned.

Then, during the evening hours of June 1, 1970, a fire was started and raged out of control. It damaged several of the buildings and destroyed the warden's residence, the lighthouse keeper's home and even badly damaged the historic lighthouse itself.

Tension now developed between federal officials and the Indians as the government blamed the activists for the fire. The press, which had been previously sympathetic toward the Native Americans, now turned against them and began to publish stories about beatings and assaults that were allegedly occurring on the island. Support for the Indians disintegrated, especially in light of the fact that the original activists had already left Alcatraz. Those who remained were seen as little more than squatters. On June 11, 1971, the Coast Guard, along with twenty U.S. Marshals, descended on the island and removed the remaining residents.

Alcatraz was empty once more.

In 1972, Congress created the Golden Gate National Recreation Area and Alcatraz Island fell under the purview of the National Park Service. It was opened to the public in the fall of 1973 and has become one of the most popular of America's park sites. During the day, the old prison is a bustling place, filled with tour guides and visitors, but at night, the buildings are filled with the inexplicable. Many believe that some of the men who served time on The Rock remain behind, lingering here for eternity. Alcatraz, they feel, is a very haunted place - a place where strange things can, and do, happen.

Hauntings have been widely reported since Alcatraz has been closed down. Despite a "no ghosts policy" meaning that staff members are not allowed to spread ghost stories park service employees and visitors to Alcatraz report weird, ghostly happenings in the crumbling old buildings. Inexplicable clanging sounds, footsteps and disembodied voices are commonly reported. Others say that they have heard screams coming from empty corridors and long-abandoned cells.

Some guides have reported strange events in certain areas of the prison, like the infamous Hole, where convicts suffered and sometimes died, during the years of the prison's operation.

Every visitor who arrives by boat on Alcatraz follows the same path once walked by the convicts who came to do time on The Rock. I Troy first visited Alcatraz on a family vacation when I was about thirteen years old. The Clint Eastwood movie, *Escape From Alcatraz,* had been released earlier that year and I was excited to see the place where the story took place. In addition, I was aware of the prison's haunted history from a book that I read a couple of years before. As far as I know that book, *Haunted Houses* by Richard Winer and Nancy Osborn, was the first to include the hauntings of Alcatraz.

After almost thirty years, I don't remember much about that trip but I recall returning to Alcatraz in 2004 when I was in San Francisco for a conference. I have never experienced anything paranormal at the famous prison but interviews with people who have encountered the unknown within its crumbling walls lead me to believe that it is an activity haunted place.

Tourists like myself who come to Alcatraz - just like the convicts from the prison's heyday -- pass through the warden's office and the visiting room and eventually enter the cell house. After passing the double steel doors, I recall looking just past C Block. I also looked opposite the visiting room and saw a metal door that looked as though it was once welded shut. Although the tour guides don't usually mention it, behind that door is the utility corridor where Coy, Cretzer and Hubbard were killed by grenades and bullets in 1946.

It was also behind this door where a night watchman heard strange, clanging sounds in 1976. He opened the door and peered down the dark corridor, shining his flashlight on the maze of pipes and conduits. He could see nothing and there were no sounds. When he closed the door, the noises started again. Again, the door was opened but there was still nothing that could be causing the sounds. The watchman did not believe in ghosts, so he shut the door again and continued on his way. The sounds continued to be heard in the years that followed and the door was eventually welded shut. It is still regarded today as one of the most haunted locations on Alcatraz.

Noises coming from behind the metal door are not the only strange sounds heard in this cell house, I've been told. Other night watchmen who have patrolled the building, long after the last tourist boats have left for the day, say they have heard the sounds of running footsteps in the upper tiers. Often thinking that an intruder is inside the prison, they have investigated the sounds, but always find nothing, and no one, out of place.

One National Park Service employee reported off the record, of course that she had been working one rainy afternoon when the sparse number of tourists were not enough to keep all of the guides busy. She went for a walk in front of A Block and was just past the door that led down to the dungeons when she heard a loud scream from the bottom of the stairs. She ran away without looking to see if anyone was down there. When asked why she didn't report the incident, she replied, "I didn't dare mention it because the day before, everyone was ridiculing another worker who reported hearing men's voices coming from the hospital ward, and when he checked the ward, it was empty."

Several of the rangers and guides have also expressed a strangeness about the one of the cells in the infamous Hole, number 14D. Several spoke of a feeling of sudden intensity in the cell that seems to come over anyone who spends much time there. One guide said, "That cell, 14D, is always cold. It's even colder than the other three dark cells. Sometimes it gets warm out here - so hot that you have to take your jacket off. The temperature inside the cell house can be in the 70s, yet 14D is still cold... so cold that you need a jacket if you spend any time in it."

Tour guides and park rangers have not been the only ones to have strange experiences in that particular cell. One former guard, who worked at the prison during its operation, told of several strange incidents that occurred in the Hole, particularly in Cell 14D. During the time when the guard was working at Alcatraz in the middle 1940s, he recalled an occurrence that took place when an inmate was locked in the punishment cell for some infraction. According to the officer, the inmate began screaming within seconds of being locked in. He claimed that some creature with glowing eyes was locked in with him. As tales of a ghostly presence wandering the nearby corridor were a continual source of practical jokes among the guards, no one took the convict's cries of being "attacked" very seriously.

The man's screams continued on into the night until finally, there was silence. The following day, guards inspected the cell and they found the convict dead. A horrible expression was frozen onto the man's face and there were clear marks of hands around his throat. The autopsy revealed that the strangulation could not have been self-inflicted. Some believed that he might have been choked by one of the guards, who had been fed up with his screaming, but no one ever admitted it. A few of the officers blamed something else for the man's death. They believed that the killer had been the spirit of a former inmate. To add to the mystery, on the day following the tragedy, several guards who were performing a head count noticed that there were too many men in the lineup. Then, at the end of the line, they saw the face of the convict who had recently been strangled in the Hole! As the guards stood staring at the man in stunned silence, the figure abruptly vanished.

It may come as no surprise to most readers, but this same cell was where Henry Young was confined after his attempted escape in 1939. He was confined there in the darkness for months and when he emerged, he was insane from the horrible isolation that he endured. Days later, he murdered Rufus McCain in the prison shop. Young found sympathy with the jury because they believed that his time in the Hole had deprived him of everything about himself that was spiritual and human. Did Henry Young leave a piece of his insanity behind in Cell 14D - or did something evil that already inhabited that grim place give a little of itself to Young?

If, as many believe, ghosts return to haunt the places where they suffered traumatic experiences when they were alive, then Alcatraz must be loaded with spirits. There have been claims made that many of the guards who served at the prison between 1946 and 1963 experienced strange happenings on Alcatraz. The guards often spoke to one another of voices sobbing and moaning, inexplicable smells, cold spots and spectral apparitions of prisoners and soldiers inhabiting every part of the island, from the cellblocks to the prison yard and on down to the caverns beneath the buildings. Phantom gunshots were known to send seasoned guards ducking to the ground in the belief that some of the prisoners had escaped and had obtained weapons. There was never an explanation. A deserted laundry room would sometimes fill with the smell of smoke, even though nothing was burning. The guards would be sent running from the room, only to return later and find that the air was clear.

Even Warden Johnston, who did not believe in ghosts, once encountered the unmistakable sound of a person sobbing while he accompanied some guests on a tour of the prison. He swore that the sounds came from inside the dungeon walls. The strange sounds were followed by an ice-cold wind that swirled through the entire group. He could offer no explanation for the weird events.

And since the prison has been closed down, the ghostly happenings seem to have intensified. Weird noises and eerie apparitions continue to be encountered. One of the most prominent ghosts still lingering on the island may be one of the most famous men to have served time there: Al Capone. It's not uncommon for rangers and tour guides to sometimes hear the sound of banjo strings being plucked on the cellblock or in the bath house, where Capone once cleaned and became known by the derogatory nickname of "the wop with the mop." Many who have experienced these strange sounds have no idea that Capone once played the banjo and one ranger even surmised that perhaps it was a ghostly echo from the time when Alcatraz was a military fort. Other have come to believe that the sound of the banjo is the only lingering part of a man who left his sanity behind on the island. Is it merely an imprint from the past, or is Al Capone still on

Alcatraz, a lonely and broken spirit desultorily plucking the strings of a spectral banjo that vanished decades ago?

Or could it be merely another of the countless ghosts who continue to haunt this place, year after year, still serving hard time on The Rock?

SOLDIERS and the SUPERNATURAL

HAUNTED BATTLEFIELDS

1836: "REMEMBER THE ALAMO"
San Antonio, Texas

My Troy's first visit to the Alamo came far too late in life, for it was a journey that I had always wanted to make. The Alamo has always been a sacred place to me. My first ancestor to come to America, an Irishman from County Kerry named Joseph Hawkins, was one of the men who gave his life in the defense of the outpost. I had been told to expect disappointment over the size and location of the Alamo. It's a tiny place, I was warned, in the middle of downtown San Antonio and I shouldn't go expecting too much. But my visit to the Alamo was anything but disappointing.

My friend, April Slaughter author of *Ghosthunting Texas,* among others , took me to the Alamo in the spring of 2012 and I was literally overwhelmed by the place. The quiet stillness of the old mission makes it easy to believe that the heroes of yesterday have left an indelible impression behind at what many consider to be the most haunted location in Texas.

The Alamo

The beginnings of the Alamo were humble ones. In the early 1500s, all of the land that would later make up the state of Texas belonged to Spain. For the next two centuries, this vast frontier was molded and shaped by famous explorers like Alvarez De Pineda, Francisco Vásquez de Coronado and others. But whatever accomplishments that were made by these men, they were overshadowed by the demands of the Catholic Church in the region. During the late 1690s, Spanish priests were enlisted to help colonize the Texas Territory in the name of the King of Spain. The key to this monumental endeavor was the conversion of the Native Americans living in the region to Catholicism. It was believed that this was an act of benevolence that would not only save the Indians' souls but would also ease their eventual assimilation into European culture.

Almost from the start, this ill-conceived and poorly executed campaign met with failure. Hampered by repeated Indian attacks and food shortages, the priests, largely Franciscan, were forced to abandon their plans for the region. Unable to admit defeat, the Church returned in the 1700s and established a series of frontier missions along a line that stretched from the present-day town of Guerrero all the way to the Rio Grande. In 1718, a group of monks constructed the Alamo in a cotton grove in San Antonio de Béxar.

Life at the mission could be brutal. Disease and starvation were rampant. In 1739, a smallpox epidemic ravished the mission and the surrounding countryside. It was in a remote location and a site almost abandoned by the Spain because there were no gold deposits nearby. Even so, the Alamo survived, and over the next several decades, it slowly expanded into a fortress-like mission, changing in both size and complexity. A small military garrison was stationed at the mission and in 1789, an eight-foot stone wall was erected around the chapel and its sixteen outer buildings. The barrier served as protection from Indian attacks for the town's two hundred and seventy-five men, women and children.

In December 1802, a full company of Spanish soldiers was posted at the Alamo in the hope that the increased military presence would dissuade the French or the Americans from planning any sort of invasion into the Texas region. But as it turned out, invasion by foreign countries was the least of Spain's worries. Between 1805 and 1821, a series of uprisings turned Mexico into a hotbed of rebellion. For sixteen years, the inhabitants fought and died for their freedom until Spain finally relinquished its dominion over Mexico in 1821.

By 1824, Mexico had developed into an independent nation and had established a democratic constitution. Around that time, American settlers began to be courted to try and get them to immigrate to Mexican Texas then part of the Mexican State of Coahuila y Tejas and establish settlements, colonies, businesses, farms and plantations. The Mexican government believed that this would accelerate civilization in that part of Mexico. The American colonists were offered large tracts of land and guaranteed protection and assistance by the Mexican government.

This practice continued without problems until the Texians, as they were called, revolted when Antonio López de Santa Anna became President of Mexico in 1835. Upon coming into power, Santa Anna rescinded the democratic constitution of 1824, dismantled the state legislatures, and proclaimed himself as dictator of Mexico.

Large groups of Americans flooded into Texas to assist in the revolt, hoping to help the Texians and the Tejanos -- former Mexicans living in the region -- achieve independence. Though most of them were untrained for military operations, and could count their time in Texas by weeks rather than years, they were a dedicated group. Together, they moved to capture Mexican military outposts and garrisons in the area. After a major conflict on December 10, 1835, in which the new Texas Army defeated the Mexican garrison at San Antonio de Béxar, they were able to drive out any remaining Mexican military from Texas.

After taking San Antonio, the spirited Texians declared their independence from Mexico, established a provisional government, and elected Davis Burnet as president. A capitol for the fledgling Republic of Texas was founded at

Washington-on-the-Brazos. The Americans and Texian colonists who had volunteered to help drive out the Mexicans believed that the revolution was over and the Republic of Texas was in place. Most of them returned to their homes and families, leaving a skeleton army to maintain the new republic's independence.

Santa Anna, a man not to be crossed, did not agree. He saw the "revolution" as nothing more than an insurrection, and one that needed to be put down immediately. With a strong show of force and a violent, unforgiving hand, he believed the Texians would suffer the consequences of their rebellious actions and not dare to rise up again.

President Santa Anna gathered an army more than six thousand strong. Within days of being informed of the loss of San Antonio de Béxar, he assumed the title of general and personally led his vast army on a march into Texas. Once in Texas, he split his army, sending nine hundred men with General José de Urrea to San Patricio. Santa Anna continued the march to San Antonio himself, as he wanted to be the one to personally put down the Texians and retake the Alamo.

After the Texians had overtaken San Antonio and evicted the Mexican military, protection from Mexican retaliatory attacks became their primary goal. Two forts blocked the entrances into Texas from the interior of Mexico: the Alamo in San Antonio de Béxar and Presidio La Bahía in Goliad. Both forts would remain frontier outposts for the protection of the new republic. Colonel James W. Fannin was put in command of the fort in Goliad and Colonel James Neill was assigned to command the Alamo.

Colonel Neill worked hard to strengthen the former mission. The walls were thick and high but they were simple masonry. The buildings were not strategically designed for protection. Their principal efforts were directed toward placing the twenty-four artillery pieces scattered around the mission inside the fort's walls for the greatest effect. There was also a severe shortage of supplies. The fort was seriously undermanned and low on both ammunition and horses. Neill complained to General Sam Houston that his men were underfed and exhausted. A message he sent to the provisional government stated: "Unless we are reinforced and victualed provided with food and supplies , we must become an easy prey to the enemy, in case of an attack."

Soon after, on January 19, Colonel James Bowie arrived with a small company of men. He was impressed with the work already done and he worked well with Colonel Neill. Complaints again went out stressing the lack of horses. There weren't even enough horses to send out scouts to watch for signs of the approaching Mexican Army. Again, a meager number of reinforcements were sent to the Alamo. Colonel William Travis arrived on February 3 with a small contingent of cavalry. Five days later, David Crockett, the famous frontiersman and former U.S. congressmen, arrived with a small group of American volunteers. Travis was unhappy to be given this post, but as a career Army officer, he followed orders. Sadly, they were still significantly low on supplies and ammunition. The number of soldiers positioned at one of the two forts protecting the whole of the Republic of Texas had risen to only one hundred and fifty men.

At noon on February 23, 1836, Santa Anna and the forward part of his army reached the crossroads just outside of San Antonio. Guards that had been positioned south of town came riding in hard with the news that what looked like the entire Mexican Army was moving in. With Neill absent as the result of a family emergency, Travis and Bowie began giving orders. Some men were sent to collect what food stores they could find and others worked to drive their few head of cattle inside the fort. Most of the Mexicans living in San Antonio were hostile to the Texians, but there were a few people living outside the walls of the Alamo who were invited inside for protection.

Two hours later, after a brief respite, Santa Anna marched his men into the village and sent word to Travis, demanding immediate and unconditional surrender. Travis answered with a cannon shot. Santa Anna initiated a bombardment of the fort and gave orders that it continue around the clock. Travis sent off an express message to Colonel Fannin in Goliad, ninety miles to the southeast, where Fannin had a contingent of three hundred soldiers. Travis described the situation at the Alamo as extremely serious and requested immediate assistance.

The thirteen-day siege of the Alamo had begun.

On February 24, Travis sent an appeal to the provisional government for supplies and reinforcements. He and Bowie knew that without them, they had no chance of withstanding the attack.

As Colonel Travis was composing his message, Colonel Bowie became ill. He was believed to have fallen victim to what was then known as "hasty consumption" rapidly active tuberculosis . Bowie would remain in his bed for the rest of the siege, except for the noon officers' meeting, when he would crawl from his bed to attend, and then crawl back to bed.

On February 26, a light skirmish between the fort's defenders and Mexican cavalry erupted, but it amounted to nothing. A storm had blown in and the temperature dropped to thirty-nine degrees. Santa Anna brought up more reinforcements and posted more guards around the Alamo. But the Texians were able to sneak out for wood and food and return safely. While they were out, they burned a few houses. The bombardment of the Alamo continued.

Early in the day on February 28, Colonel Fannin and two hundred men with four pieces of artillery left Goliad for the Alamo, leaving one hundred men to guard the Presidio La Bahía. After marching only two hundred yards, though, a wagon carrying supplies broke down. They decided to return to the Precidio La Bahia and Fort Defiance in Goliad. They would not be reinforcing the soldiers at the Alamo.

Meanwhile, the bombardment of the Alamo continued. No help was coming.

On March 1, Captain John Smith slipped into the Alamo, bringing thirty-two Texians with him. That brought the number of men inside the walls to one hundred and eighty-eight. Outside, Santa Anna's troops numbered five thousand. The defenders were holding their own, but the walls of the fort were weakening. The Mexican troops were rested and well-fed while the Texians were starving and exhausted.

By the tenth day of the siege, March 3, Santa Anna's men had erected a forth battery to the north of the fort, within musket range. Travis sent off another desperate request for reinforcements and supplies. This was to be his last appeal to the president. By then, he had ceased expecting any help to come from Colonel Fanning.

The final day came on March 6 when, just after midnight, Santa Anna pulled his entire force into town and surrounded the fort. His troops had been supplied with scaling ladders and they waited quietly for the word to attack. At 5:00 a.m., they received their orders. The troops moved forward and the ladders were placed against the wall, ready to scale. But the Texians were ready and brought down heavy fire, driving the Mexicans back. They made a second attempt with the same results, followed by a third and a fourth. Each time, they were repulsed by the Texians. For Santa Anna, the fifth try finally met with success.

The Mexican troops flooded up and over the wall and into the Alamo. Completely overwhelmed, the Texians had no chance -- but they kept fighting. Travis was one of the first to be killed. The beleaguered Texians fought until nearly all lay dead in the dirt inside the Alamo. Santa Anna had given orders that the wounded were to be killed. The Mexicans then moved through the fort, looking for anyone who might be hiding. During this search, the men came upon Colonel Bowie, still in his sickbed. Knowing he was one of the commanders of the fort, they butchered him.

After twelve days of bombardment, the Alamo was taken by the Mexican Army in just ninety minutes. By 8:00 a.m., every fighting man who had defended the Alamo lay dead.

After the dead Texians had been collected and brought into the center of the courtyard, the bodies were looted for valuables. The bodies were then stripped of their clothing and stacked like cordwood and set on fire. Witnesses related that the corpses smoldered for three days.

Despite the savagery of the attack, several people survived the day. Santa Anna distinguished between those who had fought against him and others who had not. The survivors were all released without harm. They included the wife of a slain officer and her infant daughter; Travis' black servant, and two Mexican women from San Antonio, cousins of Travis' widow. Each of the survivors were given a blanket and two dollars and sent on their way.

The Mexican Army stood victorious but at a tremendous cost. Records vary, but best estimates put the number of dead at nearly five hundred, with almost as many wounded.

The heroic defenders of the Alamo were wiped out to the last man.

And the battle that Santa Anna thought would frighten the rebels into submission became an inspiration to the people of Texas. Their battle cry for freedom became, "Remember the Alamo!" After the battles that followed, Santa Anna was defeated and the Republic of Texas was born.

The Alamo was already ninety-three years old at the time of the famous battle. The first stones for the Spanish mission were laid in 1744. There were several hundred burials in what is now Alamo Plaza. In 1793, the Catholic Church moved the religious artifacts to a nearby mission and turned the property over to the town. It officially became the Alamo, the Spanish word for cottonwood, when it was used as a barracks for Spanish soldiers in 1803. The building was vacant and abandoned between 1825 till 1835, when General Martin Perfecto de Cos of the Mexican Army made it into a military fort. It changed hands between the Mexicans and the Texans three more times, including the Battle of the Alamo in 1836. After that time, a variety of purposes were found for the structure until it was purchased by the state of Texas and opened to the public as a state shrine.

After so many different uses by so many different people, it is not unexpected that the old mission chapel and surrounding property is considered quite haunted. However, the primary reason that the Alamo is so haunted can be linked to the battle that occurred there in 1836, when hundreds of people died violent deaths over a period of just over two hours. Added to that, the bodies of the Texians were stripped, desecrated and burned, with no proper burial. Even the bodies of the Mexican soldiers were mishandled in ways that would have been considered improper in their religion and their culture. They were either burned, thrown into the San Antonio River, or left to rot as carrion for wild animals and vultures.

The land within and surrounding the old mission is essentially a cemetery. After the bodies were burned, their ashes and charred bits of bone and teeth were raked out and mixed into with the soil. Is it any wonder that spirits of the past are still believed to linger at the Alamo?

There is no record of any hauntings or ghost sightings before the battle in 1836, but one of the most prominent paranormal legends stems from just a few weeks afterwards. General Santa Anna and the bulk of his forces stayed on at San Antonio de Béxar for a few weeks before leaving to chase down General Sam Houston and the Republic of Texas Army, leaving a garrison of men at the Alamo under General Juan de Andrade's command.

Shortly before leaving, Santa Anna ordered General de Andrade to demolish the Alamo, leaving nothing standing. General Andrade then instructed Colonel Jose Juan Sanchez-Navarro to get the job done. Colonel Sanchez-Navarro took his men to the site of the Alamo. After twelve days of constant bombardment, the place was not much more than rubble. The only recognizable structure still standing was the mission chapel. The colonel ordered the men to begin demolishing of the church and the men complied, although there was some grumbling among the ranks about it possibly being sacrilege to tear down a former Catholic church.

According to legend, as the men began to work, six ghostly forms emerged from the chapel walls. The soldiers immediately stopped what they were doing and backed away, crossing themselves and muttering "*diablos!*" devils under their breath. The forms, often described as monks, slowly advanced on the soldiers, waving flaming swords and warning the men in inhuman voices, "Do not touch the walls of the Alamo!" Colonel Sanchez-Navarro and his men ran screaming from the chapel, back to their encampment.

When Sanchez-Navarro told General de Andrade what they had witnessed, the general was furious and chastised the colonel for his cowardice. Taking matters into his own hands, de Andrade collected a detail of men and marched them to the Alamo to get the work done. As added protection, he took along a small cannon and instructed the gunner to aim it directly at the front doors of the chapel. But before they could blast the doors, the six ghostly monks again took shape and issued their warning. The general's horse took fright and reared, throwing de Andrade to the ground. Before following his men in retreat, he turned to look at the building again and saw giant flames blast up from the ground. The smoke curled and twisted into the shape of a huge man. The menacing figure held balls of fire in each hand and hurled them at de Andrade.

General de Andrade affected a hasty retreat and the phantom protectors of the Alamo won out, but this part of the legend is not borne out by fact. Apparently, de Andrade was not frightened away for good, since he must have returned to complete his orders. According to official records and archeological investigations, much of what remained of the mission was demolished, including many of fort's walls.

In the 1890s, the Alamo chapel and some of the old barracks were used as a police station and local jail. Soon after moving into the old buildings, the prisoners and guards began complaining about a variety of unexplainable experiences. They reported that a ghostly sentry walked from east to west on the roof of the police station, formerly the old barracks. This and other events were described so frequently and fervently that stories about the hauntings were picked up by the newspapers.

The *San Antonio Express News* published two articles, in 1894 and again in 1897, about the ghostly goings-on. The articles described several types of "manifestations" that were witnessed within the walls of the police station and jail. These were mysterious man-shaped shadows moving about the rooms and corridors, and strange moaning sounds that could not be explained. According to the newspaper reports, these were frequent and so frightening that many of the guards refused to patrol the area after dark.

As the stories of the hauntings became more well-known, complaints were brought to the San Antonio City Council, where councilmen took the position that making the prisoners sleep in a building with ghosts roaming around and moaning amounted to "cruel and unusual punishment," and that it was unsafe for the public because of the guards refusal to walk their patrols after sunset. Shortly after the second article was published, the city moved the police station from the Alamo to a building that was not haunted.

Many of the same types of incidents that were reported in the 1890s are said to continue to happen today, except that now, the ghosts of the Alamo no longer seem to distinguish between night and day, but prefer to conduct their hauntings around the clock.

For decades, visitors, park rangers and passersby have described seeing a mysterious sentry walking his patrol. There have also been countless reports of unexplained noises: men screaming in pain, battle cries, and voices and whispers seeming to emanate from the walls of the chapel. People walking past the Alamo at night have seen distorted and disheveled human shapes emerging from the exterior walls.

A commonly seen apparition is that of a man dressed in clothing of the early 1800s, walking across the courtyard. Although visitors have described seeing this man many times over the years, the story was validated for Alamo officials by one of their own park rangers. The ranger noticed a man dressed in period costume walking toward the library. The ranger decided to follow him and see what he was up to. To his surprise, the stranger faded away to nothing as he approached the chapel.

Another commonly witnessed ghost is that of a blond boy who has been seen wandering the buildings and courtyard, but is most often seen in the gift shop. He apparently likes to interact with children and has been known to carry on conversations with them. He has told several children that he was present during the battle and believes that he died there. He seems to selectively appear to specific people, with children waving goodbye to him while their parents see no one.

The basement of the mission, which is now used mostly for storage, has also been the scene of supernatural manifestations. Staff members have often felt that someone is sneaking up on them while they are working. When they turn to see who might be approaching, a shadowy apparition is glimpsed as he quickly steps backward through the wall and disappears. Employees are - not surprisingly - often reluctant to enter the basement for fear of encountering this mysterious phantom.

Another ghost often seen on the grounds is that of actor John Wayne. In 1959, Wayne directed and starred in a movie about the Alamo. The Duke portrayed Davy Crockett in the film. He was said to be obsessed with creating a movie set that was historically accurate, down to the last detail. Filming could not take place in the original Alamo, so an exact replica was built one hundred and twenty-five miles away in Brackettsville, Texas. Wayne toured the real Alamo many times and developed a passion for the place and for the people who fought there. The reproduction that was built for the movie has become a tourist attraction in its own right. Over the years, about a dozen films about the Alamo have been shot there. Wayne's ghost is reported to be seen wearing a full set of buckskins and a coonskin cap - made famous for the fictional "Davy Crockett," not by the real man who died at the Alamo. Wayne's ghost has been seen all over the compound, but most frequently he is seen guarding the old mission chapel.

The Alamo is a sacred place, there is no doubt about that. It is also a haunted one. If the horror of war can leave psychic scars on a battlefield, a landscape or a building, then the eerie atmosphere that still surrounds the Alamo can be easily explained.

Dating back to the days that followed the battle, common, everyday people began having experiences at the old mission that they could not explain. Without a doubt, some of the stories that have survived can be dismissed as folklore or the products of overactive imaginations, but what do we make of the other encounters? The ones that cannot be explained away by logic and rational thinking?

For the countless ghost hunters, tourists and park rangers who have found themselves frightened, unnerved and even exhilarated by a brush with the lingering spirits of the Alamo, there is no question that the place is haunted. For those who journey here and walk away with an experience with something from beyond the words, "Remember the Alamo!" will always mean something very different than it did for the men who fought so bravely for their independence.

AUGUST 1861: THE BATTLE OF WILSON'S CREEK
Near Springfield, Missouri

The Battle of Wilson's Creek, also known as the Battle of Oak Hills, was fought on August 10, 1861, near Springfield, between Union troops and the Missouri State Guard. While considered by historians to be the first major battle of the Civil War that was fought west of the Mississippi - it's sometimes referred to as the "Bull Run of the West" - it's often forgotten by those who believe the war was fought only on the battlefields of the East.

The hours of bloody fighting that occurred at this lonely spot left an indelible impression on the landscape of Southwest Missouri and tales of hauntings still reverberate more than one hundred and fifty years after the last shots were fired on the battlefield.

At the start of the Civil War, Missouri declared that it would be an "armed neutral" state, and not send men or materials to either side. However, that neutrality was quickly put to the test on May 10, 1861 by Governor Claiborne F. Jackson, who leaned toward the Confederate cause. He had called out the state militia to drill on the edge of Pro-Union St. Louis and, after secretly obtaining artillery from the Confederacy, smuggled it into the militia camp at Lindell Grove that came to be known as Camp Jackson. Federal Captain Nathaniel Lyon was aware of the guns and feared that the militia was planning to attack the St. Louis Arsenal. Thomas W. Sweeny was put in command of the Arsenal's defense, and Lyon surrounded the militia camp with Union troops and home guards, forcing the surrender of the militia. He blundered, though, when he marched the captured militia through the streets, attracting crowds, many of whom were angry. Taunts and fighting eventually led to gunfire and many civilian and military deaths.

The following day, the violence in St. Louis led the Missouri General Assembly to create the Missouri State Guard, which was tasked with defending the state from attacks by perceived enemies, either from the North of the South. The governor appointed Sterling Price as the commander with the rank of Major General. The State Guard was divided into divisions, with each division consisting of units raised from a military district of Missouri and command by a brigadier general.

Fearing that Missouri would fall to the Confederacy, William S. Harney, Missouri's Federal commander, struck the Price-Harney Truce on May 12, 1861, which affirmed the state's neutrality. Governor Jackson then declared his support for the Union. However, Harney was replaced with Nathaniel Lyon, now promoted to Brigadier General, and Abraham Lincoln made a specific request for Missouri troops to enter into Federal service. With that, Jackson withdrew his support. On June 12, Lyon and Jackson met in St. Louis with hopes of resolving the matter, but things went badly. The meeting ended with Lyon's now-famous words, "This means war. In an hour, one of my officers will call for you and conduct you out of my lines."

Lyon sent a force under General Thomas Sweeney to Springfield while his own forces captured the state capital and pursued Jackson, Price and the now-exiled state government across Missouri. Skirmishes occurred at Boonville and Carthage and in light of the crisis, the delegates of the Missouri Constitutional Convention that had rejected secession in February convened again. On July 27, the convention declared the governor's office vacant and then selected Hamilton Rowan Gamble to be the new provisional governor.

By July 13, Lyon's army of about six thousand men was encamped at Springfield. The force was composed of the 1st, 2nd, 3rd, and 5th Missouri Infantry, the 1st Iowa Infantry, the 1st Kansas and 2nd Kansas Infantry, several companies of Regular Army infantry and cavalry, and three batteries of artillery. Lyon divided the units into four brigades commanded by Major Samuel D. Sturgis, Colonel Franz Sigel, Lieutenant Colonel George Andrews, and Colonel George Dietzler.

By the end of July, the Missouri State Guard was encamped about seventy-five miles southwest of Springfield and had been reinforced by Confederate Brigadier General Benjamin McCulloch and Arkansas state militia Brigadier General N. Bart Pearce. The mixed Missouri and Confederate force doubled the size of Lyon's Union force. They began making plans to attack Springfield but on August 1, Lyon marched out of the city in a bold move to try and surprise the Confederate forces. A short skirmish occurred at Dug Springs, with the Union emerging as the winner, but by then Lyon had learned that he was greatly outnumbered by the enemy and retreated back into Springfield. McCulloch went in pursuit and by August 6 was encamped at Wilson's Creek, about ten miles southwest of the city.

The pursuit was slowed by bickering between Price and McCulloch. Price favored an immediate attack on Springfield but McCulloch, doubtful about the quality of the Missouri State Guard, preferred to remain in place. After Price threatened an attack without his support, McCulloch reluctantly agreed to attack on the morning of August 10, only to be stopped by a heavy rainstorm on the night of August 9. He cancelled his plans and ordered his men back to camp.

Meanwhile, Lyon knew that his smaller force was in great danger. He began making plans to withdraw northeast to Rolla where he could reinforce and resupply - but not before he launched a surprise attack on the Missouri camp to slow the enemy's pursuit. Colonel Franz Sigel developed a flawed strategy, with which Lyon unfortunately agreed, that split the already outnumbered Union force. Sigel proposed trapping McCulloch with a pincer movement. He would lead twelve hundred men in a flanking maneuver while the main body of troops under Lyon struck from the north. Going along with the ill-conceived plan, the Union troops marched out of Springfield on the dark, wet night of August 9, leaving behind about one thousand men to protect the supplies and cover the retreat.

The Union force attacked at first light on August 10. The Confederates were taken by surprise and Lyon's force overran their camps and took the high ground at the crest of a ridge that came to be known as "Bloody Hill." But the Union's hopes for a quick victory were dashed when the artillery of the Pulaski Arkansas Battery opened up on their advance, which gave Price's infantry time to organize lines on the south side of the hill. Lyon attempted to counterattack from his position but was unsuccessful. Price launched a series of frontal and flank attacks against Lyon but was also unsuccessful. Eventually, a shortage of ammunition caused his attack to falter.

The two Union forces, commanded by Lyon and Sigel, lost contact with each other since they had no means of communicating and no way of supporting each other if anything went wrong. Sigel's attack was successful at first, with the brigade arriving in the Confederate rear just as the sun was coming up. Artillery fire routed the Confederate cavalry units that were encamped at Sharp's farm and Sigel started a pursuit that stopped along Skeeg's Branch. When he inexplicably stopped at this position, he failed to post skirmishers along his front and left his flank open for an attack. Meanwhile, McCulloch rallied several Confederate units, including the 3rd Louisiana Infantry and the 3rd Division from the Missouri State Guard, and launched a counterattack. Sigel's men mistook the 3rd Louisiana for the 3rd Iowa Infantry, who also wore gray uniforms, and withheld their fire until the Confederates were nearly upon them. His flank was consequently utterly devastated by the counterattack and his brigade was routed, losing four cannons. Sigel and his men fled the field and Lyon, Sweeny and Sturgis were left on the field alone.

After Sigel was driven from the battle, the momentum shifted in favor of the Confederacy. Nathaniel Lyon became the first Union general to be killed in the war. He was shot in the heart at Bloody Hill, at about 9:30 a.m., while leading the 2nd Kansas Infantry in a countercharge. General Sweeny was wounded in the leg, and Major Samuel D. Sturgis, as the highest ranking Regular Army officer, assumed command of the troops. By this time, the Federal men were still in a defensible position atop the hill, but supplies were low and morale was worsening by the minute. By 11:00 a.m., the Union troops had repulsed three separate Confederate charges. Finally, fearing a fourth Confederate attack, Sturgis retreated and the Federals fled toward Rolla.

In the aftermath of the bloody battle, the causalities were nearly equal -- 1,317 Union and 1,230 from the Missouri, Arkansas and Confederate troops. Though the Confederates won the day, they were unable to pursue the retreating Union forces. Once again, Price and McCulloch argued. Price wanted to start immediately in pursuit but McCulloch feared for the condition of the troops and didn't want to stretch the supply line to Arkansas any farther than he had to. This Confederate victory buoyed Southern sympathizers in Missouri and served as a springboard for a bold thrust north that carried Price and his Missouri State Guard as far as Lexington on September 20. The Confederate and Arkansas forces withdrew from the state.

After falling back to Springfield, Sturgis handed over command to Sigel. At a council of war that evening, it was agreed that the Federal troops would fall back to Rolla. However, Sigel failed to get his brigade ready at that time, forcing a delay of several hours. Along the retreat route, Sigel's men took several lengthy delays in order to prepare meals and the other officers turned on Sigel and forced him to turn command back over to Sturgis. Throughout the rest of the war, Sigel largely failed to distinguish himself, often blaming poor health for bad decisions and defeats. He was soundly defeated by Major General John C. Breckenridge at the Battle of New Market, on May 15, 1864, which was particularly embarrassing due to the prominent role that young cadets from the Virginia Military Institute played in his defeat. In July, he fought Lieutenant General Jubal A. Early at Harpers Ferry, but soon afterward was relieved of his command for "lack of aggression" and replaced by Major General David Hunter. Sigel spent the rest of the war without an active command.

The Battle of Wilson's Creek was an important moment to the Confederate sympathizers in southwest Missouri. On October 30, 1861, the Missourians under Price and Jackson formally joined the Confederate cause in Neosho, Missouri. Officials passed the resolution for Missouri's secession and Jackson was named the governor of Confederate Missouri. However, the new government never earned the favor of most of the population of Missouri, and the state remained in the Union throughout the war. To make matters worse, a series of defeats shattered what little control Jackson had and his Confederate state government was soon forced to leave the state.

War had shattered the peace of rural Missouri and it would be many years before the violence and bloodshed would come to an end.

One hundred years after the last guns were silenced at Wilson's Creek, the battlefield was dedicated as a national park. Today, visitors, travelers and history buffs visit this quiet park, which is filled with trees and prairie grass and looks almost the same as it did in 1861. The stories of bravery and bloodshed seem far in the distant past at this peaceful place but they may not be as far in the past as one might think because there are ghosts that wander the fields at Wilson's Creek.

One of the lingering haunts on the battlefield may not be linked directly to the battle. The John Ray house was built in 1850 and during the battle, was in the middle of the fighting. The house was home to Ray, his wife Roxana, and their nine children. Ray was appointed postmaster of Wilson Creek and the house was used as the local post office for more than ten years. During the battle, it served as a hospital. General Lyon's body was brought there after he was killed and the bed where his body lay is still on display in the house.

During the six-hour battle, John Ray sat on the front porch and watched the action unfold in his cornfield while his family, a hired hand, their slave, Rhoda, and her four children took shelter in the cellar. The first warning that fighting was about to erupt on their farm came when three of the Ray children, who had been hearding horses in the valley early that morning, were approached by a soldier on horseback. The soldier told them, "There's going to be fighting like hell in less than ten minutes."

The Ray family has been gone from their old home for many years, but at least one member of the family may have stayed behind. On several occasions, visitors have seen a young woman in a long dress carrying water from the Ray springhouse, a small stone building that covered a nearby spring. The family stored perishables like milk, butter and eggs there and used the water for drinking and cooking. After the battle, the Ray children made many trips to the springhouse to bring water to the suffering soldiers. Could the girl whom visitors have seen have been one of the Ray daughters? Those who spotted her believed that she was part of a living history program at the battlefield but when they tried to speak to her, she didn't respond. Park rangers stated that there were no living history programs going on at the time of the sightings.

But most of the ghostly occurrences at Wilson's Creek take place on the battlefield itself, where more than two thousand young men bled and died in August 1861. Battlefields, with all of the trauma and death that occurred on them, are common places to find ghosts and hauntings. Wilson's Creek is no exception.

Stories about ghosts date back at least as far as the 1940s, when a group of fisherman saw at least fifteen Union soldiers, wearing dirty uniforms and carrying rifles, file past them and then vanish. The same group of spectral soldiers have seen been seen several times near the creek. It was as if a supernatural recording imprinted itself on the location and now repeats itself over and over again.

Civil War reenactor Steve Cottrell told of an incident that occurred in the spring of 1983, when the park sponsored a large encampment of reenactors to present simulations of military drills, camp life and battle recreations for visitors. During that weekend, a column of Union infantry reenactors went on an early-morning march. In the predawn light, the men became aware of a solitary horseman who was following them at a distance. Although his features were not clear, he was dressed in Civil War clothing. By the time the march was over, the lone figure on horseback had disappeared. The men assumed that the rider was a cavalry reenactor out of an early morning ride. However, when the men in the cavalry unit including Cottrell heard about the incident, they were surprised because none of the men had been out riding at that time of the morning. As far as they were able to determine, no one - reenactor, visitor or park ranger alike - was on horseback in the park at the time the lone rider made his appearance.

But there is no place on the battlefield as haunted as "Bloody Hill," the site of numerous deaths during the fight. Union batteries on the hilltop dueled with Confederate artillery in the valley for more than six hours and the Federal men on high ground fought off three charges by the desperate Missouri and Arkansas men who threw themselves at the line over and over again. Hundreds of men died both attacking and defending the hill and not surprisingly, some of them have apparently remained behind.

Over the years, many people who have visited "Bloody Hill" have spoken of not feeling as if they were alone while on the hilltop. And while this could be merely be imagination at work by those knew of the violent events on the hill, other incidents suggest that there is more to the place than meets the eye. Accounts have circulated of voices, cries, shouts and screams that have been heard there, even when no living person is nearby. Some claim that have actually seen the mournful apparitions of torn and bloody soldiers on the hill, often sending the unlucky visitors hurrying back to their cars.

There is little doubt to those who have encountered something unusual out in the trees and prairie grass of the park that something of the war remains behind at Wilson's Creek.

And Wilson's Creek is not the only haunted battlefield in Missouri. There is another, and this battle also involved some of the same participants. The Battle of Pilot Knob, also known as the Battle of Fort Davidson, took place in September 1864, just outside of Pilot Knob in Iron County. Although outnumbered by more than ten to one, the Union defenders of Fort Davidson managed to hold off repeated Confederate assaults on their works and were able to slip away during the night, abandoning their position long before the Confederates realized they were gone. The attacking Confederates took possession of the fort the next day, but the useless waste of men and ammunition effectively ended Major General Sterling Price's plan to seize the city of St. Louis.

Today, a mere few hundred yards from the base of Pilot Knob mountain, it is said that the same men that fought and died there in 1864 still wander the battlefield, perhaps ready to continue their war.

By the spring of 1864, the Confederacy found itself in an increasingly desperate military situation. Unable to win any decisive victories or to obtain foreign recognition, its main strategy by this point was merely to hold on to what they had and to hope that enormous Union casualties might cause the war-weary Northern public to vote Abraham Lincoln out of office in November. Democrats, who had named General George B. McClellan as their nominee to run against Lincoln, had adopted a peace plan for the South if he was elected. McClellan backed away from the plan after the Union met with several successes that summer, but the Confederacy was still hopeful that a significant military disaster in the fall of 1864 might still embarrass Lincoln and doom his presidency.

But as the election approached, things looked even bleaker for the South. General Ulysses S. Grant had pinned down Robert E. Lee in Virginia, while General William Sherman was battling with General Joe Johnston north of Atlanta. General Crook's army held the Shenandoah Valley. The only area that seemed to offer possibilities for the Confederates to humiliate the Union was in the West. With this in mind, Major General Sterling Price was chosen for the task. He raised a mixed force of twelve thousand cavalry, mounted infantry and fourteen cannon. He named it the Army of Missouri and set about "liberating" his home state.

In early September 1864, Price left Camden, Arkansas, and marched north into Missouri. His main objective was St. Louis, not only the largest city in the state, but a major supply post for the Union military in the West. Even though Sherman had captured Atlanta by this time, which provided a tremendous boost to Lincoln's reelection campaign, the seizure of St. Louis by Price - along with the huge quantity of arms and ammunition at the Federal arsenal there - could still prove catastrophic for the Republican Party.

As the Army of Missouri moved north toward Ironton, near the terminus of the Iron Mountain Railroad from St. Louis, Price came upon Fort Davidson with a garrison of fifteen hundred men and seven guns. It was a tempting target. Price had a large force under his command and capturing the fort would not only be simple, he believed, but would prove beneficial to Southern morale.

Fort Davidson was a hexagonal-shaped fortress with walls nine feet high and ten feet thick. It was surrounded by a nine-foot-deep dry moat, with two long rifle pits running out from the walls. A reinforced wooden fence topped the thick walls. The only way into the fort was by means of a drawbridge on the southeastern corner. To further protect the position, a field had been cleared that extended in all directions beyond the walls, leaving any enemy that approached totally exposed to the soldiers inside of the fort. It lay in a valley with large hills on three sides, and in its center was a buried powder magazine.

As Price prepared to seize the garrison, he received word that Federal troops were moving south to intercept him. Ordering detachments to destroy the railroad to the north, he moved his main three brigades into the Arcadia Valley, where he focused the attention of his three divisions on the fort on the evening of September 26.

The command of Fort Davidson had fallen to Brigadier General Thomas Ewing, deputy command of the District of St. Louis and a brother-in-law of William T. Sherman. He had only recently arrived at the fort with two hundred Iowa Infantry to augment the small Union force that was already there. Ewing had been scouting the route that Price might make towards St. Louis when he got word that Iron Mountain Railroad behind him had been cut by the Confederate cavalry. Despite being outnumbered ten to one, he decided to stand and fight at Fort Davidson.

The official battle began on September 26 when the leading element of Price's army encountered Union pickets south of Ironton, which was about three miles south of the fort. The Federal troops were driven back into town and the two sides exchanged fire on the lawn of the Iron County courthouse. As more Confederates poured into town, the Union forces withdrew to the fort.

On September 27, Ewing ignored repeated demands by Confederate officers that he surrender the fort. Ewing later wrote that he considered capitulating, but he feared for the lives of the black civilians that he had in his camp after the slaughter of African American soldiers at Fort Pillow in Tennessee earlier that year. Furthermore, Ewing was uncertain of his own fate if he was captured. He had issued General Order No. 11 after William C. Quantrill's raid on Lawrence, Kansas in 1863, and had used Federal cavalry to force thousands of Missouri civilians into Arkansas as Confederate guerilla collaborators who could not prove their loyalty to the Union. The area became known as the "Burnt District," since Ewing's order virtually wiped out the entire region, causing Cass County's population to drop from ten thousand to only six hundred. Needless to say, he was hated across a large part of Missouri. Thus, Ewing decided to fight on, and Price became determined to take the fort that same day.

Price's attack came as one massive assault from several directions: One brigade went over the top of Pilot Knob, engulfing a small Union force there, while another attacked over the summit of Shepherd Mountain. A third brigade skirted Shepherd Mountain to attack the northwestern side of the fort, while a fourth attacked through the valley between the two mountains. As Federal troops were driven back by the Confederates' superior numbers, the Army of Missouri took control of Shepherd Mountain, which was southwest of the fort. Two Confederate guns were set up there and their murderous fire caused the smaller of the rifle pits inside of the fort to be abandoned.

Price's mistake was that these assaults did not occur simultaneously. This allowed the guns of Fort Davison to be directed at each Confederate force in turn. Just one brigade reached the fort itself, badly hampered by the cannon and rifle fire from inside. When they made it to the walls, they found the earthworks to be too steep to climb. As they milled about below, planning another assault on the walls, Union defenders dropped bombs on them. The wood-finned impact devices were taken from the fort's magazines and tossed over the walls, forcing the defenders to break off their attack. The attacks of the second day broke off and the disorganized Confederates fell back and prepared to assault the fort again the following day.

While Price was starting his troops on building ladders to scale the walls the next morning, Ewing was making his own plans inside the fort. He had received belated orders from St. Louis instructing him to abandon the post and he now agreed that he was trapped and needed an escape strategy. Union soldiers put all of the equipment that they could not take with them inside the powder magazine and placed a slow-burning fuse leading into the magazine itself. Soldiers draped canvas over the wooden drawbridge leading out of the fort to muffle the sounds of their movement and stealthily exited the fort after midnight. Even though the Confederates had fires burning all over the valley, Federal survivors withdrew undetected to the northwest, passing directly between two Confederate encampments. More than an hour after they had vanished, the fuse burned its way into the powder magazine and exploded with tremendous force. Fire, smoke, dirt and stone erupted in the center of the fort, startling the Confederate troops, but despite the explosion, Price did not have his men investigate the fort's condition until sunrise.

Price's officers were furious at the Union deception and demanded that their commander pursue the escaping Union troops. But Price hesitated. He had lost hundreds of men and three precious days in what turned out to be a fruitless assault. His plans of taking St. Louis were clearly dashed. Ewing's daring defense of the fort - and amazing escape through Price's lines - made newspaper headlines throughout the region and Ewing later received the personal thanks of President Lincoln. Although the exact number of Confederate casualties remains unknown, historians estimate that they at least one thousand men were lost. In comparison, only twenty-eight of Ewing's men were killed and about one hundred and sixty were wounded.

Price's campaign to "liberate" Missouri foundered after Fort Davidson. They resumed their march to the north, but instead of daring St. Louis, turned westward to Jefferson City. Finding it too heavily fortified, they continued further west toward Kansas City and Fort Leavenworth. Ultimately, at Westport, Price suffered a crushing defeat and his Missouri campaign came to a bloody end. His army was virtually destroyed and he limped back to Arkansas with less than half of the men that he started his campaign with.

More than one hundred and fifty years later, Fort Davidson is a shadow of its former self, remaining as a historic site below Pilot Knob. According to historians, Civil War buffs and locals, the ghosts of many of the Confederate soldiers who died there in 1864 still walk the battlefield today. Visitors have frequently reported seeing the apparitions of soldiers and even cannon on the field, only to see them disappear when approached. History left a dark and bloody mark on this ground and time has not yet allowed it to be forgotten.

During the Battle of Pilot Knob, wounded soldiers from both sides were treated in a field hospital inside a house in Caledonia. A quarantine room was located on the third floor for soldiers with infectious diseases. The room was padlocked and a hole was cut in the door to pass supplies back and forth.

The house was built back in 1824 using slave labor and served as an inn on the stage line that passed through the area. According to legend, the three-story, twelve-room house was once used as a station on the Underground Railroad, helping escaped slaves pass through the region on their way to freedom in the North. A secret door was cut into the back of the house and several tunnels led out of the dirt-floored basement, allowing access to a nearby creek. The tunnels were later filled in, destroying the physical evidence of the "railroad" station, and yet the legend persists.

The house went through a series of different owners over the years, serving as a private residence and an antique shop. Today, it is a restaurant, bed and breakfast and wine shop called the Caledonia Wine Cottage. It is listed on the National Register of Historic Places, and if the stories are to be believed, history has left more than a little of itself behind inside of these walls.

Stories have circulated for decades about voices being heard in the empty halls of the house. There have been numerous sightings of a shadowy Civil War soldier and sounds of boots are often heard clumping around the house. One of the stranger recent reports tells of corks suddenly popping out of wine bottles and objects being moved and thrown about. Wall hangings have inexplicably jumped been found lying on the floor. Animals watch empty rooms, wary to enter, and staring at things that humans are unable to see.

The Caledonia Wine Cottage is another of Missouri's many places where the Civil War left an indelible mark, and where the spirits of the past make their presence known to the living.

1862: BATTLE OF FORT DONELSON
Dover, Tennessee

On February 16, 1862, the course of the Civil War would be changed forever, when Union forces under the command of an obscure brigadier general named Ulysses S. Grant won the first major Northern victory of the war. This key turning point was the battle that led to the fall of Fort Donelson, located in Dover, Tennessee. This fifteen-acre earthen fort guarded the Cumberland River, a vital transportation and supply route for the South. With the taking of Fort Donelson, the South gave up its claim to southern Kentucky and most, if not all, of the western portion of Tennessee for the remainder of the war.

Following the startling Southern victories as First Manassas and Wilson's Creek in the summer of 1861, both armies maneuvered against each other in a series of attempts to break a mutual stalemate. Repeatedly, Union forces attempted to break a seemingly invincible Confederate defensive line that stretched from southwest Missouri to the Appalachian Mountains, but they achieved little success.

In January 1862, Northern commanders conducted a reconnaissance of the Confederates' western defensive positions and determined that Fort Henry, guarding the Tennessee River and Fort Donelson, which guarded the Cumberland River, were the South's weakest links.

Both Fort Henry and Fort Donelson were constructed on land that was not particularly suitable for defensive positions. Clearly, better defenses could have been built in Kentucky, but since the Kentucky was considered neutral at the start of the war, Confederate commanders had to settle for less desirable defensive locations inside territory they already controlled. The site for Fort Henry, located approximately twenty miles west of Fort Donelson, was definitely the least desirable of the two construction sites. Fort Henry was surrounded by higher ground and it frequently flooded, due to the seasonal changes in height and depth of the Tennessee River.

The attack on Fort Donelson

In early 1862, Flag Officer Andrew H. Foote and Brigadier General Ulysses S. Grant were tasked to break the back of the Confederacy by taking Forts Henry and Donelson. They formed a joint Army-Navy command and immediately set about making preparations for their attack. This would be the first true test of Ironclad ships during the Civil War.

On February 6, 1862, Foote's Ironclads, *U.S.S. Cincinnati, U.S.S. Carondolet, U.S.S. St. Louis* and the recently converted *U.S.S. Essex*, slowly approached Fort Henry, and opened fire. The resulting hour-long bombardment pounded the poorly defended fort into submission but not before almost 2,500 soldiers escaped to Fort Donelson. The ironclads had won the day, but in doing so, they had taken heavy damage and had suffered many casualties.

Compared to Fort Henry, Fort Donelson was a far superior defensive position. The fort, built over a period of seven months, consisted of two river batteries which housed twelve impressive heavy thirty-two-pound coastal artillery pieces. A ten-foot-high defensive earthen ring made of logs and dirt stretched along the high ground from Hickman Creek to the small town of Dover. Prior to the battle for Fort Donelson, all of the trees within two hundred yards of the fort had been cut down to better improve the Confederate fields of fire. The remnants of trees and waste lumber were sharpened and later used to build obstacles around the exterior of the fort. At the heart of Fort Donelson were approximately four hundred crudely built log huts. These huts, built by both soldiers and slaves, housed the Confederate defenders during the winter. These small hovels were of poor construction, and on at least one occasion, the huts had to be burned to the ground after an epidemic of measles had been reported in the camp.

Initially, the soldiers stationed at the fort were in good spirits. They had snowball fights, told stories around the campfires, and let off steam with whooping rebel yells. Their light-heartedness would change, however, on the cold morning of February 14, 1862, when more than fifteen thousand Union troops encircled around the outer defensive ring of Fort Donelson. The Union troops, who had suffered a miserable night in a ferocious snowstorm, were ready for a fight. Early on the afternoon of the 14th, the Battle of Fort Donelson officially began when Foote and his fleet of ironclads arrived at the river's edge, just below the fort. Foote's armada, consisting of the *U.S.S. St. Louis, U.S.S. Pittsburgh, U.S.S. Louisville* and *U.S.S. Carondolet* and accompanied by the wooden vessels *U.S.S. Conestoga* and *U.S.S. Tyler,* had navigated the Tennessee and Ohio Rivers and were soon heavily engaged with the twelve coastal defense cannons manned by Confederate artillerymen at the lower river battery. Foote had hoped to move his fleet close to the fort's defensive works so that he could pound the riverside Confederate positions into submission, but his plan failed miserably. The slow-moving current and the lack of space on the river required to maneuver the lumbering ironclads combined to make the Union flotilla an easy target for Confederate gunners.

Withering Confederate fire devastated Foote's ironclads, causing serious damage and wounding many sailors, including Foote himself. At one point during the battle, friendly fire nearly caused the demise of the *USS Carondelet* when it was accidentally fired upon by one of its sister ships.

The naval and land battle for Fort Donelson raged for over an hour and a half before the crippled Union fleet was forced to retreat. As the ships pulled away, the Confederate defenders filled the air with premature cheers of victory. This initial part of the battle was so furious that the impressive artillery duel could be heard up to thirty-five miles away.

As the battered and bruised Union fleet yielded the muddy Cumberland River to the besieged Southern defenders, the Confederate generals inside the fort -- John Floyd, Bushrod Johnson, Gideon Pillow, and Simon Buckner -- breathed a collective sigh of relief. They had won the day against a daunting and imposing foe. This hard-fought state of euphoria and rejoicing was cut short when the Confederate commanders of Fort Donelson realized that during the river duel with Foote's ironclads, General Grant had continued to rush reinforcements into the area, thereby bolstering his ranks.

Grant had used his reinforcements to tighten his grip on the beleaguered defenders of Fort Donelson. The Confederate leadership knew instinctively that if they did not attempt to break Grant's stranglehold on the fort, the Northern troops would completely encircle the earthen fort and starve the Confederates into surrendering without a fight. On the morning of February 15, 1862, the battle resumed as Southern forces massed against the Union right flank in an attempt to break through the Federal lines. The Southern commanders believed that if they could win the day, they would be able to clear a path through Grant's flank and eventually make their way to the safety of Nashville, Tennessee.

At first, it seemed like the Confederate plan would work. By late morning, Southern forces found their Federal counterparts slowly retreating. Instead of seizing the opportunity, though, confusion ruled in the Confederate chain of command. To the amazement of the Southern troops, their leadership ordered them back into their formerly occupied rifle pits and other defensive positions. Grant, seeing the Confederates' indecision, ordered an all-out attack. This instinctive move on General Grant's part allowed his troops to regain most of the terrain they had given up during the earlier day's fighting. It was now clear to the Confederate commanders that escape through Grant's lines was no longer an option.

It was about this time that the Confederate leadership truly started to crumble. Generals Floyd and Pillow immediately turned the command of the fort over to General Buckner. Shortly thereafter, Floyd and Pillow, along with two thousand infantrymen, quietly snuck out of Fort Donelson en route to Nashville. Later, Colonel Bedford Forrest, the acclaimed cavalryman, followed suit, as he led a small contingent of men and horses out of the fort, across Lick Creek, to safety.

The morning of February 16, 1862 heralded the dawn of a new day. But for General Buckner, it was a terrible day of reckoning. He knew he could not fight his way out of Fort Donelson and he knew his forces would not survive a long siege during the cold Tennessee winter. With this in mind, General Buckner asked General Grant for terms of surrender. Grant did not mince words. He immediately stated, "No terms, except an unconditional and immediate surrender can be accepted."

Buckner, seeing no other option, surrendered Fort Donelson to Grant and his victorious men at arms.

With the fall of Forts Henry and Donelson, the Union firmly tightened their hold on the Tennessee and Cumberland Rivers. These waterways became vital supply routes for the Federal Army throughout the remainder of the war. More importantly, the fall of these two relatively minor strongholds, forced the South to give up any intentions they may have had for securing a foothold in Kentucky and Western Tennessee.

After the cessation of hostilities at Fort Donelson, the U.S. Sanitary Commission rushed to the scene to provide food and aid to the wounded of both sides. Both Confederate and Union dead where hastily buried on the battlefield. Union forces, now in control of the tattered fort, began the arduous task of rebuilding it to support future military operations in the region. At the same time, nearly fifteen thousand Confederate prisoners of war were transported by steamboat to St. Louis, where they were incarcerated at the Gratiot Street Prison and the penitentiary in Alton, Illinois. Unknown to these brave men of the Confederacy, they would soon meet a fate much worse than a quick death in the throes of conflict.

The guns of Fort Donelson today

Following the end of the Civil War, the Fort Donelson National Cemetery was established on the Western edge of the original battlefield site. The remains of six hundred and seventy Union dead, previously buried at various locations across the battlefield and at several local cemeteries, were reinterred at this new cemetery. Due to the haste of their previous burials, five hundred and twelve Union bodies could not be identified, thereby contributing to the large number of "Unknown Soldiers" interred at this particular site. In 1933, the United Daughters of the Confederacy erected an impressive stone monument on the grounds of the Fort Donelson National Park. The exact location of the Confederate dead who were buried at Fort Donelson still remains a mystery.

It comes as no surprise that the battlefield of Fort Donelson has earned a reputation for being haunted.

The unspeakable horrors of the Battle of Fort Donelson continue to have a profound effect on those people who live near or visit the battlefield today. Visitors and employees at the Fort Donelson National Park frequently report that they have observed the spirits of dead Union and Confederate soldiers killed on the site wandering around the battlefield at night. Stranger yet, on many nights, the sound of gunfire is heard on the grounds, as if two invisible armies are still fighting for the control of Fort Donelson. There has yet to be an explanation of these mysterious occurrences, which are possibly related to the trauma of death at the site and the countless number of Confederate dead that still lay hidden at unknown locations beneath this historic battlefield.

1862: SHILOH

The Battle of Shiloh, or Pittsburg Landing as it is sometimes known, took place in April 1862 in Southwestern Tennessee. The battle involved two very different commanders, on different sides of the war. One of them, Ulysses S. Grant, was rising through the ranks and would eventual become the top man in the Union Army, while the other, Albert Sidney Johnston, was rapidly falling from the graces of Confederate President Jefferson Davis. Initially, Johnston had been held in high esteem. Davis once said, "If Sidney Johnston is not a general, we had better give up the war, because we have no general." But thanks to the fall of Fort Henry and Fort Donelson in February 1862, Johnston's reputation had suffered. He had been forced to abandon Kentucky and most of middle Tennessee. He concentrated his 42,000-man army at the major rail junction of Corinth, Mississippi, and from there, he and his commanders plotted to retake the important state of Tennessee. Johnston, though, would never leave the fields at Shiloh.

The Union Army under Major General Ulysses S. Grant had moved deep into Tennessee and was encamped principally at Pittsburg Landing on the west bank of the Tennessee River. Confederate forces led by Johnston and General P.G.T. Beauregard launched a surprise attack on the Union position - which ultimately failed. Grant may have won the battle, but it nearly derailed the sterling career that followed. In hindsight, critics questioned his tactics and he was nearly removed from command. Newspapers clamored for him to be demoted because he had been so badly surprised by the enemy. President Lincoln silenced Grant's critics. "I can't spare the man. He fights," he said.

At the time it took place, the battle at Shiloh was the bloodiest ever recorded in American history. The violence and death that occurred in those fields along the Tennessee River left an indelible impression behind, leaving Shiloh Battlefield to be regarded as one of the most haunted places in the state.

After the humiliating defeats at Fort Henry and Fort Donelson, General Albert Sidney Johnston withdrew his army into Western Tennessee, Northern Mississippi and Alabama to reorganize. Sensing an opportunity, Union Major General Henry W. Halleck, then commander in the West, responded by ordering Grant to begin an invasion up the Tennessee River. Halleck then ordered Grant to remain at Fort Henry and turn field command of the expedition over to a subordinate, C.F. Smith, who had just been promoted as a major general. Various historians assert that Halleck did this because of professional and personal animosity toward Grant. However, Halleck shortly restored Grant to full command - soon after an inquiry arrived about the action from President Lincoln, who recognized Grant's potential as a commander. Lincoln would continue to defend Grant against critics through the end of the war.

By early April, Grant had five divisions at Pittsburg Landing, Tennessee, and a sixth nearby. Meanwhile, Halleck's command was enlarged, and now having command over General Don Carlos Buell's Army of the Ohio, Halleck ordered Buell to concentrate with Grant. Buell duly commenced a march with much of his army from Nashville toward Pittsburg Landing. Halleck intended to take the field in person and lead both armies in an advance south to seize the Memphis & Charleston Railroad, a vital supply line between the Mississippi River Valley, Memphis, and Richmond.

Grant's army of nearly 49,000 men consisted of six divisions, led by Major Generals John A. McClernand and Lew Wallace and Brigadier Generals W.H.L. Wallace, Stephen A. Hurlbut, Benjamin Prentiss and William T. Sherman. In early April, all six of the divisions were encamped on the western side of the Tennessee River, Lew Wallace's at Crump's Landing and the rest farther south at Pittsburg Landing. Grant would later be criticized for the way that the army was encamped, spread out in bivouac style, many of them around the small log church named Shiloh the Hebrew word that means "place of peace." The men spent time waiting for Buell to arrive doing drills for his many raw troops, without entrenchments or other awareness of defensive measures. Grant later stated that he felt that "the troops with me, officers and men, needed discipline and drill more than they did experience with the pick, shovel and axe. Under all these circumstances I concluded that drill and discipline were worth more to our men than fortifications." Lew Wallace's division was five miles downstream at Crump's Landing, a position intended to prevent the placement of Confederate river batteries, and to strike the railroad line at Bethel Station.

On the eve of the battle, April 5, the first of Buell's divisions, under the command of Brigadier General William "Bull" Nelson, reached Savannah. Grant instructed Nelson to encamp there rather than cross the river immediately. The rest of Buell's army had not yet reached the area and, in fact, only portions of four divisions, totaling just under eighteen thousand men, would reach the area in time to take part in the battle, almost entirely on the second day.

On the Confederate side, Johnston concentrated his almost 55,000 men around Corinth, Mississippi, about twenty miles southwest of Grant's position. Of them, almost 45,000 departed from Corinth on April 3, hoping to surprise Grant before Buell arrived to join their forces together. They were organized into four large corps, commanded by Major Generals Leonidas Polk, with two divisions under Brigadier General Charles Clark and Major General Benjamin F. Cheatham; Major General Braxton Bragg, with two divisions under Brigadier Generals Daniel Ruggles and Jones M. Withers; Major General William J. Hardee, with three brigades under Brigadier Generals Thomas C. Hindman, Patrick Cleburne and Sterling A.M. Wood; Brigadier General John C. Breckinridge, in reserve, with three brigades under Colonels Robert Trabue and Winfield S. Statham and Brigadier General John S. Bowen, and attached cavalry.

As the Confederate and Union armies headed toward a collision, they were of comparable size, but the Confederates were poorly armed with aged weapons, including shotguns, hunting rifles, pistols, flintlock muskets and even a few pikes. However, some regiments, notably the 6th and 7th Kentucky Infantry, had Enfield rifles. They approached the battle with very little combat experience -- Braxton Bragg's men from Pensacola and Mobile were the best trained. Grant's army included thirty-two out of sixty-two infantry regiments who had combat experience at Fort Donelson. One-half of his artillery batteries and most of his cavalry were also combat veterans.

Johnston's second in command was Pierre G.T. Beauregard, who urged Johnston not to attack Grant. He was concerned that the sounds of marching and the Confederate soldiers' test-firing of their rifles after two days of rain had cost them the element of surprise. Johnston refused to accept Beauregard's advice and told him that he would "attack them if they were a million." Despite General Beauregard's well-founded concern, the Union forces did not hear the sounds of the marching army in its approach and remained blissfully unaware of the enemy camped just three miles away. It was a near blunder that could have cost Grant the field - and his command.

Johnston's plan was to attack Grant's left and separate the Union Army from its gunboat support and avenue of retreat on the Tennessee River, driving it west into the swamps of Snake and Owl Creeks, where it could be destroyed. Johnston's attack on Grant was originally planned for April 4, but the advance was delayed forty-eight hours. As a result, Beauregard again feared that the element of surprise had been lost and recommended withdrawing to Corinth. But Johnston once more refused to consider retreat.

Battle at Shiloh

On Sunday, April 6, Johnston's army was deployed for battle at 6:00 a.m. The army had spent the entire night undetected just a few miles away from Grant's troops and their approach and subsequent assault achieved almost total strategic and tactical surprise. For some reason, the Federal Army had no patrols in place to provide an early warning. Grant was caught unaware, as were his subordinates. Sherman, the informal camp commander at Pittsburg Landing, did not believe that the Confederates were anywhere nearby; he discounted any possibility of an attack from the south, expecting that Johnston would eventually attack from the direction of Purdy, Tennessee, to the west. When an Ohio colonel warned Sherman that an attack was imminent, the general said, "Take your damned regiment back to Ohio. There is no enemy nearer than Corinth."

Fortunately for the Union Army, Johnston and Beauregard had no unified battle plan and the confusing alignment of their troops helped reduce the effectiveness of the attack. Johnston had telegraphed Jefferson Davis that the attack would proceed as: "Polk the left, Bragg the center, Hardee to right, Breckinridge in reserve." His strategy was to emphasize the attack on his right flank to prevent the Union Army from reaching the Tennessee River, its supply line and avenue of retreat. He instructed Beauregard to stay in the rear and direct men and supplies as needed, while he rode to the front to lead the men on the battle line. This effectively ceded control of the battle to Beauregard, who had a different concept: simply to attack in three waves and push the Union Army straight eastward into the Tennessee River. The corps of Hardee and Bragg began the assault with their divisions in one line, almost three miles wide.

As these units advanced, they became intermingled and difficult to control. Corps commanders attacked in line without reserves. Artillery could not be concentrated where it needed to be. At about 7:30 a.m., from his position in the rear, Beauregard ordered the corps of Polk and Breckinridge forward on the left and right of the line, destroying their effectiveness. The attack therefore went forward as a frontal assault conducted by a single line formation, which lacked both the depth and weight needed for success. The effectiveness of the Confederates' initial surprise attack was watered down from the very start.

Regardless of its shortcomings, though, the assault was ferocious, and some of the numerous inexperienced soldiers of Grant's new army fled for safety to the Tennessee River. Others fought well but were forced to withdraw under strong pressure and attempted to form new defensive lines. Many regiments fragmented entirely and the companies and sections that remained on the field attached themselves to other commands. During this period, Sherman, who had been negligent in preparation for the battle, became one of its most important elements. He appeared everywhere along his lines, inspiring his raw recruits to resist the initial assaults, despite staggering losses on both sides. He received two minor wounds and had three horses shot out from under him that day.

Sherman's division bore the brunt of the initial attack, and despite heavy fire on their position and their right flank crumbling, they stubbornly continued to fight. The Union troops slowly lost ground and fell back to a position behind Shiloh Church. McClernand's division temporarily stabilized the position. Overall, however, Johnston's forces made steady progress until noon, rolling up Union positions one by one. As the Confederates advanced, many threw away their flintlock muskets and grabbed better rifles that had been dropped by the fleeing Union troops.

General Grant was about ten miles downriver at Savannah, Tennessee, that morning. On April 4, he had been injured when his horse fell and pinned him underneath. He was convalescing and unable to move without crutches. He heard the sound of artillery fire and raced to the battlefield by boat, arriving about 8:30 a.m. He worked frantically to bring up reinforcements that seemed near enough to arrive swiftly, including Bull Nelson's division from Savannah and Lew Wallace's division from Crump's Landing. However, he would wait almost all day before the first of these reinforcements from Nelson's division arrived.

It would be Lew Wallace's slow movement to the battlefield that day that would become controversial. The future author of *Ben-Hur* and governor of New Mexico had been left in reserve at Crump's Landing at a place called Stoney Lonesome at the rear of the Union line. When Grant reached the battlefield, he sent orders for Wallace to move his unit up to support Sherman. Wallace took a route different from the one Grant intended claiming later that there was ambiguity to Grant's order . Wallace arrived at the end of his march to find that Sherman had been forced back and was no longer where Wallace thought he was. Moreover, the battle line had moved so far that Wallace now found himself in the rear of the advancing Southern troops. A messenger arrived from Grant, demanding to know why Wallace had not arrived at Pittsburg Landing, where the Union was making its stand. Wallace was confused. He felt sure he could viably launch an attack from where he was and hit the Confederates in the rear. After the war was over, he claimed that his division might have attacked and defeated the Confederate forces if his advance had not been interrupted. Nevertheless, he decided to turn his troops around and march back to Stoney Lonesome. Rather than realign his troops so that the rear guard would be in the front, Wallace chose to march the troops in a circle so that the original order was maintained, only facing in the other direction. Wallace marched back to Stoney Lonesome and then to Pittsburg Landing, arriving at Grant's position that evening, when the fighting was practically over. Needless to say, Grant was furious. His endorsement of Wallace's battle report was negative enough to damage Wallace's military career severely - which is why he is best remembered today as an author instead of a soldier.

Along the main Union defensive line that morning, men of Prentiss' and W. H. L. Wallace's divisions established and held a position nicknamed the "Hornet's Nest," which was a dirt road that ran through a field. The Confederates assaulted the position for several hours rather than simply bypassing it, and they suffered heavy casualties during what may have been as many as fourteen assaults. The Union forces on both the right and left sides of the Hornet's Nest were forced back and Prentiss' position was left hanging in the line. Coordination among the units in the Nest was poor, and units withdrew based solely on their individual commanders' decisions. This pressure increased when W.H.L. Wallace was mortally wounded. He commanded the largest concentration of troops in the Nest and soon, regiments became disorganized and companies fell apart. However, it was not until the Confederates, led by Brigadier General Daniel Ruggles, assembled over fifty cannons into a battery that could blast the line at close range that they were able to surround the position. The Hornet's Nest fell after holding out for seven hours. Surrounded on three sides, General Prentiss surrendered himself and the remains of his division to the Confederates. A large portion of the Union survivors, numbering over two thousand men, were captured, but their sacrifice bought time for Grant to establish a final defense line near Pittsburg Landing.

While the Confederates were attempting to take the Hornet's Nest, they suffered a serious setback with their death of their commanding general. Johnston was mortally wounded at about 2:30 p.m. while leading attacks on the

Union left when he was shot in the leg. Believing that the wound was insignificant, he sent his personal surgeon away to care for some of the wounded captured Union soldiers. In the doctor's absence, he bled to death within an hour, his boot filling with blood from a severed artery. This was a severe blow to the Confederacy. Despite recent setbacks, Johnston was still considered to be one of the South's most effective leaders. He was the highest-ranking officer from either side to be killed in combat during the Civil War.

Beauregard assumed command, but from his position in the rear he may have had only a vague idea of the disposition of forces at the front. He ordered that Johnston's death be kept secret to avoid damaging morale among the soldiers. He then resumed attacks against the Hornet's Nest, which was likely a tactical error. The Union flanks were slowly pulling back to form a semicircular line around Pittsburg Landing, and if Beauregard had concentrated his forces against the flanks, he might have defeated the Union Army and then overrun the Hornet's Nest at his leisure.

The Union flanks had been pushed back, but not decisively. Hardee and Polk caused Sherman and McClernand on the Union right to retreat in the direction of Pittsburg Landing, leaving the right flank of the Hornet's Nest exposed. Just after the death of Johnston, Breckinridge, whose corps had been in reserve, attacked on the extreme left of the Union line, driving off the undermanned brigade of Colonel David Stuart and potentially opening a path into the Union rear area and the Tennessee River. However, they paused to regroup and recover from exhaustion and disorganization. When the men were recovered, they chose to follow the sound of the guns toward the Hornet's Nest - and the opportunity was lost.

After the fall of the Hornet's Nest, the remnants of the Union line established a solid three-mile front around Pittsburg Landing, extending west from the Tennessee and then north up the River Road, keeping the approach open for the expected belated arrival of Lew Wallace's division. Sherman commanded the right of the line, McClernand the center, and on the left, remnants of W. H. L. Wallace's, Hurlbut's, and Stuart's men mixed in with the thousands of stragglers. One brigade of Buell's army under Colonel Jacob Ammen, arrived in time to be ferried over and join the left end of the line. The defensive line was supported by fifty cannon and two naval gunboats on the river, the *U.S.S. Lexington* and the *U.S.S. Tyler*.

A final Confederate charge of two brigades, led by Brigadier General Jones Withers, attempted to break through the line but was repulsed. Beauregard called off a second attempt after 6:00 p.m., just as the sun was setting. The Confederate plan had failed. They had pushed Grant east to a defensible position on the river, not forced him west into the swamps.

The evening of April 6 was a dispiriting end to the first day of the bloodiest battle in American history up to that point. The eerie cries of wounded and dying men on the fields between the two armies could be heard in both camps throughout the night. A thunderstorm passed through the area and the rhythmic shelling from the Union gunboats made the night a miserable experience for both sides.

Beauregard, convinced that he had the Union troops cornered, caused considerable historical controversy with his decision to halt the assault at dusk. Braxton Bragg and Albert Sidney Johnston's son, Colonel William Preston Johnston, were among those who bemoaned the so-called "lost opportunity at Shiloh." Beauregard did not come to the front to inspect the strength of the Union lines but remained at Shiloh Church. He also discounted intelligence reports from Colonel Nathan Bedford Forrest that Buell's men were crossing the river to reinforce Grant. In defense of his decision, his troops were simply exhausted, there was less than an hour of daylight left, and Grant's artillery advantage was formidable.

Was it a "lost opportunity?" Historians will never agree if Grant could have been taken that night or not.

On Monday, April 7, the now-combined Union armies numbered 45,000 men. The Confederates had suffered as many as 8,500 casualties the first day. Because of straggling and desertion, their commanders reported no more than twenty thousand effective men. The Confederates had withdrawn south into Prentiss' and Sherman's former camps, and Polk's corps retired to a point four miles southwest of Pittsburg Landing. No line of battle was formed and few, if any, of the commands were resupplied with ammunition. During the night, the soldiers had been consumed by the need to find food, water and shelter for a much-needed rest.

That morning, Beauregard, unaware that he was now outnumbered, planned to continue the attack and drive Grant into the river. To his surprise, the Union forces started moving forward in a massive counterattack at dawn. Grant and Buell launched their attacks separately, coordinated only at the division level. Lew Wallace's division was the first to see action, at the extreme right of the Union line, crossing Tilghman Branch of the river around 7:00 a.m. and driving back the brigade of Colonel Preston Pond. On Wallace's left were the survivors of Sherman's division, then McClernand's, and W. H. L. Wallace's now under the command of Col. James M. Tuttle . Buell's divisions continued to the left: Bull Nelson's, Crittenden's, and McCook's. The Confederate defenders were so badly disorganized that there was no cooperation between units. It took more than two hours for General Polk to bring up his division from the southwest. By 10:00 a.m.,

Beauregard had stabilized his front with his corps commanders. In a thicket near the Hamburg-Purdy Road, the fighting was so intense that Sherman described in his report of the battle "the severest musketry fire I ever heard."

On the Union left, Nelson's division led the advance, followed closely by Crittenden's and McCook's, down the Corinth and Hamburg-Savannah roads. After heavy fighting, Crittenden's division recaptured the Hornet's Nest area by late morning, but Crittenden and Nelson were both repulsed by determined counterattacks launched by Breckinridge. The Union right made steady progress, driving Bragg and Polk to the south. As Crittenden and McCook resumed their attacks, Breckinridge was forced to retire, and by noon, Beauregard's line paralleled the Hamburg-Purdy Road.

In early afternoon, Beauregard launched a series of counterattacks from the Shiloh Church area, aiming to ensure control of the Corinth Road. The Union right was temporarily driven back by these assaults at Water Oaks Pond. Crittenden, reinforced by Tuttle, seized the road junction of the Hamburg-Purdy and East Corinth roads, driving the Confederates back. Nelson resumed his attack and seized the heights overlooking Locust Grove Branch by late afternoon. Beauregard's final counterattack was flanked and repulsed when Grant moved Colonel James C. Veatch's brigade forward on the field.

By this time, Beauregard realized that the day was lost. He had lost the initiative, was low on ammunition and food, and was faced with more than ten thousand of his men killed, wounded or missing. He pulled back beyond Shiloh Church, using five thousand men under Breckinridge as a covering force and massing Confederate cannon at the church and on the ridge south of Shiloh Branch. They managed to keep the Union forces in position on the Corinth Road until 5:00 p.m., when the Confederates began their withdrawal back to Corinth.

The exhausted Union troops made a half-hearted pursuit, but only as far as Sherman and Prentiss' old camps. Lew Wallace's division advanced beyond Shiloh Branch but, receiving no support from other units, halted at dark and returned to Sherman's camp. The battle was over. For long afterwards, Grant and Buell quarreled over Grant's decision not to mount an immediate pursuit with another hour of daylight remaining. Grant cited the exhaustion of his troops, although the Confederates were certainly just as exhausted. Part of Grant's reluctance to act could have been the unusual command relationship he had with Buell. Although Grant was the senior officer and technically was in command of both armies, Buell made it quite clear throughout the two days that he was acting independently. It was another case of complicated personal relations having had a strange effect on events during the war.

On April 8, Grant sent Sherman south along the Corinth Road on a reconnaissance to ascertain if the Confederates had retreated, or if they were regrouping to resume their attacks. Grant's army lacked the large organized cavalry units that would have been better suited for reconnaissance and for vigorous pursuit of a retreating enemy. Sherman marched with two infantry brigades from his division, along with two battalions of cavalry, and they met up with Brigadier General Thomas J. Wood's division of Buell's army. Six miles southwest of Pittsburg Landing, Sherman's men came upon a clear field in which an extensive camp was erected, including a Confederate field hospital, protected by three hundred Confederate cavalry soldiers, commanded by Nathan Bedford Forrest. The road approaching the field was covered by fallen trees for over two hundred yards.

As skirmishers from the 77th Ohio Infantry approached, having difficulty clearing the fallen timber, Forrest ordered a charge, producing a wild melee with Confederate troopers firing shotguns and revolvers and brandishing sabers, nearly resulting in Sherman's capture. As Colonel Jesse Hildebrand's brigade began forming in a battle line, the Confederates started to retreat at the sight of the strong force, and Forrest, who was well in advance of his men, came within a few yards of the Union soldiers before realizing he was all alone. Sherman's men attacked and a soldier shoved his musket into Forrest's side and fired, striking him above the hip, and penetrating to near the spine. Although he was seriously wounded, Forrest was able to stay on horseback and escape. He survived both the wound and the war. The Union lost about one hundred men, mostly captured during Forrest's charge, in an incident that has been remembered with the name "Fallen Timbers." After capturing the Confederate field hospital, Sherman encountered the rear of Breckinridge's covering force, and when he determined that the enemy was making no plans to renew its attack, he withdrew back to camp.

The battle of Shiloh had officially come to an end.

In the immediate wake of the battle, Northern newspapers vilified Grant for his performance. Reporters, many far from the battle, spread the story that Grant had been drunk, falsely alleging that this had resulted in many of his men being bayoneted in their tents because of a lack of defensive preparedness. Despite the Union victory, Grant's reputation suffered in Northern public opinion. Many credited Buell with taking control of the broken Union forces and leading them to victory on April 7. Calls for Grant's removal overwhelmed the White House, but President Lincoln refused to bow to pressure to get rid of Grant. Sherman emerged as an immediate hero, his steadfastness under fire and amid chaos winning him great acclaim and according to many, truly beginning his great career to come. In time, though, Grant would emerge as the hero of the day. He has since been recognized for his clear judgment under the strenuous circumstances, and his ability to perceive the larger tactical picture that ultimately resulted in victory on the second day.

At the time, though, Grant's career temporarily suffered. Henry W. Halleck combined and reorganized his armies, relegating Grant to the powerless position of second-in-command. In late April and May, the Union armies, under Halleck's personal command, advanced slowly toward Corinth and captured it, while an amphibious force on the Mississippi River destroyed the Confederate River Defense Fleet and captured Memphis. Halleck was promoted to be general in chief of all the Union armies, and with his departure for the East, Grant was restored to command. Grant eventually pushed on down the Mississippi to besiege Vicksburg. After the surrender of Vicksburg and the fall of Port Hudson in the summer of 1863, the Mississippi River was under Union control and the Confederacy was cut in two. Command of the Confederate forces in the region fell to Braxton Bragg, who was promoted to full general on April 6. In the fall of 1862, he led the Western army on an unsuccessful invasion of Kentucky, culminating in his retreat from the Battle of Perryville.

The two-day battle of Shiloh, the most horrific in American history up to that time, resulted in the defeat of the Confederate Army in the West and the frustration of Johnston's plan to prevent the joining of the two Union armies in Tennessee. The Union lost more than thirteen thousand men in those two days and the Confederacy lost more than ten thousand - a much costlier loss for the badly outnumbered Southern force. The dead included the Confederate Army's commander, Albert Sidney Johnston and Union General W.H.L. Wallace.

Both sides were shocked at the carnage. None suspected that three more years of such bloodshed remained in the war and that larger and bloodier battles were still to come.

In the 1890s, Shiloh became one of the first five battlefields restored by the federal government to commemorate its importance during the war. Government involvement eventually proved insufficient to preserve the sprawling canvas upon which the battle took place, though, and private preservation organizations like the Civil War Trust stepped in to preserve more than eleven hundred acres of his once blood-soaked site.

Every year, tourists, Civil War reenactors and history buffs return to the fields of Shiloh to experience what life - and death - was like in the days of early April 1862. In many reported instances, they have not had to look far. Death walks hand in hand with life on these fields of battle, for the ghosts of Shiloh refuse to rest in peace. There have been many reports of the sounds of men crying and moaning on the fields at night - much like it happened on the night after the first day of the battle - and stories of spectral gunfire, shouts, screams and even the pounding of hoofbeats of invisible horses.

One of the most famous ghost stories of Shiloh is that of the phantom drummer boy. There have also been reports of drums being heard on the battlefield when no drummer is present. The sounds are attributed to a young boy who helped to win a victory by mistake. Like many of the soldiers that fought over the course of those two bloody days, many of the support troops - like the young drummer boys - were inexperienced, raw recruits. During a critical moment at Shiloh, the drummer was told to sound the beat for advance, which he did. The soldiers advanced and fought bravely until they were outnumbered. The commanding officer then told the drummer boy to pound out a code that meant to retreat. Instead, the boy accidentally tapped out the beat for "advance" again. The commander was stunned as the men surged forward rather than retreating to safety. But rather than be slaughtered by the enemy, the opposing troops began to withdraw and the attack became successful - thanks to the drummer boy's ignorance of his drum cadences.

The story goes on to say that the drummer boy did not survive the battle. He was later killed and his drum was smashed into pieces. Regardless, after all of these years, his drum can still be heard in the distance across the fields of Shiloh.

Some say that the drummer was John Clem, the famous "Drummer Boy of Shiloh," whose spirit wanders the field, tapping out the cadence of the drums. But this isn't the case. Though a John Joseph Klem, born in 1851, was indeed associated with the Union Army, his name was recorded as Clem when he enlisted , he first served with the 22nd Michigan, which hadn't been formed when the battle of Shiloh was fought in April 1862. Clem, however, did ride an artillery caisson into the battle of Chickamauga, carrying a musket cut down to fit his short stature. With it, he shot a Confederate colonel who had the nerve to demand the boy's surrender. For his action, Clem was promoted to sergeant and became the youngest soldier to ever attain the rank of a noncommissioned officer in the U.S. Army.

After the battle at Chickamauga, a song was written by William S. Hays called "The Drummer Boy of Shiloh," and published in *Harpers Weekly*. Many later assumed that Clem was the subject of the song, during which the drummer boy died. But the "Drummer Boy" of Chickamauga, not Shiloh, was alive at the time. He would be captured in October 1863 and then later exchanged to participate in several other battles with the Army of the Cumberland. He would be wounded two times before being discharged in 1864. He later rejoined the army, finally retiring as a brigadier general.

The ghostly drummer boy of Shiloh continues to play after all these years - but his identity remains unknown.

One of the battlefield's most haunted sites is "Bloody Pond." During the battle, wounded soldiers and horses sought out this small pond to quench their thirsts. After a while, so many wounded men dragged themselves to the edge of the water that it was stained red by blood. Legend has it that, at certain times, the water in the pond will turn crimson once again, as if in reminder of the horrors that took place on the battlefield in 1862. Many have tried to explain this strange phenomenon, but they have never been successful.

One enduring story of an unexplained occurrence took place in the early 1990s. According to a park ranger, there was a man who often visited the battlefield who was illegally digging up relics and selling them. The rangers had been trying to catch him for a long time, but he somehow managed to elude them. He was often spotted with a metal detector, and they knew he was digging up the unmarked graves and stealing artifacts from the bodies. The problem was that they could never catch him in the act.

One night, some rangers were patrolling the woods when they found a broken metal detector. Then, sitting in a car at the edge of the woods, they found the man they had been looking for. They said that he seemed to be in shock and was incapable of talking or moving. They took him to a hospital, and while he recovered, he refused to talk about what had happened to him and later was put under psychiatric care. The story went that the man had encountered something in the woods that had scared him out of his mind. Rumor had it that he had dug up a grave and was in the act of stealing uniform buttons from a corpse when a bony hand had reached out of the ground and snatched away his ill-gotten treasure.

Sounds unlikely? Perhaps -- but something certainly scared him.

1862: ANTIETAM
"On Bloody Ground..."

Located on the far western edge of Maryland is the Antietam Battlefield, which can be found just outside of the small town of Sharpsburg. Antietam is perhaps the best preserved of all of the areas that have been turned into National Park Battlefields, looking much as it did at the time of the battle in 1862.

On a clear day, when the crisp wind is blowing across the grass, you can almost imagine yourself in another time. You feel that if you looked up, you might actually catch a glimpse of a weary soldier, trudging on toward either death or victory. Of course, some people claim to have done more than just imagined this....

The famous photograph taken near Dunker Church in the aftermath of the battle at Antietam Creek

The Battle of Antietam Creek took place in September 1862, during some of the most brutal days of the Civil War. The Union Army had been badly beaten at Manassas and was in the midst of turmoil as President Lincoln fired ineffectual general after general. At this point, it still looked as though the Confederacy might actually win the war.

The battle was fought on September 17 and marked the first of two attempts by Robert E. Lee to take the war onto Northern soil. It would become known as the bloodiest single day of the entire war with combined casualties of more than 23,000 wounded, missing and dead. The battle itself was considered a draw, but the effect on both sides was staggering.

By early September, Lee was on the move to the north. He had trounced the Union Army at Manassas in August, but his men were exhausted, low on ammunition and out of supplies. He marched them north into Maryland, a march that was not unobserved by Washington or by Army of the Potomac commander General George McClellan. As luck would have it for Lee, McClellan, already known for acting slowly and overestimating the forces against him, believed that he was greatly outnumbered by Lee's Confederates and he was slow to act in heading off Lee's march, allowing him to penetrate deep into Union territory.

During the march north, a strange occurrence took place. It is one that has never truly been explained, and it changed the course of the battle to come. If it had not taken place, it's entirely possible that the outcome of the war could have been much different.

Copies of Special Order No. 191, which was Lee's plan for the invasion of the North, were sent out to all of Lee's generals. Thomas "Stonewall" Jackson received his copy of the order, copied it and then sent it out to his brother-in-law, Harvey Hill, who also received a copy from Lee. Not realizing that Jackson had sent him an additional copy, Hill never knew that the second copy had not arrived.

On September 13, Union troops moved into a campground that had been recently vacated by Hill. A corporal with the 27th Indiana Volunteers found an envelope containing three cigars wrapped around a piece of paper lying in the grass. The paper was a copy of Lee's orders. McClellan, upon being presented with the document, realized that he was now privy to Lee's secret plans. He is reported to have jubilantly stated, "Here is a paper with which, if I cannot whip Bobby Lee, then I will be willing to go home."

Even though he now possessed a step-by-step outline of the Confederates' plans for invading Maryland and attacking Washington, McClellan did nothing. His failure to act in such situations had previously cost the Union Army dearly and he was frequently criticized by President Lincoln for being overly cautious. This time was no exception. Instead of starting out immediately in pursuit of Lee's forces, McClellan waited overnight and then started west to South Mountain. He was convinced that Lee's dirty, tired, hungry army still outnumbered him. Ironically, the Union Army outnumbered Lee by more than 35,000 men.

On September 14, Lee tried to block McClellan's pursuit at South Mountain, but he was forced to split his army and send troops to aid Stonewall Jackson in his capture of Harper's Ferry. He was able to delay McClellan for one day, and by September 15, battle lines had been drawn west and east of Antietam Creek, near the town of Sharpsburg. Harper's Ferry surrendered the same day and Jackson soon moved north and joined Lee at Sharpsburg. They moved into position along a low ridge that ran north and south of town. It was an effective defensive position, but not a perfect one. The terrain provided excellent cover for infantrymen, with rail and stone fences, outcroppings of rocks and small hollows. The creek in front of them was a minor barrier and was crossed by three stone bridges, set one mile apart. However, the position was made precarious by the fact that the Confederate rear was blocked by the Potomac River and only a single crossing point was nearby if retreat became necessary. On September 15, the force under Lee's immediate command consisted of no more than eighteen thousand men, one-third the size of the Federal Army.

The first two Union divisions arrived on the afternoon of September 15 and the bulk of the army came later that night. Although an immediate Union attack on the morning of September 16 would have given the Union an overwhelming advantage in numbers, McClellan still believed that Lee outnumbered him and had over one hundred thousand men in his command. This caused McClellan to delay his attack for a day and gave the Confederates more time to prepare defensive positions and to allow Longstreet and Jackson to arrive from Hagerstown and Harper's Ferry.

On the evening of September 16, McClellan ordered General Joseph Hooker's corps to cross Antietam Creek and probe enemy positions. George Meade's division cautiously attacked Confederates under John Bell Hood near the East Woods. After dark, artillery fire continued as McClellan tried to position his troops with plans to overwhelm the enemy's left flank. He came up with this plan because of the configuration of bridges across the Antietam. The lower bridge which would later be named Burnside's Bridge was dominated by Confederate positions on the bluffs above it. The middle bridge, on the road from Boonsboro, could be hit by artillery fire from the heights near Sharpsburg. But the upper bridge was two miles east of the Confederate guns and could be crossed safely. McClellan planned to commit more than half his army to the assault. He also planned a diversionary attack on the Confederate right and was prepared to strike the center with his reserves if either assault succeeded.

But Robert E. Lee, noting the skirmish in the East Woods, was quick to realize McClellan's plan and prepared his defenses accordingly. He shifted his men to the left flank and sent urgent messages to two commanders, Lafayette McLaws and A.P. Hill, who had not yet arrived at the battlefield.

McClellan's plans were poorly made and badly executed. He issued to each of his commanders only the orders for his own corps, not general orders describing the entire plan for battle. The terrain of the field made it difficult for the commanders to see what was happening outside of their immediate area, and with McClellan's headquarters more than a mile to the rear at the Phillip Pry house he was unable to control the separate corps. Because of this, the battle on the following day became essentially three, separate, mostly uncoordinated fights - morning in the north end of the battlefield, mid-day in the center and afternoon in the south. The disorganization of McClellan's forces nullified the numbers advantage enjoyed by the Union and allowed Lee to do heavy damage to the Federal Army.

The battle opened at dawn on September 17 with an attack down the Hagerstown Turnpike by a Union corps under General Hooker. Hooker's objective was the plateau that was home to Dunker Church, a modest, whitewashed building that belonged to a local sect of German Baptists. Abner Doubleday's division moved on Hooker's right, James Ricketts's moved on the left into the East Woods, and George Meade's Pennsylvania Reserves division deployed in the center and slightly to the rear. Jackson's defense consisted of the divisions under Alexander Lawton and John R. Jones in line from the West Woods, across the Turnpike, and along the southern end of the Miller cornfield.

As the first Union troops emerged from the North Woods and into the cornfield, artillery erupted from the horse artillery batteries under Jeb Stuart and from four batteries under Colonel Stephen Lee on the high ground across the pike from Dunker Church. The Union returned fire from nine batteries on the ridge behind the North Woods and from four batteries east of Antietam Creek. Heavy casualties were felt on both sides and Colonel Lee later referred to the scene as "artillery Hell."

Spotting the sun glinting on Confederate bayonets, hidden in the cornfield, Hooker halted his infantry and brought up four batteries of artillery, which fired canister shots into the air. The artillery, and rifle fire from both sides, acted like a scythe, cutting down both cornstalks and men alike. It was reported in eyewitness accounts that the corn in the field was "cut as closely as could have been done with a knife."

Meade's Pennsylvanians advanced through the East Woods and exchanged fire with Colonel James Walker's brigade of Alabama, Georgia and North Carolina troops. As Walker's men forced back the Federals, aided by Lee's artillery fire, Rickett's division entered the cornfield and was decimated by artillery. Union Brigadier General Abram Duryee marched his division directly into the line of fire of Colonel Marcellus Douglass's Georgia brigade and enduring heavy fire, he was forced to order a retreat. Duryee had expected reinforcements - brigades under Brigadier General George L. Hartsuff and Colonel William A. Christian - but they had difficulties reaching the field. Hartsuff was wounded and Christian dismounted and fled to the rear in terror. When the men rallied and advanced into the cornfield, they met the same infantry and artillery fire as the unlucky men before them. Eventually, though, the superior Union numbers began to overwhelm the Confederate lines. At that moment, the Louisiana "Tiger" Brigade under Harry Hays entered the fray and forced the Union troops back to the East Woods. The Tigers were beaten back when the Federals rolled a battery of three-inch guns directly into the cornfield and slaughtered the Tigers at point-blank range.

The result was a stalemate but Federal advances a few hundred yards to the west were more successful. Brigadier General John Gibbon's 4th Brigade of Doubleday's Division recently named the Iron Brigade began advancing down and across the turnpike, into the cornfield and into the West Woods, driving back Jackson's men. They were only halted by a charge of Confederates from Starke's Brigade, which opened fire from only thirty yards away. The Iron Brigade counterattacked and Starke was mortally wounded. The Union advance on Dunker Church resumed and cut a large hole in Jackson's defensive line, which nearly collapsed. The cost was steep, but Hooker was making steady progress.

Confederate reinforcements finally arrived around 7:00 a.m., consisting of two divisions that had made a night march from Harper's Ferry. Around 7:15 a.m., General Lee moved George T. Anderson's Georgia Brigade from the right flank of the army to assist Jackson.

John Bell Hood's division advanced through the West Woods and pushed the Union troops back through the cornfield again. The Texans were said to have attacked with particular ferocity because they had been called from reserve position, where they had been eating the first hot meal they had enjoyed in days. They were aided by three brigades from D.H. Hill's division, encamped near the Mumma Farm, southeast of the cornfield, and by Jubal Early's brigade, which pushed through the West Woods. Hood's men bore the brunt of the fighting and took heavy casualties, but were able to keep the defensive line from crumbling. When later asked by a fellow officer where his division was, Hood replied, "Dead on the field."

Hooker's men also paid dearly and never achieved their objective. After two hours and 2,500 casualties, they were back where they started. The cornfield, which was only about two hundred and fifty yards deep and four hundred yards wide, was a scene of nightmarish devastation. That forlorn field changed hands no fewer than fifteen times in the course of the morning. Major Rufus R. Dawes later compared the fighting ground to several other blood-soaked slaughters during the war, insisting that "the Antietam Turnpike surpassed them all in manifest evidence of slaughter."

By mid-day, the action had shifted to the center of the Confederate line. Major General Edwin Sumner had accompanied the morning attack of Sedgwick's division, but another of his divisions, under William French, lost contact with Sumner and Sedgwick and inexplicably headed south. Eager to join the fighting, French found skirmishers in his path and ordered his men forward. By this time, Sumner's aide located French and described the terrible fighting in the West Woods and relayed an order for him to divert Confederate attention by attacking their center.

French confronted D.H. Hill's division, which numbered less than half of the men commanded by French. However, Hill's men were in a strong defensive position atop a gradual ridge that overlooked a sunken road that separated the Roulette and Piper farms. It had been worn down by years of wagon traffic and had been turned into a trench from which men could fire from cover. For nearly four hours, fierce fighting occurred along this road which would later become known as "Bloody Lane." Finally, confusion and exhaustion ended the battle here.

Scores of men were killed and wounded and yet a great opportunity presented itself. If the section of line that was broken by the fighting along the sunken road was exploited, Lee's army could be divided in half and possibly defeated. There were ample Union forces to do so. There was a reserve of 3,500 cavalry and the 10,300 infantrymen waiting near the middle bridge, a mile away. A corps under command of Major General William B. Franklin had just arrived, and he was eager to exploit this breakthrough, but Sumner, the senior corps commander, ordered him not to advance. Franklin appealed to McClellan, who left his headquarters in the rear to hear both arguments. He ended up backing Sumner's decision and ordered Franklin to hold his position. Another opportunity was lost.

Later in the day, the action moved to the southern end of the battlefield. McClellan's plan called for Major General Ambrose Burnside's corps to carry out a diversionary attack in support of Hooker's corps, hoping to draw Confederate attention away from the main attack to the north. However, Burnside was specifically told to wait until he received orders to start the attack, which did not reach him until 10:00 a.m. Burnside was impatient about starting the attack. He had hard feelings against McClellan and a dislike for the man, feeling that he had been pushed aside during a recent reshuffling of the command structure.

Burnside had four divisions about twelve thousand men and fifty guns east of Antietam Creek. Facing him was a force that had been greatly depleted by Lee's movement of troops to bolster the Confederate left flank. At dawn, many of the men had been shifted away and Brigadier General David R. Jones had only about three thousand men and twelve guns left to face Burnside. Four thin brigades guarded the ridges near Sharpsburg, a low plateau known as Cemetery Hill. The remaining men, the 2nd and 20th Georgia regiments under Brigadier General Robert Toombs, defended Rohrbach's Bridge, a stone structure that was the southernmost crossing of Antietam Creek. It would come to be known as Burnside's Bridge because of the notoriety of the events of that day. The bridge was a difficult objective with the road leading up to it exposed to enemy fire. It was dominated by a high wooded bluff on the west bank, strewn with boulders from an old quarry, making infantry and sharpshooter fire from good, covered positions a dangerous impediment to anyone who dared to cross it.

Ironically, though, Burnside's men could have easily stormed across the creek without ever setting foot on the bride. Antietam Creek in this area was seldom more than fifty feet wide and most stretches were only waist deep and out of Confederate range. Burnside was oblivious to this fact, which made him a subject of derision to both Confederate soldiers and officers. Confederate staff officer Henry Kyd Douglas later wrote, "Go and look at that river, and tell me if you don't think Burnside and his corps might have executed a hop, skip, and jump and landed on the other side. One thing is certain, they might have waded it that day without getting their waist belts wet in any place."

But Burnside concentrated his plan on storming the bridge while simultaneously crossing a ford that McClellan's engineers had found a half-mile downstream - a shallow spot in the river that turned out to have banks too high for the men to climb. Unable to use this crossing, Burnside sent a division under Brigadier General Isaac Rodman downstream through woods and thick brush to find another crossing, hoping they could flank the Confederates. Meanwhile, Colonel George Crook's Ohio brigade, with the support of Brigadier General Samuel Sturgis' division, prepared to attack the bridge.

Crook's assault on the bridge was led by skirmishers from the 11th Connecticut, who were ordered to clear the bridge for the Ohioans to cross and assault the bluff. After being hammered with heavy fire for fifteen minutes, the Connecticut men pulled back with a third of their men wounded, including their commander, Colonel Henry W. Kingsbury. Crook's main assault veered off-course, thanks to the unfamiliar terrain, and his men reached the creek a quarter-mile upstream from the bridge, where they exchanged volleys with Confederate skirmishers for the next few hours.

With Rodman's division still wandering up the creek, Burnside directed a second assault on the bridge with one of Sturgis' brigades. They also fell prey to the Confederate sharpshooters, and the attack fell apart. By this time, it was noon and McClellan was losing patience. He sent a succession of couriers across the battlefield to urge Burnside forward. He ordered one aide, "Tell him if it costs 10,000 men, he must go now!" He pressured him further by sending his inspector general, Colonel Delos B. Sackett, to confront Burnside, who replied indignantly, "McClellan appears to think I am not trying my best to carry this bridge; you are the third or fourth one who has been to me this morning with similar orders."

A third attempt to take the bridge was launched by Sturgis' other brigade, commanded by Brigadier General Edward Ferrero. The men, with good artillery support and the enticing promise that a recently canceled whiskey ration would be restored if they were successful, charged downhill and took up positions on the east bank. Using a recently captured howitzer, they fired a double canister down the bridge and got within twenty-five yards of the enemy. By 1:00 p.m., Confederate ammunition was running low and word reached Toombs that Rodman's men were crossing the creek on their flank. He ordered a withdrawal. His men had cost the Union more than five hundred casualties, a fraction of what the Confederacy had lost, and had stalled Burnside's attack for more than three hours.

Although able to seize the ground given up by the Confederates, Burnside's assault stalled out on its own. His officers had neglected to transport ammunition across the bridge, which was itself jammed with soldiers, artillery and wagons, causing a two-hour delay. General Lee used this time to bolster his right flank. He ordered up every available artillery unit, but made no attempt to strengthen the badly outnumbered force with infantry units from the left. Instead, he counted on the arrival of A.P. Hill's Light Division, which was currently making a seventeen-mile march from Harper's Ferry. Hill arrived around 2:00 p.m. and he was able to confer with a greatly relieved Lee, who ordered him to bring up his men on the right.

Burnside was completely unaware that three thousand new men would be facing him and his plan was to move around the weakened Confederate right flank, converge on Sharpsburg, and cut off Lee's only escape route across the Potomac. At 3:00 p.m., he left Sturgis' division in reserve on the west bank and moved west with eight thousand men and twenty-two guns for close support.

An initial assault led by the 79th New York Cameron Highlanders succeeded against Jones' outnumbered division, which was pushed back to within two hundred yards of Sharpsburg. Farther to the left, Rodman's division advanced toward Harper's Ferry Road. They came under heavy fire from a dozen Confederate guns mounted on a ridge to their front, but they continued to push forward. There was panic in the streets of Sharpsburg, which were clogged with retreating Confederates. Of the five brigades in Jones' division, only Toombs' brigade was intact - and he only had seven hundred men.

The Union Army had pushed as far as the Lutheran Church, just east of Sharpsburg, when A.P. Hill's division arrived on the scene. At 3:40 p.m., Brigadier General Maxcy Gregg's brigade of South Carolina men attacked Rodman's left flank in the cornfield of local farmer John Otto. The line broke and as other Federals tried to counterattack they became disoriented in the high rows of corn and because many of the Confederates were wearing Union uniforms that had been captured at Harper's Ferry. They broke and ran and were driven down the hills towards Antietam Creek.

Although Burnside still possessed twice the number of Confederates confronting them, he was unnerved by the collapse of the flank and ordered his men back across the bridge they had fought so hard to take a few hours before. He urgently requested more men and guns. McClellan was able to provide only one battery. He said, "I can do nothing more. I have no infantry." In fact, however, McClellan had two fresh corps in reserve, but he was too cautious, concerned about an imminent massive counterstrike by Lee. Burnside's men spent the rest of the day guarding the bridge they had suffered so much to capture.

By 5:30 p.m., the battle was over. It was the single bloodiest day of the war and losses were heavy on both sides. The Union had 12,401 casualties with 2,108 dead. Confederate casualties were 10,318 with 1,546 dead. More Americans died on September 17, 1862, than on any other day in the nation's military history. Several generals died in the battle, including Major Generals Joseph K. Mansfield and Israel B. Richardson and Brigadier General Isaac P. Rodman on the Union side, and Brigadier Generals Lawrence O. Branch and William E. Starke for the Confederate side.

On the morning of September 18, Lee's army prepared to defend against a Federal assault that never came. After an improvised truce for both sides to recover and exchange their wounded, Lee's forces began withdrawing across the Potomac that evening to return to Virginia.

When words reached Washington of the events at Sharpsburg, President Lincoln was once again disappointed in McClellan's lackluster performance. He believed that McClellan's cautious and poorly coordinated actions had forced the battle to a draw rather than a crippling Confederate defeat. The Union military had every advantage, from men to guns and even a forewarning of the Confederate plans and yet McClellan had not even committed his entire army to the battle. One-third of his men had been left in reserve and had never fired a shot.

The president was even more astonished that from September 17 to October 26, despite repeated entreaties from the War Department and the president himself, McClellan declined to pursue Lee across the Potomac, citing shortages of equipment and the fear of overextending his forces. Lincoln relieved McClellan of his command of the Army of the Potomac on November 7, effectively ending the general's military career. McClellan would later run for president against Lincoln in 1864, but he was soundly defeated. Most of the votes cast in Lincoln's favor came from the soldiers that McClellan had once commanded.

Lee limped back to Virginia, regretting the toll that the battle had taken on his northern invasion. He would not return into northern territory until the following summer, when his army would be defeated at Gettysburg.

The Confederate wounded were left behind in Sharpsburg. Many of them were treated in homes and barns and even at the Lutheran Church in Sharpsburg, which had been the extent of the Union charge during the late afternoon of the battle. Mount Airy, or Grove Farm as it is often called, was located west of town and was used as a hospital for the wounded on both sides after the battle. President Lincoln visited the farm after the battle, seeing the aftermath for himself. The floorboards of the house were stained with so much blood that even today, it cannot be removed, no matter how much sanding and scrubbing is done. I Troy saw those bloodstains for myself a number of years ago and they are just as vivid today as they probably were back in 1862.

More men died on the banks of Antietam Creek than on any other single day of the war. The loss of American lives was tremendous, as were the stories of heroism and valor. There are many tales of Antietam that linger on the battlefield and many believe that some of the soldiers - and the deeds committed here - may linger, too.

The battle shifted several times on the morning of the battle and by mid-day was an open assault on the center of the Confederate line. Fighting erupted along a country road that divided the fields of two local farmers. The sunken wagon track now served as a sheltered rifle pit for two Confederate brigades. General Lee ordered the center of the line to be held at all costs and this task fell to Colonel John B. Gordon, the commander of the 6th Alabama. Gordon allowed the initial attack to approach within yards of the road before he gave the order to fire. Lines of Union men fell under the explosive fire from the sunken road. The troops wavered and then retreated.

The second attack, launched by raw recruits under command of Colonel Dwight Morris, were also hit with heavy fire but managed to beat back a counterattack by the Alabama Brigade under Robert Rodes. A third attack, under Brigadier General Nathan Kimball, included three veteran regiments, but they also collapsed under fired from the sunken road. William French's Union division suffered 1,750 casualties in less than an hour.

Reinforcements began to arrive on both sides and by 10:30 a.m., Robert E. Lee sent his final reserve division, under Major General Richard H. Anderson, to bolster the line and extend it to the right for an attack on French's left flank. But at the same time, four thousand men of Major General Israel B. Richardson's division arrived on French's left. This was the last of Sumner's divisions, which had been held up in the rear by McClellan as he organized his reserve forces. Richardson's fresh troops attacked the Confederate line at the sunken road.

Leading the fourth attack of the day was the 69th New York, the "Irish Brigade" of Brigadier General Thomas F. Meagher. The Brigade had been reformed in New York after the fighting at Manassas cost the lives of many of the men and many others were captured. They formed again under the command of Meagher, an Irish immigrant and a campaigner for Irish freedom. The Brigade was among the most colorful of the Union troops and brawling was common, as was heavy drinking. They brought along their own priest and he conducted mass for them on the Sabbath and on the eve of battles.

The Sunken Road at Antietam after the battle

In 1862, the 69th came to Virginia and were designated the Second Brigade of Israel B. Richardson's First Division, Edwin V. Sumner's II Corps. They saw action at Fair Oaks, Gaine's Mill, Salvage Station and a number of other places before meeting their destiny at Antietam.

As they advanced, their emerald banner snapped in the wind. The Irish Brigade announced their arrival with the sounds of drums and volleys of fire as they attacked the Confederate position. They launched their assault, cheering loudly, while their priest, Father William Corby, rode among the men offering prayers and absolution. As they charged, the brigade screamed loudly and shouted a battle cry that sounded like "Fah-ah-bah-lah," spelled Faugh-a-Balaugh which is Gaelic for "Clear the Way!"

The thunderous sound of weaponry filled the air and men fell on both sides. Father Corby, who seemed to be oblivious to the gunfire, dodged across the field, administering last rites to fallen Irishmen. Colonel Meagher fought alongside his men and when he saw the emerald banner fall, he ordered it to be raised again. The 69th lost eight color bearers at Antietam and once, the firing was so intense that the flagstaff was shattered in a man's hands.

Meagher's horse was shot out from under him as the fighting intensified. The brigade fought fiercely and fell in huge numbers. They fired all of the ammunition they had and then collected what they could from the dead and wounded and fired that, too. Eventually their cries of "Faugh-a-Balaugh" became fainter and the Irish Brigade lost more than sixty percent of its men that day -- and wrote its name in the bloody pages of American history.

As the fierce fighting continued, General Richardson personally dispatched the brigade of Brigadier General John C. Caldwell after being told that Caldwell was in rear, hiding behind a haystack , and finally, the tide turned. A number of key Confederate leaders were lost in the fighting that followed, including George B. Anderson, Colonel Charles Tew, and Colonel John B. Gordon, who was wounded four times. He was shot once in the cheek and fell, unconscious, with his face in his hat. He later told friends that he would have drowned in his own blood, except for the fact that a Yankee bullet had earlier shot a hole in his hat, which allowed the blood to drain. Robert Rodes was shot in the thigh, but remained on the field. However, the losses of the Confederate officers added to the confusion of the events that followed.

As Caldwell's brigade advanced around the right flank of the Confederates, Colonel Francis Barlow and three hundred and fifty New York men saw a weak point in the line and seized a knoll that commanded the sunken road, turning it into a deadly trap. From their vantage point, the Union troops fired down on the road's defenders. The once-impregnable position had become an abattoir. A sergeant from the 61st New York later wrote, "We were shooting them like sheep in a pen. If a bullet missed the mark at first it was liable to strike the further bank, angle back, and take them secondarily." The road, soon to be known as "Bloody Lane," rapidly filled with bodies, piled two and three feet deep.

The New York men continued to fire into the sunken lane and then poured into the roadway, kneeling on the slain Confederates to fire at the retreating survivors. "A frenzy seized each man," one soldier recalled. He remembered tossing aside his own empty rifle to pull loaded ones from the hands of the dead to continue firing.

Confederates moved in to meet the threat by the Union troops but a command from Rodes was misunderstood by Lieutenant Colonel James N. Lightfoot, who had taken over the command of John Gordon. Lightfoot mistakenly ordered his men to withdraw, an order that all five regiments of the brigade thought also applied to them. Confederates hurried toward Sharpsburg, their line broken.

Richardson's men were in pursuit of the fleeing men when massed artillery hastily assembled by General Longstreet drove them back. A counterattack, led by D.H. Hill, flanked the Federal line beside the sunken road but they were driven back by a fierce charge by the 5th New Hampshire. Unfortunately, this caused the Union center to collapse, and Richardson was forced to order his division back to the other side of the sunken road. His division lost nearly one thousand men. Colonel Barlow was wounded and Richardson later died from his wounds.

The Federal advance had been stalled and the battle at the center of the line died out.

Over the years, Bloody Lane has come to be known as the most eerie spot on the Antietam battlefield. Visitors have had many strange encounters here and even some former skeptics have come to believe that the events of the past are still very present in this place. Reports that have been collected over the years tell of phantom gunfire echoing along the old road and the smell of smoke and gunpowder that seems to come from nowhere. Other reports have included the apparitions of men in Confederate uniforms, who were believed to be reenactors - until they vanished without a trace.

Perhaps the most famous story of the Bloody Lane involves a group of boys from the McDonough School, a private school located near Baltimore. They toured the battlefield and ended the day at Bloody Lane. The boys were allowed to wander about and think about what they had learned that day. They were then asked to record their impressions for a history assignment, and some wrote brief remarks and poems. But the comments that got the most attention from their teacher were written by several boys who walked down the road to the observation tower, which is located where the Irish Brigade charged the Confederate line.

The boys described hearing strange noises that became shouts, coming from the field near the tower. Some of them said that it sounded like a chant and others described the voices as though someone were singing a Christmas song, which sounded a lot like "Deck the Halls."

Most specifically, they described the words as sounding like the part of the song that goes "Fa-la-la-la-la." The singing came strongly and then faded away. But what if the singing had not been a Christmas song at all, but the sounds of the famous Irish Brigade "clearing the way"?

Faugh-a-Balaugh.

And Bloody Lane is not the only haunted spot at Antietam.

Located overlooking the battlefield is the Phillip Pry House, a brick farmhouse that was commandeered by General George McClellan to use as his headquarters during the battle. Shortly after the battle began, General Joseph Hooker was brought to the house with wounds that he received during the fighting. He was followed by General Israel B. Richardson, who died of painful abdominal wounds at the Pry House, more than six months after the battle ended.

The house today is owned by the National Park Service and is not open to visitors, but this does not stop strange stories from being told about the place. For many years, the house was simply used for storage, then in 1976, the Pry house caught fire and about one-third of it was gutted. It was during the restoration of the house that many strange events were recorded.

One day, during a meeting of park personnel, the wife of one of the men in the meeting met a woman in old-fashioned clothing coming down the staircase. She asked her husband who the lady in the long dress was but he had no idea who she was talking about.

A short time later, workers arrived at the house to see a woman standing in an upper window. It was the same room in which General Richardson had died. They searched the house and after going upstairs, they realized the room where the woman had been standing had no floor. On another occasion, a new contracting crew was hired to work in the house at night. They caught a glimpse of the spectral woman and abandoned the project.

Could the apparition be that of Richardson's wife, Frances, who cared from him on his deathbed? Mrs. Richardson had traveled to Sharpsburg from their home in Michigan when she heard her husband had been injured. His wound had not been considered life threatening but infection set in and he sickened and died.

In addition to sightings of the spirit, a more common experience is for people to hear her. The sounds of footsteps have often been heard going up and down the main staircase of the house. Many believe it's the memory of Fannie Richardson climbing up and down the stairs as she did so many times, checking on her dying husband.

Those who have spent time at Burnside Bridge on the battlefield, especially those who have been there after dark, say that strange things are still taking place there after all these years. Historians report that the fighting that took place here in September 1862 left a number of fallen soldiers behind, and many of them were hastily buried in unknown locations near the bridge. Could these restless souls be haunting the area? Visitors to the bridge at night have reported seeing blue balls of light moving about in the darkness and hearing the sound of a phantom drum that beats out a cadence and then fades away.

Near the center of Sharpsburg is another site connected to the battle, St. Paul Episcopal Church. It was used as a Confederate field hospital following the battle. Although it was heavily damaged during the fighting it was later rebuilt. Those who have lived close to the church claim they have heard the screams of the dying and injured coming from inside of the structure. They have also seen unexplained lights flickering from the church's tower.

In 1998, I spent the night at the Piper House, which is located on the battlefield. During the battle, it served as the headquarters of Confederate General James Longstreet and the barn was used as a field hospital after the fighting had ended. The house was directly in the heat of the battle, and after the fighting ended, the bodies of three dead soldiers were removed from under the piano in the parlor. The Piper House is no longer open to the public.

Stories by others who have stayed in this house claim that the apparition of a soldier is often seen standing in the doorway of an upstairs bedroom. Strangely, the section where the ghost is most often seen is a newer part of the house that was added in 1900, long after the battle occurred. In addition to the shadowy form of the soldier, guests have also told of hearing muffled voices and odd sounds.

The only explanation as to why this newer part of the house might be haunted is that it is believed to have been built over the graves of hastily buried Confederate soldiers. After a number of dead men were found in and around the house, Union troops buried them in a mass grave out back - exactly where the new section of the house was added thirty-eight years later.

I have to add, with some regret, that I never experienced anything unusual in the Piper House that night. I stayed up most of the night in hopes that a soldier from the past might reveal himself but my patience didn't pay off. I can't say for sure whether or not the old house is actually haunted, but many who came before me certainly believed that it was.

As for the Antietam battlefield itself, again, I can't say for sure. However, this is a place where time seems to stand still and the events of the past seem to be so close that you can almost reach out and touch them. Whether by actual ghosts or not, Antietam is a place that is definitely haunted by its past.

1862: FREDERICKSBURG

The Battle of Fredericksburg was fought between December 11 and 15, 1862, in and around Fredericksburg, Virginia. It became a bloody fight between Robert E. Lee's Army of Northern Virginia and the Union Army of the Potomac, commanded by Major General Ambrose Burnside. The battle would be the perfect illustration of why military tactics of the past were no longer feasible in modern warfare. Due to the blunderings of this awkward - and ultimately unsuccessful campaign - Ambrose Burnside's career was forever destroyed.

The Union Army's losses at Fredericksburg were more than double those of the victorious Confederates and at times, so many men were killed that even the enemy soldiers had trouble believing what they seeing as man after man fell to heavy fire.

Is it any wonder that Fredericksburg is reputed to have so many ghosts?

By November 1862, President Lincoln was desperate to demonstrate the success of the Union war effort before the American public lost all confidence in his administration. After several embarrassing losses, as well as a bloody draw at Antietam, Lincoln needed a rousing success to aid in the Union's propaganda campaign.

Fredericksburg in December 1862

Confederate armies had been on the move earlier in the fall, invading Kentucky and Maryland, and although each had been turned back, those armies remained intact and capable of further action. Lincoln urged Major General Ulysses S. Grant to advance against the Confederate stronghold of Vicksburg, Mississippi. He replaced Major General Don Carlos Buell with Major General William S. Rosecrans, hoping for a more aggressive posture against the Confederates in Tennessee. And on November 5, seeing that his replacement of Buell had not stimulated Major General George B. McClellan into action, he issued orders to replace McClellan in command of the Army of the Potomac in Virginia. McClellan had stopped Robert E. Lee at the Battle of Antietam in Maryland, but had not been able to destroy Lee's army, nor did he pursue Lee back into Virginia in the aggressive manner that Lincoln had ordered.

McClellan's replacement was Major General Ambrose E. Burnside, the commander of the IX Corps. Burnside had established a reputation as an independent commander, with successful operations earlier that year in coastal North Carolina. Unlike McClellan, he had no apparent political ambitions. However, he felt himself unqualified for army-level command and objected when offered the position. He accepted only when it was made clear to him that McClellan would be replaced in any event and that an alternative choice for command was Major General Joseph Hooker, whom Burnside disliked and distrusted. Burnside assumed command on November 7.

In response to prodding from Lincoln and general-in-chief Major General Henry W. Halleck, Burnside planned a late fall offensive, sending his plans to Halleck on November 9. The plan relied on quick movement and deception. He would concentrate his army in a visible fashion near Warrenton, feigning a movement on Culpeper Court House, Orange Court House, or Gordonsville. Then he would rapidly shift his army southeast and cross the Rappahannock River to Fredericksburg, hoping that Robert E. Lee would wait, unclear as to Burnside's intentions, while the Union Army made a rapid movement against Richmond, south along the Richmond, Fredericksburg and Potomac Railroad from Fredericksburg. In the early days of the war, it seemed that every commander's plan was to seize Richmond, the capital of the Confederacy.

Burnside concocted this plan because he was concerned that if he were to move directly south from Warrenton, he would be exposed to a flanking attack from General Thomas J. "Stonewall" Jackson, whose corps was at that time in the Shenandoah Valley south of Winchester. He also believed that the Orange and Alexandria Railroad would be an inadequate supply line.

While Burnside began assembling a supply base at Falmouth, near Fredericksburg, the Lincoln administration entertained a lengthy debate about the wisdom of his plan, which differed from the president's preference of a movement south along the railroad and a direct confrontation with Lee's army instead of the movement focused on the city of Richmond. Lincoln reluctantly approved the plan on November 14, but cautioned his general to move with great speed, certainly doubting that Lee would cooperate as Burnside anticipated.

Burnside organized his Army of the Potomac into three so-called grand divisions, organizations that included infantry corps, cavalry, and artillery, comprising 120,000 men, of whom 114,000 would be engaged in the coming battle.

The Right Grand Division, commanded by Major General Edwin V. "Bull" Sumner, consisted of the II Corps of Major General Darius N. Couch divisions of Brigadier Generals Winfield S. Hancock, Oliver O. Howard, and William H. French and the IX Corps of Brigadier General Orlando B. Willcox divisions of Brigadier Generals William W. Burns, Samuel D. Sturgis, and George W. Getty . A cavalry division under Brigadier General Alfred Pleasonton was attached.

The Center Grand Division, commanded by Major General Joseph Hooker, consisted of the III Corps of Brigadier General George Stoneman divisions of Brigadier Generals David B. Birney, Daniel E. Sickles, and Amiel W. Whipple and the V Corps of Brigadier General Daniel Butterfield divisions of Brigadier Generals Charles Griffin, George Sykes, and Andrew A. Humphreys . A cavalry brigade under Brigadier General William W. Averell was attached.

The Left Grand Division, commanded by Major General William B. Franklin, consisted of the I Corps of Major General John F. Reynolds divisions of Brigadier Generals Abner Doubleday and John Gibbon and Major General George G. Meade and the VI Corps of Major General William F. "Baldy" Smith divisions of Brigadier Generals William T. H. Brooks, Albion P. Howe, and John Newton . A cavalry brigade commanded by Brigadier General George D. Bayard was attached.

The Reserve, commanded by Major General Franz Sigel of the XI Corps, was in the area of Fairfax Court House. The XII Corps, under Major General Henry W. Slocum, was called from Harpers Ferry to Dumfries, Virginia, to join the reserve force on December 9, but none of these troops arrived in time to participate in the battle.

Robert E. Lee's Army of Northern Virginia had nearly 85,000 men, with 72,500 engaged.

The First Corps of Lieutenant General James Longstreet included the divisions of Major Generals Lafayette McLaws, Richard H. Anderson, George E. Pickett, and John Bell Hood, and Brigadier General Robert Ransom, Jr. The Second Corps of Lieutenant General Thomas J. "Stonewall" Jackson included the divisions of Major Generals D.H. Hill and A.P. Hill, and Brigadier Generals Jubal A. Early and William B. Taliaferro. Lee's Army also had artillery held in reserve under Brigadier General William N. Pendleton and a cavalry division under Major General J.E.B. Stuart.

When the two armies met at Fredericksburg, they represented the largest number of armed men to ever confront each other for combat during the Civil War.

The Union Army began marching on November 15, and the first elements arrived in Falmouth on November 17. Burnside's plan quickly went awry. He had ordered pontoon bridges to be sent to the front and assembled for his quick crossing of the Rappahannock, but because of administrative bungling, the bridges did not arrive on time. Burnside first requisitioned the pontoon bridging along with many other provisions on November 7 when he detailed his plan to Halleck. The plan was sent to the attention of Brigadier General George Washington Cullum, the chief of staff in Washington, and he received them on November 9. It took five days to get everything together and on November 14, the 50th New York Engineers were ready to move - except for the fact that the two hundred and seventy horses required to move them were missing. Unknown to Burnside when he reached Falmouth, the bridgework was still on the upper Potomac.

When Major General Edwin V. Sumner arrived, he strongly urged an immediate crossing of the river to scatter the token Confederate force of five hundred men in the town and occupying the commanding heights to the west. Burnside became anxious, concerned that the increasing autumn rains would make the fording points unusable and that Sumner might be cut off and destroyed. Thanks to this, he ordered Sumner to wait in Falmouth.

Lee had originally assumed that Burnside would beat him across the Rappahannock and that to protect Richmond, he would assume the next defensible position to the south, the North Anna River. But when he saw how slowly Burnside was moving, he directed all of his army toward Fredericksburg. By November 23, all of Longstreet's corps had arrived and Lee placed them on the ridge known as Marye's Heights to the west of town, with Anderson's division on the far left, McLaws' directly behind the town, and Pickett's and Hood's to the right. He sent for Jackson on November 26, but his Second Corps commander had anticipated the need and began forced-marching his troops from Winchester on November 22, covering as many as twenty miles a day. Jackson arrived at Lee's headquarters on November 29 and his divisions were deployed to prevent Burnside crossing downstream from Fredericksburg: D.H. Hill's division moved to Port Royal, eighteen miles downriver; Early's twelve miles downriver at Skinker's Neck; A.P. Hill's at Thomas Yerby's house, "Belvoir," about six miles southeast of town; and Taliaferro's along the RF&P Railroad, four miles south at Guinea Station.

The boats and equipment for a single pontoon bridge arrived at Falmouth on November 25, much too late to enable the Army of the Potomac to cross the river without opposition. Burnside still had an opportunity, however, because by then he was facing only half of Lee's army, not yet dug in, and if he acted quickly, he might have been able to attack Longstreet and defeat him before Jackson arrived. Once again he squandered his opportunity. The full complement of bridges arrived at the end of the month, but by this time Jackson was present and Longstreet was preparing strong defenses.

Burnside originally planned to cross his army east of Fredericksburg at Skinker's Neck, but an advance movement by Federal gunboats to that position was fired upon and drew Early's and D.H. Hill's divisions into that area, a movement spotted by Union balloon observers. Now assuming that Lee had anticipated his plan, Burnside guessed that the Confederates had weakened their left and center to concentrate against him on their right. So he decided to cross directly at Fredericksburg. In addition to his numerical advantage in troop strength, Burnside also had the advantage of knowing his army could not be attacked effectively. On the other side of the Rappahannock, two hundred and twenty artillery pieces had been located on the ridge known as Stafford Heights to prevent Lee's army from mounting any major counterattacks.

While Burnside shuffling his troops around the landscape and wasting precious time, Union engineers began to assemble six pontoon bridges before dawn on December 11, two just north of the town center, a third on the southern end of town, and three farther south, near the confluence of the Rappahannock and Deep Run. The engineers constructing the bridge directly across from the city came under punishing fire from Confederate sharpshooters, primarily from the Mississippi brigade of Brigadier General William Barksdale, in command of the town defenses. Union artillery attempted to dislodge the sharpshooters, but their positions in the cellars of houses rendered the fire from the one hundred and fifty guns mostly ineffective. Eventually Burnside's artillery commander, Brigadier General Henry J. Hunt, convinced him to send infantry landing parties over in the pontoon boats to secure a small bridgehead and rout the sharpshooters. Colonel Norman J. Hall volunteered his brigade for this assignment. Burnside suddenly turned reluctant, lamenting to Hall in front of his men that "the effort meant death to most of those who should undertake the voyage." When his men responded to Hall's request with three cheers, Burnside relented.

At 3:00 p.m., the Union artillery began a preparatory bombardment and one hundred and thirty-five infantrymen from the 7th Michigan and the 19th Massachusetts crowded into the small boats. The 20th Massachusetts followed soon after. They crossed successfully and spread out in a skirmish line to clear the sharpshooters. Although some of the Confederates surrendered, fighting proceeded street by street through the town as the engineers completed the bridges. Sumner's Right Grand Division began crossing at 4:30 p.m., but the bulk of his men did not cross until December 12. Hooker's Center Grand Division crossed on December 13, using both the northern and southern bridges.

The clearing of the city buildings by Sumner's infantry, and by artillery fire from across the river, began the first major urban combat of the Civil War. Union gunners lobbed more than five thousand shells into the town and onto the ridges to the west. By nightfall, four brigades of Union troops occupied the town, which they looted with a fury that had not been seen in the war up to that point. This behavior enraged Lee, a man of principle who did not believe in such behavior. The destruction also angered the Confederate troops, many of whom were native Virginians. Many on the Union side were also shocked by the destruction inflicted on Fredericksburg. Civilian casualties were unusually sparse in the midst of such widespread violence, probably amounting to no more than four civilian deaths.

River crossings south of the city by Franklin's Left Grand Division were much less eventful. Both bridges were completed by 11:00 a.m. on December 11, while five batteries of Union artillery suppressed most of the sniper fire raining down on the engineers. At 4:00 p.m., Franklin was ordered to cross his entire command, but only a single brigade was sent over before dark. Crossings resumed at dawn and were completed by 1:00 p.m. on December 12. Early on December 13, Jackson recalled his divisions under Jubal Early and D.H. Hill from downriver positions to join his main defensive lines south of the city.

Burnside's verbal instructions on December 12 outlined a main attack by Franklin, supported by Hooker, on the southern flank, while Sumner made a secondary attack on the north. His actual orders on December 13 were vague and confusing to his subordinates - a problem that occurred frequently during the Civil War, when both written and verbal orders were often presented so eloquently and politely that they were often left to the interpretation of the listener or reader.

At 5:00 p.m. on December 12, Burnside made a cursory inspection of the southern flank, where Franklin and his subordinates pressed him to give definite orders for a morning attack by the grand division, so they would have adequate time to position their forces overnight. However, Burnside demurred and the order did not reach Franklin until either 7:15 or 7:45 a.m. When it arrived, it was not as Franklin expected. Rather than ordering an attack by the entire grand division of almost sixty thousand men, Franklin was to keep his men in position, but was to send "a division at least" to seize the high ground Prospect Hill around Hamilton's Crossing. Sumner was to send one division through the city and up Telegraph Road, and both flanks were to be prepared to commit their entire commands. Burnside was apparently expecting these weak attacks to intimidate Lee, causing him to withdraw. Franklin, who had originally advocated a vigorous assault, chose to interpret Burnside's order very conservatively. Brigadier General James A. Hardie, who delivered the order, did not ensure that Burnside's intentions were understood by Franklin, and map inaccuracies about the road network made those intentions unclear. Furthermore, Burnside's choice of the verb "to seize" was less forceful in nineteenth-century military terminology than an order "to carry" the heights.

December 13 began cold and overcast. A dense fog blanketed the ground and made it impossible for the armies to see each other. Franklin ordered his I Corps commander, Major General John F. Reynolds, to select a division for the attack. Reynolds chose his smallest division, about 4,500 men commanded by George G. Meade, and assigned John Gibbon's division to support Meade's attack. His reserve division, under Abner Doubleday, was to face south and protect the left flank between the Richmond Road and the river. Meade's division began moving out around 8:30 a.m., with Gibbon following behind. At around 10:30, the fog started lifting. They moved parallel to the river initially, turning right to face the Richmond Road, where they began to be struck by fire from the Virginia Horse Artillery under Major John Pelham. Pelham started with two cannons – a twelve-pounder Napoleon smoothbore and a rifled Blakely – but continued with only one after the latter was disabled by counter-battery fire. "Jeb" Stuart sent word to Pelham that he should feel free to withdraw from his dangerous position at any time, to which Pelham responded, "Tell the General I can hold my ground."

The Iron Brigade formerly Gibbon's command, but now led by Brigadier General Solomon Meredith was sent out to deal with the Confederate horse artillery. This action was mainly conducted by the 24th Michigan Infantry, a newly enlisted regiment that had joined the brigade in October. After about an hour, Pelham's ammunition began to run low and he withdrew. General Lee observed the action and commented about Pelham, age twenty-four, "It is glorious to see such courage in one so young." The most prominent victim of Pelham's fire was Brigadier General George D. Bayard, a cavalry general who was mortally wounded by a shell while standing in reserve near Franklin's headquarters. Jackson's main artillery batteries had remained silent in the fog during this exchange, but the Union troops soon began to receive direct fire from Prospect Hill, principally five batteries directed by Lieutenant Colonel Reuben Lindsay Walker, and Meade's attack was stalled about six hundred yards from his initial objective for almost two hours by these combined artillery attacks.

Around 1:00 p.m., the Union artillery fire lifted and Meade's men moved forward to Jackson's force of about 35,000 men, who remained concealed on the wooded ridge to Meade's front. His formidable defensive line had an unforeseen flaw. In A.P. Hill's division's line, a triangular patch of the woods that extended beyond the railroad was swampy and covered with thick underbrush and the Confederates had left a six-hundred-yard gap there between the brigades of Brigadier Generals James H. Lane and James J. Archer. Maxcy Gregg's brigade stood about a quarter mile behind the gap. Meade's 1st Brigade under Colonel William Sinclair entered the gap, climbed the railroad embankment, and turned right into the underbrush, striking Lane's brigade in the flank. Following immediately behind, his 3rd Brigade turned left and hit Archer's flank. The 2nd Brigade came up in support and intermixed with the leading brigades. As the gap widened with pressure on the flanks, thousands of Meade's men reached the top of the ridge and ran into Gregg's brigade. Many of these Confederates had stacked their arms while taking cover from Union artillery and were not expecting to be attacked at that moment, so were killed or captured unarmed. Gregg at first mistook the Union soldiers for fleeing Confederate troops and ordered his men not to fire on them. While he rode prominently in front of his lines, the partially deaf Gregg could not hear the approaching Federals or their bullets flying around him. He was shot through the spinal cord, dying two days later.

Confederate reserves – the divisions of Brigadier Generals Jubal A. Early and William B. Taliaferro – moved into the fray from behind Gregg's original position. Inspired by their attack, regiments from Lane's and Archer's brigades rallied and formed a new defensive line in the gap. Now Meade's men were receiving fire from three sides and could not withstand the pressure. Brigadier General Conrad Feger Jackson attempted to flank a Confederate battery, but after his horse was shot and he began to lead on foot, he was fatally shot in the head and his brigade fell back, temporarily without a leader.

At around 1:00 p.m., on Meade's right, Gibbon's division prepared to move forward. Brigadier General Nelson Taylor proposed to Gibbon that they supplement Meade's assault with a bayonet charge against Lane's position. However, Gibbon stated that this would violate his orders, so Taylor's brigade did not move forward until 1:30 p.m. The attack did not have the benefit of a gap to exploit, nor did the Union soldiers have any wooded cover for their advance, so progress was slow under heavy fire from Lane's brigade and Confederate artillery. Immediately following Taylor was the brigade of Colonel Peter Lyle, and the advance of the two brigades ground to a halt before they reached the railroad. Committing his reserve at 1:45 p.m., Gibbon sent forward his brigade under Colonel Adrian R. Root, which moved through the survivors of the first two brigades, but they were soon brought to a halt as well. Eventually some of the Federals reached the crest of the ridge and had some success during hand-to-hand fighting. Men on both sides had depleted their ammunition and resorted to bayonets and rifle butts, and even empty rifles with bayonets thrown like javelins, but they were forced to withdraw back across the railroad embankment along with Meade's men to their left. Gibbon's attack, despite heavy casualties, had failed to support Meade's temporary breakthrough.

After the battle, Meade complained that some of Gibbon's officers had not charged quickly enough. But his primary frustration was with General David B. Birney, whose division of the III Corps had been designated to support the attack as well. Birney claimed that his men had been subjected to damaging artillery fire as they formed up, that he had not understood the importance of Meade's attack, and that Reynolds had not ordered his division forward. When Meade galloped to the rear to confront Birney with a string of fierce profanities that, in the words of one staff lieutenant, "almost makes the stones creep," he was finally able to order the brigadier forward under his own responsibility, but harbored resentment for weeks. By this time, however, it was too late to accomplish any further offensive action.

Early's division began a counterattack, led initially by Colonel Edmund N. Atkinson's Georgia brigade, which inspired the men from the brigades of Colonel Robert Hoke, Brigadier General James J. Archer, and Colonel John M.

Brockenbrough to charge forward out of the railroad ditches, driving Meade's men from the woods in a disorderly retreat, followed closely by Gibbon's. Early's orders to his brigades were to pursue as far as the railroad, but in the chaos many kept up the pressure over the open fields as far as the old Richmond Road. Union artillery crews proceeded to unleash a blast of close-range canister shot, firing as fast as they could load their guns. The Confederates were also struck by the leading brigade of Birney's belated advance, commanded by Brigadier General J. H. Hobart Ward. Birney followed up with the brigades of Brigadier Generals Hiram G. Berry and John C. Robinson, which broke the Rebel advance that had threatened to drive the Union into the river. Any further Confederate advance was deterred by the arrival of the III Corps division of Brigadier General Daniel E. Sickles on the right.

General Burnside, who by this time was focused on his attacks on Marye's Heights, was dismayed that his left flank attack had not achieved the success he assumed earlier in the day. He ordered Franklin to "advance his right and front," but despite repeated entreaties, Franklin refused, claiming that all of his forces had been engaged. This was not true, however, as the entire VI Corps and Abner Doubleday's division of the I Corps had been mostly idle, suffering only a few casualties from artillery fire while they waited in reserve.

The Confederates withdrew back to the safety of the hills south of town. Stonewall Jackson considered mounting a resumed counterattack, but the Federal artillery and impending darkness changed his mind. A fortuitous Union breakthrough had been wasted because Franklin did not reinforce Meade's success with some of the 20,000 men standing in reserve. Neither Franklin nor Reynolds took any personal involvement in the battle, and were unavailable to their subordinates at the critical point. Franklin's losses were about 5,000 casualties in comparison to Stonewall Jackson's 3,400, demonstrating the ferocity of the fighting. Skirmishing and artillery duels continued until dark, but no additional major attacks took place, while the center of the battle moved north to Marye's Heights.

On the northern end of the battlefield, Brigadier General William H. French's division of the II Corps prepared to move forward while being subjected to Confederate artillery fire as it rained down on the fog-enshrouded town of Fredericksburg. General Burnside's orders to General Sumner was to send "a division or more" to seize the high ground to the west of the city, assuming that his assault on the southern end of the Confederate line would be the decisive action of the battle. The avenue of approach was difficult: mostly open fields, but interrupted by scattered houses, fences, and gardens that would restrict the movement of battle lines. A canal stood about two hundred yards west of the town, crossed by three narrow bridges, which would require the Union troops to funnel themselves into columns before proceeding. It was just one more bit of poor planning that would ultimately lead to slaughter and defeat.

About six hundred yards west of Fredericksburg was the low ridge known as Marye's Heights, which were actually several hills that were cut with ravines. Near the crest of one hill was a narrow lane that ran through a cut called the Telegraph Road -- known after the battle as the Sunken Road – and it was protected by a four-foot stone wall, which was enhanced in places by logs and heavier bricks. It became a perfect infantry defensive position. Confederate Major General Lafayette McLaws initially had about two thousand men on the front line of Marye's Heights and there were an additional seven thousand men in reserve on the crest and behind the ridge. Massed artillery provided almost uninterrupted coverage of the plain below. General Longstreet had been assured by his artillery commander, Lieutenant Colonel Edward Porter Alexander, "General, we cover that ground now so well that we will comb it as with a fine-tooth comb. A chicken could not live on that field when we open on it."

The fog lifted from the town around 10:00 a.m. and Sumner gave his order to advance an hour later. French's brigade under Brigadier General Nathan Kimball began to move around noon. They advanced slowly through heavy artillery fire, crossed the canal in columns over the narrow bridges, and formed in line, with fixed bayonets, behind the protection of a shallow bluff. In perfect line of battle, they advanced up the muddy slope until they were cut down at about one hundred and twenty-five yards from the stone wall by repeated rifle volleys. Some soldiers were able to get as close as forty yards, but having suffered severe casualties from both the artillery and infantry fire, the survivors clung to the ground. Kimball was severely wounded during the assault, and his brigade suffered tremendous casualties. French's brigades under Lt. Col George Andrews and Colonel Oliver Palmer followed, and each lost more than half their men. They were foolishly ramming against approximately three thousand Confederate infantrymen, lined up in multiple ranks behind a heavy stone wall, with another three thousand men in support on the high ground behind them. And above those ranks was heavy artillery commanded by Alexander.

Attempting to take the wall was almost a suicide mission.

Sumner's original order called for the division under General Winfield S. Hancock to support French and Hancock sent forward his brigade under Colonel Samuel K. Zook behind Palmer's. They met a similar fate. Next was his Irish Brigade under Brigadier General Thomas F. Meagher. By coincidence, they attacked the area defended by fellow Irishmen of Colonel Robert McMillan's 24th Georgia Infantry. A few of the Confederate Irish expressed lament at being forced to fire at their former countrymen, but did so anyway. Hancock's final brigade was led by General John C. Caldwell. Leading his two regiments on the left, Colonel Nelson A. Miles suggested to Caldwell that the practice of marching in formation, firing, and stopping to reload, made the Union soldiers easy targets, and that a concerted bayonet charge might be effective in carrying the works. Caldwell denied permission. Miles was struck by a bullet in the throat as he led his men to within forty yards of the wall, where they were pinned down -- just as their predecessors had been. Caldwell himself was soon struck by two bullets and put out of action.

The commander of the II Corps, Major General Darius N. Couch, was dismayed at the carnage wrought upon his two divisions in the hour of fighting and, like Miles, realized that the tactics were not working. He first considered a massive bayonet charge to overwhelm the defenders, but as he surveyed the front, he quickly realized that French's and Hancock's divisions were in no shape to move forward again. He next planned for his final division, commanded by Major General Oliver O. Howard, to swing to the right and attempt to envelop the Confederate left, but upon receiving urgent requests for help from French and Hancock, he sent Howard's men over and around the fallen troops instead. The brigade of Colonel Joshua Owen went in first, reinforced by Colonel Norman Hall's brigade, and then two regiments of Brigadier General Alfred Sully's brigade. The other corps in Sumner's grand division was the IX Corps, and he sent in one of its divisions under Samuel Sturgis. After two hours of desperate fighting, four Union divisions had failed in the mission Burnside had originally assigned to one. Casualties were heavy: the losses for II Corps in a single afternoon were more than four thousand men.

While the Union Army paused, Longstreet reinforced his line so that there were four ranks of infantrymen behind the stone wall. General Thomas R. R. Cobb of Georgia, who had commanded the key sector of the line, was mortally wounded by an exploding artillery shell and was replaced by General Joseph B. Kershaw. General Lee expressed concerns to Longstreet about the massing troops breaking his line, but Longstreet assured his commander, "General, if you put every man on the other side of the Potomac on that field to approach me over the same line, and give me plenty of ammunition, I will kill them all before they reach my line."

By midafternoon, Burnside had failed on both flanks to make any progress against the Confederates. Rather than reconsidering his approach in the face of heavy casualties, he stubbornly decided to continue on the same path. He sent orders to Franklin to renew the assault on the left which, as described earlier, the commander ignored and ordered his Center Grand Division, commanded by General Joseph Hooker, to cross the Rappahannock into Fredericksburg and continue the attack on Marye's Heights. Hooker performed a personal reconnaissance something that neither Burnside nor Sumner had done, both remaining east of the river during the failed assaults and returned to Burnside's headquarters to advise against the attack.

Brigadier General Daniel Butterfield, commanding Hooker's V Corps, while waiting for Hooker to return from his conference with Burnside, sent his division under General Charles Griffin to relieve Sturgis's men. By this time, General George Pickett's Confederate division and one of General John Bell Hood's brigades had marched north to reinforce Marye's Heights. Griffin smashed his three brigades against the Confederate position, one by one, and gained nothing. Couch sent six guns to within one hundred and fifty yards of the Confederate line, but they were hit so hard by Confederate sharpshooters and artillery fire that they provided no relief to Sturgis.

As if things weren't going badly enough, a soldier in Hancock's division reported movement in the Confederate line that led him to believe that the enemy might be retreating. Despite this unlikely turn of the events - since the Confederates were trouncing the Union forces - the V Corps division of Brigadier General Andrew A. Humphreys was ordered to attack and capitalize on what was thought to be a situation that was beneficial to the Union. Humphreys led his brigade on horseback, with his men moving over and around fallen troops with fixed bayonets and unloaded rifles; some of the fallen men clutched at the passing pant legs, urging their comrades not to go forward, causing the brigade to become disorganized in their advance. The charge reached to within fifty yards of the Confederate line before being cut down by concentrated rifle fire. Brigadier General George Sykes was ordered to move forward with his V Corps regular army division to support Humphreys' retreat, but his men were caught in a crossfire and pinned down.

By 4:00 p.m., Hooker had returned from his meeting with Burnside, having failed to convince the commanding general to abandon the pointless and costly attacks. While Humphreys was still attacking, Hooker reluctantly ordered the IX Corps division of General George W. Getty to attack as well, but this time to the left section of Marye's Heights, which was called Willis Hill. Colonel Rush Hawkins' brigade, followed by Colonel Edward Harland's brigade, moved along an unfinished railroad line just north of Hazel Run, approaching close to the Confederate line in the gathering twilight. When they were suddenly detected and began taking fire, the sneak attack was repulsed.

Seven Union divisions had been sent in, generally one brigade at a time, for a total of fourteen individual charges, all of which failed, costing the Union between six thousand and eight thousand casualties. Confederate losses totaled less than twelve hundred men. The falling of darkness and the pleas of

Burnside's subordinates were enough to put an end to the attacks. Longstreet later wrote, "The charges had been desperate and bloody, but utterly hopeless."

Thousands of Union soldiers spent the cold December night on the fields leading to the heights, unable to move or assist the wounded because of Confederate fire. That night, Burnside attempted to blame his subordinates for the disastrous attacks, but they were having none of it. Burnside would bear the responsibility for the disaster alone - and it would end his career.

But he was not yet finished with Fredericksburg.

During a dinner meeting on the night of December 13, perhaps burdened down by the blame that had been cast on him for the Union's ongoing failure during the battle at hand, Burnside dramatically announced that he would personally lead his old IX Corps on one final attack against Marye's Heights. But despite the bluster, his generals managed to talk him out of it the next morning.

The armies remained in position throughout the day on December 14. That afternoon, Burnside asked Lee for a truce to attend to his wounded, which the latter graciously granted. The next day the Federal forces retreated across the river, and the campaign sputtered to an end.

The Fredericksburg campaign was the most savage of the war at that point and a testament to the extent of the carnage and suffering during the battle was the legend of Richard Rowland Kirkland, a Confederate sergeant from South Carolina. According to the often re-told and likely embellished tale, he was stationed at the stone wall by the sunken road below Marye's Heights during the fight. Kirkland had a close-up view of the suffering and like so many others was appalled at the cries for help of the Union wounded throughout the cold winter night of December 13, 1862. After obtaining permission from his commander, General Joseph B. Kershaw, Kirkland gathered canteens and in broad daylight, without the benefit of a cease-fire or a flag of truce, provided water to numerous Union wounded lying on the field of battle. Union soldiers held their fire as it was obvious what Kirkland's intent was. Kirkland was nicknamed the "Angel of Marye's Heights" for these actions, and is memorialized with a statue on the battlefield today.

Fredericksburg turned out to be a humiliating defeat for the Union. The Federal Army suffered 12,653 casualties - killed, wounded, captured or missing - and two Union generals were mortally wounded. The Confederate Army lost 5,377 and most of those were lost in the early fighting on Jackson's front. The casualty numbers paint a bloody picture of how disastrous the Union Army's tactics were. Although the fighting on the southern flank produced roughly equal casualties of between four thousand and five thousand on each side, the northern flank was completely lopsided, with about eight Union casualties for each

Confederate. Burnside's men had suffered considerably more in an attack that had originally been meant as a diversion than in his main effort.

The dead at Fredericksburg

The South erupted in jubilation over their great victory. The *Richmond Examiner* described it as a "stunning defeat to the invader, a splendid victory to the defender of the sacred soil."

Reactions were opposite in the North, and both the army and President Lincoln came under strong attacks from politicians and the press. The *Cincinnati Commercial* wrote, "It can hardly be in human nature for men to show more valor or generals to manifest less judgment, than were perceptible on our side that day."

Pennsylvania Governor Andrew Curtin visited the White House after a trip to the battlefield. He told the president, "It was not a battle, it was a butchery." Curtin reported that the president was "heart-broken at the recital, and soon reached a state of nervous excitement bordering on insanity." Lincoln himself wrote, "If there is a worse place than hell, I am in it."

Burnside was relieved of his command a month later, following an unsuccessful attempt to purge some of his subordinates from the army. This "man of magnificent failures" was never content to take responsibility for his own actions when blaming someone else suited his purposes better.

Fredericksburg has been preserved today as testament to the bloody struggle that took place in and around the small town in December 1862. Hundreds of acres remain around the town, while the streets of buildings of Fredericksburg itself still stand as scenes of bloody conflict where the dead and wounded once suffered and died. Many of the buildings that line these quaint streets are the same brick, wood and stone that stood as mute witnesses to the horrific battle, and many of them still hold the spirits of the men who were slain and then bled to death in their bedrooms and parlors as they were converted to makeshift field hospitals.

Much of the fighting on December 11 actually occurred on the streets of the town, and as the Confederates withdrew to the heights above the city, where they would repulse the bloody Union attacks to come, they left behind the homes and businesses unprotected. Union soldiers occupied the town, prying into private pantries, taking what they needed, breaking into homes, looking for the enemy or even hiding from their own commanding officers.

In modern times, such historic homes seem to reverberate with the chaos that once occurred within their walls. Renovations to these homes seem to stir up more than their share of strange activity: doors open and close, lights turn on and off, water faucets come to life, footsteps are heard and eerie voices often ring out in otherwise empty rooms. One strange event was reported a few years ago when the owner of a home tore out all of the old carpets and placed them out by the curb to be picked up by the local trash service. The next morning when he arrived back at the house to continue the remodel, he found that the carpet had mysterious been returned to the house - and was laid out and tacked down exactly as it had been the day before. There had been no one in the house after he had left!

One local house, built in the 1740s by a Scottish merchant named John Allan, was one of the few houses that withstood a Union bombardment in the area in 1862. The house was in the midst of the shelling and fighting that took place during the battle - and that has become the source of its ghostly legend. The story states that the spirit of a young Federal soldier, a casualty of the battle, has taken up residence in the house. Apparently, he had taken shelter in the building, perhaps using it to take cover during the fighting. He was standing behind one of the double doors in the back hall of the house when a bullet ripped through the door and killed him. The soldier was later buried in the back garden and a plug was placed in the door, which remains to this day. In the years that followed, the soldier was often reported to enter the house by the side porch door. The many witnesses who saw him described him as wearing a Union Army uniform.

In time, the young soldier appeared less and less often and eventually, he faded away - returning to the unseen world where he now belonged.

1862: STONES RIVER

The greatest battle for the state of Tennessee began in the last days of 1862 with fierce and bloody fights at places like Chattanooga, Lookout Mountain, Nashville and Franklin. The Union and Confederate armies raged back and forth across the landscape, each hoping to claim this western state as their own. The spilled blood of thousands of Northern and Southern boys seeped into the frozen ground and left a permanent mark on the land. Neither army achieved a victory that season, but then in the waning days of that same year -- over the holiday season -- another battle occurred near Murfreesboro. It is a place that has since become known as Stones River and it remains one of the most eerie and most haunted battlefields of the war. It was a Christmas season unlike any that the young soldiers on both sides of the battle had experienced before, and probably because of this, an especially poignant moment took place here on Christmas Eve that has caused this battle to be remembered by history buffs and ghost enthusiasts alike.

The Battle of Stones River, which was fought near Murfreesboro, Tennessee, occurred in late December of 1862 and lasted through January 2, 1863. The prelude to the battle began a short time earlier, after General Braxton Bragg retreated from Perryville, Kentucky, and started moving his troops into position near Murfreesboro. Because of a number of cavalry raids that occurred around this time, Union General William S. Rosecrans decided to move his troops out of Nashville and attack Bragg. The Confederate raids were designed to disrupt Federal communication lines but had little effect. Rosecrans, however, wanted to take advantage of the depleted Confederate cavalry forces and take the fight to Murfreesboro.

Murfreesboro was a small town in the Stones River Valley, a former state capital named for a colonel in the American Revolutionary War, Hardy Murfree. All through the war it was a center for strong Confederate sentiment, and Bragg and his men were warmly welcomed and entertained by the locals during the month of December. The town was located in a rich agricultural region, and the generosity of the people made it possible for Bragg to re-supply his troops and make plans to block a Federal advance into Chattanooga. The area offered him no particular advantages, but thanks to the ready food supply, he was reluctant to move farther south, to the arguably more defensible Duck River Valley, or north to Stewart's Creek, where Rosecrans expected to encounter Bragg's army.

Instead, Bragg chose to encamp in a relatively flat area northwest of the city, straddling the Stones River. It was a rough place, filled with thick cedar forests and outcroppings of stone that impeded the movement of wagons and artillery. Bragg placed Major General William Hardee's corps in Triune, about twenty miles to the west. General Leonidas Polk's corps were on the west bank of the river and a detached division from Hardee's corps under Major General John C. Breckenridge were on the low hills east of the river. None of the troops were ordered to construct field fortifications.

By the time Rosecrans had arrived in Murfreesboro on the evening of December 29, Bragg's Army of Tennessee had been in the area for a month. By nightfall of that day, Rosecrans' army had begun moving into position along the Nashville Turnpike and by the next day, numbered over 45,000 men. Bragg's army consisted of about 38,000 troops, but was strengthened by the skill of his cavalry commands under Nathan Bedford Forrest and John Hunt Morgan, who raided deep into Union lines, while a third cavalry force under Joseph Wheeler slowed the Federal movement with hit-and-run skirmishes. On December 29, Wheeler's men rode completely around the Union army, destroying supply wagons and capturing reserve ammunition. They captured four wagon trains and took one thousand Union prisoners.

On December 30, the Union force moved into line two miles northwest of Murfreesboro. The two armies were in parallel lines, about four miles long, oriented from southwest to northeast. Bragg's left flank was weak at the start, and Rosecrans could have attacked there when he arrived and wheeled left, around the flank and directly into the town of Murfreesboro, but feeling nervous after the cavalry attacks of the day before, he faltered. Both armies made very similar battle plans for the following day: envelop the enemy's right, get into his rear, and cut him off from his base. Since both plans were the same, the victory would probably go to the side that was able to attack first. Rosecrans ordered his men to be ready to attack after breakfast, but Bragg ordered an attack at dawn.

The Confederate division under John C. Breckinridge was left across the river, while two other divisions moved into position on the Federal right. The center was held by two divisions under Leonidas Polk and planned to attack at dawn. Alexander McCook's corps held the Federal right, where the initial Confederate attack was to fall. They had a strong center and extended their line to the river with a number of divisions to outnumber the Confederates.

As the battle opened at dawn, Federal brigades under Edward N. Kirk and August Willich were driven back. Although Kirk's outposts saw the enemy advance, Willich's brigade was taken by surprise. The Confederates kept up the momentum of the attack by moving up Major General John P. McCown's right, but a single Federal Division under Phillip Sheridan managed to hold off three divisions on their own. Sheridan's right flank was only exposed after a retreat by Davis and they suffered heavy losses. Around 9:30 a.m., though, Sheridan counterattacked and gained the time he needed to set up a new position behind the Nashville Pike. They routed a Confederate division under Johnson and Davis followed them to the rear while a Rebel cavalry brigade harassed his western flank.

The battle at Stones River

A renewed attack, all along the Federal front, finally forced Sheridan, whose ammunition was exhausted, to withdraw. This left a gap between trrops commanded by Brigadier Generals James S. Negley and Lovell H. Rousseau, which the Confederates quickly filled. Shepherd's brigade of regulars lost twenty officers and 518 were killed and wounded in covering a general withdrawal of the Federal right half of the line to a new position. The right of Colonel Oliver H. Palmer's division also had to withdraw but his left flank held its strong position on a wooded ridge astride the railroad. This was a four-acre oak grove that reports of the battle call the Round Forest, but which the troops dubbed "Hell's Half Acre." By noon, the Federals had been forced back to what turned out to be their final defensive line.

As Rosecrans raced across the battlefield directing units, his uniform was covered with the blood of his friend and chief of staff, Col. Julius Garesché, who was beheaded by a cannonball while riding alongside him.

The Federal divisions of Generals Horatio P. Van Cleve and Thomas J. Wood, which were supposed to move north of the river and make Rosecrans' main attack, had been called back to bolster the Federal defense. Van Cleve had crossed the river, and Wood was ready to follow, when the Confederate attack started. Wood was held back and put into position on the Federal left. Van Cleve was ordered back and arrived about 11:00 a.m., just in time to reinforce the final defensive line.

Bragg was rallied by the way the battle was going and in preparation for what he hoped would be a death blow to the Federal troops, he called on Breckinridge to send two of his five brigades to reinforce Hardee. Only one of them arrived in time to be of any use, though. To make matters worse, cavalry units had reported the arrival of a Federal division to face off against Breckinridge but had not seen its subsequent withdrawal. Because of this, Breckinridge believed that he was in danger of being overwhelmed and refused to spare the brigades that he was supposed to send to Hardee. It would not be until late afternoon before Breckinridge's other brigades were brought south of the river and committed to action against "Hell's Half Acre." They were all beaten back with heavy losses.

The Confederate assaults were well-driven but were effectively repulsed by the now-organized Federal defense. One brigade had been waiting for forty-eight hours in shallow trenches and without fires for the attack to take place. When the Confederates charged across the open field toward them, they cut the Rebels to pieces with rifle and artillery fire. After desperate fighting, in which some regiments lost six to eight color bearers, the Confederates were driven back. Donelson's brigade made the next effort. After some initial confusion when they reached the field, and in the face of heavy fire, the brigade penetrated the Union line and took one thousand prisoners and eleven guns. Before they could advance, though, a Federal position in the Round Forest forced them to retreat.

The counterattacks drove back the Confederate army but after some hesitation, Rosecrans decided to remain on the field during the night and to resume the offensive if Bragg did not attack. The battlefield was quiet the next morning but Confederate cavalry under Wheeler and Wharton were doing damage along Rosecrans' line of communications and supply to Nashville. Wheeler attacked a wagon train near Lavergne, dispersed the guards and destroyed about thirty wagons.

For some reason, the Federals had abandoned the Round Forest position during the night, so the Confederates took possession of the position. Bragg then became determined to have Breckinridge cross the river again and take the high ground, from which they could force the Union troops from their position. Breckinridge went on record to say that he felt the task was not only impossible, but pointless, but Bragg insisted, so he attacked with about 4,500 men.

The rebel forces stormed the hill and managed to drive the Federals from it. However, as the Confederates pursued them down the forward slope, they were slaughtered by the massed fire of fifty-eight guns that had been posted across the river. Breckinridge was driven back to his line of departure. He had lost almost two thousand men in a matter of minutes.

By January 3, Rosecrans was holding a defensive position west of the river and Bragg was withdrawing through Murfreesboro through Shelbyville. Rosecrans did not pursue them and it was not until June that Rosecrans renewed operations in the area, when his Tullahoma Campaign set the stage for the Chickamauga and Chattanooga Campaigns.

In the end, Stones River was declared a tactical victory for the Confederates, even though Bragg lacked the strength to destroy Rosecrans' larger army or drive it from the field. Casualties were so high during the fighting that there was little cause to celebrate any sort of victory. The battle was carried out over a seventy-two-hour period and when the carnage ended, the opposing forces counted their losses. The Confederates suffered more than 10,000 casualties among the 38,000 men engaged. Meanwhile, the Union forces counted 13,249 dead, wounded, missing or captured among the 43,400 men they entered the battle with. The horrendous losses of men at Antietam and Gettysburg are more widely known today than those in Tennessee, yet Stones River saw the highest percentage of casualties compared to numbers engaged of any Civil War battle.

Today, the battlefield stands as a monument to the bitter fighting that took place. Near the battlefield is the Stones River National Cemetery, one of the oldest national cemeteries in the country. Visitors to the modern battlefield can take a walking, or driving, tour of the area and various stops on the tour are marked with numbers. These designate the sites where major events took place during the battle.

The location known as Stop No. 4 is also known by the more colorful, and graphic, name of the "Slaughter Pen." It was at this point on the battlefield where Sheridan's division was able to hold the Confederates back long enough for a proper defense to be organized. Sheridan fought a confusing battle in the heavy forest and the Federals soon found themselves in a tightening pocket that was collapsing on three sides. The Confederates, headed by troops from Alabama and South Carolina, rushed out of the woods towards Sheridan's position, only to be met with artillery fire and small arms volleys from the Yankees. However, the defense did not hold and soon, the borders of Sheridan's defense began to collapse. Only his brigade of men from Illinois and Missouri stood strong.

Sheridan's three brigade commanders were killed in the "Slaughter Pen" and a third of his division was destroyed. Finally, the Federals ran out of ammunition and turned to fighting hand-to-hand with bayonets, scrambling through the forest and the underbrush. As the Rebels rushed their position, in devastating wave after wave, the Union soldiers cut, slashed, and continued to drive the enemy back. Sheridan lost fourteen pieces of artillery, but not without a fight. The cannon crews defended their guns with everything they had, turning from guns to knives and even their bare knuckles. Captain Charles Houghtaling had been ordered to hold his artillery at all costs and it was a command he took literally. Only at the very last moment were his guns abandoned and even then, Houghtaling had to be carried from the field.

There were a couple of odd events that occurred during the battle. Much was written in journals and letters about the strange behavior of the animals at Stone River. While the men were lying behind a crest waiting for the fighting to begin, a brace of frantic wild turkeys, so paralyzed with fright that they were incapable of flying, ran between the lines and endeavored to hide among the men. What was even stranger was the flight of other birds and rabbits. When the roar of battle rushed through the cedar thickets, flocks of little birds fluttered and circled above the field in a state of bewilderment and scores of rabbits fled for protection to the men lying down in line, nestling under their coats and creeping under their legs in a state of utter panic. They hopped over the field, as perfectly tamed by fright as household pets. Many officers witnessed it, remarking it as one of the most curious spectacles ever seen upon a battlefield.

Perhaps the most memorable event of the battle took place one night after fighting had ended for the day. It was the holiday season and on both sides of the line, soldiers wished for home and were saddened by spending the holidays without their families. In order to keep up morale, a military band played for the soldiers' entertainment. The battle lines were so close together that the sounds of the opposing army's music carried through the forest. As the night wore on, the troops battled each other in another way --- as one side played a rousing rendition of "Dixie," the other band would try to drown it out with the equally loud strains of "Yankee Doodle." Finally, one of the bands struck up the chords to the song "Home, Sweet, Home" and the rival band joined in.

Soldiers on both sides began to sing the familiar words and for one brief moment, the war was forgotten and the soldiers shared their mutual longings for the comforts of home. The spirit of Christmas drew them together and for just a brief few hours, the men were no longer "Rebels" and "Yankees" but comrades in arms who equally missed the warmth of hearth and home. Grown men wept and raised a toast across the battle lines to the men on the other side. Cheers resounded and Northern and Southern men greeted one another in good cheer, but it was not to last. When dawn came, the bloody fighting began once again.

Even so, this was not the only melancholy event to occur during the battle. As night fell on the second day of fighting, a group of men from the 74th Illinois heard a wounded Confederate begging for help. He was found near a battery that had been overrun by the Federals and since he was unable to walk, the Illinois men picked him up and carried him behind their lines. He was given a drink of water but his only request, as he lay dying, was that his mother be informed of his end.

Henry R. Freeman, one of the Illinois soldiers, took down the man's address and promised to write her a letter. The Confederate died there on the cold ground that night and Freeman kept his promise. Sadly, though, he was unable to carry it out in full. In late 1865, a letter that had been addressed to "Relatives of M.W. Wildy, Davis Creek Post Office, Fayette County, Alabama" was returned to Freeman's home and was never delivered because the address was inadequate to reach the dead man's family.

There is no question that Stop No. 4 on the battlefield tour, the Slaughter Pen, was the scene of the bloodiest fighting at Stones River. Today, the area is a wooded section with a number of rocks and sinkholes and it is regarded as a haunted place. Civil War reenactors and living history groups often camp near the Slaughter Pen when they come to Stones River. There is something about the bravery displayed here by Sheridan's men that seems to appeal to them and to draw them to the place. Visitors often report a strange stillness to the area that should not be found in a wooded area, where birds and wildlife should be active, but are not. Many of them also speak of eerie feelings here -- feelings that let them know they are not always among the living in this place.

The legends of the Slaughter Pen tell of a mysterious soldier who often appears here. Reenactors claim they have seen him around the campfire, or on the edge of the darkened camp. He is also seen leaning against a tree, or lingering in the shadows, aware of, and yet separate from, the activity around him. His uniform allows him to often blend in with the reenactors, yet he is known to simply disappear if anyone tries to speak to him.

Park rangers, and visitors that I have interviewed, often report the Slaughter Pen to be about ten or twenty degrees colder than the park around it. They also claim that you can sometimes hear the sound of someone following you if you walk there after dark.

Aside from the Slaughter Pen, there are other haunted places on the battlefield as well, including Site No. 6. In 1978, according to an interview given to author Richard Winer, a park ranger named Jeffrey Leathers was involved in a Civil War reenactment on the battlefield and was encamped near Tour Stop No. 6. He woke up in the middle of the night feeling thirsty. Finding his canteen empty, he walked back to the administration building and along the way, noticed a man lurking in the bushes near the path. Thinking that it was one of his friends waiting to play a prank on him, he yelled for the man to come out of hiding.

The soldier, who like Leathers was dressed in a period uniform, raised a hand and walked out. He appeared to be very serious, but many reenactors stay in character during the mock battles and apparently the mysterious man was pretending to be captured by the enemy. The soldier continued walking toward Leathers, who then ordered him to stop. Still playing his part in the "engagement," Leathers raised his rifle and just as he did, the man fell to the ground -- and vanished.

Still thinking this was all part of the reenactment, Leathers looked around in the shadows, but quickly became convinced that the man had actually disappeared. The next morning, he returned to the spot in the company of several friends, but they found no footprints or any other trace of the soldier. In fact, there was nothing to say that he had ever existed at all!

I Troy had the chance to visit Stones River for the first time in May 1997. When I arrived at the battlefield, it had turned into a gloomy and overcast day. That first visit was a short one, thanks to an approaching storm and as it turned out, a tornado that moved through shortly after I left the area. Even though I didn't have much time, I did go to the Slaughter Pen that afternoon, interested in soaking up some of the atmosphere of this reportedly haunted place. When I reached the area, I stopped the car in a small parking lot and got out to take a look around.

The woods beyond the field were dark and filled with shadows but then I did notice something odd. I saw a small light appear and start to bob along the edge of the trees. It traveled about forty yards and then it vanished as quickly as it had come. I could see nothing behind it in the gloom and quickly walked to the edge of the woods for a closer look. There was no one there who was carrying a light or walking around, so what could this have been? Could it have been a reflection from a car or another natural explanation? Electricity was certainly in the air from the approaching storm and perhaps this caused the strange light...

Or could it have been something else? The light of a lost soldier still searching for a way to get a message home, a lone sentry from Sheridan's brigade still patrolling the picket line, or even perhaps the mysterious man who has been seen in so many reenactors' camps over the years, still fighting a battle that ended many years before?

1863: GETTYSBURG

Most Civil War enthusiasts would say the battle that was fought near the small Pennsylvania town of Gettysburg in 1863 was the greatest conflict of the war. At the very least, it is considered the turning point that led to the fall of the Confederacy. For ghost hunters, the mere mention of Gettysburg conjures up images of haunted buildings, strange battlefield encounters and restless ghosts.

I Troy honestly believe there is no place in America that is as haunted as Gettysburg - both the official battlefield and the small town that around it. During the bloody fighting that took place here in July 1863, the fighting raged not only in the woods, fields and hills around the town, but in the homes and up and down the streets as well. Those events left an indelible mark on this community and it's one that is still being felt today.

By early summer of 1863, the war in the East was going well for the Confederacy. Lee, confident after his victories at Fredericksburg and Chancellorsville, urged President Jefferson Davis to once again take the war to the North. By doing so, this would take the fighting out of Virginia and relieve the pressure being felt by the government in Richmond. It would also ease the load on the Confederate supply lines because if the invasion could be pushed far enough to the north, it would allow the soldiers to live off the land. In addition, Lee's invasion would also draw attention away from Grant's siege of Vicksburg, plus, if the Confederates could capture any Northern towns, it just might push the war-weary citizens of the North into discussion of a settlement between the two nations.

It seemed as though the outlook for a Northern invasion was completely positive, and if a downside existed, Lee couldn't find it. So, moving in secret, Lee began his northern thrust on June 3, 1863. He marched his troops into the Shenandoah Valley and pushed them on, using the mountains as a shield. After the death of Thomas "Stonewall" Jackson a short time before, the Army of Northern Virginia had been re-organized into three corps, commanded by A.P. Hill, Richard S. Ewell and James Longstreet. The cavalry was commanded by the magnificent J.E.B. Stuart.

Although unaware of Lee's plans, the Army of the Potomac, under the command of Joseph Hooker, realized that a major enemy troop movement was underway, following a cavalry engagement at Brandy Station, later known as the Battle of Fleetwood Hill, on June 9. Hooker then cautiously followed Lee's march to the north, keeping his army east of the mountains and between Washington and the Confederates. On June 15, Lee overwhelmed a Union force at Winchester, Virginia, and then continued northward. By June 28, all of the Confederate troops had crossed over into Union territory. They were still widely scattered, but all were converging on the Pennsylvania capital of Harrisburg.

Meanwhile, tension between Washington and General Hooker was increasing. Once again, Lincoln was disappointed by the inaction of one of his generals and on June 28, he appointed George Meade to replace Hooker as the head of the Army of the Potomac.

Coincidentally, on this same day, General Lee received a message that the Federal Army was on the move, heading toward his new location. This came as a shock to the old campaigner, as he had been depending on Stuart to keep him aware of all enemy activity. Although no one knew it at the time, Stuart had seemingly vanished. He was involved in a daring raid east of the Federal army and all communications with the main Confederate force had been cut off.

With the news that the Federal Army, now under command of General Meade, was aware of his plans, Lee sent out an order to concentrate the Confederate forces at Cashtown, a small village between Chambersburg and Gettysburg. There, Lee would prepare to confront the Federal advance troops. The Confederate Army was now in place to the north and west of Gettysburg, while Meade pushed the Federal Army from the south, moving northward from Maryland.

Both armies were in the dark as to the whereabouts of the other on June 30, the day that cavalry units under command of General John Buford rode into Gettysburg.

Before this time, there was nothing to set Gettysburg apart from hundreds of other small communities in America. The population of the town was of about 2,400 and aside from a thriving carriage-building industry, its only claims to fame were its two colleges, the Lutheran Theological Seminary and Pennsylvania College Gettysburg College . It was nothing more than a sleepy little Pennsylvania town in the summer of 1863, but that was about to change.

Buford's cavalry rode into town on June 30 and established a picket line near the Lutheran Seminary to guard approaches to the town from the west. By coincidence, a brigade of Confederate Infantry under General John Pettigrew, of A.P. Hill's Corps, had been sent to Gettysburg from Cashtown to scout out the area that same day. Legend has it that the Confederates were in town looking for shoes, but they were actually on a reconnaissance mission. With two large armies so close to one another, it was inevitable that they would collide. When the Confederates spotted the Union pickets, they returned to the west to report the enemy's presence.

Early in the morning of July 1, two Confederate brigades were sent to investigate the Federal presence in Gettysburg. Within a short time of the Confederate arrival, a skirmish broke out between the Rebels and Buford's men. Although Buford knew that he was greatly outnumbered, and in a bad position, he chose to stand his ground and send for help from two Union corps that were a short distance to the south. The Confederates also sent for reinforcements and soon, both armies were headed toward Gettysburg - a place where neither Lee nor Meade planned to fight.

For the next two hours, Buford's cavalrymen, fighting dismounted, managed to hold off a number of Confederate attacks from the area known as McPherson's farm. Buford was later relieved by the arrival of General John Reynolds' corps. One division crossed an unfinished railroad cut to the north of the Chambersburg Pike and formed a battle line. Another Confederate brigade was at the same time attacking McPherson's Woods, which lay to the south of the Pike. General Reynolds himself led the Federal Iron Brigade into the woods, where he was killed instantly by enemy fire. Reynolds was the second in command to the Army of the Potomac and would be the highest-ranking officer to perish during the three days of fighting at Gettysburg.

Around the middle of the day, the fighting broke off and the field was fairly quiet until the middle of the afternoon. The corps commanded by Hill and Ewell advanced against the Federals along a two-mile stretch that ran between the western and northern approaches to Gettysburg. Confederate reinforcements continued to arrive throughout the afternoon and around 4:00 p.m., General Jubal Early's division struck the right flank of the Union's XI Corps, which was under command of General Francis Barlow. The attack caused Howard's entire line to begin to crumble.

The corps began retreating into Gettysburg, where they almost collided with other retreating Federal troops, who at the same moment had collapsed to Confederate pressure near the McPherson farm. Falling back from two different directions, the Union troops became confused and disoriented in the small town and stumbled along to the shelter of Cemetery Hill, a reserve position located on the southern outskirts of Gettysburg. Here, Union General Winfield Scott Hancock rallied the men into defensive positions on Cemetery and nearby Culp's hills.

The jubilant Confederates stormed after them and not only captured the entire town, but over 2,500 Union prisoners. And then, they halted. Strangely, Lee's forces made no attempt to storm Cemetery Hill that night. One has to wonder what may have been the outcome of the battle if they had. Instead, Lee had given orders to Ewell to renew the attack before nightfall "if practicable." Unfortunately, Ewell took Lee's courteous order as giving him a choice of whether to fight or to retire from the field. He chose incorrectly. Ewell decided his men needed a rest and the first day's fighting came to an end.

Lee arrived in Gettysburg that afternoon. He established his headquarters in a house along the Chambersburg Pike and began to make plans for the following day. Even though he was in poor health and suffering from diarrhea, Lee remained confident about the Confederate chances in the battle ahead. He felt the Union Army was weakened by its recent defeats at Fredericksburg and Chancellorsville and by yet another change in command. If he pressed hard enough, he believed, the Federals would break.

Throughout the night, the two armies continued to gather, and by morning about 65,000 Confederate troops faced a Union force of around 85,000 men. The Northern lines had assumed what has become known as the "Fishhook" formation. Cemetery Hill became the curve of the fishhook, while Culp's Hill, located just to the east, became the hook, and right flank, of the Union line. Hancock's corps occupied the shank of the formation, and they stretched south through the open fields to Cemetery Ridge. The Union left was to be defended by troops under General Daniel Sickles, a former politician who was best known for killing his wife's lover before the war. Secretary of War Edwin Stanton had been his attorney and had gotten him off by using the first-ever plea of "temporary insanity."

Sickles spent the entire morning of July 2 disobeying orders. He had shifted his corps' position on lower Cemetery Ridge out into the Peach Orchard, which stood on a flat-topped ridge about a half-mile in front of the Union line. This managed to leave the hills known as Little Round Top and Big Round Top, and the Union's left flank, completely undefended. When Meade learned of this, he angrily ordered him back into position, but before the corps could be moved, Longstreet had begun his attack.

As Lee studied the Union formation on the field that morning, he noted that the Federal fishhook was overlooked by hills on both ends. Culp's Hill and Cemetery Hill stood above the right and the Big and Little Round Tops loomed over the left. Lee's plan called for the Confederates to take the hills, sending Ewell to attack Culp's Hill and Longstreet the Round Tops.

Little fighting took place during the morning and afternoon, aside from scattered fire from skirmishes. Lee's plan called for attack on both Union flanks at the same time, but the assault was delayed for several hours as Longstreet shifted his two corps into position on the southern edge of Seminary Ridge.

At the same time, Sickles was shifting his own line to the more forward position. By the time Longstreet was ready to attack, Sickle's new line extended northwestward from the tangle of boulders at Devil's Den, through Rose Woods and the Wheatfield, and then sharply to the northeast where it crossed the Peach Orchard and continued along the Emmitsburg Road. The new position was nearly impossible to defend and not only did it fail to connect its right flank to the left flank of II Corps, but it also left Little Round Top completely unoccupied.

The Confederate attack against the left Union flank began just after four in the afternoon. One of the first points to be struck was the rocky promontory known as Devil's Den, which fell to Hood's men after a bitter struggle that lasted for several hours. In waves, Longstreet's brigades swept over the Rose Woods and the Wheatfield and then advanced on the Federal positions at the Peach Orchard and along the Emmitsburg Road.

The fighting continued on through the afternoon and while Sickles' beaten line was reinforced by troops under George Sykes, Sickles himself was severely wounded. The Confederates were relentless and after four hours of battle, all of the Union positions along Sickle's' line were overrun.

Meanwhile, during the initial attack, the 15th Alabama managed to reach the summit of Big Round Top. From there, Colonel William C. Oates realized that the summit of Little Round Top was virtually undefended. If he could haul guns to the top of the hill, he would be directly above the Federal lines and could destroy them.

As luck would have it, Little Round Top had also come under the scrutiny of the Union command. Meade had dispatched the army's chief engineer, General

Gouverner Warren, and a lieutenant of engineers named Washington Roebling to the summit of Little Round Top to bring back a report of the state of the battle. They found only a handful of Union signalmen on the hill and one look around sent them into shock. Warren quickly realized what was going to happen as he saw Sickles corps pinned down below and Confederate troops coming up the ravine that separated the Round Tops.

He sent for reinforcements at once and the last of the four regiments ordered to the hill was the 20th Maine, under the command of Colonel Joshua Lawrence Chamberlain, a professor of rhetoric and languages at Maine's Bowdoin College. The colonel's orders were to hold Little Round Top "at all hazards" and with three hundred and fifty men, he started up the south slope and they took shelter behind rocks and trees. Fortunately, at the last moment, Chamberlain sent a company of men across the hollow between the hills to bolster the left flank of the defense. Less than ten minutes later, Oates and his Confederates arrived, attacking before the company could take shelter on the left. The Rebels opened fire and Chamberlain later stated that he assumed his men had been wiped out with the first volley of fire.

The Maine men attacked but the Confederates regrouped and charged again and again, slowly gaining ground and swinging around to Chamberlain's left. He ordered that portion of his line to drop back, forming again at right angles to the rest of the regiment. The men dropped back, continuing to fire as they regrouped.

In less than an hour, over forty thousand rounds had been fired on Little Round Top and still the Federals held firm. The Rebels had driven them from their position five times and yet each time, Chamberlain's men fought their way back again. He would lose one hundred and thirty of his men, a loss of nearly one-third of his force. He would describe the conflict by saying: "At times I saw around me more of the enemy than my own men; gaps opening, swallowing; closing again and all around, a strange, mingled roar."

The sounds of battle behind Chamberlain grew louder and he assumed they had been surrounded. His men had finally run out of ammunition and the only choices that remained were to surrender or die. Instead, Chamberlain ordered his men to fix bayonets. Then, while the right corner of the regiment stood firm, the men were told to wheel around like a great hinge toward the right.

The attacking Confederates were so stunned by the maniacal charge of the Federals that many of them actually dropped their weapons and surrendered. Others began to run, only to get another, more gruesome surprise -- the company of men that Chamberlain had sent over to guard the left flank had not been killed by the initial Confederate attack. They suddenly appeared from behind a stone wall and opened fire on the retreating Rebels.

The remaining Confederates broke and ran. As Colonel Oates would later admit, "we ran like a herd of wild cattle." The Confederate dead literally covered the ground and while fighting continued on other parts of the slope, the summit of Little Round Top was secure.

Joshua Lawrence Chamberlain would go on to receive the Congressional Medal of Honor for his actions that day.

While the heroics of the men from Maine had saved Little Round Top, things were not going as well on other parts of the Union front. Sickles' corps was in desperate straits as the Confederates continued to attack. A Confederate artillery blast amputated the lower portion of General Sickles' leg and he was carried from the field, still calmly smoking a cigar.

Union reinforcements began to arrive and fighting raged through the Devil's Den and the Valley of Death. The Federal troops, as they crossed the Wheatfield, opened a gap on Cemetery Ridge and a Confederate brigade began a drive toward it. Hancock spotted the opening and ordered a single, small regiment, the 1st Minnesota, to counthercharge and hold the gap. The Minnesota regiment, made up of only two hundred and sixty-two men, raced toward the opening with fixed bayonets and came face to face with 1,600 Confederates. The stunned Rebels fell back and the gap in the lines was closed, although only forty-seven members of the 1st Minnesota came through the skirmish unhurt. They had lost most of their men in less than five minutes.

By the end of the day, the lack of coordination in Lee's attacks cost them the fight. Despite Longstreet's limited success against Sickles, the Confederate offensive had only worked in some locations and the plan of attacking both flanks at the same time had not worked at all. In fact, it was almost sundown before two divisions of Ewells' corps even began their assault on the hook and curve of the Union's right flank.

The Confederates had clashed with Union troops on the eastern slopes of the hill, which had previously been fortified with earthworks, strengthened by felled trees and rocks. The Federals, although badly outnumbered, used the works to their advantage and the Rebels failed to dislodge them from the hill.

Meanwhile, two brigades under Jubal Early met with even less luck in their attempt to capture Cemetery Hill. The Confederates initially managed to break through the Federal lines at the northern base of the hill in the early evening but soon suffered a devastating blow from Union artillery on Steven's Knoll. The fighting on the hill became hand-to-hand combat but with no reinforcements from the Confederate infantry units on the south edge of Gettysburg, the Rebels soon retreated.

At the end of the second day of battle, Meade's fishhook remained intact.

The third day began badly for the Confederates, further adding to the conclusion that Lee had reached during the night that he must attack the Federal forces at the center. The failure of his attempts to crush the Union flanks suggested that Meade had fortified these areas at the expense of the center. By midday of July 3, Lee decided that the Confederates would take one last shot. It would be a direct frontal assault against Cemetery Ridge. Lee's plan called for an artillery bombardment to weaken the Union line on the ridge, followed by an infantry attack.

During the morning hours, even Jeb Stuart had suffered at the hands of the Yankees. The cavalry commander had arrived in Gettysburg the afternoon before to be greeted by Lee's anger. One officer recalled later that Lee had even raised a hand as if to strike Stuart, as one would discipline an errant child, which perhaps was how Lee saw his relationship with the younger man. "I have not heard from you in days, and you the eyes and ears of my army," he was said to have chastised the cavalryman.

But Lee's anger quickly passed and on the morning of the third day, he put Stuart's men to work, launching an attack on the Federal rear. But the once-weak Union cavalry stopped him, thanks to a series of reckless charges led by a young and dashing officer named George Armstrong Custer.

Now, everything depended on the success of Longstreet's assault on the Union center. Longstreet opposed attacking in this manner, knowing what his own gunners had accomplished at Fredericksburg when Union troops had advanced across an open expanse. But Lee disagreed and ordered Longstreet to prepare the advance. "The enemy is there," he reportedly told Longstreet," and I am going to strike him."

The man that Lee chose to lead the advance was a friend and compatriot of Longstreet, General George Pickett, a rather peculiar, but well-liked officer with a beard and long, curly hair. Pickett's men waited in the wood on the opposite side of a long field from the Union center. They passed the time by throwing green apples at each other. They laughed and joked, knowing that what faced them was a nearly impossible task.

At just after 1:00 p.m., the Confederate artillery assault on Cemetery Ridge began. The earth shook as the cannons pounded the ridge, trying to weaken the Union line. General Meade had just left his commanders at the lunch table when the barrage started. As an orderly was serving butter, a shell literally tore him in two.

The top of the hill seemed to be tearing apart. Great mounds of earth were catapulted into the air and shells furrowed into the hillside, destroying grave markers and upending stones. Soon, the Union guns began to return fire and the casualty rate began to climb for the Confederate infantry, who were waiting in the woods for the signal to advance. But after about an hour, Meade ordered the Federal guns to silence, hoping to conserve ammunition for the fight that he was sure was coming. The eerie stillness, he also knew, would serve to lure the Confederates out into the open fields.

Pickett came to Longstreet and asked if his men should go forward. The Federal guns had been destroyed, they believed, and nothing lay between the Confederates and the destruction of the Federal center but Union infantry. The time was now ripe for an attack.

Longstreet was too overcome with emotion to speak and he merely nodded his head, convinced that he was sending his friend to his death. Pickett hurriedly scribbled a note to his fiancée and handed it to Longstreet to mail and then gave the order to attack.

Three divisions, numbering about thirteen thousand men, started out of the woods and towards the stone wall at the edge of Cemetery Ridge. Although history remembers this advance as "Pickett's Charge," it was hardly a quick attack. The men walked at a brisk pace, covering only about one hundred yards of the open field by the minute. "It was," one Union officer who watched the charge from the opposite side of the field recalled, "the most beautiful thing I ever saw."

Union cannons on Cemetery Ridge and Little Round Top began to sound, opening fire on the right side of the advancing line. Men were killed with every shot but the Confederates still kept coming. Behind the stone wall, Union troops waited, holding their fire until the Rebels came closer. Finally, the order was given by General Alexander Hays and eleven cannon and seventeen hundred muskets went off at once.

Hundreds died in the first volley but the rest continued to come. The Confederates reached the line at just one place, a crook in the wall that has become known as "The Angle." They were led by General Lewis A. Armistead, who jumped the wall and managed to capture a Union battery before he was shot down. All of the other Confederates who breached the wall were captured, killed or wounded. Soon, those Confederates remaining on the field broke and ran or gave themselves up as prisoners.

The assault was over -- a complete and utter failure.

As the Confederates staggered back to Seminary Ridge, Lee rode out among them, urging them to regroup. "It was all my fault," he was said to have told them, "Get together and let us do the best we can towards saving what is left of us."

Pickett had watched the advance with disbelief. Half of his men, over 6,500, had been killed or captured; sixteen of his seventeen field officers were gone, along with three brigadier generals and eight colonels. When Lee ordered him to rally his division for possible counterattack by the Federals, Pickett replied, "General Lee, I have no division now." In the years to come, Pickett would never forgive Lee for what happened that day, always believing that his commander had sent his men into the field to be needlessly slaughtered.

By the end of the third day, the Battle of Gettysburg was over. The fighting had spilled across the hills and through the forests and even into the streets of Gettysburg itself.

The next day, July 4, both armies remained on the battlefield, with Meade and Lee each waiting for the other to move. When nothing of significance occurred that day, Lee realized that his invasion of the North had come to an end. He was now far from his supply line and was running low on ammunition, not to mention the fact that the Confederacy could not afford the tens of thousands of casualties they had sustained. It was time to return home. That afternoon, Lee began his long retreat back to Virginia while Meade, despite urgings from Washington, declined to attack the retreating force.

Behind them, the streets and fields of Gettysburg were littered with the bodies of the dead, slowly decaying in the heat of the Pennsylvania summer. The people of the town were left with thousands of the wounded to attend to and homes and businesses were quickly turned into field hospitals. "Wounded men were brought into our houses and laid side-by-side in our halls and rooms," one local woman recalled. "Carpets were so saturated with blood as to be unfit for further use. Walls were bloodstained, as well as books that were used as pillows."

The dead also lined the streets and walkways, rotting in the summer sun. "Corpses, swollen to twice their original size," wrote a Federal soldier, "actually burst asunder.... several human, or inhuman, corpses sat upright against a fence, with arms extended in the air and faces hideous with something very like a fixed leer..."

In terms of significance, Gettysburg will always be remembered as one of the greatest battles in American history. It was the turning point in the war and it was probably not a coincidence that the day after the battle ended also marked the fall of Vicksburg to General Grant. The war had just taken a darker turn for the Confederacy.

The battle would have a lingering effect on the country, not only for the armies of the Civil War, but for the America itself -- an effect that still lingers today. It goes without saying that the Battle of Gettysburg left a tremendous mark on the small town and on the fields where the fighting actually took place. Few are surprised to learn that many of the buildings in Gettysburg and many locations on the battlefield are now believed to be haunted. In places where so much death and destruction took place, stories of ghosts and spirits often follow.

Gettysburg Haunts

There are numerous places throughout the town of Gettysburg where spirits from the battle are still said to linger: homes, shops, hotels, restaurants and scores of other places are allegedly infested by ghosts. The very idea of ghosts has become a cottage industry in the town, catering as a secondary market to those who come to the area with a taste for Civil War history.

I have visited Gettysburg dozens of time and have had my share of encounters with the unusual, from strange incidents on the battlefield to the phantom odor of peppermint on the city streets. Fighting took place throughout the town when the Federals retreated on that first day of the battle, they poured into Gettysburg, fleeing to the relative safety of Cemetery Hill. Many were killed here, their bodies left to await burial on the streets of the town. The fact that these bodies were left to decompose in the July heat has given rise to one of the many ghostly tales of Gettysburg. According to the story, the ladies of the town were only able to walk the streets after the battle with scented handkerchiefs pressed to their faces to combat the horrible smell of death. The stories say these odors of peppermint and vanilla are still present today, lingering as a bit of forgotten history that a few people myself included have inexplicably encountered.

But there are other places where the past still lingers within the confines of Gettysburg.

Located in town is Gettysburg College, or as it was known in 1863, Pennsylvania College. This small, attractive campus seems a quiet place today, and anyone who visits here would probably be surprised to learn that during the battle, the college was in the midst of the fighting. At the time, the college consisted of only three brick buildings, which provided lodging and classrooms for little more than one hundred students. When the battle erupted, the campus was thrown into the midst of the fight, providing shelter for the wounded and dying as a field hospital. Today, the college is still marked with the physical effects of the battle - and some spiritual residue, as well.

One of the most haunted places on campus is said to be Pennsylvania Hall, a large building fronted with stately white columns. It once served as a dormitory and now houses the campus administrative offices. The hall was constructed in 1837 and is often referred to as Old Dorm. The large structure was taken over by the Confederates during the battle for use as a field hospital and also as a lookout post. A number of officers, including General Lee, climbed to the cupola of Old Dorm to keep an eye on the progress of the battle.

It has been said that on certain nights, students and staff members have reported seeing the figures of soldiers pacing back and forth in the building's cupola. The descriptions of the men vary but it is believed they may be sentries who were placed on duty there to guard the safety of Lee, or to deliver messages to the battlefield.

One student reported that he and his roommate, who lived in a dorm about fifty yards away from Pennsylvania Hall, saw a shadowy figure in the tower over a period of several nights. On another occasion, a figure was seen to be gesturing wildly, apparently to a student below. When the student called out to him, believing that perhaps someone was trapped in the tower, the figure vanished. An investigation by campus security found the building to be empty.

It is believed to be the terrible conditions of the field hospital, however, which have left the strongest impressions on Old Dorm. According to the records of the time, blood sprayed the walls and floors of the rooms as doctors operated on screaming men without anesthetic, dealing with serious bullet wounds by the preferred treatment of the time, which was amputation. Outside the operating rooms was an area where those who could not be saved were left to die. There is no way that we can even imagine the horrible wails, groans and cries that echoed in this area.

Perhaps the most famous story connected to the time of the battle was related by author Mark Nesbitt. He told of two college administrators who were working on the building's fourth floor one night. As they were leaving, they stepped into the elevator and punched the button for the first floor. Instead of taking them to their destination, the elevator mysteriously passed it and came to a stop on the basement level. The elevator doors then opened to a terrifying scene. The basement storage room had vanished and in its place was the blood-splattered operating room of 1863. Wounded men were writhing on the floor and administering to them were doctors and orderlies in blood-splattered clothing. The entire scene was completely silent, although it was obvious that it was one of chaos.

Stunned and horrified, the administrators repeatedly pushed at the elevator button, desperately trying to close the doors and escape the hellish scene that lay before them. Just before the doors closed, though, one of the spectral orderlies was said to have looked up, directly at the two panicked administrators, and gestured to them to come and assist in the operations that were taking place. The administrators, frozen with fear, were unable to move. The man put aside his surgical instruments and started to walk toward them. Before he reached them, however, the elevator doors mercifully closed.

Whatever happened that evening, the two administrators were shaken and frightened by it. They reported what they had seen in the basement to a security guard, who went to investigate, thinking it was a fraternity prank. He found nothing out of the ordinary. Needless to say, the administrators never forgot their strange experience. Although both of them continued to work in the building, whenever they had to work at night, they always departed by way of the stairs.

The home of the widow Mary Thompson was located on Seminary Ridge, on the north side of the Chambersburg Pike. It is best remembered today as the headquarters of General Robert E. Lee during the battle, although Lee actually slept in a tent that was pitched in an apple orchard on the south side of the pike.
Not far from Lee's encampment was the Thompson barn. During the battle, both the barn and house were used as field hospitals. The house was only used for a short time, but the barn was used even after the fighting had ended. Local lore recalls that Mrs. Thompson tending the dying as best she could and was even seen "wrapping the dead up in her carpets."
Across the road in the barn, however, the dead were not treated so kindly. The records say that they were piled like "cordwood" in what was called the "stone room" of the cellar beneath the building. During this, and other Civil War battles, icehouses and cool corners of cellars were often used as temporary storage places for the dead. In this way, they could be placed out of the way, in cold storage, until they could be properly buried. The bodies of the dead soldiers were carried down into the cellar of the barn and stacked there, literally in piles. During the first day of the battle, the body count began to increase and soon stretcher carriers were placing more men there by the hour. The corpses were unceremoniously tossed one atop the other in a grisly pyramid of death. Nothing more could be done for the dead until the battle was over.
Unfortunately, not everyone piled in that gruesome stone cellar was dead. One of those men, lying beneath dozens of his fallen comrades, was badly wounded but alive. He awakened to find himself buried alive under the stiffening bodies of his fellow soldiers.
A few days later, the battle was over and the Confederates had begun their retreat back to Virginia. Slowly, the Union troops moved into the area that was once behind the Rebel lines. It was not long before someone discovered the horrible pile of bodies rotting beneath the Thompson barn.
As the burial crews came along, they began removing the bloated cadavers one by one, carrying them out to wagons to be taken away for burial. As they eventually reached the bottom of the pile, they tugged on the legs of one of the bloody corpses -- only to see the man's eyes fly open and his limbs began to twitch and shake. Maniacal screams emerged from his lips and the Union crew hurriedly dropped him and scrambled away. The man had been alive, buried beneath the festering bodies for four days, imprisoned there to go slowly and

terribly insane. They fetched a doctor, but by this time, the man was raving mad. He never recovered his senses and died a few days later.

Regardless of the fact the man was taken from the cellar alive, something of him remained there in the Thompson barn. Perhaps a bit of insanity, or perhaps the stark impression of his terror, we'll never know. However, it would make itself known in the years to come.

In the late 1800s, the barn burned down and a few decades later, a house was constructed on the site that incorporated the stone cellar room into the basement of the new dwelling. The room was closed off from the rest of the basement by a door, hiding an earthen floor and plain stone walls.

Not long after taking up residence in the new dwelling, occupants of the house began to report hearing odd sounds coming from the basement. These were not the usual creaks and groans associated with a house; they were sounds for which no one could provide an easy explanation. And they were coming from the stone cellar room.

At first the family was disturbed by the sounds, but soon, they grew used to them. Then, one summer night, a sound like the furnace exploding roared from the basement. The family had been asleep at the time and they ran from their beds to see what was going on. As one family member entered the kitchen, she realized that everything there was shaking. "The appliances, the cutlery and glasses were shaking violently and falling off the shelves," she recalled. "The furniture in the hallway was moving from one side of the hall to the other. It felt like an earthquake."

The woman, now joined by other members of the family, descended into the basement and soon discovered the source of the sounds was behind the door to the stone cellar room. It was as if someone were on the other side of the door with a sledgehammer, pounding away at it. They could actually see the door bend outward with each blow, the wood seemingly straining against the pressure being applied to it. It seemed as if the heavy oak door was literally going to fly off its hinges and hurtle across the room.

Terrified, they fled the house that night. They refused to return to what had become a fearsome place without some sort of assistance. Despite what they may have initially believed, the family could find no explanation for what had occurred that night other than a supernatural one. The strange sounds in the house had progressed far beyond the unusual creaks and groans and so they turned to the church for help.

A few days later, an elderly priest arrived to bless the house. He explained that he had many years of experience with sending spirits on their way from homes and other locations and most considered him to be somewhat sensitive to the supernatural. One visit downstairs to the stone room convinced him that the house was indeed haunted, although not by a spirit the family should fear, but one they should pity. The ghost who was trapped in the house was not evil, but terrified. The priest explained that he believed the spirit to be that of a young Confederate soldier who was still desperately trying to free himself from the horrible place that he was in just before his death.

A short time later, the old priest performed his ceremony, and when he was finished, he used a white paste to place the sign of the cross on the oak door and around it, he drew a circle. From that time on, no further sounds were heard coming from the basement.

But the family who lived in the house, regardless of the priest's assurances, sold the place in 1987 and moved out. It is now owned by the Lutheran Seminary in Gettysburg and while it is believed that no further disturbances have taken place there, no one will say for sure.

Battlefield Hauntings

There are scores of ghostly stories and supernatural incidents that have been unexpectedly experienced by everyday people across the official confines of the Gettysburg Battlefield. Factor into this number the encounters of those ghost seekers who have purposely traveled to the battlefield in search of spirits, and the number of strange tales becomes an amazing one.

There are a number of once-private residences scattered across the battlefield that have reportedly played host to spirits in the years that have passed since the battle. Most of these homes are now the property of the National Park Service and often they serve as residences for park rangers and personnel who stay in the houses to keep them occupied and in good repair.

Nearly all of the nearby homes were used during the battle as makeshift field hospitals and as shelters for the wounded, which, in turn, have given these places reputations for being haunted. However, the rangers are usually very reluctant to discuss their supernatural encounters on the battlefield. Those who do speak usually do so off the record, which nevertheless creates a fairly impressive documentation of events beyond our understanding.

The George Weikert House is one such odd battlefield location. Weikert moved to the Gettysburg area from Maryland in 1838. He bought the farm north of Little Round Top in 1852. He and his family left the farm during the fighting. Afterwards they returned to scenes of desolation familiar to many Gettysburg residents. The house was a field hospital, with wounded filling the parlor and amputated arms and legs piled outside the windows. According to family history, six men died in the parlor, and the yard was filled with graves. When the corpses were exhumed to be re-buried in the National Cemetery, the missing parlor rug was found, cut into strips as the top and bottom layers of the burial trench.

Over the years, this home has had a surprising number of different occupants, many of whom have not stayed for long. One of the previous residents spoke of a door on the second floor that refused to stay closed, no matter what was done to it. One ranger even nailed the door shut with a small wire nail, and yet it refused to stay closed.

Possibly connected to this, other tenants reported the sounds of footsteps pacing back and forth in the attic. They would hear a heavy tread cross the area above their heads, and then cross back, as if someone up there were worried or deep in thought. Needless to say, when they would go up to the attic to check for an intruder, they would find no one there.

Another seemingly haunted residence is the Jacob Hummelbaugh House, where stories say the cries of Confederate Brigadier General William Barksdale can still be heard on certain nights.

Jacob Hummelbaugh was a widower. His son, Leander, was in the 138th Pennsylvania Infantry Regiment, which was not at Gettysburg. It was assigned to the Harpers Ferry garrison, and at the time of the battle was escorting stores to Washington to prevent them from falling into the hands of Lee's army. Leander was badly wounded at the Battle of the Wilderness in 1864.

The farm was located on Taney Town Road, just behind the Union lines, and it was set up as a 2nd Corps field hospital. General Barksdale was wounded while leading a charge on Seminary Ridge and was brought to the Hummelbaugh House. According to an officer from the 148th Pennsylvania Volunteers, Barksdale was last seen lying in front of the house and a young boy was giving him water with a spoon. The general continued to call for water, as though he could not see the boy --- calling over and over again. In the years since, the legends say the sound of Barksdale's voice can still be heard.

And that is not the only story connected to the house, or to General Barksdale. The other story tells of the days after the battle, when Barksdale's wife journeyed to Gettysburg to have her husband's remains exhumed and returned to their home in Mississippi. She was accompanied on her trip by the General's favorite hunting dog. As the old dog was led to his master's grave, he fell to the ground and began to howl. No matter what Mrs. Barksdale did, she was unable to pull the animal away.

All through the night, the faithful dog watched over the grave. The next day, Mrs. Barksdale again tried to lure the dog away, but he refused to budge, even though the general's remains had already been loaded onto a wagon to begin the journey back to Mississippi. Finally, saddened by the dog's pitiful loyalty, she left for home.

For those who lived nearby, the dog became a familiar fixture during the days that followed. He would occasionally let out a heart-breaking howl that could be heard for some distance. Many locals came and tried to lead the dog away, offering him food, water and a good home. The dog refused all of their gestures and eventually died from hunger and thirst, still stretched out over his master's now-empty burial place.

Within a few years, a tale began to circulate that the animal's spirit lingered at the Hummelbaugh Farm. It has been said that on the night of July 2, the anniversary of Barksdale's death, an unearthly howl echoes into the darkness as the faithful hunting dog still grieves from a place beyond this world.

In addition to these former private residences, spirits on the battlefield itself abound. There are numerous reports of apparitions of phantom soldiers seen marching in formation, riding horses, and still seemingly fighting the battle from various parts of the park. These ghosts haunt the fields where Pickett's Charge took place, the slopes of Little Round Top, the Peach Orchard, the Wheatfield, and many other places.

McPherson's Woods

The Edward McPherson farm played an important role in the fighting during the first day of the Gettysburg battle and marks a spot today that is one of the lesser-known sites for hauntings on the battlefield.

The farm was located close to the picket line that the Union Army set up to intersect the Chambersburg Road, three miles west of Gettysburg. Dawn was breaking on July 1, 1863 when Federal soldiers spotted a large group of approaching men on the road. When a young sergeant began to discern the sounds of muffled conversation, the clinks of metal cups and canteens, and the shuffle of boots and shoes on the road, he ran to find his commanding officer. Lieutenant Marcellus Jones of the 8th Illinois Cavalry was in charge of the picket line and had just returned to the position with bread and butter that he had purchased from a nearby farm. Jones rode with the sergeant to the post and peering through the morning haze, they spotted a column of soldiers on the road ahead. Borrowing a carbine from the sergeant, the lieutenant took aim at a mounted figure at the front of the column and fired. The column abruptly stopped and the horseman who had been narrowly missed pointed out the Yankee picket line. Behind, a breeze revealed a red banner and Jones was assured that the men on the road were Confederates. Jones handed a brief message to a courier, instructing him to ride as fast as possible to General John Buford. Seconds later a cannon ball bounded down the road, scattering the Union troopers and Confederate bullets whined overhead. The Battle of Gettysburg had begun.

The Confederate troops spotted by the picket line were men from Major General Henry Heth's division, leading the march to Gettysburg that morning.

Well-liked by Lee Heth was the only officer Lee addressed by his first name , the general was uncertain of what lay ahead of them on the road, whether they were Pennsylvania militia or Federal troops, so he ordered his lead unit into a skirmish like to drive away the enemy soldiers. Infantry from the 5th Alabama advanced on the position and met fire from groups of cavalrymen who fired on them from behind trees and fences. Three miles away in Gettysburg, General Buford waited for a report from the picket line. He knew that his thin line of cavalrymen were no match for a solid force of infantry, but hoped that they could slow the Confederate approach until Reynolds' corps arrived.

The skirmishing continued for over an hour. The fighting occurred over a series of rolling ridges and fields until Buford's men reached Willoughby Run, a shallow stream that bordered the McPherson farm. From the observatory atop the Lutheran Seminary, Buford watched his horsemen gather on a ridge that cut across the farm and he knew that time was running out. His men had been lucky up until that point. The Confederates had only advanced as skirmishers and had not pushed forward in battle lines, but clouds of dust on the Chambersburg Pike made it clear that more Confederates were approaching the town. Confederate artillery was just pulling into line on Herr's Ridge, west of Willoughby Run, which meant that an infantry attack was soon coming. General Heth had discovered how thin the Union line actually was and having arrived at Herr's Ridge, he could direct an artillery attack to wipe out Buford's men. With his artillery set up and ready to fire, Heth ordered his two lead infantry brigades under Brigadier General James Archer and Brigadier General Joseph Davis to move forward.

From his post in the observatory of the Seminary roof, General Buford was intently observing the fighting when he was startled by a familiar voice calling from below: "How goes it, John?" the voice yelled out.

Buford immediately recognized the voice of his old friend, John Reynolds. "The devil's to pay!" he replied and hurried down to meet with the infantry commander. The two men quickly discussed the situation and rode together to McPherson's farm. Reynolds chose the ridge where the cavalrymen had gathered as the best location to establish an artillery and infantry battle line, but Confederate pressure on Buford's men was mounting and Reynolds knew his men would have to move fast. With a casual salute, Reynolds rode off to hurry his troops forward. It was the last time Buford would see his friend alive.

Within a half-hour, the vanguard of Reynolds' corps arrived near the Seminary and moved toward the McPherson Farm. By this time, Confederates from General Archer's brigade had reached the woods and fields south of the McPherson farm and turned their attention to the Union infantry that was forming ahead of them. This was the famous "Iron Brigade," which had won its reputation on the battlefields of Second Manassas, Antietam, and Fredericksburg, and was commanded by Brigadier General Solomon Meredith. Meredith had just ordered the first regiment of the brigade, the 2nd Wisconsin Infantry, to deploy into battle line when the first volley from Archer's men struck them from the edge of the woods. The Wisconsin men had not even had a chance to load their rifles, but with bayonets fixed, they stormed into the woods. Surprised by the sudden counterattack, the Confederates fired a few scattered shots and then retreated in disorder through the woods and across Willoughby Run, with the Union soldiers in hot pursuit. Many of the Confederates found themselves cut off and many were taken prisoner, including General Archer himself.

Riding behind the 2nd Wisconsin, General Reynolds cheered the men on as they scrambled into the woods. The general turned toward Seminary Ridge to see what troops and officers were following, when he suddenly slumped in his saddle. A staff officer rushed to the general's side as he toppled from his horse. As he scooped Reynolds up in his arms, cradling his head, he found his hands covered in blood. A bullet had struck the general in the right temple, blowing out the back of his head, and Reynolds had died instantly.

John Reynolds was the highest-ranking officer of either side to lose his life at Gettysburg and was the man who had recommended to President Lincoln that General Meade replace Joseph Hooker in command of the Army of the Potomac. The general's body was taken from the field in an ambulance, escorted by his heartbroken staff officers.

Casualties were severe for both sides in this early fighting and though the Union Army had lost one of its most distinguished generals, the Confederates had suffered more than their Union counterparts. General Archer was captured and the better part of two brigades was taken out of the action for the remainder of the day. Realizing that he was facing more than just Pennsylvania militia, General Heth wisely decided to wait for the remainder of his division and artillery before continuing the attack.

The lull in the battle allowed both sides time to regroup and for many of the wounded to be removed from the woods around McPherson's farm. The cries of the maimed and the dying echoed in the trees and brush, making the woods sound, as one soldier later put it, "like one of the circles of Hell." There were so many bodies in the narrow creek that Willoughby Run was stained red with blood.

Over the years, the remaining woods near the McPherson farm have become known as one of the battlefield's least known, but most haunted spots. It's not uncommon for ghost hunters - and even ordinary tourists - to encounter phantom soldiers among the trees. There are also reports of crying, screaming and moaning that often come from the woods with no explanation and more than one person has told of hearing the eerie cry of a young man calling for "Lucy" down near the water of Willoughby Run.

This is a strange and unsettling place, and a spot where the faint of heart would do well to avoid after dark.

Iverson's Pits

Perhaps one of the most infamous locations on the battlefield, at least in Confederate military history, is Oak Ridge, a northern extension of Seminary Ridge, and a place that has since been dubbed "Iverson's Pits."

On the first day of fighting at Gettysburg, Brigadier General Alfred Iverson's Brigade of North Carolina troops set off to flank the Union positions at Oak Ridge and to the southwest of the hill. It turned out to be a costly blunder, carried out by a lawyer turned Confederate general whose entire career was destroyed in a few short minutes at Gettysburg.

Alfred Iverson, Jr. was born in Clinton, Georgia, the son of a fiery United States Senator and ardent secessionist. The elder Iverson decided that a military career was a fitting one for his son and after a term at the Tuskegee Military Institute, the younger Iverson fought in the Mexican-American War at the age of just seventeen. His father had raised and equipped a regiment of Georgie volunteers and Iverson left for Mexico as a second lieutenant in the regiment. He left the service in 1848 to become a lawyer and contractor but returned to service in 1855 as a first lieutenant in the 1st U.S. Cavalry regiment.

At the start of the Civil War, Iverson resigned his U.S. Army position and received a commission from his father's old friend, Confederate President Jefferson Davis. He was now a colonel in the 20th North Carolina Infantry. His regiment was initially stationed in North Carolina, but was called to Virginia in June 1862 for the Seven Days Battles. He distinguished himself at the Battle of Gaines' Mill, in a division commanded by Major General D.H. Hill, by leading the only successful regiment of the five that were assigned to capture a Union artillery battery. The regiment took heavy casualties and Iverson himself was wounded, but was praised for his daring and quick thinking on the field. Unfortunately, the battle would turn out to be the high point of his career.

After recovering from his wounds, Iverson rejoined the Army of Northern Virginia in the Maryland Campaign. From this point on, it was almost as if he were cursed. At the Battle of South Mountain, his entire brigade retreated after their commander, Brigadier General Samuel Garland, was mortally wounded. Iverson's men also ran away from the Battle of Antietam a few days later, although he was able to rally them to return to the battle. After this battle, Iverson was promoted to brigadier general and given command of the brigade -

a promotion that caused the senior colonel who had been in temporary command to resign from the Army in disgust.

Iverson's first assignment was to command his new brigade at the Battle of Fredericksburg, but he was assigned to the reserve and saw no action. Regardless, he managed to get himself involved in a new conflict. When he attempted to name a new colonel for the 20th North Carolina, a personal friend from outside of the regiment, twenty-six of his field officers signed a letter of protest against the action. Iverson attempted to arrest all twenty-six men, but eventually cooled off. He decided not to name his friend as the new colonel, but he also refused to promote any of the men who had signed the letter to the position.

At Chancellorsville, Iverson's brigade suffered serious damage and Iverson himself was wounded in the groin by a spent shell. His poor relations with his men continued and rumors started that he was shirking his duty when he returned to the rear to get support for his flank. His performance at Gaines' Mill had been forgotten and most concluded that he had achieved his command only by his family's political influence. But it would be at Gettysburg that his career would be destroyed.

As Iverson's men were sent to flank the Union positions, they moved southwest toward Oak Ridge in perfect alignment, closing on the suspected Union line without actually seeing the Union positions. Suddenly, a horde of enemy soldiers, the regiments of Brigadier General Baxter's brigade, rose from behind a stone wall on the ridge and loosed a volley into the Confederate ranks, killing scores of men and officers and stopping Iverson's brigade in its tracks. Many of the men fell over dead in a straight line.

For those who survived the initial volley, the next minutes were filled with horror. Every shot fired from the Confederate ranks was returned by hundreds from the Union line. A number of soldiers in one regiment were able to evade the deadly fire by hiding behind a slight rise of ground, but others were frozen in place while Union bullets decimated their ranks.

Captain Lewis Hicks of the 20th North Carolina recalled, "We carried three hundred soldiers in to action. The result of two and one-half hours battle forced us to surrender, and only sixty-two men left. A little ravine in the hillside saved this number. In the absence of white flags the wounded men hoisted their boots and hats on their bayonets to show their desperation. The firing continued about ten minutes, our firing ceased and the Federals moved on us to affect our capture. The smoke was so dense you could not perceive an object ten feet from you. The awful gloom of the moment is beyond description... We felt and heard the tread of the enemy, our minds were in tumult, whether to lie still, to yield, or to die fighting. I jumped up and found myself confronted with a bayonet of a

Union soldier pointed at my breast. I grasped the blade and reversed the handle of my sword in a twinkle and offered to surrender. The soldier said in the excitement, he thought I had run him through and he dropped his gun. By that time I was almost over-powered by other Federals rushing at me, so to protect myself I grabbed up the half-dazed Yankee... In a few more seconds their passions cooled and they gave me my life."

Despite efforts to get support to his trapped regiments, Iverson was helpless to stop the destruction of his command. He had made the crucial error of not scouting the ground in front of his brigade and had failed to go with them and to provide orders that might get them out of the trap. It was Iverson's failure to accompany his brigade during the assault that was considered so galling to most and, when the helpless survivors surrendered to hold off further Union fire, he raged in anger that they were cowards. His conduct became so irrational some accounts suggest that he was drunk that he was removed from brigade command for the rest of the battle.

His military career was essentially over. Robert E. Lee made Iverson a temporary provost marshal, which removed him from combat command, and, in October 1863, removed him from the Army of Northern Virginia altogether, ordering him back to Georgia to organize cavalry. He commanded the cavalry of the Georgia State Guard until its enlistment expired in February 1864.

In 1864, he commanded a cavalry division against General William T. Sherman's Atlanta Campaign and then remained on duty in North Carolina until the end of the war. As a commander in Greensboro, he suffered his final military insult as his garrison ignored his commands and plundered part of the city.

After the war, Iverson ran a business in Georgia until moving to Florida to raise oranges in 1877. He died in 1911 and was buried in Atlanta's Oakland Cemetery, all but forgotten save for his disastrous defeat at Gettysburg.

After the smoke had cleared at Gettysburg, burials began to take place on the battlefield. Confederate soldiers were interred where they had fallen, and on Oak Ridge, the men from Iverson's brigade were placed in shallow graves that were often "as straight as a dress parade," as some of the soldiers said. The long, narrow graves were soon referred to as "Iverson's Pits" and even in the late 1800s, it became known as an area where supernatural activity was common.

Strange activity seems to manifest on the ridge mainly as sounds. Witnesses have described hearing Southern-accented voices calling for help, screams, cries and even the booming thunder of musket fire as the past replays itself over and over again. In some cases, however, the past seems to be mixed in with the present in a very tangible way. Some claim that they have been touched by unseen hands near the location of Iverson's Pits. Others say they have been pushed, pinched, had their hair pulled and have even been knocked to the ground by a presence that seems solid and yet cannot be seen by the human eye.

After all of these years, Iverson's Pits remains a frequent location for visits by those with an interest in the supernatural and is one of the most haunted spots on the battlefield.

Devil's Den at Gettysburg in 1909

Devil's Den

If asked to name the one spot on the battlefield that is the most haunted, there is little doubt that I would point the reader to the Devil's Den.

The events that created the lore and legend of the place is undoubtedly the fighting which took place there on July 2, 1863, the second day of the battle at Gettysburg. However, stories surrounded this intimidating tangle of rocks long before the Civil War was ever fought.

According to early accounts from the area, the rocky area was a Native American hunting ground for centuries. Some stated that a huge battle was once fought here, called the "Battle of the Crows" during which many perished. A Gettysburg writer named Emmanuel Bushman wrote in an 1880 article of the "many unnatural and supernatural sights and sounds" that were reported in the area of the Round Tops and what he called the Indian Fields now Devil's Den . He wrote that the early settlers had told stories of ghosts that had been seen there and that Indian "war-whoops" could still be heard on certain nights. In addition, he reported that strange Indian ceremonies also took place there.

Also according to local legend, the name "Devil's Den" was actually in use before the battle took place. How the area got its name remains a mystery but many believe that the strange atmosphere of the area itself may have contributed to the designation. Another legend persists that the Devil's Den was always known for being infested with snakes. The legends say that one gigantic snake in particular eluded local hunters for many years and they were never able to capture or kill him. He was allegedly nicknamed "the Devil" and thus, the area of rocks was called his "den."

No matter how the area got its name, it was apparently already considered a strange and haunted spot before the battle, at least according to Emmanuel Bushman. In the years that would follow, the Devil's Den would gain an even more fearsome reputation. The fighting there, which took place on the second day of the battle, was especially brutal and bloody. Control of the rocky area went back and forth between the Confederate and the Federal troops and hundreds were mowed down in the narrow rocky field that has been dubbed the "Slaughter Pen."

After hours of bloody fighting the Confederates finally controlled the area. The fight for the Devil's Den may have been the most confusing and intense skirmish on the battlefield that day. The heat of the afternoon and the collapse of the battle lines, thanks to the difficult terrain, had caused the entire chain of events to happen so fast that many of the men were almost stunned to find the battle was over.

Stranger yet were the reports from the men who were ordered to stand guard in the tangle of boulders that night. Many of them later spoke of the macabre and unnerving surroundings and of sharing the space in the looming boulders with the bodies of the dead.

Days later, the Union Army would return to the Devil's Den, this time triumphant as the battle had come to an end with a Confederate defeat. As men approached, they were stunned by the scene that greeted them. The hills and boulders were covered in blood and carnage and the dead lay scattered about in every direction. One of the first soldiers to enter the area recalled that some of the dead men "had torn and twisted leaves and grass in their agonies and their mouths filled with soil... they had literally bitten the dust."

Another Federal soldier, A.P. Chase of the 146th New York described a scene of horror that July 4 afternoon. As he climbed the stones, he found "those rocky crevices full of dead Rebel sharpshooters, most of them still grasping their rifles."

That afternoon, the rain began to fall in a heavy downpour that lasted for several hours. The dead men, who were already bloated beyond recognition, were now drenched and beginning to decay. No one knows just how long the Confederate dead remained unburied around the Devil's Den but it could have been days or even weeks. And many of the bodies were said to not have been buried at all, but merely tossed into the deep crevices between the rocks.

New stories about the Devil's Den being haunted began not long after the battle. Even those who are skeptical about the hauntings at Gettysburg, and who claim that the stories of ghosts here are a recent addition to the battlefield, admit that there have always been tales recalled about supernatural doings at the Devil's Den. While admittedly, most of these stories are of a rather recent vintage, Emmanuel Bushman wrote of "many unnatural and supernatural sights and sounds" back in 1880, and local lore has always included odd happenings in the area.

In the late 1800s, local legend had it that two hunters had wandered onto the battlefield one day and had gotten lost in the woods near the rocky ridge. They had completely lost their way when one of them looked up and saw the dim figure of a man standing atop the boulders. He gestured with one hand as if pointing the way and the hunter realized it was in that direction they needed to travel. He looked back to thank the man but the apparition had vanished.

One afternoon in the early 1970s, a woman was said to have gone into the National Park Service information center to inquire about the possibility of ghosts on the battlefield. One can imagine just how many times this question must come up and, although the official position of the park is to neither confirm nor deny the ghostly tales, the ranger on duty was reported to have asked why the woman wanted to know.

The visitor quickly explained that she had been out on the battlefield that morning, photographing the scenery. She had stopped her car at the Devil's Den and had gotten out to take some photos in the early morning light. The woman stated that she had walked into the field of smaller boulders, which are scattered in front of the Den itself and had paused to take a photo. Just as she raised the camera to her eye, she sensed the uncomfortable feeling of someone standing beside her. When she turned to look, she saw that a man had approached her. She described this man as looking like a "hippie," with long, dirty hair, ragged clothing, a big floppy hat and noticeably, no shoes.

The man looked at her and then simply said, "What you are looking for is over there," and pointed over behind her. The woman turned her head to see just what the unkempt fellow was pointing at and when she turned around again, he had vanished. There was no trace of him anywhere.

A month or so later, the same ranger was on duty at the information desk when another photographer came in and asked almost the same question. He too had been taking photos at the Devil's Den, only this time, he had taken a photo about a month before in which the image of a man had appeared on the exposed frame -- a man who had not been there when the photo was taken! When asked what the man had looked like, he described him as looking like a "hippie" remember, this was the early 1970s and also mentioned his long hair, ragged clothing and the fact that he was barefoot.

Could this have been the same man? And if so, who was he?

During the war, many of the Confederate soldiers, and especially those connected with the fighting at the Devil's Den, were from Texas. At that time, this was America's most remote frontier and most of these men did not receive packages from home containing shoes and clothing as many of those from states in the immediate vicinity did. Because of this, the "wild" Texas boys were often unkempt and dirty, lacking shoes and new clothing.

Could this reported specter be one of the soldiers from Texas, still haunting the rocks of the Devil's Den? Since those reports from the 1970s, this same soldier — or at least one fitting his description — has been reported several times in and around the rocks of the Devil's Den. According to some of the stories, a number of visitors have mistaken the man for a Civil War reenactor and have even had their photographs taken with him. The accounts go on to say that when they return home and have their film developed, the man is always missing from the photo.

In addition to this apparition at the Devil's Den, there are also reports of a ghostly rider who has been seen and who in turn vanishes, the sounds of gunfire and men shouting that cannot be explained — not unlike Bushman's phantom "Indian whoops" from long ago — and literally dozens of photographs that allege to be evidence of supernatural activity.

I have long been a believer in the hauntings of the Gettysburg battlefield, dating back to my first visit to the town in the early 1990s. During that trip, I had my first encounter with the phantom smell of peppermint while walking along Baltimore Street and would later have another encounter in the garret of the Farnsworth House. Since that time, I have seen and heard enough things on the battlefield itself to convince me that this is one of America's most haunted places. Perhaps my most convincing - and unsettling - encounter occurred at the Devil's Den.

In the spring of 1998, I had the chance to conduct a number of investigations on the battlefield with my friend Chris Waterston and several other investigators. Chris and I obtained permission to do some research at the home that had been used as General Lee's Headquarters during the battle and then we went on to several locations on the battlefield itself. The night was largely uneventful until we reached the Devil's Den.

After climbing in and around the rocks for a while, plus setting up some cameras and recording equipment, Chris and I were walking along the edge of the road at the base the rocks. We were silent as we walked and then suddenly, both of us were startled by a bizarre sound that came from just behind us. The noise we heard was the loud snorting of a horse, followed by the distinct sound of a jingling bridle and the strong smell of a sweaty animal. Both Chris and I spun around at the same time and looked behind us. There was nothing there!

I asked him: "What was that?" I must have jumped about three feet when the sound occurred. It had come so suddenly, and was so close behind us, that I was totally unnerved and I know that Chris was, too.

"What did you hear?" Chris asked.

I answered quickly: "It sounded just like a horse to me and it definitely smelled like one."

He nodded quickly. He had experienced the same thing, and at the exact same time. How could we explain away such a unique, shared experience, except to say that we had a brush with the paranormal!

1863: CHICKAMAUGA
"The River of Death"

The year 1863 was a triumphant one for General Ulysses S. Grant. After the fall of Vicksburg, many believed that Grant could do no wrong. By the following season, he would be the commander of all of the Union forces and would achieve another great victory at Chattanooga, Tennessee, in the autumn of that same year.

Chattanooga stood above the bend of the Tennessee River in the southeastern corner of the state. It was there where two important railroad lines met and was a place that many considered to be the gateway to the Confederacy. Just a short distance beyond were the Rebel war industries in Georgia, and from Chattanooga, the Confederates launched expeditions into Tennessee and Kentucky. If the Union could capture the region, they could drive south into Georgia and divide the eastern Confederacy.

Throughout 1862, the Union had been trying to push the Confederates from Tennessee. The Northerner who had been placed in charge of this task was William Rosecrans, a well-liked General from Ohio. His Confederate rival was Braxton Bragg, a Louisiana sugar planter who was a graduate of West Point and a friend to Jefferson Davis. Many say that this was the only reason he was able to hang onto his command. He was hated by the soldiers, disliked by his own officers and despised by most of the other Southern commanders.

The two armies had previously met at Stones River, and while the battle was considered a Confederate victory, Rosecrans never believed it to be anything but a draw. The Confederates had been beating them badly until Rosecrans rallied his men by riding up and down the lines. He seemed unaware of the heavy shelling that was going on all around him, even when the aide who was riding next to him had his head blown off. Each army had lost about one-third of its men and Bragg had retreated to Tullahoma.

For almost six months after Stones River, the two armies clashed and feinted at one another. Confederate cavalry commander John Hunt Morgan led a raid into Ohio, where he was captured, while the Union cavalry headed into Alabama, where they attempted to cut the Chattanooga-Atlanta Railroad. The Federals were captured by Nathan Bedford Forrest.

President Lincoln pushed Rosecrans for more action but the commander refused, demanding more troops and always a little more time. Finally, threatened with dismissal, Rosecrans executed a series of flanking maneuvers that pushed Bragg back more than eighty miles, first past Tullahoma, and then to Chattanooga. Rosecrans again pushed him back but then ran into trouble when Confederate reinforcements under Longstreet arrived by train. The Rebels succeeded in luring the army out of Chattanooga and then attacked them along Chickamauga Creek - a name that translated in Cherokee to mean "River of Death."

It would be a calamitous clash of two armies on the fields and in the rough hills and mountains of southeastern Tennessee and the battle would leave a bloody mark on the area. It would also leave behind one of the strangest - and most terrifying - supernatural tales of the Civil War.

The campaign that brought the Union and Confederate armies to Chickamauga began in late June 1863, when the Union Army of the Cumberland under Major General William S. Rosecrans advanced southwestward from Murfreesboro, Tennessee, against the Confederate Army of Tennessee, commanded by General Braxton Bragg.

The Union army arrived in late August, crossing the Tennessee River at several points west and southwest of Chattanooga. Numbering almost sixty thousand men, they advanced southeastward in three widely separated columns over rough mountain and valley terrain in an attempt to threaten Bragg's crucial railroad supply line. When Bragg learned of the enemy threat at his back, he abandoned Chattanooga on September 9 and moved southward, just as Confederate reinforcements were arriving from Mississippi and East Tennessee.

As his army passed through LaFayette, Georgia, Bragg learned of the widely scattered condition of the Union army and quickly planned an offensive movement against the enemy. During the second week of September, he had several chances to destroy isolated portions of the Union army, but command dissension resulted in several bungled attempts to do much damage. At the same time, Rosecrans began ordering a concentration of his troops, realizing that the three isolated corps of his army were in danger.

Lee & Gordon's Mill on Chickamauga Creek

By September 17, two of Rosecrans' corps were joined and were moving north toward Lee and Gordon's Mill on Chickamauga Creek to join up with the third corps. Bragg, believing that the Union troops at the mill constituted the northernmost elements of Rosecrans' force, developed a battle plan to cross Chickamauga Creek north of the mill and drive the Union army southwestward against the mountains and away from Chattanooga.

The first day of fighting began almost by accident when Confederate advance cavalry units encountered Union troops guarding one of the bridges across the creek. The battle raged throughout the day as the Confederates attempted to seize the crossing points on the river. Union cavalrymen delayed the Confederates at Reed's Bridge, but eventually Southern forces seized the span and advanced southwestward toward Lee and Gordon's Mill. Union mounted infantrymen at Alexander's Bridge also fought a successful delaying action before being forced back. The Confederates eventually crossed the Chickamauga but the delays prevented them from reaching the left flank of the main Union force.

The actions on September 18 led Rosecrans to believe that Bragg might try to drive the Confederate army between the Union forces, so he ordered one of his corps commanders, Major General George H. Thomas, to extend his lines northward from Lee and Gordon's Mill to the area of the Kelly farm. On the morning of September 19, Thomas sent brigades eastward from the farm to destroy what he thought was a small and isolated enemy force. Instead, the Union soldiers encountered Confederate cavalrymen under General Nathan Bedford Forrest and became embroiled in a confused general engagement that lasted all day and spread southward for nearly four miles. Both Rosecrans and Bragg sent brigades into the fighting, although the thick forests made it difficult for large bodies of troops to maneuver. At one point, a body of Confederates achieved a breakthrough and threatened to seize the LaFayette Road, but Union reinforcements regained the lost ground. At the end of the day, the Union troops had withstood repeated attacks without losing their connection to Chattanooga. That night, they pulled back to a defensive position along the LaFayette Road, which they strengthened by constructing log breastworks.

During the night and early morning of September 19 and 20, Bragg divided his army into two wings, the northern wing under Lieutenant General Leonidas Polk, and the southern wing under Lieutenant General James Longstreet, who had arrived from Virginia with additional troops. Bragg's plans for September 20 called for an attack to begin at dawn on the Confederate right and continue southward, driving the Union troops away from Chattanooga. But nothing went as planned. Polk's ineptitude caused the attacks to begin several hours late. Although a small force of Confederates briefly turned the enemy troops left, Union reinforcements drove back the Rebel forces. Union soldiers protected by breastworks bloodily repulsed the rest of the attacks launched by Polk's troops.

Shortly after 11:00 a.m., Rosecrans came to believe that a Union division in the center of his line had created a gap by moving out of position. In order to rectify the situation, Rosecrans ordered another division under Brigadier General Thomas J. Wood northward to fill the alleged hole. But a massive Confederate attack led by Longstreet began at the same time, with thousands of Rebels charging into the real gap created by Wood's movement.

The result was disaster.

By noon, the Confederates had overwhelmed the Union's center and the army's right flank, sending Rosecrans, many of his brigade commanders and their troops into a retreat northward to Chattanooga. Some of the Federal soldiers eventually formed a line on a series of steep, wooded knolls known as Snodgrass Hill. Although the Confederates continued to attack Snodgrass throughout the afternoon, they were unable to capture the position. Union General George Henry Thomas, a Unionist from Virginia who was called "Pap" by his men, somehow managed to arrange his troops into a defensive withdrawal, which protected the army's rear flank. This feat earned him the nickname of the "Rock of Chickamauga." Late in the afternoon, he managed to get the Union troops off the battlefield and headed back toward Chickamauga to the safety of a gap in Missionary Ridge.

Chickamauga turned out to be an extremely costly battle for both armies. Rosecrans lost more than sixteen thousand men, killed, wounded and missing, while the Confederate troops sustained more than eighteen thousand casualties. While the battle was considered a Confederate victory because it pushed the Union army back to Chattanooga rather than letting them proceed into Georgia, Rosecrans achieved his objective for the campaign -- the capture of Chattanooga. Union troops had to be pulled from Virginia and Mississippi to reinforce Rosecrans's besieged army in Chattanooga, but otherwise the staggering losses sustained in both armies produced few immediate tangible results.

The aftermath of the battle would have strange results for some of those involved.

The Confederates had won the day, but Bragg refused to follow-up on their advantage, infuriating the other officers. Longstreet was so angry that he demanded Bragg's removal. A short time later, Jefferson Davis actually traveled to Bragg's headquarters to settle a dispute among the officers. Bragg had dismissed three members of this staff for failing to obey orders and was blaming everyone for his decision not to follow through against Rosecrans at Chickamauga. Nathan Bedford Forrest was so enraged by Bragg that he refused to serve under him. He departed the battlefield and left for Mississippi to set up an independent command. He warned Bragg that if he interfered with him, it would be "at the peril of your life."

Davis finally asked each corps commander whether or not Bragg should be replaced. All said yes, but Davis disliked both of Bragg's possible replacements, Gustave Beauregard and Joe Johnston, so he paid no attention to his commanders and left Bragg in charge.

Meanwhile, the Federal troops were holed up in Chattanooga. They were hungry and cut off from all but a thin line of supplies. They had demolished houses and had hacked down every tree and fence line they could find for fuel, and to make matters worse, the fall rains were beginning. They were in miserable shape and were badly in need of a morale boost.

In October, President Lincoln placed General Ulysses S. Grant in charge of all of the Federal troops between the Appalachians and the Mississippi. He quickly headed for Chattanooga and replaced Rosecrans with Thomas as head of the Army of the Cumberland. Suddenly, things began to come together as Grant opened a hole in the Southern lines and laid a pontoon bridge across the Tennessee River. Soon, food and supplies began arriving by way of the new line.

The Confederate troop placement was still strong, however. Bragg's army occupied the six-mile crest of Missionary Ridge, east of the city. They also had heavy guns on the summit of Lookout Mountain, which commanded a field of fire to the south and west.

Grant's plan was to drive them off, and the Battle of Chattanooga began on November 24. Sherman attacked Bragg on his left flank in a rather ineffectual thrust that merely opened the way for Hooker to storm Lookout Mountain. They succeeded in planting the Union flag atop the mountain in such dense fog that the fight was nicknamed the "Battle Above the Clouds."

The following day, the troops under Thomas made an attack on the first line of Confederate trenches below Missionary Ridge, while Hooker attacked on the right. Despite the nearly impregnable Confederate placements artillery on the crest of the hill, rifle pits on the slopes, and trenches at the base Thomas' men quickly swarmed over the trenches and then waited for orders.

Attacking with Thomas was General Philip Sheridan, who recklessly pulled a flask from his pocket and toasted the Confederate gunners on the ridge. "Here's to you," he shouted and rifles opened fire at him, showering Sheridan and his officers with dirt. The volatile general was furious. "That was ungenerous!" he shouted at them. "I'll take your guns for that!"

Sheridan's boast was all of the incentive the men needed and they began charging up the hill toward the Confederate artillery. Worried, Grant was said to have asked an officer just who had ordered the men up the hill. "No one," his aide was said to have answered. "They started up without orders. When those fellows get started, all hell can't stop them!"

And apparently he was right. The Federals were determined to avenge themselves for their recent defeat and as they scrambled up the ridge, they shouted "Chickamauga!" at the top of their lungs. They soon overran the rifle pits and kept going, whopping and hollering as they went. Sections of the slope were so steep that the men had to sometimes crawl, using tree branches and bayonets to haul themselves up. The Confederates on the top began to break and run and those who remained became more desperate as the Federals grew closer, screaming as they came. The rebels fired and fired again and began rolling shells with lighted fuses down the slope, but nothing slowed the force of the charge. In moments, the Confederate gunners and defenders began to run. Bragg tried to rally them, but it was no use. Not surprisingly, he would blame everyone but himself for the defeat, saying that their position "was one which ought to have been held by a line of skirmishers."

True or not, four thousand Confederate prisoners were taken on Missionary Ridge and sent north to the prison camps. The Union had won the day and gained their revenge for the defeat at nearby Chickamauga a few months before.

The battles at Chickamauga Creek and Lookout Mountain will be forever connected in Civil War history, but when it comes to ghosts, it is Chickamauga that is still haunted to this day.

Many years before the Civil War, before the white man brought his armies to die on the banks of the creek, the Native Americans of the region had already done their share of dying in this place. The Cherokee Indians had christened the stream "Chickamauga" or the "River of Death." The white armies who later followed would cause this river to run red with blood.

When Bragg's Army of Tennessee, reinforced by Longstreet and his troops from Virginia, dealt a stunning blow to Rosecrans' Army of the Cumberland, no one knew that it would be one of the last major Confederate victories of the war. The fighting was especially hazardous at Chickamauga because of the rough terrain and the heavily wooded areas. Men became lost in the forest and separated from their units. Messages sent by commanders to their troops vanished without a trace and much of the fighting was chaotic and deteriorated into hand-to-hand combat. The enemy had a way of appearing among the trees and brush and then disappearing again in a haze of gunsmoke. At almost no time was a brigade commander on either side able to see all of the men under his command.

When the battle was over, thousands were dead. Bragg's army had pushed Rosecrans back into Chattanooga, although strangely enough, both of the generals left the battlefield before the fighting was over. It was Longstreet instead of Bragg and Thomas instead of Rosecrans who saw the battle to the last volley of fire. Bragg was angry because the battle plan that he had devised had not been followed and he removed himself from the command of the battle and went to sulk at Reed's Bridge. His staff had to convince Bragg that the Confederates had been victorious, even bringing in Confederate soldiers to swear that the Federals had retreated in such haste that they had left wounded behind.

Rosecrans had retreated with the fleeing Federal troops. Charles Dana, an observer at the battle, and a military liaison with Washington, would later remark that he believed Rosecrans never forgot the tragedy of Chickamauga.

After darkness fell on the last day of the battle, within hours of the last shots being fired, women were seen searching the battlefield by lantern light. It has been reported that these eerie lights, along with the voices and cries of the women, are still present on the field today.

Thirty years after the war, a camp was established on the old battlefield to train men for the Spanish-American War. The camp was named after Thomas, the "Rock of Chickamauga." During the brief time the camp was in operation, disease ran rampant throughout the population and men died by the score -

resulting in more deaths than the American forces suffered during all of the fighting in Cuba.

And the long record of death did not end there. The sprawling park has been the continuing scene of death by murder and suicide over the years. It has been reported that at least one death each year occurs in the huge park, which is accessible at night by many public roads. Thanks to this fact, the park is also used a dumping ground for victims who are murdered elsewhere.

One notable murder attempt in the recent past involved a woman and her boyfriend who plotted the death of the woman's husband. The murder did not go as planned and the husband escaped, badly injured. He was chased screaming through the park and was discovered by rangers with the killers still in pursuit, both of them carrying knives.

But is not these strange and bizarre happenings, or even the hauntings, which bring thousands of tourists to Chickamauga each year, it is the history. Many thousands come to see the battlefield where the Confederate and Union forces clashed with such fury. There are also those tourists who come to search for ghosts, and those who come looking for the supernatural are often not disappointed. The park is one of the oldest and the largest of the battlefield parks. It is peaceful and tranquil in the daylight hours, but after the sun goes down, strange things are reported to happen.

The battlefield has long been associated with the macabre. Many of the corpses of the Union soldiers lay where they fell in battle for more than two months before they were buried -- and they were buried everywhere in the park. One report claimed they were often buried in rows, from head to foot, and one grave would hold up to three or four bodies. There are no stones to mark these graves and it is said that even today, a park maintenance crew will occasionally uncover bodies where none were previously thought to be located.

There are said to be many ghosts roaming the woods and fields of Chickamauga. Rangers and visitors report hearing odd noises on the grounds, including sounds of men moaning and crying, shouts and screams when no one is present, and the sounds of horses galloping where no horses ever appear. Some visitors, and even park employees, tell of feeling as though they are being watched in the woods at night. Others report seeing the underbrush move inexplicably, as though a squad of invisible soldiers were passing by. One of the rangers was even told by a "well-known minister" that he had witnessed a headless man on horseback ride past him at Chickamauga.

One popular legend of the battlefield is that of the ghostly Lady in White. She has been seen many times, by a wide variety of different people, roaming about the park. The legends say that she was the wife of a soldier who was slain in the battle and that she is still searching for his spirit. Even after all of these years, she has reportedly never found him.

But despite all of the tales and stories of strange activity, there is one legend of Chickamauga that remains the most famous of all: "Old Green Eyes." The mysterious entity was given this colorful nickname by park visitors and rangers who have encountered him over the years. Who is this chilling creature? Well, that's a good question, because there happens to be two very different legends to explain his presence in the park.

The first story claims that "Old Green Eyes" was a Confederate soldier who had his head blown off during the battle. When he was buried, all that could be found of him was his head. The stories say that his spirit now roams the battlefield at night, moaning and searching for his missing body. Visitors and staff members claim to have seen green, glowing eyes coming toward them in the darkness and have heard the sounds of a soldier moaning in despair. In the early 1970s, two different and unrelated people had accidents near the same place in the park, wrecking their cars after reportedly seeing these glowing eyes.

The other legend of "Old Green Eyes" is apparently a much older one -- and a much more unnerving one. In this case, reliable witnesses have reported the creature to be, not a slain soldier, but a creature that barely resembles a person. The story also states that "Old Green Eyes" was present at Chickamauga Creek long before the Civil War. Some accounts also claim that the monster was seen moving among the dead at Snodgrass Hill, after the battle was over. The legends claim that the creature is human-like, although he has glowing green eyes, waist-length, light-colored hair and huge, misshapen jaws from which fangs protrude. This is not a creature that anyone would want to meet in a secluded location in the dark - which is unfortunately where most people claim to have encountered him.

One of the most notable encounters occurred to a park ranger named Edward Tinney, who described his brush with the creature in a 1981 interview. He was walking through the park one night when he was struck by a strange chill, one unlike anything he had ever felt before. A moment later, he saw the creature appear out of the darkness. He recalled, "When it passed me, I could see his hair was long like a woman's. The eyes -- I'll never forget those eyes -- they were glaring, almost greenish-orange in color, flashing like some sort of wild animal. The teeth were long and pointed like fangs. It was wearing a dark cape that seemed to be flapping in the wind, but there was no wind. I didn't know whether to run or scream or what. Then the headlights of an approaching car came blazing through the fog, and the thing disappeared right in front of me."

Tinney said he had no doubt that the creature was real. He said, "I've seen Green Eyes. You know he's watching. We all know he's watching us. It's enough to make the hair stand up on the back of your neck... and I'm not a superstitious man."

But wandering creatures are not the only strange things to occur in the park. The incident that occurred at Wilder Tower in 1970 was one of the weirdest to ever happen at Chickamauga. Whether it was supernatural or not is anyone's guess, but it's never been explained.

Wilder Tower at the Chickamauga Battlefield

Wilder Tower is a monument that marks the center of the Union lines where the Confederates finally broke through and routed the Federal forces. It is a stone structure that stands eighty-five feet high. It was built in 1903 by men who served under Colonel John T. Wilder at Chickamauga. The colonel's mounted infantry, armed with Spencer repeating rifles, managed to hold off the attacking Confederate troops long enough for the Union men to make a somewhat orderly retreat. When Wilder had been commissioned, the Union army was so poorly equipped that his men were given mules to ride and hatchets for weapons. He used every political favor that he could to get horses for his troops and he used his own money to purchase rifles. Wilder bought each of his men a Spencer

Repeating Rifle that was designed to hold seven shots. It was the most advanced infantry weapon in the world at the time. He purchased more than two thousand of them for $13 each. Wilder's men used the rifles very effectively to hold off the Confederates as the Union army retreated.

The tower was erected in Colonel Wilder's memory by survivors of the mounted infantry. Souvenirs of the war were sealed into the cornerstone of the structure, which was scheduled to be opened again in 1976, to celebrate the nation's Bicentennial. Strangely, although the stone showed no signs of being disturbed in any way, the contents placed inside in 1903 were missing when the cornerstone was unsealed.

But that's not the strangest thing that has occurred at the tower.

One night in 1970, a young man decided to climb the tower after dark. The park is open at night, but the tower is kept locked in order to keep people from going out onto the observation deck at the top. The young mand didn't let this didn't stop him. He merely climbed the lightning rod, which was attached to the back of the tower. He then slipped into a gun slot about fourteen feet off the ground. He went inside and ran up the steps to the top, where he called to his friends, who were about fifty feet away from the tower, drinking beer.

Suddenly, the young people outside heard a scream from inside the tower. Panicked, the boy ran down the winding staircase and quickly jumped out of the small window from which he had entered the tower -- or so he thought. Instead, he jumped out of a higher window by mistake and fell about twenty-five feet on the concrete below. Although he survived the fall, he was paralyzed for the rest of his life.

He was never able to explain - or remember - what had scared him so badly inside the tower.

1876: LITTLE BIGHORN

The legendary Battle of Little Bighorn, popularly known as "Custer's Last Stand," was the most famous battle of the American Indian Wars of the late nineteenth century. It was a three-part battle, although the most important and well-known part ended with the annihilation of five companies of the U.S. 7th Cavalry and the death of its commander, Lieutenant Colonel George Armstrong Custer.

It also left a terrifying haunting in its wake.

The United States had been at war with the American Indians almost since the first Europeans set foot on the continent. After the Civil War, as the nation began moving west, it became more and more important to move the Native

Americans from their traditional lands to make way for American settlement. The events that led to the Battle of Little Big Horn began as the Black Hills wars of the era.

The Cheyenne Indians had migrated west to the Black Hills and Powder River Country before the Lakota and had introduced them to horses as early as 1730. By the late eighteenth century, the growing Lakota tribe had expanded west of the Missouri River. They pushed out the Kiowa and formed an alliance with the Cheyenne and Arapaho to gain control of the buffalo hunting grounds of the northern Great Plains. The Black Hills, located in what is now western South Dakota, became not only a source of game and wood for lodge poles, it also came to be considered sacred by the Lakota.

In 1868, the Lakota and the Northern Cheyenne signed an agreement with the government called the Fort Laramie Treaty, which set aside a large portion of the Lakota territory as the Great Sioux Reservation. It included the Black Hills region, which was designated for their exclusive use. But it was not meant to last...

The growing number of miners and settlers flooding into the Dakota Territory soon nullified the treaty. The U.S. government could not keep the settlers out. By 1872, territorial officials were considering harvesting timber in the Black Hills and were wondering about the possibility of rich mineral resources in the region. When a commission approached the Red Cloud Agency about the possibility of the Lakota giving up the Black Hills, Colonel John E. Smith noted that this was "the only portion of their reservation worth anything to them." He grimly concluded "nothing short of their annihilation will get it from them."

In 1874, an expedition led by Civil War hero George Armstrong Custer was sent in to explore the Black Hills. The Lakota were alarmed by this development, but there was little they could do about it. Before Custer and his men had returned to Fort Abraham Lincoln, news that they had discovered gold had been telegraphed across the country. The discovery was confirmed the following year and prospectors began to trickle into the Black Hills, ignoring the treaty that was still in place. The trickle soon became a flood and thousands of prospectors invaded the hills before the gold rush was over.

Initially, the U.S. Army struggled to keep the gold seekers out of the region. In December 1874, for example, a group of miners led by John Gordon from Sioux City, Iowa, managed to evade military patrols and reached the Black Hills. The military ejected them three months later. Such evictions, however, increased political pressure on the Grant administration to secure the Black Hills from the Lakota.

In May 1875, Sioux delegations, led by Spotted Tail, Red Cloud and Lobe Horn, traveled to Washington, D.C., in an attempt to persuade President Ulysses S. Grant to honor the existing treaties and stem the flow of miners into their territories. They met with Grant, Secretary of the Interior Columbus Delano and the Commissioner of Indian Affairs, Edward Smith. The Sioux were told that Congress wanted to pay the tribes $25,000 for the land and relocate them to the Indian Territory now Oklahoma but they refused to sign a new treaty under those conditions. The three chiefs went away disappointed, but none of them joined Crazy Horse and Sitting Bull in the war that followed.

Later that fall, a U.S. commission was sent to each of the Indian agencies to hold council with the Lakota. They hoped to gain the people's approval and thereby bring pressure on the Lakota leaders to sign a new treaty. This attempt also failed, which made the Black Hills the center of a growing crisis.

Grant and his administration began to consider alternatives to the failed diplomatic venture. In early November 1875, Major General Philip Sheridan, commander of the Division of the Missouri, and Brigadier General George Crook, commander of the Department of the Platte, were called to Washington to meet with Grant and several members of his cabinet to discuss the Black Hills issue. They agreed that the Army should stop evicting trespassers from the reservation, thus opening the way for the Black Hills gold rush. In addition, they discussed initiating military action against the non-treaty bands of Lakota and Northern Cheyenne who had refused to come to the Indian agencies for council. Indian Inspector Erwin C. Watkins supported this option. "The true policy in my judgment," he wrote, "is to send troops against them in the winter, the sooner the better, and whip them into subjection."

Concerned about launching an unprovoked war against the Lakota, the government instructed Indian agents in the region to notify the various non-treaty bands to return to the reservation by January 31, 1876, or face potential military action. This request was impossible to carry out. As noted by the agent at the Standing Rock Agency, the winter weather restricted travel and the distance could not be crossed in such a short amount of time - which, of course, was the point. He asked for an extension of the deadline, but the request was refused.

As the deadline passed, it was decided that Sitting Bull, who had formed the Sun Dance Alliance between the Lakota and the Sioux, was not going to submit. His confederation was seen as hostile, gathering new recruits from reservations throughout the region, and military operations were ordered to commence against him at once. New Secretary of the Interior Zachariah Chandler stated that the Indians "are hereby turned over to the War Department for such action on the part of the Army as you may deem proper under the circumstances." On February 8, 1876, General Sheridan telegraphed Generals Crook and Terry and ordered them to commence their campaigns against the hostile Indians and the Great Sioux War began.

By May 1876, the Dakota Territory was infested with soldiers. Under General Sheridan's command, the military planned to strike a decisive blow against the Indians of the Northern Plains. But this was not the Civil War and fighting was much different this time around. Among other things, it brought a final and fatal blaze of glory for Sheridan's favorite young officer, an extraordinary cavalryman named George Custer.

While still vastly outnumbered, white soldiers poured into the region. Colonel John Gibbons' column of six companies of the 7th Infantry and four companies of the 2nd Cavalry had marched east from Fort Ellis in western Montana on March 30 to patrol the Yellowstone River. Brigadier General George Crook's column of ten companies of the 4th Infantry, and three companies of the 9th Infantry, moved north from Fort Fetterman in the Wyoming Territory on May 29, marching on the Powder River area. Brigadier General Alfred Terry's column, including twelve companies of the 7th Cavalry under the immediate command of Lieutenant Colonel George Armstrong Custer, Companies C and G of the 17th U.S. Infantry, and the Gatling gun detachment of the 20th Infantry, left Fort Abraham Lincoln in the Dakota Territory on May 17. They were accompanied by teamsters and mule drivers with one hundred and fifty wagons and a large contingent of pack mules, all reinforcing Custer. Companies C, D, and I of the 6th U.S. Infantry moved along the Yellowstone River from Fort Buford on the Missouri River to set up a supply depot. On May 29, they joined Terry at the mouth of the Powder River.

Things began to go wrong on June 17, 1876 when Crook's column was delayed after the Battle of the Rosebud, in the Montana Territory between the U.S. Army and its Crow and Shoshoni allies and an Indian force consisting mostly of Lakota Sioux and Northern Cheyenne. Surprised by the unusually large number of Indians that fought against him, a defeated Crook was forced to pull back, halt and regroup. Unaware that Crook had been attacked, Gibbon and Terry joined forces near the mouth of the Rosebud River. They reviewed Terry's plan calling for Custer's regiment to proceed south along the Rosebud, while Terry and Gibbon's united forces would move in a westerly direction toward the Bighorn and Little Bighorn rivers. As this was the likely location of Indian encampments, all army elements were to converge around June 26 or 27 and attempt to overwhelm the Native Americans.

On June 22, Terry ordered the 7th Calvary, composed of thirty-one officers and five hundred and sixty-six enlisted men under Custer, to begin a reconnaissance and pursuit along the Rosebud, with the prerogative to "depart" from orders upon seeing "sufficient reason." Custer had been offered the use of

Gatling guns but declined, believing they would slow down their advance.

On the evening of June 24, Terry and Gibbon began marching toward the mouth of the Little Bighorn while Custer's scouts arrived at an overlook known as the Crow's Nest, about fourteen miles east of the Little Bighorn River. At sunrise on June 25, Custer's scouts reported seeing a massive herd of ponies and signs of an Indian village about fifteen miles from their position. After a long night's march, the tired officer who had accompanied the scouts was unable to see what they were looking at. Custer joined them on the hill and he was also unable to see any signs of an encampment. The bad news for Custer's men was that while they were unable to see the enemy, the enemy could see *them* -- the smoke from their fires had already given away their position.

Finally convinced that the scouts' sighting was valid, Custer began making plans for a surprise attack against the Indian encampment to occur early the next morning. In the midst of his planning, though, he received word that the trail left by his troops had been discovered by hostile Indians. Assuming that his presence had been exposed, Custer decided to attack the village without delay. On the morning of June 25, he divided his twelve companies into three battalions in anticipation of the battle that was to come. Three companies were placed under the command of Major Marcus Reno; three placed under Captain Frederick Benteen and five would be under Custer's direct command. The final company, under Captain Thomas McDougald, was assigned to protect the pack train, which carried provisions and ammunition.

Unknown to Custer, the group of Native Americans that discovered his trail were actually leaving the encampment on the Bighorn and did not alert anyone in the village. Custer's scouts warned him about the size of the encampment. One of them, Mitch Bouyer, reported, "General, I have been with these Indians for thirty years, and this is the largest village I have ever heard of." But Custer was less concerned with the size of the village and more worried that its occupants might break up and scatter in different directions before he could get to them.

With that thought in mind, Custer began his approach to the Native American village at noon and prepared to attack in full daylight. It would be a frontal attack against an overwhelming and motivated foe.

Custer: "Boy General"

By almost any rational definition, Custer was a dangerous and reckless fool. He was a bad commander and most of his men disliked him, distrusted him and feared him - and did so with good reason. He was personally undisciplined, but those who served under him found him to be strict and uncompromising. He had a tremendous ego that had to be constantly fed. Something odd in emotional makeup allowed him to kill without flinching, but would make him break down and weep while watching a melodrama in a theater. His marriage to the beautiful Elizabeth Bacon was a great love story. She adored him with every fiber of her being and spent nearly sixty years of widowhood glorifying his memory. He was a man of many contradictions whose lust for adulation would eventually get him killed.

General George Armstrong Custer

Custer was the son of an Ohio blacksmith. He managed to talk himself into West Point, where he earned a reputation for slovenliness and a record number of demerits. He graduated thirty-fourth in a class of thirty-four, and yet had a flair that caught the attention of powerful men. General George McClellan, Commander of the Army, put Custer on his staff after a chance meeting with the young officer. When McClellan was replaced, Custer returned to the cavalry and promptly made perhaps the most extraordinary series of leaps in rank in the history of the U.S. military. Between July 1862 and July 1863, he went first from first lieutenant to brigadier general of volunteers and was given command of a brigade of cavalry. In 1865, when Philip Sheridan held command of all of the Union cavalry, Custer became a major general and took over one of Sheridan's three divisions. He was only twenty-five years old.

There was no question that Custer cut a dashing figure. He was a natural horseman and athlete who stood just under six feet tall. He had broad shoulders and curly blond hair that he wore to his shoulders. His eyes were a startling, vivid blue, made even more so when his face was tanned by the sun. He wore a black velvet uniform of his own design with puffed sleeves and loops of gold braid. He carried a heavy sword, a trophy that he had taken from a Confederate officer whom he had shot in the back while pursuing him through the woods. In a letter home, he described the killing as "the most exciting sport I ever engaged in."

Despite his enormous ego and glaring character flaws, there was something about Custer that made men follow him, often to their deaths. When he sighted the enemy, his instinct was immediate and unswerving - he charged. He did not bother to find out how many troops were against him, what reserves they might have, or what problems of tactics or terrain might come against him. He simply charged at full speed.

And rarely did such a charge fail. Once, during the Civil War, he stormed against General James "Jeb" Stuart's men in the Blue Ridge Mountains, only to find himself surrounded and forced to cut his way out with his sword. But otherwise, his headstrong tactics generally worked, and General Sheridan liked them. When Sheridan pillaged the Shenandoah Valley, Custer led the way. When Sheridan blocked Robert E. Lee's final retreat, it was Custer's division that shattered the Confederate cavalry and destroyed Lee's infantry. After Grant and Lee met at Appomattox to end the war, Sheridan paid $20 in gold for the table on which the articles of surrender were signed and presented it to Mrs. Custer with a note that read: "I know of no person more instrumental in bringing about surrender than your most gallant husband."

When the war ended, Custer was dropped to the rank of captain. However, in 1866, partly because he had attracted the attention of President Andrew Johnson, he was given the rank of lieutenant colonel in the 7th Cavalry, which was then being formed at Fort Riley in Kansas. Technically he was second in command, but the regiment's colonel always seemed to be posted elsewhere on staff duties, so Custer effectively became the commander for the rest of his life. Soon, partially because of Custer's ferocious discipline and drilling, the 7th Cavalry became the best - and most famous - horse soldiers on the Plains. But Custer was not out to make a reputation merely as a drillmaster. He wanted to be known as a famous military leader, known to both "present and future generations," as he put it. In an effort to make himself known, he began to engage in a series of fame-seeking missions that raised serious doubts in the minds of his patrons at headquarters. General Sherman noted in a letter to his brother that Custer had "not too much sense."

Custer adored his wife, whom he called Libbie. When they were apart, he wrote her long letters every night. They often romped together like children, running through the house, playing tag and shrieking with laughter. When Custer had good news to tell, he became so excited that he charged through the house, knocking over furniture. But despite the laughter at home, Custer tended to be distant with his officers. He rarely had anything to do with them socially. At parties, he would frequently hide in his study, sending his orderly occasionally to invite Libbie to dance with him. He could be petulant, like a child, and was offended by any slight, real or imagined. And yet he found it hard to hold a grudge and quickly forgave his enemies, a gesture that rarely returned.

He was often reckless in the field, a trait that got him into trouble. One morning, deep in Indian country and miles from help, Custer abandoned his marching regiment and galloped off to test his hunting dogs against a herd of antelope. He was completely alone. The chase went on for miles until Custer's attention was diverted by a buffalo, the first he had seen. He followed it as it ran off in another direction. Custer pulled his pistol to shoot the animal, but it suddenly lunged at him, slamming into his horse. Custer's gun went off and the bullet killed his horse. The animal fell like a stone, throwing its rider to the ground. Custer was now alone and on foot in hostile Indian country, miles from his regiment and without the faintest idea of where he was or in what direction his men might be. Eventually, the dogs chose the direction and their master followed. After walking for miles, he finally saw the regiment's dust on the horizon. When he caught up with them, he learned that no one had any idea that he had been missing.

That kind of reckless behavior was typical of Custer. Whenever he went into the field, he was a fierce driver, setting a demanding pace that he expected everyone to keep up with. He could ride all day with nothing to drink but a cup of tea or coffee at noon, keep his energy up with only a small amount of food, fall to the ground and sleep like a log for an hour or two and then be refreshed and ready to move on. He often pushed his men through the day and then, as they wearily made camp, order a fresh horse and ride off to hunt or scout the trail ahead. While everyone around him slept, he sat in his tent and wrote long letters to Libbie.

The men who did not share his frantic energy found the pace that he set to be cruel, especially when ordered on a whim, but the fact that he never noticed their distress was just another example of his narcissism. He only looked to his own comfort. His scouts supplied him with fresh game while his men ate moldy bacon and hardtack. Sometimes he even brought along a large iron stove for his tent, as well as a woman to cook for him, neither one of which was much help to a supposedly mobile column that was out on its own in Indian country.

On one occasion, Custer was leading his men on a hot, exhausting summer reconnaissance through Kansas, hoping to engage Kiowa and Comanche warriors in battle. The Indians stayed one step ahead of them and finally Custer ordered a desperate march with no precise military objective beyond a wild hope of possibly running into some Indians along the way. The regiment blundered over sixty-five miles of alkali flats toward the Platte River without a single break, marching through heat so intense that all of the dogs that were brought along on the campaign died from exhaustion. At nightfall, they were still miles from the river. Custer summoned a handful of officers and several orderlies and they galloped off, leaving the troops to plod along behind them. His purpose, Custer later wrote, was to find a good camping ground. But without further explanation he added that on reaching the river he had a long, satisfying drink and spread out his blankets to sleep. He slept so soundly that an Indian raid on a stagecoach station less than a mile away never disturbed him. Meanwhile, his regiment eventually struck the river three miles below his camp. It was daybreak before the worn-out, thirsty men finally reached water.

Besides caring little about his men's welfare on the trail, Custer could become murderous toward them when he felt that he had been crossed. The 7th Cavalry always had a high desertion rate, and after that wretched march a number of men quenched their thirst in the river and then simply walked away. Custer was furious. That day, the column halted at noon, well past the Platte, and a dozen men headed back toward the river, five of them on foot. Custer ordered the officer of the day to pursue them and "to bring in none alive." The seven mounted men escaped, but Custer's zealous officer overtook the five men on foot and opened fire on them. One was killed, two were wounded and two survived by pretending to be dead. For the men of the 7th, the incident gave them a chillingly clear indication of how little they were worth to their commander.

Days later, the tired and demoralized 7th Cavalry made their way to Fort Wallace in western Kansas. Orders awaited Custer from his commanding officer, General W.S. Hancock, telling him to remain in the field, using Fort Wallace as a base, and to patrol between the Platte and Arkansas rivers. The orders ended explicitly: "The cavalry will be kept constantly engaged."

The commander who had just ordered deserters to be shot proceeded to abandon his own troops. Claiming that Fort Wallace was short on supplies, Custer readied a column of seventy-five men to travel one hundred and fifty miles to Fort Hays and sixty more miles to Fort Harker, the nearest supply depot. The column was to return with a wagon train of food and ammunition. But Libbie was at Fort Riley, in eastern Kansas, and Custer wanted to see her so he joined the column and forced it to move at a terrible pace. Some of the men could not keep up and near Downer's Station Indians attacked the rear guard and killed two of the stragglers. The survivors caught up with Custer and told him of the attack, but Custer did not attempt to punish the Indians or even pause to recover the bodies of the dead soldiers. He left that chore to the men who occupied Downer's Station.

The column made the one hundred and fifty miles to Fort Hays in fifty-five hours, arriving with both men and horses exhausted. Custer rode on to Fort Harker, accompanied by two officers and two orderlies, making sixty more miles in less than twelve hours. When they arrived, he roused the commander from bed and insisted that supplies be sent to the 7th at Fort Wallace, and then rushed off to catch a train to Fort Riley, where Libbie was waiting.

This direct disobedience of Hancock's orders was too much for even Custer's high-placed admirers to overlook. In September, a court-martial convened to try Custer on no fewer than seven charges, including not only his disregard of orders, but his treatment of the deserters at the Platte River. He was convicted on all counts but his punishment was mild, explaining that his "anxiety to see his family at Fort Riley overcame his appreciation of the paramount necessity to obey orders." The court sentenced him to a year's suspension without pay and yet General Sheridan, wielding his rank to override the court, rescued Custer from even that lenient sentence by calling him back to the 7th for a winter campaign.

During that campaign, Custer's indifference toward his troops had fatal results when, in November 1868, he attacked Chief Black Kettle's village on the Washita River. In the course of the battle, Major Joel Elliott galloped off with nineteen men in pursuit of fleeing Indians and did not return. Twice during the day, a young officer told Custer that he heard heavy firing in the direction Elliott had taken and suggested that the detachment was likely in trouble. Custer paid no heed; he simply gathered his regiment and marched it away without even looking for Elliott.

Weeks later, the bodies of Elliott and his men were found within two miles of the battle site. Evidence around the bodies indicated that the men had held out for most of the day - with plenty of time for Custer to have rescued them, had he been so inclined. He could offer no excuse for his failure to come to Elliott's aid, only saying that he didn't want his men to be attacked. He had brought over seven hundred men into battle that day and had something that he could point to as a clear-cut victory. Had he risked an Indian counterattack, which chasing after Elliott might have provoked, his victory could have been written off as an indecisive action. Custer chose the road to fame and abandoned Elliott, but he never again had the loyalty of most of his officers. Years later, Captain David Stanley, who headed an expedition in which the 7th Cavalry took part, called

Custer a "coldblooded, untruthful and unprincipled man" who was "despised" by most of his officers.

The incident at Washita also emphasized Custer's inadequate tactical skills. During the Civil War, he had fared well with full-frontal attacks, but he was no longer dealing with troop formations and battlefield orders. The fight against the Indians was guerrilla warfare and Custer was poorly equipped to handle it. At Washita, he had divided his force, a gamble that didn't always pay off. If such an attack worked, it could be devastating to the enemy but if it failed, each unit could be surrounded and destroyed. Even more important, Custer had attacked the village without scouting it first. He had never forgotten the success of his blind, smashing attacks during the war but now, because he didn't order a reconnaissance to be done, he did not know that there were other Indian encampments near Black Kettle and had no idea how many warriors were in those camps. He saw the attack as a success and because of this, never bothered to reassess his tactics and thus overcome his tragic shortcomings. It would be a mistake that would soon have fatal consequences.

Over the next two years, the 7th Cavalry saw no action on the plains. Then, in 1873, it joined up with an expedition that was seeking a northern railway route through Dakota and Montana. During this expedition, Custer led his men into battle with Sioux warriors who fled so quickly that Custer began to dangerously underestimate their fighting abilities. Later that year, he also led the reconnaissance into the Black Hills from Fort Abraham Lincoln. One day while the men were at the fort, Sioux raiders drove off a herd of mules and Custer immediately galloped after them, leaving his troopers strung out across the prairie for miles. In his haste, he had left the fort completely defenseless. Libbie Custer, who had come to live at the post, never forgot the terror she and the other women felt as the result of being left unprotected at Fort Abraham Lincoln that day.

Late in the fall of 1875, General Sheridan drew up the plans for the climactic campaign against the Indians on the Northern Plains. While these plans were developing, Custer and Libbie, apparently having found life at Fort Abraham Lincoln during a Dakota winter too dull, traveled to New York City. During the fall of 1875, Custer had taken off on an extended leave and he and Libbie were enjoying themselves. They went to parties, dinners and plays and Custer addressed both the Century Society and the New York Historical Society. He also demonstrated his ability at charming important men, like James Gordon Bennett, publisher of the *New York Herald*.

Thanks in part to Bennett, a national scandal was in the works - a scandal in which Custer came to play an important and possibly career-ending role. That fact that 1876 was a presidential election year made the scandal even worse.

Democrats charged that W.W. Belknap, Secretary of War to Republican President Ulysses S. Grant, was profiteering from sales at Army posts. According to their stories, the traders at the posts were cheating soldiers and Indians alike and then funneling profits back to Belknap. Even though Belknap quickly resigned as soon as the scandal broke, the Democrats pushed for an impeachment trial before the Senate. Custer himself had experienced trouble with traders at Fort Abraham Lincoln, who imposed outrageous prices on the men of the 7th. When he brought this matter to Belknap's attention, the Secretary had found in favor of the trader and in so doing, earned Custer's permanent hatred. Later, when the scandal broke, Custer helped to fan the flames. He offered to give evidence against Belknap and was probably the author of at least one of the devastating articles that ran in Bennett's newspaper. He was soon summoned to Washington to testify before Congress.

Custer now faced a dilemma. It was March 1876 and he was supposed to be in Dakota preparing his regiment for the important campaign ahead. That year on the Northern Plains, Custer hoped to regain some of the national fame that he had enjoyed during the Civil War and after the battle at Washita. Anxious to return to the West, Custer appeared before the committee and proved himself more righteous than wise. He offered a collection of hearsay evidence against Belknap - evidence that he could not hope to prove - and on equally flimsy grounds, he also accused President Grant's brother, Orville, of influence peddling and receiving payoffs. This testimony did not endear him to the president.

Custer had blundered into a mess. After the Congressional hearings, he was summoned to testify at the trial. He won release from that duty, but President Grant ordered that another officer lead the Dakota column against the Indians. Custer went to the White House, hat in hand, and sat in an anteroom for hours, waiting to plead his cause. Grant refused to see him.

Custer was frantic. The chance of a lifetime was slipping away from him. With a new scandal making the rounds, the Democrats saw the opportunity for their first presidential victory since the end of the Civil War. To pull it off, they needed a popular candidate, strong, well known and perhaps a war hero. While never discussed openly, as is usually the case with politics, Custer may have been led to believe that with a fresh military victory behind him, followed by good newspaper coverage, he could be that candidate.

Desperate, he fled Washington without orders. Under instructions from the Commander of the Army, William Sherman, General Sheridan had an aide meet Custer's train at Chicago to place him under arrest. With Sheridan's permission, Custer sent telegrams to Sherman, pleading his case. He never received an answer. Then he turned to General Alfred Terry, who had been named by Sheridan to lead the Dakota column. When he met with Terry in St. Paul,

Minnesota, it was said that he got down on his knees to plead with him to intercede on his behalf. Terry did so, perhaps out of pity, perhaps out of decency, or perhaps because Terry had no experience fighting against Indians and felt he needed someone like Custer to come to his own rescue.

With Terry's help, Custer composed a penitent telegram to President Grant asking, as one solider to another, not that he be allowed to lead the expedition, but to be spared the shame of having his men go into battle without him. Terry sent the telegram with a message of his own that stated he would lead the command, but would appreciate having a man with Custer's experience at his side. Sheridan endorsed the plea and Grant relented. Within hours of his reprieve, Custer reportedly told other officers that he would find a way to get free of Terry and run the campaign on his own. Custer also did one other thing. Against Sherman's specific orders, he permitted Mark Kellogg, a reporter for the *New York Herald* to come along with the 7th during the campaign.

By the time Custer returned to the West, the campaign had gone from the planning stages into action and soldiers began pouring into the region, intent on defeating the Native Americans once and for all. Ignorant of everything but the Indians' approximate location, General Terry divided his forces. Custer would take the 7th up the Rosebud to follow a trail that had been discovered by scouts. Terry expected the trail to turn westward from the Rosebud and cross over the divide to the valley of the Little Bighorn. To complete the plan, he and Gibbon would go up the Yellowstone to the mouth of the Bighorn, and up that river to the Little Bighorn. There, the Gibbon and Custer columns would be in a position to trap the Indians between them.

The entire plan was based on a powerful conviction that the Indians would flee when attacked. They had often done so in the past, fighting mainly in guerilla fashion, running, striking, and running again. For years, these same officers had been repeatedly frustrated by Indians who raided settlers' farms and stagecoach stations and then vanished when the Army arrived.

The Indians would run, both Custer and Terry believed this, and their best escape would be to flee south into the Big Horn Mountains. There, if they split up into two smaller groups, they would be hard to find. Custer was not supposed to attack them, merely block their escape, as Terry instructed him. But those instructions had been purposely vague, issued to an officer who was known for being insubordinate, and whose fame had been created by striking hard and quickly. Terry had to have suspected that Custer would attack the Indians when he found them, without regard to orders. If he didn't, Custer believed his career would be over - a fate that seemed to him to be the equivalent of death. He had become obsessed with the idea that no Indian would ever stand and fight. If they were given the chance to escape, they always would, but if they could be trapped, he would annihilate them.

It was a belief that would prove to be fatal.

It wasn't only Custer's immense ego that put him and his men at risk. His most fundamental and dangerous weakness was the problem he had with his officers. Even since he had abandoned Major Elliott and his men on the Washita River in 1868, he had been unable to command the loyalty and respect of all of his junior officers. Soon after the Washita incident, one of them had written a letter to a friend angrily accusing Custer of cowardice. The letter was published anonymously in the *Missouri Democrat*, and Custer was enraged. It was obvious that an officer in the regiment had written it. Custer summoned his officers and with the newspaper in one hand and a whip in the other, he promised the thrash the man who had written the letter, if his identity was ever revealed.

Captain Frederick Benteen, the regiment's senior captain with the brevet rank of colonel, six years older than Custer, and a close friend of Elliott's, glanced at the newspaper. He spoke quietly, addressing Custer by the brevet rank that he had held during the Civil War: "If there's to be a whipping, General, you can start in. I wrote that letter."

His bluff called, Custer's face turned crimson. He barked out, "Colonel Benteen, I will see you later, sir." He stormed away but the matter was never mentioned again.

As much as he could, Custer surrounded himself with a clique of admiring officers and his own family members. His brother, Captain Tom Custer, and his brother-in-law, Lieutenant James Calhoun, were members of the regiment. Another brother, Boston Custer, and a nephew, Armstrong Reed, came along on the campaign as civilian fighters. But Custer was estranged from most of his officers.

While camped along the Rosebud, and before launching the campaign, Custer held a meeting of his officers at which he addressed the subject of loyalty. Some of his officers, he reminded the staff, had gone to headquarters to criticize his conduct. He was willing to hear complaints, he said, but they should be made within the regiment. Now, as never before, he needed the backing of his men. Again, it was Benteen who challenged his commander. He asked Custer if he wanted to be specific as to who was at fault and Custer reddened. "I'm not here to be chastised by you," he snapped. "But for your own information, I will state that none of my remarks have been directed toward you." With that he dismissed the men. It was an inauspicious start to the campaign ahead.

The regiment was on the march by 5:00 a.m. on the morning of June 23. Custer set a terrible pace and as the sun climbed into the sky and the heat grew more intense, the column stretched out with stragglers dropping so far behind that they eventually arrived in camp hours after their leaders. The hard riding had caused blisters to form and then burst on the men's legs and the horses began to suffer from saddle sores. In some parts of the Indian trail they were following, the ground was cut to powder six inches deep. Alkaline dust covered the riders and their mounts, burning their eyes and throats. Swarming buffalo gnats stung them and caused their eyes to swell shut, while deerflies tortured the exhausted horses. It was a brutal day and so far, there had not been an Indian in sight.

The next day was no better. The trail was clear and so rutted by Indian lodge poles and horses that it resembled a plowed field, and was just as difficult to walk and ride on. The grass all around it had been cropped to the roots and the Indian herds had left little fodder for the suffering cavalry horses and mules. As the march continued, the soldiers passed one abandoned campsite after another in quick succession. It seemed to them that individual bands of Indians must have been moving very slowly, a mile or two at a time. But the scouts knew what they were seeing: These were not a series of camps but a single camp made by a group so large that it had stretched for miles. They came to a great camp circle where a framework of lodge poles that were still in place showed that a great sun dance had been held. Custer had no way of knowing it, but at this point three weeks earlier Chief Sitting Bull had experienced a vision of soldiers falling into his camp, signifying that they would attack and be killed.

At first, the droppings that had been left by Indian ponies had been dry, but as the command moved along, the trail became fresher. The men began to notice the remains of fires so recent that ashes still flew in the wind, and roasted buffalo ribs that, while picked clean, had not yet dried in the summer sun.

With their worn-out horses laboring along the trail, the troopers traveled over more than thirty miles of hard terrain on June 23 and about twenty-eight miles on June 24 before stopping at sundown along the upper reaches of Rosebud Creek. They camped under a high bluff where a little grass had been left behind by Indian ponies. The men ate and then went to sleep in their clothes, for they knew that they might be making a night march. Custer had sent three of his Crow Indian scouts ahead to follow the trail. They returned at about 9:00 p.m. to announce that, as expected, the trail turned westward to cross the divide between the Rosebud and the valley of the Little Bighorn.

For the last several days, the scouts, white men as well as Arikara and Crow, had understood the meaning of the trail they were following and had become increasingly cautious. One the first night out, a mixed-race scout named Mitch Bouyer, who had spent more than thirty years in the West, asked a young officer if he had ever fought the Sioux. When the young man confidently replied that the 7th could handle them, Bouyer replied, "Well, I can tell you that we are going to have a damned big fight."

Lonesome Charley Reynolds had scouted the region during the winter and early spring. The Indians had been gathering guns for months, he told Terry and Custer, and he was convinced that they planned to stand and fight. Reynolds had an infected finger that forced him to keep his arm in a sling and he planned to use this as an excuse to avoid the campaign. He asked Terry to relieve him on two occasions, but each time, Terry had shamed him into staying.

The scouts had spent their lives tracking animals and men. They could follow a trail that consisted of little more than broken twigs and a blade of grass that was pressed in the wrong direction, but now they were following a trail that was sometimes as much as one-half mile wide, leaving broken ground and near devastation behind. They knew that this was not the only trail leading in the same direction and that it must involve several tribes of Sioux, as well as Northern Cheyenne. They were certain that the Army was about to face more Indian warriors than anyone had ever seen together at one time.

Custer's favorite scout, an Arikara named Bloody Knife, warned him of the danger in plain language. The Crow and Arikara scouts were commanded by another Custer favorite, Lieutenant Charles Varnum, and they were enemies of the Sioux and eager to help wipe out their traditional foes. The Arikara had been disturbed by bad signs during the campaign: the unusually high water in the streams, a freak snowstorm just three weeks earlier and now, by the terrifying size of the trail they were following. While the regiment was still at the Yellowstone, they had ridden in a somber circle, singing their death songs. At some of the stops along the trail, they had engaged in rites seeking the protection of the spirits. Finally, Bloody Knife approached Custer and solemnly warned him that there were more Sioux ahead of them than there were bullets in the belts of the soldiers.

It was a more accurate prediction than anyone knew, for even the most pessimistic scout did not expect to find more than two thousand Indian warriors waiting for Custer's six hundred men.

Custer had to have known that the Indian force was huge but he rejected Bloody Knife's warnings that the odds against him would be overwhelming. He was more concerned that the enemy might get away from him. He was supremely confident in the capacity of the 7th Cavalry to defeat any Indians that it met and it was likely that the presence of a larger force made him even more eager to fight. The greater the number he defeated, the greater would be the fame of his victory.

With thoughts of glory pulsing in his head, he ordered the troops to march again at 11:00 p.m. He was now officially disobeying orders. Terry had told him to swing well to the south, then double back to prevent any possibility of an

Indian escape. Instead, Custer had pushed his troops at such brutal speed that he was far beyond the point that Terry would have expected him to reach. He was now prepared to attack immediately on his own. Waiting for Terry and Gibbon to come up the Little Bighorn from the other side would have meant sharing the victory. Continuing south, as he had been directed to do, would have risked a meeting with Crook's column and that would have reduced Custer to a subordinate and made the victory Crook's.

So Custer started his exhausted men and horses on a night march that extended ten miles up the divide between the Rosebud and the Little Bighorn. The men noisily clomped along through the darkness, dragging, pushing, cursing and kicking their way along the steep and dusty trail. Their voices, as well as the occasional brays of the thirsty, ill-tempered mules, advertised the presence of a marching army for miles in every direction.

At 2:00 a.m., the head of the column reached a deep, wooded ravine. It took hours before the rest of the regiment caught up to them and stopped. The water in the ravine was too alkaline to drink and the horses wouldn't touch it. Some of the men removed their saddles and rubbed down the lathered mounts with handfuls of dry grass and dust, while others simply lay down on the ground to sleep. Six hours later, they were on the march again.

They continued on for another ten grueling miles and then stopped at another ravine, just below the crest of the divide. The noise and the clouds of dust that hung over the moving column provided a clear sign of the soldiers' presence but it mattered very little since Sioux scouts had been watching the regiment for some time. The soldiers were somewhat aware of this since their scouts had reported fresh Sioux tracks on several occasions, and one claimed he had been close enough to a Sioux to converse with him in sign language. The only advantage Custer now had was the speed of his movement gained by the night march. Once he had left the Rosebud, orders or not, he was committed to attack. His decision to turn rather than continue south was a crucial moment that led to the battle.

During the previous night, Custer had sent Lieutenant Varnum and a party of scouts to a high knob that later became known as the Crow's Nest. Perched high over the divide, it offered a vantage point for the valley of the Little Bighorn, about fifteen miles away. Varnum had not slept for nearly thirty-six hours at this point and during those hours, he had ridden more than sixty miles on constant forays away from the main column. While waiting for the sun to rise, he napped for about forty-five minutes and when he awoke, he and his scouts were astonished by what they saw in the emerging light.

The Little Bighorn was a smallish river, running in horseshoe bends through a broad valley. On the eastern side, from which the scouts were looking, the river cut against bluffs eighty to one hundred feet high. One the western side was a wide flat plain, sometimes as much as two miles across. In the growing light, while Varnum slept, the scouts began to sense that something about the hills beyond the plain, about twenty miles from their lookout point, looked odd. They soon realized that they were looking at horses. Horses covered the hills like a carpet of brown shrubs and all of the men agreed that it was the largest pony herd they had ever seen. They awakened Varnum and with his eyes blurred with sleep, he was unable to see what they were pointing at. They urged him to look for the horses and though he still couldn't see them, Varnum trusted his scouts. At 5:00 a.m., with the sky growing brighter, he sent word to Custer.

When the message arrived, Custer rode through the camp issuing orders. Soon, the troops moved out at a steady walk, reaching the woods below the Crow's Nest in a little less than an hour. They waited while Custer rode to the lookout point. The sun was climbing higher into the sky and the day promised to be another scorcher.

When Custer reached the observation point, the valley was filled with humid fog. Even with field glasses, he was unable to make out the horses that the scouts had seen in the early morning light with the sun at their backs. Bouyer told him that it was the largest encampment that he had ever seen in his three decades among the Indians. But it was clear to everyone by now that Custer did not care how big the village was. He might be outnumbered, but he believed that he was more than a match for anything that might come his way. Bloody Knife had warned him of impending doom and the night before, Lonesome Charley Reynolds had given his few possessions to his friends, since he did not expect to survive the day. But Custer was undeterred. He was determined to take the fight to the enemy and even though he could not see them that morning, he knew they were there. Fame and glory awaited him.

Custer returned to the regiment, but Varnum, still at his lookout post, saw something that had a critical effect on the situation. A group on Indians was moving downstream and he assumed they were trying to escape. He sent a runner galloping after Custer to alert him to what was happening. In truth, the group of Indians was actually hurrying to the main camp for safety after seeing the soldiers. Their actions helped to trigger the attack.

Custer put the regiment into motion and at about noon, the command passed over the divide toward the valley of the Little Bighorn. They were still nearly fifteen miles from the Indian encampment, but they were moving quickly. The encampment lay on the far side of the river, which ran between banks from five to ten feet high in places and offered a number of convenient crossings. One of the shallow spots was upstream in the direction from which the cavalry was coming. One was near the center of the Indian camp, which was about three miles long. A third ford lay farther downstream, just below the camp.

Near the headwaters of Ash Creek which would later be named Reno Creek , which ran down to the river at the first ford, Custer stopped the regiment and divided his command. He assigned one entire company and details from each of the others to guarding the slow-moving pack train. He assigned three companies of about one hundred and twenty-five men to Benteen and told him to sweep the bluffs well south of the valley, searching them thoroughly for Indians. After Benteen departed, Custer assigned three more companies to Reno and ordered him to go directly down the creek, cross the river and charge the southern end of the Indian camp. Custer, with a five-company main force of about two hundred and fifteen men, would support him. Reno supposed that Custer would be riding behind him, coming in to deal a decisive blow after the initial collision with the Indian forces. But instead of following Reno across the ford, Custer swung to the right, remaining on the other side of the river. Hidden behind the high bluffs, he rode downstream, parallel to the Little Bighorn.

The true motives behind Custer's actions, and his intentions in dividing his force, will forever remain a mystery. However, it's possible that the key lies in Custer's personality. Every victory that he had ever won had come from rushing into an attack. He was a man of intense courage - perhaps too courageous in fact, as once observed by General Sherman - and he likely never felt the same inner stirrings of mortality that warned other men of danger and doom. His confidence in himself, and by extension in his regiment, was boundless and it was a confidence that would kill them all.

Custer's only fear, it seemed, was that the Indians would flee to the south and elude him. It was a fear that he need not have worried about.

The "Last Stand"

Custer's was adamant about the fact that he could not let the enemy escape. He sent Benteen to the west to block them if they broke through and sent Reno to the south in a diversionary attack that would have the effect of holding them in place. Custer would strike them at their heart.

With his command divided, the odds against his five-company force were overwhelming. Bouyer protested against marching into the valley and Custer accused him of cowardice. Bouyer simply shrugged. "If we go in there, we will never come out," he said. Bloody Knife bade farewell to the sun, telling it that he would not "see you go down behind the hills tonight."

On his ride, Reno was joined by Lieutenant Varnum and most of his scouts. Only Bouyer and a few of the others remained with Custer, who watered his horses at a small branch of the Ash Creek before continuing on. At least twice he halted his men and rode up on the bluffs to look down on the river. For the first time, he could see the actual size of the Indian encampment - and he was thrilled by the sight. Because no effort had been made to strike the lodges, Custer apparently believed that he had caught the Indians unprepared. He waved his hat and gleefully yelled to the men, "We've got them this time!" From the bluffs, he sent a sergeant hurrying down to bring up the packs. The sergeant gleefully told the men in Benteen's column, which had begun to circle back to the regiment, "We've got 'em, boys!"

Custer's column rode on. Just before turning into Medicine Tail Coulee, which led down to the river at the central crossing, Custer sent back another message, this time to Benteen. Scrawled hastily by an adjutant, Lieutenant W.W. Cooke, it read: "Benteen. Come on. Big village - be quick - bring packs. W.W. Cooke. PS. Bring packs." The message reflected Custer's confidence - it was not so much Benteen's men that he wanted, it was their packs filled with ammunition. There was no indication Custer was worried, either in the message or in the report of the messenger, a trumpeter named Giovanni Martini. But Martini did say that he had paused at the top of the coulee and had looked back and seen Indians rising and firing from the brush on both sides of Custer's position. Martini had been shot at and his horse wounded as he galloped back toward Benteen. Custer's two hundred men had ridden down to meet an enemy numbering in the thousands.

Reno had asked no questions when he was ordered to attack the southern end of the camp. His total force amounted to one hundred and thirty-four officers and men and sixteen scouts, but he assumed that Custer would be right behind him. When that assumption turned out to be wrong, his charge began to fall apart. Although Reno had fared well in the Civil War, he had never fought against Indians. He took his three companies across the river at a trot and then launched his attack on the village, galloping across the valley at a pace that was faster than some of his men had ever ridden a horse.

Indian warriors came out of the village on foot and on horseback to meet them. They sped toward them and then wheeled about, raising a great cloud of dust. As Reno neared them, they seemed to fall back toward the camp so rapidly that Reno suspected a trap. Ahead of him, Reno saw - or thought he saw - a shallow ravine that contained hundreds of warriors. He suddenly ordered his men to halt and dismount. The order caught his men by surprise since, at that point, no shots had been fired, even though several hundred Indians were on the field in front of them. Cavalryman George F. Smith's horse ran away with him, carrying him straight into the Indians. He was knocked from his horse and killed. Then Reno ordered every fourth man to take four horses and retreat to a stand of trees near the river. The remaining men, about eighty in number, formed a thin skirmish line, its right end anchored in the trees. Each man stood about nine feet from the next and many, especially the new recruits, began firing wildly and rapidly, even though most of the Indians were still hundreds of yards away.

Reno's attack was halted almost before it began. Technically, he had disobeyed the order to attack the camp and some believed that he had left Custer without support. Others have argued that he would have been cut down within five hundred yards. Whatever the truth of the situation, one fact was clear: In halting and dismounting, Reno had shifted from offense to defense. In addition, he had no chance of holding his position. The mounted Indians soon swept around the end of his line, turning his left flank and putting him in a deadly crossfire. His men reflexively bunched up, making them better targets, and several were hit. As the Sioux turned Reno's flank, they also slipped up the river on his right flank, preparing to take his men and horses in the woods.

Reno began calling for the men on the skirmish line to retreat to the woods, but the men who didn't hear the orders began to collapse from the pressure of the attack. Most of them stopped firing immediately and as the Sioux moved in closer, several more were hit. Defense was easier in the woods, which were heavy with brush and undergrowth, but finding a better position did not help Reno to carry out his orders. He and his men were at least one thousand yards from the nearest lodge in the encampment and any chance of an attack was gone. At that point, they were thinking in terms of sheer survival.

The Indians set fire to the dry grass along the river bottom and the flames swept through the brush and trees. Warriors slipped in on their bellies under the smoke, rising, shooting and then dropping out of sight. Horses were shot with bullets and arrows, sending them into a panic while the frightened, and now effectively blind soldiers fired wild shots in every direction.

Reno knew that he was in a serious situation, but it was not a desperate one - not yet anyway. He looked upriver, still waiting for Custer's promised support, which, of course, never came. Custer was miles away by this time, heading into the encampment. As more Indians surrounded Reno's position, he ordered a move to the bluffs on the other side of the river. A captain shouted, "Men, to your horses; the Indians are at our rear!" Some of the men were perplexed by the order. One of the other scouts turned to Reynolds and asked, "What damn fool move is this?"

In the commotion, many of the soldiers failed to hear the order. They were still firing when they heard from others that they were getting out. Uncertain, they looked around, searching for their officers, their friends, their horses, anything that looked familiar. As they attempted to scramble to safety, they stopped shooting. In the lull that followed, a group of Sioux suddenly pushed toward them and fired a deadly volley from less than thirty yards. Reno was next to Bloody Knife when an enemy bullet struck the scout between the eyes. His skull shattered, spraying Reno with blood and brains.

That horrifying moment apparently released the panic that had been rising in the inexperienced Reno. Even though he and a number of the soldiers managed to get mounted, Reno lost sight of the immediate plan, which was to leave the woods and escape across the river to safer ground. Shouting maniacally, he ordered the men to dismount and, as they began to do so, to mount up again. He himself swung back into his saddle and his horse leaped out of the timber without being spurred. The other soldiers thundered after him, leaving their wounded behind - which meant certain death for the helpless men. It was a frantic scene of panic, but it was impossible to blame Reno, who was drastically outnumbered. He might not have saved any of his men if he had continued to try and hold that patch of timber. However, his reputation will always be blotched by the fact that he abandoned his wounded and that, as he led his men through a brutal crossfire, he made no attempt to maintain order or to cover the rear. If they had withdrawn in even a somewhat orderly manner the soldiers would have kept up fire as they moved and kept the enemy busy. By running, the Indians were able to pick off scores of them like animals in a hunt. They rode beside them and shot down the soldiers as they fled from the woods.

Reno galloped for more than a mile alongside the river and away from the encampment, making for a high bluff on the far side. At the bank opposite the bluff, the horses were forced to jump four and five feet into the river. As they struggled across, the Indians followed and ran them down, pulling soldiers from their mounts and smashing their heads with clubs. For those who made it across the river, they faced a sheer, eight-foot bank. Varnum's horse threw itself against the bank and managed to reach the top, but others were not so lucky. Many of them toppled backward, crashing back on the men and horses below. The panicked animals thrashed about in the water, fighting the current, frantic with fear and rearing backward as their riders pushed them toward the steep bank.

Meanwhile, Sioux warriors were coming along the bluffs from downstream and shooting down the soldiers as they emerged from the river. Lieutenant Benjamin Hodgson, Reno's adjutant, was hit by a bullet that passed through his leg and killed his horse. A trooper thrust a stirrup at Hodgson and pulled him to the riverbank. He was climbing out of the water when a bullet fired from above split his skull and killed him instantly.

The fight in the woods and the chase across the river had lost Reno about one-third of his men. They straggled to the top of the highest bluff before the Indians could reach it, and lay there, demoralized, exhausted and terrified, fearing another attack at any moment.

Charley Reynolds had died on the way to the river crossing, trying to cover the retreating soldiers. His horse had been shot out from under him and the litter of shells found next to his body showed that he had fought long and hard from the shelter of the animal's body before he had finally been killed. Reynolds had taken his share of enemy lives, and he was not the only one. One of the men had shot an Indian off his horse and came up the bluff with a bloody scalp swinging in his hand.

At the same time, Reno, at least temporarily safe, was already re-writing the history of what had occurred. Told by the company doctor that the men had been demoralized by the rout, Reno snapped at him, "That was a cavalry charge, sir!"

The men set up posts to meet the next attack but by now, except for a few snipers firing from a distance, the Indians were leaving, riding hard downstream toward the center of the encampment. Some of the men heard firing coming from that direction. Custer was giving it to them, the soldiers told one another, grinning and pleased with this small bit of revenge for their lost men.

They were on the bluff for nearly a half hour when Reno saw Benteen's column approaching his position. He ran out and waved to the captain. "For God's sake, Benteen," he called, "halt your command and help me. I've lost half my men."

Soon after riding off at Custer's order, Benteen had decided that he was on a fool's errand. He moved west as he had been instructed and searched the countryside for hour after hour but after seeing no Indians, he turned back and headed for the Little Bighorn, where he knew he would be needed. He was ahead of the pack train when he received Custer's written order to hurry forward with the packs. The order apparently made no sense to Benteen. If Custer's men were going into a hard fight, they needed his men more than they needed him to herd pack animals. He moved forward at a brisk trot and when he saw Reno, he assumed that he had found the regiment since he had no idea that Custer had further divided his command after sending Benteen away. But Reno had no idea where Custer was. He only knew that he had not received the support that Custer had promised him and he believed that Indians would soon overrun his position.

The two officers were now bogged down with confusion and indecision. Custer's written order to Benteen had obviously come from some position ahead, and Reno and Benteen both knew that a lively battle was taking place there. They could hear the pounding of the guns and the cries of the Sioux warriors. And yet Benteen did not obey the order to swiftly join Custer, nor did either man follow the classic military dictum that, in the absence of orders, one marches toward the sound of the guns. Reno refused to move at all, in fact, until the pack train arrived to resupply his men.

Finally, a junior officer forced their hand. Captain Thomas Weir, who admired Custer as much as Benteen disliked him, set off downstream without his commanders' authority. He and his company reached a high point - known later as Weir Point - from which he could look down on both the Indian camp and the field into which Custer had ridden. By this time, the heavy fire had died down. Weir saw no sign of Custer and his men, but he did see clouds of dust and warriors milling about in the distance.

Meanwhile, Reno and Benteen finally moved the rest of the command in Weir's direction. When they reached the vantage point, Benteen for the first time realized the enormity of the situation. Across the river, he saw at least eighteen hundred Indian lodges. The air was filled with smoke and dust but he could see the size of the pony herd that was spread across the hills - the same sight that had startled the scouts earlier that morning.

The Indians saw the soldiers on the point and began moving toward them, rushing the slopes and attempting to surround them on two sides. With the position clearly untenable, the soldiers retreated back to the bluff. More men were lost in this second retreat and more wounded soldiers were left to be tortured by the Sioux. Once on the bluff, though, they had a defensible position and were able to hold off the attack for more than three hours. When darkness finally came, the shooting dropped off and the Indians, as usual, broke off the attack for the night. Safe for the time being, the soldiers worked all night to fortify the bluff, using hatchets, knives, tin cups and even their bare hands to dig rough trenches. In the distance, the exhausted men could see great fires burning in the encampment. Figures danced among the flames and the rapid beat of drums could be heard echoing across the fields. No one knew what had become of Custer and his men but at that point, the men could only fear for their lives.

What exactly happened to Custer that day is still unknown. The messenger Giovanni Martini was the last soldier to see him alive and when Martini rode off with his message to Benteen, he believed that all was well. Soldiers studied the evidence of the battlefield afterward and over the years Indians offered their own accounts - often conflicting ones - of what happened that day. The accounts conflict for several reasons, the most important being that the Indians tended to see the battle from their own point of view. They had no command structure or clear orders, which made it difficult for them to reconstruct what happened in terms of overall battlefield movements. Each warrior recounted what he did and saw from his own perspective. And even then, many of them, fearing retribution, preferred not to talk about what happened at all.

Based on the battlefield evidence and the personal accounts, historians have put together a "best guess" scenario of what happened to Custer during what has been called his "Last Stand" against the Sioux.

Custer led his command to Medicine Tail Coulee, where Martini saw him come under the initial attack. Custer's next move from there would have been to cross the river near the center of the camp and enter the battle against a larger body of Indians. There would have been at least one thousand warriors facing his two hundred men in that area alone. The Indians came across the ford and swarmed up the gullies all around the soldiers. Custer, who never cared about the odds, likely charged against them, despite their superior numbers. Sheer numbers, though, can turn even the fiercest charge. In the midst of flying arrows, a rain of bullets, blue powder smoke, clouds of dust, horses crashing into one another, screams and war cries of the Sioux, Custer's firing, shouting and cursing men surely knew that they were in trouble.

Some of Custer's men may have been turned back at the river crossing, while others likely never reached the river at all. It's likely that some of them were driven to high, open ground downstream, where they hoped to mount a counterattack and hold on until reinforcements arrived - but the Indians were driving them there. What none of them could know was that Crazy Horse, one of the few great battle leaders among the Sioux, was in the camp they were attacking. Although the Indians had no generals in a structured military sense, many of them followed Crazy Horse because the tactics that he suggested always seemed to work. He had fared well in earlier battles, including a recent fight with Crook at the Rosebud, and he now played a leading role in the tactics that destroyed Custer.

Custer moved to high ground and took up an offensive at the front and set up a defensive position at the rear. Then Sioux Chief Gall, leading the attack on Reno, heard the firing downstream and entered the battle. With hundreds of warriors, Gall charged away from the bluffs where Reno's exhausted men had retreated. Crossing the river, these warriors hurled themselves against Custer's rear flank. Custer discovered Company L, commanded by his brother-in-law, Lieutenant Calhoun, and I Company, commanded by Captain Myles Keogh, a battling Irishman who was beloved by the regiment. The men moved backward step by step, firing as they went, covering the rear.

But Crazy Horse, with hundreds of fighters, had gone down through the encampment on the other side of the Little Bighorn, and had crossed the river at the lower ford. He charged toward Custer's position, leading his warriors up the same hill that Custer was climbing from the other side. The Indians topped the final rise, on a high point ahead of Custer's retreating forces, and crashed into Custer and his three forward companies like a battering ram. But Custer rallied once again. He grouped his men back to back for a final stand.

At Custer's rear flank, most of Gall's warriors had dismounted and crawled as close to L Company as they could, picking them off one by one with bows and arrows. A warrior armed with a bow could hug the ground and shoot without making a sound that might reveal his position. He would fire up in the air, the arrow arching high on its trajectory and falling to strike a soldier silently in the back. Many of the soldiers died this way, and lay face down with arrows standing upright in their backs.

Gall's fighters crept closer and finally took L Company by storm. The Indians on the ground rose and fired as one and then mounted warriors leaped over them, falling on the soldiers and beating and hacking them to death. No soldiers broke and ran. They held their position, fighting and dying in place, where they bodies were later found. The Indians moved forward, fighting their way toward Custer.

Custer was still frantically organizing his defense. He remained clear-minded until the very end, as was evident from the strong placement in which the men's bodies were later found. Their positions could not have been better. They fought hard but their carbines eventually failed in the heat. As the metal grew hot, the soft copper shells expanded and the ejectors cut through the cartridge rims and left them jammed in place. When this happened, the men had to work the cartridge out with a knife - while bullets and arrows thudded into the ground around them. The men's eyes burned with sweat and smoke, but they held their places in the line, their pistols ready for the moment when there was no time left to dig out another shell from a fouled carbine. That they were brave was well known - and respected - by the Indians. A year later, Sitting Bull stated, "I tell no lies about dead men. These men who came with 'Long Hair' ffiCusterffl were as good men as ever fought." Another chief, Brave Wolf, said, "It was hard fighting; very hard all the time. I have been in many hard fights, but I never saw such brave men."

The Indians stormed over Company I, just as they had Company L. Again, the soldiers died in place, swinging their rifles as clubs, protecting the rear, emptying their pistols – except for the last shot, which some of the men saved for themselves. A sergeant caught a horse near the end and made a desperate half-mile ride through a rain of gunfire before a bullet finally brought him down. Afterward, an Indian spoke of his courage. There was an officer in a buckskin shirt who rode through unbelievable gunfire. Finally, his horse fell but he managed to catch another and leap into the saddle, riding back and forth, rallying his men and holding his position. The Indians lost sight of him moments later and it was assumed he was killed at that point.

Finally, Crazy Horse, with his warriors behind him, rode over Custer and his men, cutting them down to the ground. The Indians came in a great cloud of dust, which hid the bloody killing that followed. When the dust settled, the soldiers were dead. A handful of white men broke away, running downhill in a panic, but the Indians galloped behind them and killed them as they ran. And then it was over.

The soldiers were all dead, the battlefield suddenly quiet, and the Indians, as they said later, were as surprised as people are when a tornado passes and leaves behind silence after its terrible roar. Custer and one-third of the 7th Cavalry had been wiped out in less than an hour.

The next day, the Indians renewed the siege of Benteen and Reno in hard fighting that lasted until the middle of the afternoon. Then, unexpectedly, the Indians stuck their camp and by sunset were moving south and away from the battlefield. Finally, on June 27, General Terry's troops came up the river from the north. His men counted one hundred and ninety-seven bodies on the hill. Custer was among them. He had been stripped naked, but he was not scalped or mutilated in any way. He had two clean wounds, one in the temple and one in the heart, either of which could have been fatal. The Indians themselves never knew who had killed Custer or even how or when he had been killed. Many didn't even know that Custer had been on the battlefield that day until much later.

The Battle of Little Bighorn was the U.S. Army's most decisive defeat during the Indian Wars of the late 1800s. It also sealed the fate of the Indians and destroyed whatever chances remained for men of goodwill to bridge the gaps that separated Native Americans from whites. After the death of Custer and his men, the national mood hardened and in Washington and on the battlefields of the West, government officials and military commanders began planning to crush the Native American resistance once and for all. Companies of cavalry were expanded from sixty-four to one hundred and new recruits hurried to join the "Custer Avengers." General Crook took to the field and drove his men to their limit, as if to make up for the foundering campaigns of the spring. Nelson Miles dressed his men in thick buffalo coats and rampaged across the Sioux lands all winter and into 1877. Other columns attacked Indian encampments from all sides, wiping out the Sioux. Their warriors were killed, their villages destroyed, their food supplies burned and their women and children left starving and homeless in the cold. Although fighting flared up periodically for the next decade and a half, but there was never again a real war or even a battle on the scale of what happened at Little Bighorn.

Custer's death marked the end of an era. New railroad lines were built across the West, towns and cities sprang up and settlers spread across the land. And as the country changed, the role of the frontier soldier changed along with it. In time, the frontier forts slowly vanished and the cavalry soldier vanished too. The Indian Wars slowly faded into history, leaving only silent stone markers and designated historic sites behind.

Hauntings at Little Bighorn

The site of Custer's final battle was first preserved as a national cemetery in 1879, to protect the graves of the 7th Cavalry troopers who were buried where they fell. It was re-designated in 1946 as the Custer Battlefield National Monument and later renamed Little Bighorn Battlefield National Monument in 1991. The site is under the care of the National Park Service and many of the staff members as well as visitors at the battlefield are quick to assure you that this is one of the most haunted locations in the West.

The dead are restless at the Little Bighorn Battlefield

Many of those who experience strange things on the battlefield are among the nearly 400,000 visitors who tour the windswept ravines and ridges of the site each year. Standing on the hill where Custer and the last of his men died, they can only imagine the last moments of the soldiers as they met their fate at the hands of the Lakota and Cheyenne. Many of the men lay wounded, helpess and horrified on the bloody grass, their heads filled with the screams and groans of their comrades in arms. When the battle was finished, most of the bodies were mutilated beyond recognition. If there was ever a place where ghosts might linger, it's the Little Bighorn Battlefield.

According to visitors and staff members, the dead are restless at Little Bighorn. Whether all of those who come to the site are believers in ghosts or not, the mysterious happenings on the battlefield are an indeible part of the place. As historian and author Robert Utley wrote, "Stories of the supernatural seem to revolve around legendary spots."

The encounters on the field date back many years. The Crow people were apparently aware of ghostly events at the site long before any others. They called the site superintendent, "ghost herder" because he lowered the flag at dusk, which the Crow believed allowed the spirits to rise from their graves and walk amongst the living. When the flag was raised, in the morning, the dead came back to rest.

Robert Utley was a ranger at the battlefield between 1947 and 1952 and reported no ghost sightings during his tenure there, but one experience involving author Charles Kuhlman did take place during that time period. It has been reported that Custer's spirit visited Kulhman. It has also been reported that Kuhlman would visit Last Stand Hill alone, in hopes of making some form of contact with the other world. Utley denies these events happened. However, it could explain Kuhlman's fantastic interpretation of the battle in a book that he wrote about the events at Little Bighorn.

In the late 1950s, visitors began to tell of hearing the sounds of Indian warriors charging on horseback through the cemetery at the site. Others, who walked through the cemetery at night, spoke of cold spots that seemed to spring up from nowhere. A visitor from New Orleans claimed to have been transported back in time to witness the battle. While driving along Battle Ridge, a cab driver from Minneapolis reported witnessing soldiers and Indian warriors fighting to the death. He came shaken and distraught into the visitor's center, where the employees calmed him. Such stories continued to be recounted for years.

One evening in August 1976, a National Park Service law enforcement officer visited Last Stand Hill. He was alone when he felt a sudden drop in temperature go through his body. The cold was accompanied by the soft murmuring of voices. He did not stay long enough to discover whether they were talking to him.

In August 1987, on a moonless night, a psychic from Colorado visited the battlefield. Although she had never been there before, and knew little about the battle, she provided details of the action at Medicine Tail Ford and Nye-Cartwright Ridge. Standing beside the 7th Cavalry Monument and the mass grave of the soldier dead, she felt the presence of restless spirits from the Custer battalion. While visiting the cemetery, the same psychic saw a spirit warrior charge a seasonal employee, then turn and ride past the visitor's center down Cemetery Ridge.

Many other stories come from park employees, who are willing to accept that there is more about the battlefield than first meets the eye. Former Custer Battlefield Park Ranger Mardell Plainfeather had an experience on the battlefield in 1980. Mardell is a member of the Crow tribe and still faithfully practices her people's ceremonies. She and her family regularly visited their sweat lodge that sat quietly in the thick timber along the Little Bighorn River across from the battlefield. Late one evening Mardell and her daughter, Lorena, went to the sweat lodge to make sure the fire was extinguished. While walking across the battlefield after sunset, she saw two Indian warriors on horseback silhouetted upon the bluffs. The warriors were on the battlefield proper within the confines of the fence. They were dressed for war, faces and bodies painted, feathers placed in the long flowing hair of one, while the other wore braids. They carried shields and one had a bow. They were there one moment and then gone the next.

Employees report bizarre stories inside the Stone House, a two-story building that was constructed as a residence for the site superintendent in 1894. It has since been converted into a library, the park historian's office and conference rooms. The lower level was once used to house bodies awaiting burial in the nearby national cemetery. Before being turned into the library, parts of it were used as a summer residence for staff members and was closed up tightly and left empty during the harsh winter months.

While living on the battleground, former ranger Neil Mangum remembered walking home on many winter nights through the cemetery and seeing the lights on in the Stone House's upstairs apartment, despite the fact that he was always careful to turn off the lights when he left the building. Once, he couldn't get the front door open. Frustrated, Neil went home, returning an hour later. The door opened easily. He walked up the stairs, and calmly turned off the lights one more time.

The Stone House can be an unsettling place. A woman's figure has been seen coming down the stairs. Footsteps are heard upstairs when no one is there. During the summer season of 1986, a new battlefield ranger was housed for two nights in the upstairs apartment. He awoke the first night feeling someone was sitting at the foot of his bed. He first thought it was his wife, but he remembered she was visiting family overseas, and he was alone. As he reached for the pistol that he kept on his nightstand, he saw a shadowy figure move from the foot of his bed. The ranger distinctly saw a torso of a soldier with the head and legs missing as the apparition disappeared into the other room.

A wooden wall complete with a padlocked door was built to make two bedrooms in the lower level of the Stone House. One night early in the 1989 season, two staff members were sound asleep. One was suddenly awakened by loud bangs on the partition wall. The sound was coming from the opposite side of the wall. The door was locked. The padlock was on the employees' side of the wall. The strong knocks occurred again. The other staff member was awakened, but the sounds had stopped. The only entrance to the other side of the wall is through a window that was securely locked. Neither employee was able to explain the anomalous sounds.

In August 1997, just before the Stone House was converted into a library, four people spent the night there. One man slept in the upstairs apartment bedroom while a father and son shared the sleeper sofa in the apartment's living room. A young woman slept downstairs. She awoke in the middle of the night to the sound of footsteps moving across the floor upstairs. She figured it was one of the fellows heading to the bathroom. The footsteps exited the bedroom, went through the upstairs hall to the bathroom then back again. Then, moments later, more footsteps sounded, but this time they were louder. They became so forceful that she noticed flakes of paint falling from the edge of the downstairs windows. Her first thought was that whoever it was would wake up the whole house. She became very concerned when the sounds became louder and more forceful, almost vibrating the entire downstairs. Suddenly, the downstairs kitchen door slammed shut with a loud bang. Startled, the young woman jumped up from her bed. She knew it wasn't a gust of wind because all the windows had been covered with heavy plastic and taped very secure during the renovation. It wasn't wind that slammed shut the door -- it was something else.

She left the house that night and tried to sleep in her car, but spent a very restless night. The next morning she shared this experience with the men who slept upstairs. All were perplexed because none of them heard footsteps banging around the apartment. However, the father who spent the night on the sleeper sofa remembered being awakened by a loud bang from downstairs around 2:30 a.m. It had been the kitchen door as it mysteriously closed on its own!

The visitor's center for the site rests at the bottom of the hill where Custer met his end. Tourists come in to escape the heat of the Montana sun, to browse the bookstore and visit the museum. After they have left for the day and the doors are locked, the spirits sometimes are said to wreak havoc in the building. Voices are heard, footsteps wander the halls and the lights come on by themselves, long after the living have departed.

On a summer's day in 1985, an employee had an odd experience in the museum basement. He had just presented a program to the public and was returning some items to the audio visual room. Before he reached the inventory storage room, he noticed a figure standing in a dark corner. Although it appeared to him to be a soldier, he thought it was a fellow employee who was trying to play a trick on him. He pretended not to see the soldier and walked past him. As the employee turned left to enter the audio room, he noticed, out of the corner of his eye, the shadowy figure of the soldier moving into the hall. The apparition proceeded to walk through the locked door of the inventory room and disappear.

Recently, a ranger was giving a live presentation to visitors when he was suddenly interrupted by the sensation that something was pulling at his leg and trying to force him to the ground. He looked down to find nothing there. One woman working in the bookstore by herself felt someone tap her on the shoulder. She turned around to find she was alone.

With such tales still being told, it's obvious that Little Bighorn remains a haunted place and that the ghosts of the battle-scarred dead are still restless there. This is a place where history literally remains alive and where the ghosts of the past are still very relevant in the present.

SOLDIERS and the SUPERNATURAL

Epilogue:
Ghosts of Abu Ghraib
By Dave Goodwin

The final story in this book holds a special place in this chronicle of military ghosts because it's one that that I discovered myself. It's a ghostly adventure that has an unlikely beginning. It started inauspiciously enough when I and sixteen other members of the 35th Engineer Brigade, Design Management Section, Missouri Army National Guard, were mobilized for active duty at Fort Leonard Wood in October 2004. We knew even before we reported for duty that our ultimate destination was Baghdad.

Overnight, I traded my ghost-hunting gear for an M-4 rifle and I planned to essentially set aside my otherworldly interests for a year. But then again, I have always had a knack for sniffing out a good ghost story and those of you who have been seriously seeking the paranormal for any length of time know that once a ghost hunter, always a ghost hunter. I was not going to let a little thing like combat curtail something that has been a passion of mine for over fifteen years. For some reason, I just knew that an opportunity would present itself.

At the time of my activation in support of Operation Iraqi Freedom, the heinous events that had transpired at the infamous Abu Ghraib Prison, located approximately thirty-two kilometers west of Baghdad, were no longer headline news.

Prior to that, however, the inhumane treatment of Iraqi detainees there by a few American service men and women in the fall of 2003, galvanized the world's attention. Stark images of hooded and bound prisoners piled like animals in a myriad of compromising positions and those of inmates with their hands and genitalia connected to non-electrified wires only served to ignite anti-coalition fervor within Iraq. The scandal was serious enough that it had given a black eye to U.S.-led initiatives throughout the Middle East.

By the time I arrived at Camp Victory, Baghdad, in December 2004, all of the past tabloid media hype about the prison and its ghastly history under Saddam Hussein was the furthest thing from my mind. I had more pressing things to worry about, primarily the random insurgent mortar and rocket attacks on the very place I was to call home for the next three hundred and sixty-five days.

In February 2005, the Design Management Section was tasked with developing plans for a military detention facility that would eventually replace the one at Abu Ghraib. To accurately assess the requirements for a new confinement center, it was imperative that we know what currently worked and what did not work from a technical design standpoint at Abu Ghraib. To find the answers to these questions, myself and seven other members of the Design Management Section were sent on a one-day fact-finding tour of Abu Ghraib. Our mission was simple: conduct an onsite reconnaissance. Little did I know what laid in wait for us there!

The Baghdad Central Confinement Facility or "Saddam's Torture Central" was an American-designed reformatory that had been built by British contractors. It officially opened its doors in March 1970. The modern, sprawling two hundred and eighty-acre prison complex, complete with numerous imposing guard towers, was originally built to house more than four thousand prisoners. The facility was further broken down into five separate cellblocks, each designated to hold different categories of inmates: foreign prisoners, those serving long sentences, those serving short sentences, those prisoners who committed capital crimes and those who committed "special" crimes. Each individual walled compound contained cramped four-by-four-meter cells, crude dining and washing facilities, a prayer room and exercise yard. When the prison opened, it adhered to strict international prison standards but when Saddam Hussein took power in 1979, overcrowding became a problem.

It was not uncommon for each cell to hold up to forty prisoners at any given time. Here, men who were sentenced to twenty years for stealing a chicken lived side by side with murderers, rapists, and other hardcore criminals. During the first Gulf War, members of a captured British Special Air Services SAS commando team known as "Bravo Two Zero" were housed at Abu Ghraib while undergoing physical torture and interrogation.

The area reserved for Saddam's favorite type of scofflaws, better known as "political prisoners," was separated into two sections: "open" and "closed." Shi'ite

Muslims were imprisoned in the "closed" wing and were for all intents and purposes held incommunicado from the outside world until they were either released or executed.

Dave at Abu Ghraib

When Abu Ghraib was under the control of Saddam and his Ba'athist cronies, the prison was a place synonymous with brutality and death. It was a symbol of terror that Saddam used to control the free people of Iraq. Guards at Abu Ghraib routinely beat prisoners, many of whom were being held without being charged with any specific crime. In some instances the guards fed shredded pieces of plastic to inmates just for fun. Those detainees fortunate enough to be paroled from "Saddam's Torture Central" were gaunt shadows of their former selves. It was said that "those who go in are lost and those who come out are reborn." Life at Abu Ghraib was a unique form of hell.

Unfortunately, many who entered the gates of Abu Ghraib were never heard from again. In 1984, over four thousand political prisoners were murdered in Saddam's "Death House," which was sequestered in an isolated section of the prison. Amnesty International reported that between 1994 and 2001, at least three hundred and thirty-three Shia Muslims were killed at Abu Ghraib. It is believed that hundreds of unidentified prisoners were executed there in November 1996 alone. Sadly, these numbers are misleadingly low. Fearing negative international reaction to the Amnesty International claims of vicious treatment of inmates at the prison, Saddam had his henchmen carry out exterminations in secret. Worse yet, it was alleged that some of the prisoners at Abu Ghraib were used as human guinea pigs in horrendous Iraqi military chemical and biological weapons tests.

In 2001, Abu Ghraib reportedly housed over fifteen thousand prisoners. Prior to the start of Operation Iraqi Freedom in 2003, plans were made to expand the facility, but construction was put on hold at the onset of hostilities. When U.S. forces toppled Saddam's government, many of his former enemies and previous Abu Ghraib's alumni boldly returned to loot and pillage the prison. They defaced images of the former dictator and literally stole anything that was not bolted down.

Today, Abu Ghraib is a kaleidoscope of both the old and the new. The U.S. currently operates a detention facility at the site known as "Camp Redemption." It is staffed by a professional, caring cadre made up of U.S. and coalition forces. At any given time, the prison can house several thousand alleged criminals or captured insurgents. In 2004, the oldest part of Abu Ghraib was returned to the Iraqi government for use as a civilian correctional facility. Other than a few technical improvements, the archaic buildings look the same as they did when Saddam was in power.

When we started our journey to Abu Ghraib on that sunny winter morning in February, no one really knew what to expect. First, we had to make the perilous trip from Camp Victory to the prison itself. Going outside the wire is always a knuckle-biting experience in Iraq. Accompanied by an ominous-looking security escort team, our tiny convoy of up-armored vehicles left the main gate of Camp Victory loaded for bear and looking for trouble. We traveled the pot-holed roads at breakneck speed hoping to avoid roadside bombs and ambushes. We slowed only slightly as we traveled through the various small villages and hamlets that dot the countryside between Baghdad and our final destination. When we passed through each town, small children approached our convoy, hands held high, asking for food and candy. We prayed that the presence of these innocent kids was not an insurgent ploy to get us "bottled-necked" or worse yet, stopped in a "kill zone." Once we were sure the children were safely off to the side of the road, we picked up speed and in no time at all, we reached Abu Ghraib. After our short but intense ride, we breathed a collective sigh of relief when we finally entered the base. In a country where death is random for friend and foe alike, we were again as safe as we could be in a war zone.

From the start, I was surprised by our reception. Many times, when you show up to visit a location, you are treated like a bastard stepchild, but in this instance it was just the opposite; we were treated like real VIPs. Our tour guide, Major Anderson, not his real name had been assigned to Abu Ghraib for the majority of his tour and in that time he had cultivated many friendships there. As a result, we were treated to a rare, behind-the-scenes glimpse of life at the prison. This included a walk-through of the prisoner in-processing buildings, tours of the various detainee holding areas within Camp Redemption, and the soldiers' living quarters, which were nothing more than retrofitted old cellblocks. Along the way, Major Anderson interjected personal comments, observations and quotes from his tenure at Abu Ghraib. This human touch brought a whole new dimension to our stopover.

Everywhere we went, we snapped numerous pictures using our digital cameras. There is dust everywhere in Iraq. Despite that, every one of our pictures up to this point had been crystal clear and free of anomalies.

Towards the end of our tour we stopped by the old Iraqi portion of the prison and met with a U.S. contractor who was advising the new Iraqi warden on the best way to run the facility. This is the portion of Abu Ghraib that is reserved for the incarceration of Iraqi criminals. The contractor was a very talkative, good-natured mountain of a man. We learned that he had previously run the prison when it was still under coalition control, so he knew the history and the layout of the place like the back of his hand. He offered to show us the exact location in the prison where all of the recently sensationalized prisoner abuse photographs had been taken.

As we made our way to the cellblock in question, I mentioned to the former warden that the prison seemed to be immersed in a blanket of despair. He agreed without question, saying that the older parts of the prison "played tricks with your mind" and that it was in those deepest, darkest recesses that he himself and other people on his staff had seen strange shadows and heard disembodied voices when no one else was present. I would not have expected these kinds of statements from a prominent civilian contractor. He didn't strike me as a believer in the paranormal. Neither did he come across as a skeptic. He was just telling me, matter-of-factly, what it was like to work inside the prison, especially at night when Abu Ghraib had what he called an "energy" all its own.

The last place we visited at Abu Ghraib was Saddam's "Death House." It now stands totally empty, devoid of all human life except for the occasional visiting dignitary. It is kept from the prying eyes of the world by a large gate that is always kept locked. There was no one standing guard at the gate, but when you walk past the entrance, you cannot help but feel the sting of seemingly a thousand unblinking eyes watching you. As Major Anderson fumbled with the lock, he mentioned something that had happened one time when he and several of his peers had entered the inner courtyard of the Death House to look around. He said that he was standing there looking in the direction of the Death House when he suddenly had the unnerving feeling that someone or something was going to slam the huge gate behind him and his party, locking them all inside. Anderson said that no matter how hard he tried to reason with himself, he was unable to shake his irrational fear, even though he knew he had the keys to the gate in his pocket. After recounting the story, and with a grin on his face, Major Anderson pushed open the gate and ushered us into the courtyard where he had his unsettling experience.

"Saddam's Death House"

The Death House is a one-and-a-half story building, which had been constructed by Saddam Hussein to rid himself of unwanted human pests and political prisoners. Those awaiting execution were corralled into eight small and I mean *very* small holding cells until there was just enough room to stand up. Once the Death House was filled to overflowing with the living, the condemned were escorted to the gallows, where they were hanged two at a time. Others were taken to an area just below the gallows where their pitiful lives were unceremoniously snuffed out in a small gas chamber.

According to Major Anderson, Saddam brought his sons Uday and Qusay to the Death House when they were nine and ten years old to teach them how to torture and kill. It turned out to be a skill the two brothers perfected to a fine art, all the way up until the start of the U.S. invasion in 2003.

On the day of our visit, the Death House was lit in the scarlet rays of a waning winter sun. I noted that as our small group stood in its shadow, a pall of uneasiness seemed to settle over us. Smiles were quickly replaced by straight faces. There was without a doubt, a dark presence emanating from the silent whitewashed monolith that seemed to dare us to enter.

Cautiously, we walked around the Death House, snapping pictures, amazed that one man could build such a testament to horror. One by one, we entered the building and were almost instantly enveloped in a cloud of cool damp air that was laced with the scent of rot and decay. I turned to my left and entered the cellblock where the condemned were held. Before me were eight open doors. To me they were nothing more than rusted metal cell doors but for those unfortunates who looked upon them for the last time, they must have seemed like toothless mouths, ready to devour their very souls.

As I entered one of the small cells, I closed my eyes and listened. With only eight people inside the building the echoes and resulting noise was almost intolerable. I could only imagine what it must have been like at night, when the cries and pleas for mercy of hundreds of panicked inmates congealed into one woeful death song. It must have been an unearthly racket, a resonant energy that undoubtedly embedded itself into the very fabric of the ghastly building over the years it was in operation. It was a stir of echoes that you could literally feel. For me, it was as real as the electrical current running through the walls. The only other time I had felt emotion of that magnitude was when I had toured Dachau, the German concentration camp, in 1996. Feeling more than a little skittish, I took a few photographs of the area and rejoined the rest of the group at the gallows.

Saddam did not go out of his way to put much creative thought into the design of his gallows. They were crude, simple and chillingly effective. Gone now were the two hangman's nooses that had been tied to large iron beams in the ceiling. Prisoners stood over one of two trapdoors, which were separated by the long metal switch that activated them. The gas chamber lay neatly tucked away beneath the floor. It was reached by a small set of stairs. As I stood there in awe, I noticed cameras flashing around me and I instinctively pulled mine out of its case and clicked off a few frames for posterity. I also noticed another thing: relative silence. No one in the group was talking, just mumbling to themselves. We were all suddenly very contemplative and somber.

A short time later, we gathered in the courtyard where we talked about our impressions and feelings while inside the Death House. I found that it was strange that almost all of us had experienced an overwhelming feeling of sadness when we walked through the gallows and the prisoner holding area. I was even more disturbed when we started to compare our photographs.

As I mentioned previously, up until the time we arrived at the Death House, our pictures had been relatively free of what might have been spectral anomalies. However, almost every photograph that I and the rest of the group had taken while inside the ghastly place was filled with strange mists and flickering images. Even our commanding officer commented that he could not explain why the strange, ghostly lights only appeared in the photos taken while we were in and around the Death House. Abu Ghraib is covered in sand and dust like any other place in Iraq. If the objects in the photos had been caused by airborne particles then they should have been in virtually every picture we had taken that day, but they were not.

Several weeks later, a security element from HHD, 20th Engineer Brigade, known as the "Thunder Cats" toured Abu Ghraib. I can attest that the "Thunder Kittens," as we jokingly call them, were unaware of our previous experiences at the Death House. Upon their triumphant return to Camp Victory, they regaled everyone who would listen with a description of their exploits, specifically the strange photographs they had taken while inside the Death House. Like us, they had toured the facility, taking normal, anomaly-free photographs, but the tenor of their pictures took on a more paranormal aspect when they were in the very heart of Saddam's chamber of death.

For these phenomena to manifest themselves in one specific location in such a prolific manner for two completely different groups at two different times is unheard of. In my opinion it is without question a convergence of documented facts that should make the hair stand up on the back of the necks of any naysayers who refuse to believe that the paranormal world co-exists with our own. The only other place that I have visited in my travels that excreted the same kind of melancholy and sometimes malevolent psychic energy I found at Abu Ghraib was Dachau. I can assure you I will never forget either visit.

Abu Ghraib prison, known to the Iraqis as "Saddam's Torture Central" was taken from relative obscurity and thrust into the public limelight by a scandal that rocked the foundations of the U.S. military. As brutal and egregious as these acts were, they pale in comparison to the despicable crimes Saddam and his sons, Uday and Qusay, committed against the Iraqi people.

During his reign of terror, Saddam imprisoned thousands of people, many without charges, within the walls of Abu Ghraib. The former inmates who lived long enough to finally see a free Iraq tell stories of how the guards beat and tortured them. It was not until Amnesty International began to investigate Abu Ghraib that the true horrors of life inside the prison's walls became known to the rest of the world.

In 1984 alone, more than 4,000 prisoners entered Abu Ghraib and were never heard from again. As the years ticked away, the murder of innocent Iraqis continued at the prison, unabated by world opinion or pressure until the U.S.-led invasion ousted Saddam in 2003. Invariably all of this death, hatred and emotional distress were absorbed by the very walls of Abu Ghraib, creating an impermeable barrier between this world and the next. Abu Ghraib became a prison for the dead as well as the living.

But gone are the days of torture and death at Abu Ghraib. Following several intense inquiries into the 2003 scandal, sweeping changes were made at the prison. The soldiers' living areas were vastly improved and safeguards put into place to preserve the safety of those detained there. The "old guard" was replaced with better-trained and better-equipped soldiers. These brave men and women strap on their body armor every single day and face not only a defiant insurgency but also the constant reminders of the prison's haunting past.

Here in the desert, just a scant few miles away from Baghdad, the ghostly images of Abu Ghraib's former inmates refuse to remain silent. It is a place where the sweat and blood of heroes co-exists with a lineage of tears and pain, making "Saddam's Torture Central" one of the most haunted locations in all of Iraq.

SOLDIERS and the SUPERNATURAL

BIBLIOGRAPHY & RECOMMENDED READING

Aron, Paul -- *Unsolved Mysteries of American History*, 1997
Blue & Gray Magazine - *Guide to Haunted Places of the Civil War*, 1996
Chariton, Wallace O. with Charlie Eckardt and Kevin R. Young -- *Unsolved Texas Mysteries*, 1991
Coleman, Elaine -- *Texas Haunted Forts*, 2001
Crain, Mary Beth - *Haunted U.S. Battlefields*, 2008
Davis, Burke - *Sherman's March*, 1980
Davis, Kenneth C. - *Don't Know Much About the Civil War*, 1996
Denney, Robert E. - *Civil War Prisons and Escapes*, 1993
Farwell, Lisa -- *Haunted Texas Vacations*, 2000
Frassantio, William - *Gettysburg: A Journey in Time*, 1975
Goodwin, David - *Ghosts of Jefferson Barracks*, 2002
Hart, Herbert M. -- *Old Forts of the Southwest*, 1961
Hauck, Denis William -- *Haunted Places the National Directory*, 1996
Hesseltine, William B. - *Civil War Prisons*, 1962
Holzer, Hans - *Travel Guide to Haunted Houses*, 1998
Leckie, Robert - *None Died in Vain*, 1990
Myers, Arthur - *The Ghostly Register*, 1986
Nesbit, Mark - *Civil War Ghost Trails*, 2012
--------------- - *Ghosts of Gettysburg Series*, 1991 - Present
Norman, Michael & Beth Scott - *Haunted America*, 1994
-------------------------------- - *Historic Haunted America*, 1995
Rainey, Rich - *Haunted History*, 1992

--------------- -- *Phantom Forces,* 1990
Riccio, Dolores & Joan Bingham - *Haunted Houses USA,* 1989
Scott, Beth & Michael Norman - *Haunted Heartland,* 1985
Slaughter, April - *Ghosthunting Texas,* 2009
Spaeth, Frank editor   -- *Phantom Army of the Civil War and other Southern Ghost Stories*, 1997
Speer, Lonnie - *Portals to Hell: Military Prisons of the Civil War,* 1999
Taylor, Troy - *Haunted St. Louis,* 2003
----------------- - *Haunting of America;* 2010
--------------- - *Spirits of the Civil War;* 1999
Toney, B. Keith - *Battlefield Ghosts;* 1997
Winer, Richard & Nancy Osborn - *Haunted Houses; 1979*
Wlodarski, Robert and Anne P. -- *Spirits of the Alamo;* 1999

Personal Interviews & Correspondence

ABOUT THE AUTHORS

DAVID GOODWIN

David Goodwin works as a commissioned police officer in the St. Louis metropolitan area. He has a Bachelor's degree in law enforcement and has worked in the law enforcement and campus security field for over 20 years. He enlisted in the Army National Guard in 1986 and was commissioned as a 2nd Lieutenant in 1992 and currently holds the rank of Major. Dave deployed to Iraq in 2004-2005 and 2007-2008 in support of Iraqi Freedom. Dave is currently stationed at Jefferson Barracks, Missouri.

Dave has actively investigated numerous haunted locations for the last twenty years. Dave's love of military history and ghosts culminated in his first book "Ghosts of Jefferson Barracks" which was published in 2001. He has been a member of the American Ghost Society AGS for over sixteen years and has been a guest speaker at several prestigious paranormal conferences over the years where he has spoken about haunted military posts, battlefields and his ghostly experiences as a member of the Army Reserve.

Dave lives with his wife and daughter in a historic farmstead located in north St. Louis County.

TROY TAYLOR

Troy Taylor is an occultist, crime buff, supernatural historian and the author of more than 100 books on ghosts, hauntings, history, crime and the unexplained in America. He is also the founder of the American Hauntings Tour Company.

When not traveling to the far-flung reaches of the country in search of the unusual, Troy resides part-time in Decatur, Illinois.

See Troy and Dave's books, along with other great titles at:
www.whitechapelpress.com

www.ingramcontent.com/pod-product-compliance
Lightning Source LLC
Chambersburg PA
CBHW070959160426
43193CB00012B/1836